TOEFL® MAP

MAP

New TOEFL® Edition

Listening

Advanced

DARAKWON

TOEFL® MAP
New TOEFL® Edition

Listening Advanced

Publisher Chung Kyudo
Editor Cho Sangik
Authors Michael A. Putlack, Stephen Poirier, Angela Maas, Maximilian Tolochko
Proofreader Talib Din
Designers Park Narae, Chung Kyuok

First published in April 2023
By Darakwon, Inc.
Darakwon Bldg., 211, Munbal-ro, Paju-si, Gyeonggi-do 10881
Republic of Korea
Tel: 82-2-736-2031 (Ext. 250)
Fax: 82-2-732-2037

ISBN 978-89-277-8035-9 14740
978-89-277-8025-0 14740 (set)

www.darakwon.co.kr

Photo Credits
Shutterstock.com

Components Main Book / Answers, Explanations, and Scripts
8 7 6 5 4 3 2   24 25 26 27 28

Introduction

Studying for the TOEFL® iBT is no easy task and is not one that is to be undertaken lightly. It requires a great deal of effort as well as dedication on the part of the student. It is our hope that by using *TOEFL® Map Listening Advanced* as either a textbook or a study guide, the task of studying for the TOEFL® iBT will become somewhat easier for the student and less of a burden.

Students who wish to excel on the TOEFL® iBT must attain a solid grasp of the four important skills in the English language: reading, listening, speaking, and writing. The Darakwon *TOEFL® Map* series covers all four of these skills in separate books. There are also three different levels in all four topics. This book, *TOEFL® Map Listening Advanced*, covers the listening aspect of the test at the advanced level. Students who want to listen to lectures and conversations, learn vocabulary terms, and study topics that appear on the TOEFL® iBT will have their wishes granted by using this book.

TOEFL® Map Listening Advanced has been designed for use both in a classroom setting and as a study guide for individual learners. For this reason, it offers a comprehensive overview of the TOEFL® iBT Listening section. In Part A, the different types of questions that are found on the TOEFL® iBT Listening section are explained, and hints on how to answer these questions properly are also provided. In Part B, learners have the opportunity to build their background knowledge of the topics that appear on the TOEFL® iBT by listening to the lectures and conversations of varying lengths that are found in each chapter. Each lecture and conversation is followed by the types of questions that appear on the TOEFL® iBT, and each chapter also has a vocabulary section, which enables learners to test their knowledge of vocabulary that is specific to the particular topics covered in each chapter. Finally, in Part C, students can take several TOEFL® iBT practice tests. These are full-length lectures and conversations that also have the same numbers and types of questions that appear on actual TOEFL® iBT Listening section passages. Combined, all of these should be able to help learners prepare themselves to take and, more importantly, to excel on the TOEFL® iBT.

TOEFL® Map Listening Advanced has a great amount of information and should prove to be invaluable as a study guide for learners who are preparing for the TOEFL® iBT. However, while this book is comprehensive, it is up to each person to do the actual work. In order for *TOEFL® Map Listening Advanced* to be of any use, the individual learner must dedicate him or herself to studying the information found within its pages. While we have strived to make this book as user friendly and as full of crucial information as possible, ultimately, it is up to each person to make the best of the material in the book. We wish you luck in your study of both English and the TOEFL® iBT, and we hope that you are able to use *TOEFL® Map Listening Advanced* to improve your abilities in both of them.

Michael A. Putlack
Stephen Poirier
Angela Maas
Maximilian Tolochko

TABLE
OF
CONTENTS

How Is This Book Different?   6
How to Use This Book   7

Part A | Understanding Listening Question Types

Question Type 01   Gist-Content   10
Question Type 02   Gist-Purpose   12
Question Type 03   Detail   14
Question Type 04   Understanding the Function of What Is Said   17
Question Type 05   Understanding the Speaker's Attitude   20
Question Type 06   Understanding Organization   23
Question Type 07   Connecting Content   26
Question Type 08   Making Inferences   29

Part B | Building Background Knowledge of TOEFL Topics

Chapter 01
Life Sciences 1 & Conversations

Mastering Question Types with Lectures A1, A2   32
Mastering Question Types with Conversations A3   36
Mastering Topics with Lectures B1, B2, B3, B4   38
Mastering Topics with Conversations B5, B6   42
TOEFL Practice Tests C1, C2, C3   44
Star Performer Word Files   49
Vocabulary Review   50

Chapter 02
Life Sciences 2 & Conversations

Mastering Question Types with Lectures A1, A2   52
Mastering Question Types with Conversations A3   56
Mastering Topics with Lectures B1, B2, B3, B4   58
Mastering Topics with Conversations B5, B6   62
TOEFL Practice Tests C1, C2, C3   64
Star Performer Word Files   69
Vocabulary Review   70

Chapter 03
Social Sciences 1 & Conversations

Mastering Question Types with Lectures A1, A2   72
Mastering Question Types with Conversations A3   76
Mastering Topics with Lectures B1, B2, B3, B4   78
Mastering Topics with Conversations B5, B6   82
TOEFL Practice Tests C1, C2, C3   84
Star Performer Word Files   89
Vocabulary Review   90

Chapter 04
Social Sciences 2
& Conversations

Mastering Question Types with Lectures A1, A2	92
Mastering Question Types with Conversations A3	96
Mastering Topics with Lectures B1, B2, B3, B4	98
Mastering Topics with Conversations B5, B6	102
TOEFL Practice Tests C1, C2, C3	104
Star Performer Word Files	109
Vocabulary Review	110

Chapter 05
Physical Sciences 1
& Conversations

Mastering Question Types with Lectures A1, A2	112
Mastering Question Types with Conversations A3	116
Mastering Topics with Lectures B1, B2, B3, B4	118
Mastering Topics with Conversations B5, B6	122
TOEFL Practice Tests C1, C2, C3	124
Star Performer Word Files	129
Vocabulary Review	130

Chapter 06
Physical Sciences 2
& Conversations

Mastering Question Types with Lectures A1, A2	132
Mastering Question Types with Conversations A3	136
Mastering Topics with Lectures B1, B2, B3, B4	138
Mastering Topics with Conversations B5, B6	142
TOEFL Practice Tests C1, C2, C3	144
Star Performer Word Files	149
Vocabulary Review	150

Chapter 07
Arts 1
& Conversations

Mastering Question Types with Lectures A1, A2	152
Mastering Question Types with Conversations A3	156
Mastering Topics with Lectures B1, B2, B3, B4	158
Mastering Topics with Conversations B5, B6	162
TOEFL Practice Tests C1, C2, C3	164
Star Performer Word Files	169
Vocabulary Review	170

Chapter 08
Arts 2
& Conversations

Mastering Question Types with Lectures A1, A2	172
Mastering Question Types with Conversations A3	176
Mastering Topics with Lectures B1, B2, B3, B4	178
Mastering Topics with Conversations B5, B6	182
TOEFL Practice Tests C1, C2, C3	184
Star Performer Word Files	189
Vocabulary Review	190

Part C | Experiencing the TOEFL iBT Actual Tests

Actual Test 01	192
Actual Test 02	206

How Is This Book Different?

When searching for the ideal book to use to study for the TOEFL® iBT, it is often difficult to differentiate between the numerous books that are available on a bookstore's shelves. However, *TOEFL® Map Listening Advanced* differs from many other TOEFL® iBT books and study guides in several important ways.

A large number of TOEFL® iBT books arrange the material according to the types of questions that are asked on the test. This often results in learners listening to a lecture on astronomy, which is then followed by a lecture on history, which is then followed by a conversation between a student and a professor, and so on. Simply put, there is little cohesion except for the questions. However, *TOEFL® Map Listening Advanced* is arranged by subject. There are eight chapters in this book, all of which cover the subjects that appear on the TOEFL® iBT. For instance, there are two chapters on life sciences, two chapters on social sciences, two chapters on physical sciences, and two chapters on the arts. By arranging the chapters according to subjects, learners are able to listen to lectures that are related to one another all throughout each chapter. This enables them to build upon their knowledge as they progress through each chapter. Additionally, since there are many vocabulary terms that are specifically used in certain subjects, learners will be able more easily to recognize these specialized vocabulary terms, understand how they are used in sentences, and, most importantly, retain the knowledge of what these terms mean. Finally, by arranging the chapters according to subjects, learners have the opportunity to cover and become familiar with all of the TOEFL® iBT question types in each chapter rather than just focus on a single type of question.

TOEFL® Map Listening Advanced, unlike many other TOEFL® iBT books and study guides, does not have any translations into foreign languages within its pages. All too often, learners rely on translations of the passages, questions, or difficult vocabulary terms into their native language. They learn to use these translations as a crutch to help them get through the material. However, the actual TOEFL® iBT does not have any translations into foreign languages, so neither does this book. This will better prepare learners to take the actual test in that they must try to learn difficult terms or expressions through context, just as native speakers of English do when they encounter terms or expressions that they fail to understand. Additionally, by not being able to resort to their native language for help through translations of the material, learners will find that their fluency in English will improve more rapidly when they use *TOEFL® Map Listening Advanced*.

Finally, the lectures and conversations in *TOEFL® Map Listening Advanced* are based on topics that have appeared on the actual TOEFL® iBT in the past. Therefore, by using this book, learners can get the opportunity to see what kinds of topics appear on the TOEFL® iBT. This will enable them to recognize the difficulty level, the style of TOEFL® iBT lectures and conversations, and the difficulty of the vocabulary that appears on the test. Second, learners will also get the opportunity to enhance their knowledge of topics that have appeared on the TOEFL® iBT before. By knowing more about the topics about which they are listening to when they take the actual test, test takers will be sure to improve their TOEFL® iBT scores. Third, learners will also gain knowledge of the specialized vocabulary in particular topics, which will help them more easily to understand lectures and conversations on the actual test. Finally, many topics appear multiple times on the TOEFL® iBT. Thus, students who study some of these topics will be pleasantly surprised on occasion to find almost the exact same topic when they take the actual TOEFL® iBT, which will no doubt help them improve their test scores.

How to Use
This Book

TOEFL® Map Listening Advanced is designed for use either as a textbook in a classroom in a TOEFL® iBT preparation course or as a study guide for individuals who are studying for the TOEFL® iBT on their own. *TOEFL® Map Listening Advanced* has been divided into three sections: Part A, Part B, and Part C. All three sections offer information which is important to learners preparing for the TOEFL® iBT. Part A is divided into 8 sections, each of which explains one of the question types that appear on the TOEFL® iBT Listening section. Part B is divided into 8 chapters. There are two chapters that cover each of the four subjects that appear on the TOEFL® iBT. Part C has 10 lectures and 5 conversations that resemble those which appear on the TOEFL® iBT.

Part A   Understanding Listening Question Types

This section is designed to acquaint learners with each question type on the TOEFL® iBT Listening section. Therefore, there are 8 sections in this chapter— one for each question type. Each section is divided into 4 parts. The first part offers a short explanation of the question type. The second part shows the ways in which questions of that particular type often appear on the test. The third part provides helpful hints on how to answer these questions correctly. And the fourth part has either a lecture or a conversation followed by one or two questions.

Part B   Building Background Knowledge of TOEFL Topics

The purpose of this section is to introduce the various subjects that most frequently appear on the TOEFL® iBT. There are 8 chapters in Part B. Each chapter covers one subject and contains 10 Listening lectures and 5 Listening conversations of various lengths as well as vocabulary words and exercises. Each chapter is divided into several parts.

Mastering Question Types with Lectures

This section contains 4 Listening lectures that are between 500 and 600 words in length. Following each lecture, there are 4 Listening questions. Each question is identified by type. The first and third Listening lectures always ask the same types of questions while the second and fourth also always ask the same types of questions. This ensures that all 8 question types are covered in this section. In addition, there is a short summary of each lecture after the questions with 4-5 blanks for learners to fill in.

Mastering Question Types with Conversations

This section contains 2 Listening conversations that are between 300 and 400 words in length. Following each conversation, there are 4 Listening questions. Each question is identified by type. The conversations ask different questions so that all of the question types that appear following Listening conversations are covered in this section. In addition, there is a short summary of each conversation after the questions with 4-5 blanks for learners to fill in.

Mastering Topics with Lectures

This section contains 4 Listening lectures that are between 600 and 700 words in length. There is a graphic organizer for learners to fill out as they listen to the lecture. This will help learners improve their organizational skills. Following each lecture, there are 3 Listening questions. These questions may be from any of the 8 types of Listening questions. In addition, there is a short summary of the lecture after the questions with 4-5 blanks for learners to fill in.

Mastering Topics with Conversations

This section contains 2 Listening conversations that are between 400 and 500 words in length. There is a graphic organizer for learners to fill out as they listen to the conversation. This will help learners improve their organizational skills. Following each conversation, there are 3 Listening questions. These questions may be from any of the 8 types of Listening questions. In addition, there is a short summary of the conversation after the questions with 4-5 blanks for learners to fill in.

TOEFL Practice Tests

This section contains 2 full-length Listening lectures and 1 full-length Listening conversation. Each lecture has 6 Listening questions of any type while the conversation has 5 Listening questions of any type. The purpose of this section is to acquaint learners with the types of lectures and conversations they will encounter when they take the TOEFL® iBT.

Star Performer Word Files and Vocabulary Review

This section contains almost 150 vocabulary words that were used in the lectures in each chapter. The words include nouns, verbs, adjectives, and adverbs. There are also 20 vocabulary questions that review the vocabulary words learners have covered in each chapter. The purpose of this section is to teach learners specific words that often appear in lectures on certain subjects and to make sure that learners know the meanings of these words and how to use them.

Part C Experiencing the TOEFL Actual Tests

This section contains 2 actual tests with 10 full-length TOEFL® iBT Listening lectures and questions and 5 full-length TOEFL® iBT Listening conversations and questions. The purpose of this section is to let learners experience actual full-length Listening lectures and conversations and to see if they can apply the knowledge they have learned in the course of studying *TOEFL® Map Listening Advanced*.

Understanding Listening Question Types

Gist-Content questions cover the test taker's basic comprehension of the listening passage. While they are typically asked after lectures, they are sometimes asked after conversations as well. These questions check to see if the test taker has understood the gist of the passage. They focus on the passage as a whole, so it is important to recognize what the main point of the lecture is or why the two people in the conversation are having a particular discussion. The test taker should therefore be able to recognize the theme of the lecture or conversation in order to answer this question correctly.

Gist-Content questions often appear on the test like this:

- What problem does the man have?
- What are the speakers mainly discussing?
- What is the main topic of the lecture?
- What is the lecture mainly about?
- What aspect of X does the professor mainly discuss?

Solve Gist-Content questions more easily by doing the following:

○ Pay close attention and be sure to listen for the overall idea of the listening passage. Gist-Content questions are not about the minor parts of the listening passage. They are concerned with the entire passage, so avoid answers that are only minor themes in the passage.

○ Recognize the key words that should enable you to determine what the main idea is. In most cases, speakers use certain phrases that indicate what they intend to speak about. Try to listen for the key words and disregard answer choices that are either unconnected with the passage or too general.

○ Determine the main idea by recognizing the various examples, explanations, and summaries that are associated with it. For example, focus on what problem and solution the speakers in the conversation are referring to.

○ Pay close attention to the beginning of the passage. When the passage is a lecture, the professor often indicates at the beginning what the topic of the lecture is going to be. However, be sure that the professor is describing the contents of the lecture and is not talking about a previously discussed topic or giving background information. When the passage is a conversation, listen to the beginning, which is where the student, professor, or employee often states what the problem is or the reason for having the conversation.

Example of a Gist-Content Question

Listen to part of a lecture in a biology class.

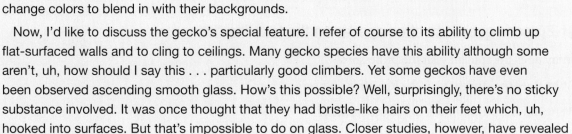

W Professor: One of the more unusual members of the lizard family is the gecko. It's notable mainly for its ability to climb walls and cross ceilings. Geckos are found in warm climates, are usually nocturnal, and eat insects. They lack eyelids but instead have a, uh, a thin, transparent membrane over their eyes. Many species actually lick their eyelids with their long tongue to keep them moist . . . Yuck! The largest geckos range from about eleven to fourteen inches long. They vary in color, and some have the ability to change colors to blend in with their backgrounds.

01-01

Now, I'd like to discuss the gecko's special feature. I refer of course to its ability to climb up flat-surfaced walls and to cling to ceilings. Many gecko species have this ability although some aren't, uh, how should I say this . . . particularly good climbers. Yet some geckos have even been observed ascending smooth glass. How's this possible? Well, surprisingly, there's no sticky substance involved. It was once thought that they had bristle-like hairs on their feet which, uh, hooked into surfaces. But that's impossible to do on glass. Closer studies, however, have revealed the truth.

The structure of the gecko's foot is what makes wall climbing possible. Their feet have large, soft pads that are covered in bristle-like hairs called setae . . . That's S-E-T-A-E . . . Setae are much smaller than human hairs. In fact, there are tens of thousands of them on each toe. Imagine how small each one must be to fit that many on a lizard's toe. Then, on each seta, there are many spatula-shaped pads . . . Oh, I see frowns on some faces, so let me explain. By spatula, I mean the kitchen utensil you use for frying and flipping over eggs or pancakes. Got it? Good . . . These spatula-shaped features are so tiny they're impossible to see without a microscope.

These physical features interact with smooth surfaces under the influence of van der Waals forces. That's a physics term named after a Dutch scientist. Now, I don't want to get into it too much since this isn't, well . . . I'm not teaching a physics class . . . but van der Waals forces deal with how things are attracted and repulsed at the molecular level. Essentially, geckos use moisture, which is always found at least in low levels on surfaces like walls and ceilings, to create a temporary bond with the setae on their toes. This then lets them utilize their wall-climbing abilities.

Q What is the lecture mainly about?

   (A) The features that let geckos scale walls and hang from ceilings

   (B) A description of setae and how they are utilized by geckos

   (C) The effects of van der Waals forces on the way geckos climb structures

   (D) The behavior and physical characteristics of geckos

⊗ Explanation

> Choice (A) best describes what the lecture is mainly about. After providing some background information on geckos, the professor mentions that she wants to talk about their special features. She then spends the rest of the lecture describing how exactly geckos can climb walls and hang from ceilings. Choices (B), (C), and (D) are all wrong because they only cover minor parts of the lecture.

Gist-Purpose questions cover the underlying theme of the passage. While they are typically asked after conversations, they are sometimes asked after lectures as well. Because these questions focus on the purpose or theme of the conversation or lecture, they begin with the word "why." They focus on the conversation or lecture as a whole, but they are not concerned with details; instead, they are concerned with why the student is speaking with the professor or employee or why the professor is covering a specific topic.

Gist-Purpose questions often appear on the test like this:

- Why does the student visit the professor?
- Why does the student visit the Registrar's office?
- Why did the professor ask to see the student?
- Why does the professor explain X?

Solve Gist-Purpose questions more easily by doing the following:

- Recognize the reason for the lecture or conversation. For example, during office hours, a student may ask the professor for help with a paper on glaciers. Their conversation might include facts about glaciers, but the reason for the conversation is that the student needs help writing his paper. So be sure to avoid answer choices that claim the purpose of the conversation is to provide information about glaciers.

- Determine the purpose of the conversation by recognizing the solution to the problem. For example, during a service encounter, a student will often try to solve his or her problem. Recognizing and determining what the student's problem is and how it can be solved will help you answer Gist-Purpose questions.

- Pay close attention to the beginning of the passage. The student will often explain why he or she is visiting the professor, or the professor will often state why he or she is interested in speaking with the student. Likewise, the reason for a service encounter is often explained at the very beginning of the conversation.

- In addition, pay close attention to the end of the passage. The speakers may sum up the conversation, or the professor may explain the purpose of his or her lecture at the end.

- Avoid answer choices that only cover a small part of the conversation or that contain incorrect information. In many cases, incorrect answer choices use words that appear in the conversation yet do not refer to the actual problem.

Example of a Gist-Purpose Question

Listen to part of a conversation between a student and an employment office employee.

W Student: Excuse me. This is the student employment office, isn't it?

M Employment Office Employee: Yes, it is. Come on in. I take it that you're here for a job, right?

01-02

W: Uh, yes . . . So, uh, what, um, exactly do I need to do?

M: First of all, do you have any particular job in mind?

W: I haven't really given it much thought to be honest. I'm a work-study student, so I'm supposed to get a job for a few hours a week this semester.

M: Ah, okay. That was going to be my next question. Since you're a work-study student, it means that you get priority over other students when it comes to hiring.

W: That's good to know. So, uh, how hard is it to get a job?

M: Well, um . . . it's really not that difficult at all. There are a ton of jobs available on campus. It really depends on what kind of work you're interested in doing. For example, there are lots of positions available at the student cafeteria and at the restaurant and coffee shop in the campus center.

W: Oh, no. I don't think I could do anything in the food industry. I tried that a couple of summers ago, and, uh, it was . . . uh, let's just say it was a complete and utter disaster.

M: Okay. I don't even want to know.

W: So what else is available?

M: Let's see . . . We have a couple of openings at the campus gym . . . Ah, I can tell by the look on your face that you're not interested in that . . . Let me check something else here . . . Buildings and Grounds is hiring.

W: What do they do?

M: They take care of the campus. You know, they cut the grass, trim the hedges . . .

W: Stop right there. That's definitely not the job for me.

M: How about a library job? They're kind of boring, but they're nice and quiet.

W: I can deal with quiet. Let me see what you've got available there, please.

M: Sure. Here's the information.

Q   Why does the student visit the employment office?

  (A) To apply for a job at the school library

  (B) To get some information on the work-study program

  (C) To inquire about how to get an on-campus job

  (D) To complain about the lack of good jobs

⊘ Explanation

> Choice (C) best describes the reason why the student visited the employment office. The employment office employee asks the student if she has come to the office to find a job, and she agrees with him. The student does apply for a library job (Choice (A)), but that is not the reason she went to the office. Choices (B) and (D) are both untrue statements.

Detail questions cover the test taker's ability to understand facts and data that are mentioned in the listening passage. These questions most commonly appear after lectures; however, they may sometimes come after conversations. Detail questions require the test taker to listen for and remember details from the passage. The majority of these questions concern major details that are related to the main topic of the lecture or conversation rather than minor ones. However, in some cases where there is a long digression that is not clearly related to the main idea, there may be a question about the details of the digression.

Detail questions have two basic formats:

1 Most Detail questions are traditional multiple-choice questions with four answer choices and a single correct answer. One-answer questions normally appear on the test like this:

- According to the professor, what is one way that X can affect Y?

- What are X?

- What resulted from the invention of the X?

- According to the professor, what is the main problem with the X theory?

2 Some detail questions, however, have two or more correct answers. These questions may require you to click on two answers or to indicate whether a number of statements are true or not. Two-answer questions normally appear on the test like this:

- According to the professor, what information should the student include in her statement of purpose?
  [Choose 2 answers.]

- In the lecture, the professor describes a number of facts about extinction level events. Indicate whether each of the following is a fact about extinction level events. Place a checkmark in the correct box.

Solve Detail questions more easily by doing the following:

○ Recognize the main topic of the passage. Then, listen carefully for any facts or details mentioned about the main topic. Ignore the minor facts and details mentioned in the passage. They are merely detractors.

○ Be sure to take good notes and to record as many details about the main topic as you can. Sometimes answers to detail questions are paraphrased, so they do not use the same words as they appeared in the passage. So check if the correct answers have been paraphrased by consulting the notes you take while listening to the passage.

○ When you are not positive about the answer, select the answer choice that most closely concerns the main topic of the passage. In addition, remember that words or concepts that are repeated are clearly important, so you should pay close attention to them.

Examples of Detail Questions

Listen to part of a lecture in a performing arts class.

01-03

W1 Professor: Have any of you ever been involved in a stage production? What kind of work did it involve? Lisa? Yes?

W2 Student: Well, I acted in my high school's drama club, and we were constantly busy preparing for our performances.

W1: Well stated. After watching a play, we may often comment on how hard the actors must have rehearsed. However . . . have any of you ever stopped to think about the other people who contributed to the overall success of the performance? Ah, yes. That's what I thought . . . Well, there are three elements critical to the success of a staged performance yet which are frequently ignored. They are . . . the stage setup, the costumes, and the lighting. Let's look at them in brief.

When the lights turn off and the curtains open, the audience sees what's on stage. This includes the scenery, the furniture, and the props. We call this the stage setup. It's critical to the play's success since it imparts to the audience the director's concept of the production. In addition, a properly created stage setup does many things. It sets the style and the tone of the overall production and establishes the mood and the atmosphere of individual scenes. It also lets the audience know the time and the location of a particular scene.

A good director uses the setup to keep certain things hidden from the audience, thereby building suspense. Oh, I mentioned props, too . . . This is a short word for "stage properties," and they include items like furniture, drapes, lamps, and other decorations. Props help set the mood and can add necessary detail and authenticity to a setup.

Next are costumes. These are critical in that they provide the audience with information about the characters. They can show a performer's occupation, social status, gender, age, and sense of style. What else can they do? Let's see . . . They help distinguish between characters. After all, you need to know who the king is and who his servants are. Costumes also suggest relationships and show how people are developing or even aging through the course of the performance. And let's not forget that accessories are a part of any costume. Accessories include, but aren't limited to, jewelry, canes, hats, gloves, shoes, and masks.

Lighting is the third element. The first spotlight was invented in 1911. Since then, stage lighting has made huge advances. Professional lighting designers can do all sorts of tricks with lights today. They can spotlight individual actors and their surroundings or use light to help set the mood of a scene. Furthermore, lighting can be used to indicate the time of day or location. It can emphasize certain places or props on stage, and it can reinforce the action going on.

That's a very brief look at three important elements of the stage. So, now that you know a little about them, I'm going to go back over them in more detail by showing you some slides. Can someone hit the lights, please? Thanks. Okay, let's look at some stage setups first.

Q1 According to the professor, how do props contribute to a performance?

    (A) They show the audience the differences between characters.

    (B) They make the stage appear to be more realistic.

    (C) They give the performance a more professional look.

    (D) They can highlight individual actors on stage.

⊘ Explanation

Choice Ⓑ best describes how props contribute to a performance. The professor mentions that props can add "authenticity to a setup," which therefore makes the stage more realistic in its appearance. Choice Ⓐ refers to costumes. Choice Ⓒ is never mentioned in the lecture. Choice Ⓓ refers to the lighting.

Q2 In the lecture, the professor describes a number of facts about stage lighting. Indicate whether each of the following is a fact about stage lighting.

Choose 2 answers.

Ⓐ Stage lights tend to detract from the action going on.
Ⓑ Stage lights are often used to add feeling to a scene.
Ⓒ The first spotlight was used in the nineteenth century.
Ⓓ Stage lights can leave some parts of the stage dark.

⊘ Explanation

Choices Ⓑ and Ⓓ best answer the question about stage lighting. For Choice Ⓑ, the professor notes that lights can "help set the mood of the scene." For Choice Ⓓ, the professor mentions how spotlights can focus on individual actors and scenery, which indicates that parts of the stage may remain dark. Choice Ⓐ is incorrect. The opposite is true. Choice Ⓒ is incorrect as well. The first spotlight was used in the twentieth century, not the nineteenth century.

Understanding the Function of What Is Said questions cover the test taker's ability to determine the underlying meaning of what has been said in the passage. This question type often involves replaying a portion of the listening passage. There are two types of these questions. Some ask the test taker to infer the meaning of a phrase or a sentence. Thus, the test taker needs to determine the implication—not the literal meaning—of the sentence. Other questions ask the test taker to infer the purpose of a statement made by one of the speakers. These questions specifically ask about the intended effect of a particular statement on the listener.

Understanding the Function of What Is questions have two basic formats:

1. Some Understanding Function questions ask about what the speaker is inferring. These are typically replay questions. They may appear like this:

- What does the professor imply when he says this: (replay)
- What can be inferred from the professor's response to the student? (replay)

2. Other Understanding Function questions ask about the purpose of a particular statement or a topic in the lecture or conversation. These can be regular questions or replay questions. They may appear like this:

- What is the purpose of the woman's response? (replay)
- Why does the student say this: (replay)
- Why does the professor ask the student about his grades?
- Why does the man tell the student about the library?

Solve Understanding the Function of What Is questions more easily by doing the following:

○ Remember that you should not always take what the person is saying or asking literally. Learn how to read between the lines of what people are saying. By understanding what people are implying, you will be able to answer these questions properly.

○ Listen to the speaker's tone of voice. In most cases, secondary meanings—those that can be inferred—are embedded in the speakers' tone of voice. Recognizing the speaker's tone can help you determine the real meaning of what has just been said.

○ Pay close attention to the dialog between the professor and student in a lecture. These questions may appear after both conversations and lectures. However, when they appear in lectures, they often concern dialog—such as when a student asks a question and the professor answers it—that occurs in the course of the lecture.

○ Listen carefully to the entire part of the conversation or lecture that is excerpted for replay questions. The rest of the dialog will help you determine what the speaker means or is implying.

Examples of Understanding the Function of What Is Said Questions

Listen to part of a conversation between a student and a professor.

01-04

M1 Student: Good afternoon, Professor Jennings. I'm sorry I'm late for our meeting. I was trying to print a report, but my printer got jammed.

M2 Professor: That's quite all right, Matthew. I was just reading a book here while I waited for you.

M1: So did you, uh, get an opportunity to check out the rough draft of the paper I turned in? I was hoping you could give me some pointers on how to improve my work.

M2: Yes, I took a look at it.

M1: And, um, what did you think, sir?

M2: Well, let me stress that I didn't go over it in detail because I'm a little pressed for time these days.

M1: That's fine, sir. Any help you can offer me would be great.

M2: Okay . . . Now, I liked the idea you came up with. I thought your thesis statement was well done as was your entire introduction.

M1: And the body? What about that part?

M2: Matthew, I need to emphasize to you just how important having a good outline is for your writing.

M1: An outline? What do you mean?

M2: You know, a plan of what you're going to write. The problem with the body of your text was that, uh, while you had some good ideas, they weren't organized very well at all. That's where I believe an outline could really help you.

M1: How so?

M2: It would enable you to organize your thoughts better. Think of an outline as, uh, as a road map. Would you drive across the country without a map?

M1: No way! I'd get lost in no time.

M2: Thanks for proving my point. That's exactly what I'm talking about. The body of your paper lacked cohesion because you were jumping around aimlessly from point to point. You really need to sit down and think about what points you want to make, and then you should write an outline for them. That way, you'll be able to organize your paper much better.

M1: Is that all I have to do?

M2: I think so. Put everything together better, and you'll be looking at an A paper.

Q1   Listen again to part of the conversation. Then answer the question.

> **M2:** Okay . . . Now, I liked the idea you came up with. I thought your thesis statement was well done as was your entire introduction.
>
> **M1:** And the body? What about that part?
>
> **M2:** Matthew, I need to emphasize to you just how important having a good outline is for your writing.

What does the professor imply when he says this: 🎧

M2: Matthew, I need to emphasize to you just how important having a good outline is for your writing.

- (A) He feels that the student is not working as hard as he should.
- (B) The student needs to come up with some better examples.
- (C) He wishes the student had turned in the outline along with the paper.
- (D) He was not impressed with the body of the student's report.

✅ Explanation

Choice (D) best describes what the professor is implying. The student asks what the professor thought of the body of his work, but the professor refuses to answer. Instead, he mentions that the student needs to come up with an outline when he is writing a paper. This implies that the professor did not think positively of the body of the student's report. Choice (A) is incorrect. Choices (B) and (C) were never mentioned in the conversation.

Q2 Listen again to part of the conversation. Then answer the question.

M2: That way, you'll be able to organize your paper much better.

M1: Is that all I have to do?

M2: I think so. Put everything together better, and you'll be looking at an A paper.

Why does the professor say this: 🎧

M2: Put everything together better, and you'll be looking at an A paper.

- (A) To promise the student what grade he will receive
- (B) To encourage the student to follow his advice
- (C) To ask the student to submit an outline along with his paper
- (D) To insist that the student work harder in the future

✅ Explanation

Choice (B) best describes why the professor makes that statement. The professor gives the student advice during the conversation. Then, at the end, he encourages the student by saying that if he follows his advice, he should get an A on the paper. Choice (A) is incorrect because the professor is not promising the student a grade. Neither Choice (C) nor Choice (D) is mentioned by the professor.

Understanding Attitude questions cover the speaker's attitude or opinion toward something. These questions may appear after both lectures and conversations. This question type often involves replaying a portion of the listening passage. There are two types of these questions. Some ask about one of the speakers' feelings concerning something. These questions may check to see whether the test taker understands how a speaker feels about a particular topic, if a speaker likes or dislikes something, or why a speaker might feel anxiety or amusement. The other category asks about one of the speaker's opinions. These questions may inquire about a speaker's degree of certainty. Others may ask what a speaker thinks or implies about a topic, person, thing, or idea.

Understanding the Speaker's Attitude questions have two basic formats:

1 Some Understanding Attitude questions ask about one of the speaker's feelings. These can be regular questions or replay questions. They may appear like this:

- What is the professor's attitude toward X?
- What is the professor's opinion of X?
- What does the woman mean when she says this: (replay)

2 Other Understanding the Speaker's Attitude questions focus on one of the speaker's opinions. These can be regular questions or replay questions. They may appear like this:

- What can be inferred about the student?
- What can be inferred about the student when she says this: (replay)
- What does the professor imply about the student's paper?

Solve Understanding the Speaker's Attitude questions more easily by doing the following:

○ Listen to the speaker's tone of voice to determine his or her opinion of some topic. In addition, pay attention to the speaker's intonation and sentence stress. These are crucial to answering the question properly.

○ Listen carefully when the speaker begins to give his or her opinion of some topic. Try to distinguish between the opinions and facts that the speaker is giving. More specifically, focus on the attitudes and opinions concerning the main theme of the lecture or conversation. Ignore opinions or attitudes about secondary topics.

○ Be sure to read between the lines of what is being said. You must remember that not every statement is meant to be taken literally. Statements can often convey messages that are quite different from their literal meanings.

○ For replay questions, listen carefully to the entire part of the conversation or lecture that is excerpted. The rest of the conversation can help you make inferences about the student or professor or understand what the speaker means.

Examples of Understanding the Speaker's Attitude Questions

Listen to part of a conversation between a student and a professor.

01-05

M1 Professor: Okay, now that we've got that matter settled, we need to move on to something a little more important, Rick.

M2 Student: What's that, sir?

M1: It's about the photos that you're taking. Have you taken all of the snapshots that you need for the journal? The deadline is coming up soon, and I don't want to be shorthanded. That happened to us last year, and, let me tell you, it was an absolute disaster.

M2: Well, I've taken a huge number of photos, so I'm pretty confident that I've got enough. We'll be all right.

M1: That sounds good.

M2: Nevertheless, I still intend to take some more. I prefer to be on the safe side. After all, it's better to have too many than to have too few.

M1: Bravo. Well spoken. You take after me.

M2: Thank you, sir.

M1: In that case, I've got a personal favor to ask of you.

M2: Yes?

M1: Would you mind taking some pictures for me so that I can use them in my research? You would be helping me out tremendously.

M2: It would be my pleasure, sir. Uh, but, um, what kind of photos would you like for me to take?

M1: Exactly the same kind that you've been taking. Different rock formations . . . Various minerals . . . You know. Like that.

M2: That's a piece of cake. Oh, say. I've got an idea. Would it be all right if I tagged along with the geology club on its hike in the Rockies this weekend? I'm sure I could get some great shots.

M1: Well, you're not a member, so, uh, technically, you're not supposed to go.

M2: Oh, please. I'd really love to go.

M1: Hmm . . . I suppose I could pull some strings and get you a seat on the bus.

M2: That's great. I can't wait to go. I'll get you some of the best photos you've ever seen.

Q1 Listen again to part of the conversation. Then answer the question.

> **M2:** Nevertheless, I still intend to take some more. I prefer to be on the safe side. After all, it's better to have too many than to have too few.
>
> **M1:** Bravo. Well spoken. You take after me.

What does the professor mean when he says this?

> **M1:** You take after me.

(A) The student will be a professor someday.

(B) The student needs to take some more photographs.

(C) The student resembles the professor in how he thinks.

(D) The student can take some of the professor's pictures.

⊘ Explanation

Choice (C) is what the professor means. When the professor says, "You take after me," he means that the student is acting just like the professor. Thus, the student resembles the professor. Choices (A), (B), and (D) are not connected with what the professor is saying.

Q2 What can be inferred about the professor?

(A) He values the student's assistance.

(B) He is the faculty advisor for the geology club.

(C) He does not have his own camera.

(D) He is going to go on the upcoming field trip.

⊘ Explanation

Choice (A) is the best possible inference to be made about the professor. The professor states, "You would be helping me out tremendously," when asking the student for a favor. He also offers to "pull some strings" to help the student be able to go on the field trip. He is clearly interested in having the student assist him. While the geology club is mentioned, there is no inference that the professor is the faculty advisor, so Choice (B) is incorrect. Choice (C) is incorrect because it is the student's photographic skills, not the professor's, that are being discussed. And Choice (D) is incorrect because there is no implication that the professor will or will not go on the upcoming field trip.

Understanding Organization questions cover the test taker's ability to determine the overall organization of the passage. These questions almost always appear after lectures. They rarely appear after conversations. These questions require the test taker to pay attention to two factors. The first is the way that the professor has organized the lecture and how he or she presents the information to the class. The second is how individual information given in the lecture relates to the lecture as a whole. To answer these questions correctly, test takers should focus more on the presentation and the professor's purpose in mentioning the facts rather than the facts themselves.

Understanding Organization questions have two basic formats:

1. Some Understanding Organization questions ask about the organization of the material in the professor's lecture. They may appear like this:

- How does the professor organize the information about X that he presents to the class?
- How is the discussion organized?

2. Other Understanding Organization questions ask about specific information in the lecture. They ask about why the professor discussed or mentioned certain pieces of information. They may appear like this:

- Why does the professor discuss X?
- Why does the professor mention X?

Solve Understanding Organization questions more easily by doing the following:

○ Pay attention to how the professor organizes the information in the lecture. Some common ways that lectures are organized are by chronology, by complexity, by comparing or contrasting, by giving examples, by classifying, by categorizing, by describing a problem and a solution, and by describing a cause and an effect.

○ Listen carefully to both the beginning and the end of the lecture. The professor may explain why he or she is going to present the lecture material or why he or she presented the lecture material in a certain way.

○ Try to determine how the various pieces of information that the professor provides are related to the lecture as a whole. When the professor provides some information that seems to be unrelated to the topic, try to determine why he or she brought that up in the lecture.

○ Pay close attention to the words and phrases the speakers use to signal the organization of their ideas. Professors often introduce the material by indicating what type of organizational format they intend to use. For example, a professor may say, "There are several differences between termites and ants," or, "Let's start from the beginning of Mozart's life."

Examples of Understanding Organization Questions

Listen to part of a lecture in a history class.

01-06

M Professor: When you think of Leonardo da Vinci, what comes to mind?

W Student: As for me, I always think about his great paintings.

M: Such as . . .

W: Well, the *Mona Lisa* for one.

M: Naturally. The *Mona Lisa* and *The Last Supper* are probably Leonardo's two most famous paintings. But can you name any of his other works of art? Most likely the answer is no. Although Leonardo started dozens of paintings, he only completed seventeen of them. Yes, that's a rather startling fact, isn't it? While his paintings are all noteworthy, none is as famous as the two I just mentioned. For instance, one painting he completed was a portrait of Ginevera de' Benci, which he did in 1478. He also painted a self-portrait, which is the only known picture of Leonardo. That painting was completed in 1515 near the end of his life. Those two are known to art historians, but that's about it.

So you may be asking yourself why Leonardo is so famous considering his relatively small corpus of paintings. Well, Leonardo was the quintessential Renaissance man. In other words, he didn't just have one specialty; he had a large number of them, and he excelled at them all.

Not only was he a painter, but he also wrote an instruction manual on how to paint called *Treatise on Painting*. In this hard-to-find work, Leonardo discussed the science of art and broke it down into a set of rules artists should follow. So we've established that Leonardo was both a painter and writer. What else was he? Well . . . I hope you have your pencils ready . . . He was a musician, anatomist, inventor, engineer, sculptor, and geometer, among other things. Didn't know that, did you? Sadly, these skills remain an obscure part of his life and are overshadowed by his two famous paintings.

Leonardo was fascinated with the workings of the most mysterious machine of all. I'm referring, of course, to the human body. You've probably seen his drawing of the Vitruvian Man, right? How did he manage to draw such anatomically correct pictures? Simple. He conducted autopsies. He's believed to have dissected around thirty bodies until the pope ordered him to stop. Times were different back then, so autopsies weren't nearly as common as they are today.

As an inventor, Leonardo was ahead of his time. You've probably heard that he worked on designs for both an airplane and a helicopter. He also came up with a self-propelled vehicle and a dredger that could clean out canals. Oh, let me note that these weren't new inventions but were instead improvements that he made to designs which already existed. The Renaissance was a violent age, so it should be no surprise that he designed various weapons of war. He devised numerous cannons, catapults, and even machine guns. He even came up with a tank which modern experts have said would have worked.

You're starting to get an idea about his greatness now, aren't you? Well, there's more. Let's get into some of the other fields he worked in.

Q1 Why does the professor mention *Treatise on Painting*?

    (A) To describe its influence on the paintings Leonardo finished

    (B) To start talking about the wide variety of skills Leonardo excelled at

    (C) To compare its instructions on paintings with Leonardo's beliefs

    (D) To explain some of the rules that artists are supposed to follow

⊘ Explanation

Choice (B) best describes why the professor mentions *Treatise on Painting*. The lecture emphasizes the many special skills Leonardo had, and the professor mentions *Treatise on Painting* to show that Leonardo was a writer. Choice (A) is never mentioned in the lecture. Choice (C) cannot be correct because since Leonardo wrote the book, his beliefs are the ones found in it. Be careful with Choice (D). While the book includes rules for artists, the professor does not explain any of the rules in the lecture. Therefore, Choice (D) is incorrect.

Q2 How does the professor organize the information about Leonardo da Vinci that he presents to the class?

    (A) By discussing each one of his specialties in detail

    (B) By noting the skills for which he was most famous

    (C) By describing his accomplishments in chronological order

    (D) By starting with his successes and ending with his failures

⊘ Explanation

Choice (A) best describes how the professor organizes the lecture. He focuses on the different skills that Leonardo had and then goes into detail on each one of them. Choice (B) is incorrect because the professor notes how some of Leonardo's skills that he discusses "remain an obscure part of his life." Choice (C) is incorrect because dates are not emphasized in the lecture. And Choice (D) is incorrect because there are no failures discussed in the lecture.

Connecting Content questions almost exclusively appear after lectures, not after conversations. These questions measure the test taker's ability to understand how the ideas in the lecture relate to one another. These relationships may be explicitly stated, or you may have to infer them from the words you hear. The majority of these questions concern major relationships in the passage. These questions also commonly appear in passages where a number of different themes, ideas, objects, or individuals are being discussed.

Connecting Content questions have two basic formats:

1. Many Connecting Content questions appear as charts or tables. They will have some four sentences or phrases, and the test taker must match them with a theme, idea, cause, effect, object, or individual. They may appear like the first example question below.

2. Other Connecting Content questions ask the test taker to make inferences from the relationships that are mentioned in the passage. They may appear like this:

   - What is the likely outcome of doing procedure X before procedure Y?

   - What can be inferred about X?

   - What does the professor imply about X?

   - What comparison does the professor make between X and Y?

Solve Connecting Content questions more easily by doing the following:

○ These questions frequently appear as charts or tables, or they may require the test taker to put sentences or phrases in the proper order. When the professor is noting various steps in a procedure, take notes to make sure you understand the correct order.

○ Pay attention to the relationships between the facts, concepts, or ideas that were mentioned in the lecture. For example, try to understand if the professor is mentioning similarities and differences between the various points he or she makes in the lecture and try to recognize how he or she is doing so.

○ These questions often involve making comparisons, recognizing cause and effect, following a sequence, or identifying a contradiction or agreement. You may be asked to identify these relationships and to classify items and ideas in some categories.

○ Try to infer as much information as possible out of the relationships that are described in the passage. Pay attention not only to the relationships and the information given about them but also to the possible results of future actions. You may have to predict an outcome, draw a conclusion, extrapolate some additional information, or infer a cause-effect relationship.

Examples of Connecting Content Questions

Listen to part of a lecture in a geology class.

01-07

M Professor: Today, we're talking about geysers. First, can anyone tell me what a geyser is?

W Student: Isn't that when, you know, hot water starts shooting out of the ground and, uh, up in the air?

M: That's a fairly accurate description, Jean. In actuality, a geyser is simply a hot spring that has become unstable, which is what causes them to, uh, spew water into the air. Now, before I tell you about geysers in detail, let me give you a brief overview. Geysers are quite rare. As a matter of fact, there are only about fifty known geyser fields on the Earth. Of them, about two-thirds have five or fewer active geysers . . . Not too many, huh? The field with the most geysers is Yellowstone National Park in Wyoming and Montana. Because it has so many, Yellowstone has been the subject of extensive studies by researchers trying to learn about geysers' properties and characteristics.

Geysers have three basic characteristics. First, they require a water supply. That's kind of obvious, huh? They're typically found near rivers, yet rainwater and groundwater are important sources, too. Second, geysers require a heat source. In order to have an eruption of water or gas, the hot and cool water sources first have to, uh, interact with one another. To achieve this, there must be a constant, steady supply of heat. That's why it's not unusual to see geysers in areas with volcanoes, even dormant or extinct ones. The third characteristic is that geysers must have a reservoir and a plumbing system. These systems are extremely complex, but . . . but there are six generic classifications of reservoir types from which all geysers originate. Let me cover them in brief.

Geysers are conveniently divided into types A, B, C, D, E, and F. That should be easy to remember. As for type A geysers, they have a single standpipe, which connects to an underground reservoir, and they have a raised cone on the surface, where the water comes out of the ground. You've all heard of Old Faithful in Yellowstone, right? Well, it's a type A geyser. Ah, some other characteristics of type A geysers are that they erupt at fairly regular intervals, and their eruptions can eject water high into the air for a considerable amount of time. But keep in mind that Yellowstone has geysers of all six types. It's just that Old Faithful is by far the, uh, well, the most famous.

Type B geysers, meanwhile, have deep, narrow shafts for their plumbing systems. Type C geysers, on the other hand, have standpipes that resemble those in a type A system. But . . . They lack a cone around their surface openings. Instead, their surface openings have slightly raised rims and are located in pools of water. Types D, E, and F are similar in that they have reservoir systems typical of fountain geysers. Yet type D geysers are part of a complex set of interconnected reservoirs while types E and F have other configurations for fountain or pool geysers.

That's a brief description of the different types of geysers. Now let's look at some pictures and see if we can identify which kind of geysers they are.

Q1 Which type of geyser do the following sentences refer to?

Click in the correct box for each sentence.

	Type A	Type B	Type C
1 Their plumbing system consists of deep and narrow shafts.			
2 They have a raised cone where they open on the surface.			
3 They have interconnected reservoirs of water.			
4 They may spew water high into the air.			

⊘ Explanation

Choice 1 describes a type B geyser. Choices 2 and 4 both describe a type A geyser. And Choice 3 describes a type C geyser.

Q2 What comparison does the professor make between type A and type C geysers?

- Ⓐ The types of plumbing systems they have
- Ⓑ The frequency with which they erupt
- Ⓒ The kind of water they are located in
- Ⓓ The types of cones their openings have

⊘ Explanation

Choice Ⓐ is the correct answer. The professor describes the plumbing systems for both type A and type C geysers. Choices Ⓑ, Ⓒ, and Ⓓ are incorrect because the professor either discusses each particular aspect for only one of the geysers, or he does not describe it for either one of them.

Making Inferences questions cover the test taker's ability to understand implications made in the passage and to come to conclusions about what these implications mean. These questions appear after both conversations and lectures. These questions require the test taker to hear the information being presented and then to make conclusions about what the information means or what is going to happen as a result of that information.

Making Inferences questions often appear on the test like this:

- What does the professor imply about X?
- What will the student probably do next?
- What can be inferred about X?
- What does the professor imply when he says this: (replay)

Solve Making Inferences questions more easily by doing the following:

○ Listen carefully to the end of the lecture or conversation. The information spoken here will typically indicate what the student, professor, or employee is going to do next.

○ Learn to read between the lines and to understand the implications the speaker is making. The literal meaning is often not the only meaning of a statement. Speakers can often have a secondary meaning that they are implying when they say something.

○ Most of the words in the correct answer choice will not be used in the lecture or conversation. Instead, the words will be different but will have similar meanings.

○ Listen carefully to the entire part of the conversation or lecture that is excerpted. The rest of the talk will help you determine what the speaker means or is implying.

Example of a Making Inferences Question

Listen to part of a lecture in a music class.

M Professor: How many of you have ever seen the movie *The Sting*? Okay, not too many of you, but I suppose that's not surprising since it, uh, it came out in 1974. But tell me . . . at least, those of you who have actually seen the movie . . . What did you think about the music that was played throughout the film? How about you, Carmen?

01-08

W Student: Oh, I loved the music. It was so, you know, lively and upbeat. I wouldn't say that it was anything you could dance to, but I sure enjoyed listening to it.

M: The music you heard in the film is called ragtime. Oh, and by the way, class, Carmen's right. You can't dance to it. Anyway, now, first of all, don't trust everything that you saw in the movie. After all, *The Sting* is a classic example of how Hollywood tries to, hmm . . . I guess you'd say, how Hollywood tries to rewrite history. It's not exactly historically accurate. For instance, the film was set in the 1930s, but the music is from twenty to thirty years earlier. Nevertheless, it perfectly underscores and supports the action on screen.

Ragtime is a uniquely American musical phenomenon. Although its birth is tied to the date of the first published rag, which happened in 1895, ragtime was being played by African-Americans long before then. In fact, they were making enough tip money from playing the rags to allow them to make a nice living.

While the end of the American Civil War in 1865 signaled the end of slavery, it didn't really give the former slaves, er, true freedom. Times were hard for many, and the only types of jobs available to them were frequently poor-paying menial labor. Oh, but there were three exceptions: teachers, preachers, and musicians. Interesting combination, huh? Well, white Americans had long accepted black musicians but only within, uh, shall we say . . . low-class establishments. Scott Joplin, one musician who played in these clubs, became one of the greats of ragtime both as a composer and player. Known as the King of Ragtime, his composition *Maple Leaf Rag* was a hit and helped spark a nationwide ragtime craze. It also helped give ragtime some much-needed respectability.

But I'm getting ahead of myself. Let me go back to the beginning of ragtime. Ragtime has its roots in the plantation lives of slaves. When they were brought from Africa, they took their rhythms, which were a part of their musical heritage, with them. These rhythms were incorporated into a wide variety of musical genres, one of which eventually became ragtime. Aside from rhythm, syncopation was also a prominent feature of African-American music. This too was a major feature of rag music. Finally, the banjo, which was a specifically southern version of the guitar, was also another important influence on ragtime.

So those three things were brought together and formed ragtime. Now, before I continue my lecture, I'd like you to listen to a couple of rags, as they were commonly called. Let's see if you can hear what I was just talking about.

Q   What will the professor probably do next?

  Ⓐ Play some ragtime music for the students
  Ⓑ Ask the students about the impression of ragtime
  Ⓒ Show the students how to dance to ragtime
  Ⓓ Continue describing the early history of ragtime

⊘ Explanation

Choice Ⓐ best describes what the professor will do next. The professor tells the students that he wants them to listen to some ragtime music so that they can hear what he was just talking about. It can therefore be inferred that he will play some ragtime music for them. The professor asks about the students' thoughts about ragtime music at the beginning of the lecture, so Choice Ⓑ is incorrect. Choice Ⓒ is incorrect because the professor says ragtime cannot be danced to. Choice Ⓓ is incorrect because the professor says he wants to stop talking about ragtime to play some music.

Building Background Knowledge of TOEFL Topics

Chapter 01 Life Sciences 1 | Conversations

zoology • biology • marine biology • medicine • virology • ecology • biochemistry • botany • public health

02-001

Listen to part of a lecture in a zoology class.

TYPE 1 What is the lecture mainly about?

(A) How some animals convert their prey into water

(B) Why ostriches and camels are well adapted to the desert

(C) How animals can survive in the desert without water

(D) The most ideal way for animals to get water in the desert

TYPE 2 What comparison does the professor make between camels and Gila monsters?

(A) How swiftly each of them can move

(B) Their method of creating metabolic water

(C) The number of days they can go without drinking water

(D) Where in their bodies they store fat

TYPE 3 Why does the professor mention the kangaroo rat?

(A) To say that it is a swift-running creature

(B) To state that it stores fat in its tail

(C) To explain how it creates metabolic water

(D) To compare its method of water creation with that of snakes

TYPE 4 Listen again to part of the lecture. Then answer the question.
Why does the professor say this: 🎧

(A) To note that camels do not often obey their riders

(B) To mention that camels do not usually like to run

(C) To claim that camels are not as fast as they appear

(D) To state that camels can move faster than most animals

Summarizing ▶ Fill in the blanks to complete the summary.

The professor explains what deserts are and then asks how some animals can live there when
_____ . He states that animals adapt to the desert in many ways. He notes that some animals
can _____ without water. The camel is one such creature. He then says another adaptation is
the animal's ability to _____ from one oasis to another. Camels, hyenas, and ostriches can all
do this. Finally, some animals, like kangaroo rats, create _____ . This means they never have to
_____ since they make it from the food they eat.

02-002

Listen to part of a lecture in a biology class.

TYPE 5 What is the main topic of the lecture?

Ⓐ How the beaver dominates the other animals in its region

Ⓑ What kind of role the beaver plays in its environment

Ⓒ How the beaver negatively alters the area in which it lives

Ⓓ How the beaver manages to construct its dam

TYPE 6 What is the student's opinion of beavers?

Ⓐ He states that their pelts make them worth hunting.

Ⓑ He believes that they should be exterminated.

Ⓒ He claims that they bother most of the other animals.

Ⓓ He thinks they are generally beneficial to the land.

TYPE 7 Which contribution of beavers to their environment do the following sentences refer to?
Click in the correct box for each sentence.

	Biodiversity	Water Purification	Preventing Flooding
1 Their dams keep the water level low.			
2 Their dams keep silt out of the water.			
3 They help attract animals to wetlands.			
4 Pesticides are broken down by the wetlands made by beavers' dams.			

TYPE 8 What does the professor imply about keystone species?

Ⓐ They are generally large animals such as the elephant.

Ⓑ They are needed to maintain the existing state of an ecosystem.

Ⓒ Most of the keystone species in various ecosystems are mammals.

Ⓓ Without them, the animals in an ecosystem would likely migrate.

Summarizing ▷ Fill in the blanks to complete the summary.

The professor begins by showing _____ and asking the students to identify it. A student says
it is a beaver and that beavers are somewhat helpful despite their _____ streams and creeks.
The professor agrees and then calls beavers a _____. According to her, beavers greatly affect
_____ in three ways. The dams create wetlands, so many animals live in them. This creates a
great amount of _____. The dams also help to purify the water that flows downstream. And the
dams help prevent flooding in the spring when water levels begin to rise.

02-003

Listen to part of a lecture in a zoology class.

TYPE 1 What aspect of reindeer does the professor mainly discuss?

    (A) Their adaptations to their frigid environment

    (B) How their bodies convert fat to nourishment

    (C) The structures of their bodies

    (D) Their weights and the places they are commonly found

TYPE 2 According to the professor, why do reindeer give birth in the spring?
Choose 2 answers.

    (A) This gives their babies time to adjust to their environment.

    (B) They need to have time for their hair to grow longer.

    (C) There is more food for them to eat during this season.

    (D) Their babies can survive better in warmer weather.

TYPE 3 How is the discussion organized?

    (A) By describing the reindeer's characteristics and then how they adapt to the cold

    (B) By explaining how the reindeer use subcutaneous fat to survive during winter

    (C) By covering the lives of reindeer from birth all the way to adulthood

    (D) By asking the students questions and then requiring them to provide answers

TYPE 4 Listen again to part of the lecture. Then answer the question.
Why does the professor say this: 🎧

    (A) The students are making too many errors.

    (B) He thinks they are having trouble understanding.

    (C) He is going to make an important point.

    (D) The material is about to get more complicated.

Summarizing ▶ Fill in the blanks to complete the summary.

The professor's lecture begins with him describing _____ of the reindeer and noting where they live. Afterward, the professor states that it must be difficult to survive in the harsh, cold environment, so he explains how reindeer _____. They give birth in the spring, so their babies can slowly _____ the cold weather. They also regularly stay active to _____. Their bodies have much _____, which they rely upon for heat and nourishment in the winter. Finally, their hooves and the length of their legs help them during cold weather.

02-004

Listen to part of a lecture in a public health class.

TYPE 5 What is the lecture mainly about?

(A) The difference between inactive and active vaccines

(B) The viruses for which there are vaccines

(C) The most effective types of vaccines

(D) The purpose and types of vaccines

TYPE 6 What is the professor's attitude toward live vaccines?

(A) She is in favor of researching them more.

(B) She would like to see their use restricted

(C) She feels that they can be useful.

(D) She offers no opinion on them.

TYPE 7 The professor gives some characteristics of inactive and active vaccines. Indicate for each example which vaccine it refers to.
Click in the correct box for each sentence.

	Inactive Vaccines	Active Vaccines
1 The virus in them is merely weakened.		
2 They must be given every few years.		
3 The virus in them has been killed.		
4 They may result in the person getting the virus that individual is being vaccinated against.		

TYPE 8 What will the professor probably do next?

(A) Describe a different kind of vaccine

(B) Continue explaining active vaccines

(C) Compare active and inactive vaccines

(D) Mention some viruses that have vaccines

Summarizing ▶ **Fill in the blanks to complete the summary.**

The professor tells the students she wants to talk about vaccines. A student asks about vaccines
_____, but the professor states she believes that does not happen. Then, she explains how
vaccines give the body _____ from certain viruses. She also mentions that there are two types of
vaccines: _____. Inactive vaccines use _____ but must be renewed every
few years. Active vaccines use live virus material, so a body only needs to be boosted once. However, active vaccines
may sometimes not work properly and might give the person the virus instead of _____.

TYPE 1 • Gist-Content   *TYPE 2* • Detail   *TYPE 3* • Understanding Organization   *TYPE 4* • Function of What Is Said

02-005

Listen to part of a conversation between a student and a housing office employee.

TYPE 1 Why does the student visit the housing office?

ⓐ To inquire about how to get a single room

ⓑ To ask about how to defer payment on his room

ⓒ To complain about his current roommates

ⓓ To request a change to another dormitory room

TYPE 2 Why does the woman give the student a form to fill out?

ⓐ To encourage him to leave the office

ⓑ To enable him to apply for a scholarship

ⓒ To help him complete his request

ⓓ To get him to put his complaint in writing

TYPE 3 Why does the student mention his father's business?

ⓐ To attempt to gain sympathy from the employee

ⓑ To mention why he feels the need to apply for a scholarship

ⓒ To explain why he lacks the funds to pay for the room

ⓓ To answer the employee's question about his parents

TYPE 4 Listen again to part of the conversation. Then answer the question.
What does the employee imply when she says this: 🎧

ⓐ She does not understand the student's motive.

ⓑ She believes that the student has misspoken.

ⓒ She wants the student to repeat his request.

ⓓ She feels that the student is making a mistake.

Summarizing ▷ Fill in the blanks to complete the summary.

A student visits the university's housing office to inquire about _____ . The housing employee says that he needs a clear reason for wanting to move, or the school will _____ . The student responds that he is in a single room but _____ , so he would like to move into _____ . The employee is surprised by his response but indicates that she can probably accommodate his request. She gives the student _____ to request a room change.

02-006

Listen to part of a conversation between a student and a professor.

TYPE 5 What are the speakers mainly discussing?

    Ⓐ A textbook that the student is supposed to purchase

    Ⓑ A class assignment the student must complete

    Ⓒ A project that the student is about to finish

    Ⓓ An exam that the professor will give the class

TYPE 6 What does the professor tell the student about plumerias?

    Ⓐ They do not take well to grafting.

    Ⓑ They can be difficult to raise in pots.

    Ⓒ They are plants that grow in the tropics.

    Ⓓ They need sunlight in order to grow well.

TYPE 7 What is the professor's opinion of the student's idea?

    Ⓐ He is very supportive of her idea.

    Ⓑ He thinks her idea needs improvement.

    Ⓒ He feels that her idea might not work.

    Ⓓ He believes her idea is not unique.

TYPE 8 What can be inferred about the student?

    Ⓐ She has just transferred from another university.

    Ⓑ She has taken a class with the professor in the past.

    Ⓒ She feels that the class will require a lot of work.

    Ⓓ She does not like to delay work she must do.

Summarizing ▶ Fill in the blanks to complete the summary.

The professor invites the student to come in to his office and apologizes for making her wait outside. The student responds that she wants to _____ . The professor is surprised because it is the first week of class, and the project is due _____ . The student says she wants to _____ , so it might take a long time. The professor mentions that they are _____ , but the student grows them in pots indoors. The professor supports the student's idea and says that he is interested in _____ .

Listen to part of a lecture in a paleontology class.

02-007

Amber Fossils

Fossilization Process:		Modern-Day Uses:
	➡	

---

1 What is the lecture mainly about?

Ⓐ The value of amber as jewelry

Ⓑ Life forms that were trapped in amber

Ⓒ The era when creatures were incased in amber

Ⓓ DNA samples taken from animals in amber

2 Why does the professor mention bees?

Ⓐ To show that they were frequently captured in amber

Ⓑ To say that DNA has been taken from their blood

Ⓒ To ask the students about a lecture the previous week

Ⓓ To explain the basis for a theory he talked about before

3 Listen again to part of the lecture. Then answer the question.
What does the professor mean when he says this: 🎧

Ⓐ DNA taken from blood cannot clone dinosaurs.

Ⓑ It is unlikely that mosquitoes incased in amber ever bit dinosaurs.

Ⓒ Mosquitoes never sucked the blood of any dinosaurs.

Ⓓ It is possible to clone dinosaurs if one has access to their blood.

Summarizing ▶ Fill in the blanks to complete the summary.

The professor describes amber's characteristics and notes how it forms and that people use it
_____ . He then mentions where it is commonly found and states that it is important to the
study of _____ . A student asks about _____ from the blood of animals
in amber, but the professor claims that is impossible. He mentions that DNA has been extracted from some amber-
encased animals though. The professor claims much can be learned about _____ by examining
creatures in amber, and he states how studying _____ might explain something that happened
100 million years ago.

Listen to part of a lecture in a zoology class.

02-008

The Characteristics of Bats

General Information:

Life Spans:

Pups:

Special Ability:

---

1   How is the discussion organized?

     Ⓐ   By comparing myths about bats to the facts about them

     Ⓑ   By providing details about the characteristics of bats

     Ⓒ   By describing in detail bats' lives from birth to death

     Ⓓ   By mentioning what information is not yet known about bats

2   Based on the information in the lecture, do the following sentences refer to myths or facts about bats? Click in the correct box for each sentence.

	Myth	Fact
1 Bats have incredibly poor eyesight.		
2 Bats often live in large groups.		
3 Bats have occasionally attacked people.		
4 Bats tend to suck the blood of their victims.		

3   Listen again to part of the lecture. Then answer the question.

     What does the professor imply when she says this: 🎧

     Ⓐ   Some students might not believe what she just said.

     Ⓑ   She made a mistake when giving them a figure.

     Ⓒ   She had to consult the book to check on her facts.

     Ⓓ   She wants the students to confirm what she told them.

Summarizing ▶ Fill in the blanks to complete the summary.

The professor mentions that there are many _____ about bats. She then notes where they live and some bat species' _____ . In response to a question about bats sucking blood, the professor claims that some bats _____ but that they do not suck the blood of animals. This is where their connection to _____ occurs. The lecture then continues by noting how bats raise their young. The professor concludes by commenting that bats have _____ , so they use a kind of radar in order to guide their flight and to find various objects.

Mastering Topics with Lectures

Listen to part of a lecture in a biology class.

02-009

Cicadas and Their Life Cycles

General Information:	Life Cycles:	Dog-Day Cicada:
		Magicicada:

---

1 What aspect of cicadas does the professor mainly discuss?

Ⓐ Their life cycles

Ⓑ Their mating habits

Ⓒ The locations of their broods

Ⓓ Their methods of communication

2 According to the professor, how do cicadas survive while underground?

Ⓐ They endure a period of hibernation underground.

Ⓑ They feed on various creatures that live there.

Ⓒ They use nearby plants as their food sources.

Ⓓ Their bodies do not require food while they are underground.

3 Based on the information in the lecture, indicate whether the sentences refer to cicadas in the United States or in Asia.

Click in the correct box for each sentence.

	United States	Asia
1 They have life cycles that are longer than average.		
2 They are found residing in tropical climates.		
3 They belong to the Magicicada family.		
4 People know when their broods are going to emerge from underground.		

Summarizing ▶ Fill in the blanks to complete the summary.

The professor comments on the number of cicada species and where on the Earth they primarily live. He describes how cicadas make _____ and notes that it is believed to be a _____ . He describes some common characteristics of cicadas, particularly the fact that they _____ for several years. He then mentions the two most prevalent species in America and explains what makes one of them, the _____ , so unique. According to the professor, the Magicicada spends a long period of time underground and then _____ in enormous numbers.

Listen to part of a lecture in a biology class.

02-010

─ **Spider Webs** ─

How It Makes Its Web:

➡

How It Uses Its Web:

Unique Feature of Some Webs:

1 What does the professor say about decorations in spider webs?

- Ⓐ They are used to attract and to capture birds.
- Ⓑ They may be made from plants or animals.
- Ⓒ They are effective at camouflaging the spiders.
- Ⓓ They distract prey, thus making them easier to catch.

2 What is the professor's attitude toward spider webs?

- Ⓐ He thinks they are very interesting.
- Ⓑ He believes they have many uses.
- Ⓒ He thinks they often waste the spiders' time.
- Ⓓ He feels they are not particularly complicated.

3 Why does the professor mention orb webs?

- Ⓐ To describe their advantages and disadvantages
- Ⓑ To say that spiders tend to decorate these webs
- Ⓒ To note that they are the webs most usually spun
- Ⓓ To show how they can easily ensnare the spiders themselves

Summarizing ▷ Fill in the blanks to complete the summary.

The professor begins by describing spider silk and saying that there are ...., yet
no one spider can spin all seven. He notes the strength of spider silk and the fact that it can be a
.... He mentions how spiders use webs to ...., which they must
do since spinning a web expends .... He describes orb webs and the process by which
spiders weave sticky and non-sticky webs to create them. He then mentions how spiders ....
in different ways but comments that no one knows exactly why they do so.

Listen to part of a conversation between a student and a student center employee.

02-011

Service Encounter

Problem:

Solution:

1 Why does the woman visit the student center?

Ⓐ To visit her friend Anne Parkins

Ⓑ To apply for a job there

Ⓒ To get some job training

Ⓓ To submit her résumé to Mr. Walker

2 Why does the man tell the woman about the coffee shop?

Ⓐ To indicate where she should apply for a job

Ⓑ To invite her to have a drink with him later

Ⓒ To tell her where Anne is working at the moment

Ⓓ To give her directions on how she can get there

3 Listen again to part of the conversation. Then answer the question.
What does the man mean when he says this: 🎧

Ⓐ He approves of what the woman says she will do.

Ⓑ He wants the woman to follow him behind the counter.

Ⓒ The woman is welcome to work at the student center.

Ⓓ The woman needs to speak with her friend Anne.

Summarizing ▷ Fill in the blanks to complete the summary.

A woman goes to the .... to apply for a job. The employee mentions that he is currently hiring
and tells the student about a job and its hours. The student can do the job, but the hours ....
her schedule. Then, the employee describes another job that is currently available, but the woman's
.... again is not a good match for the job. The employee then recommends that the woman
go to the .... and apply for a job there. He says that he will put in a good word for her with
the ....

Listen to part of a conversation between a student and a professor.

02-012

Office Hours

Problem:

Solution:

1 Why does the student visit the professor?

 Ⓐ To ask about getting a special arrangement for her class

 Ⓑ To find out about Professor Giovanni's schedule

 Ⓒ To talk to the professor about getting an internship

 Ⓓ To try to sign up for the professor's seminar

2 What is the student's problem?

 Ⓐ She does not want to take the seminar with the professor.

 Ⓑ She cannot fit a class she needs in her schedule.

 Ⓒ She thinks a certain class is unnecessary for her.

 Ⓓ She is having difficulty managing a double major.

3 Listen again to part of the conversation. Then answer the question.
What can be inferred from the professor's response to the student?

 Ⓐ The professor is having difficulty understanding the student's language.

 Ⓑ The professor is displeased with the student's request.

 Ⓒ The student is proposing something the professor has never considered.

 Ⓓ The student is trying to avoid following the university's class guidelines.

Summarizing ▷ Fill in the blanks to complete the summary.

A student visits a professor to talk about a _____ . The student says she has an _____ at the same time as the seminar, but she really wants to take the class. Then, she suggests that she not attend the class but _____ for the class. The professor disagrees. The student wonders if a class she took _____ could substitute for the seminar, but the professor claims the two classes are different. The professor suggests that the student _____ of the internship, and the student agrees to speak with her professor about doing that.

02-013

Listen to part of a lecture in a biology class.

Metamorphosis

1   What is the main topic of the lecture?

   Ⓐ The process by which tadpoles become adult frogs and toads

   Ⓑ The amount of time spent in each stage of an insect's lifecycle

   Ⓒ The way that hemimetabolism occurs in some insects

   Ⓓ The different ways in which metamorphosis in insects occurs

2   What is an example of an insect in its larva stage?

   Ⓐ A caterpillar

   Ⓑ A butterfly

   Ⓒ A tadpole

   Ⓓ A grasshopper

3   Based on the information in the lecture, indicate whether the sentences refer to simple metamorphosis or complex metamorphosis.
    Click in the correct box for each sentence.

	Simple Metamorphosis	Complex Metamorphosis
1 The insects undergo four different stages.		
2 The insects look dramatically different when they reach their adult stage.		
3 There is a slow change from the nymph to the adult stage.		
4 Some insects may molt and then change while they are instars.		

4   How does the professor organize the information about metamorphosis that he presents to the class?
    Ⓐ By discussing the life cycles of insects in simple metamorphosis
    Ⓑ By noting how insects undergoing complex metamorphosis have more advantages
    Ⓒ By describing both types individually and providing examples of each
    Ⓓ By mentioning insects and then noting which type of metamorphosis they undergo

5   Listen again to part of the lecture. Then answer the question.
    Why does the professor say this: 🎧
    Ⓐ To criticize his students
    Ⓑ To introduce some humor
    Ⓒ To point out an important fact
    Ⓓ To describe the caterpillar's lifestyle

6   Listen again to part of the lecture. Then answer the question.
    What can be inferred about the professor when he says this: 🎧
    Ⓐ He wants a student to describe the term to him.
    Ⓑ He thinks the students should look up the definition in their book.
    Ⓒ He assumes the students know what he is talking about.
    Ⓓ He believes the students should ask him about this.

02-014

Listen to part of a lecture in a marine biology class.

Marine Biology

1   What aspect of the ocean depths does the professor mainly discuss?
   Ⓐ The way oxygen reaches the bottom
   Ⓑ The creatures that survive there
   Ⓒ The abyssal and hadal zones
   Ⓓ The purpose of the thermocline

2   Why does the professor explain marine snow?
   Ⓐ To describe a unique meteorological phenomenon
   Ⓑ To mention how creatures deep in the ocean get food
   Ⓒ To explain the process of photosynthesis
   Ⓓ To note how deep-sea creatures can survive the intense pressure in the ocean

3   What comparison does the professor make between the abyssal and hadal zones?
   Ⓐ The depths they reach beneath the ocean's surface
   Ⓑ The amount of life that exists in them
   Ⓒ The existence of the thermocline in each
   Ⓓ The pressure that they exert on other objects

4   Why does the professor mention thermal vents?

    Ⓐ To explain why some places deep in the ocean have a micro-ecosystem

    Ⓑ To describe the types of creatures that live near them

    Ⓒ To note why shrimp, clams, and tubeworms can become so large

    Ⓓ To examine how they counteract the intense pressures in the ocean

5   What does the professor imply about the anglerfish?

    Ⓐ It is larger than most other creatures deep in the ocean.

    Ⓑ It only mates with one fish for its entire life.

    Ⓒ It is the only fish that can produce its own light.

    Ⓓ It is unable to survive on its own.

6   Listen again to part of the lecture. Then answer the question.
    What does the professor mean when she says this: 🎧

    Ⓐ There are some fascinating creatures living deep in the ocean.

    Ⓑ Scientists are just now learning about deep-sea creatures.

    Ⓒ There is very little known about creatures in the ocean's depths.

    Ⓓ It is surprising that creatures can live at the bottom of the ocean.

02-015

Listen to part of a conversation between a student and a professor.

1 Why does the student visit the professor's office?

- Ⓐ To say that he has not returned a library book
- Ⓑ To inquire about a term paper that he is writing
- Ⓒ To find out some information on Sir Francis Bacon
- Ⓓ To ask about changing the date of an upcoming test

2 What does the student say about his term paper?

- Ⓐ It is due this coming Friday.
- Ⓑ He lacks enough information to write it.
- Ⓒ He has almost completed it.
- Ⓓ He expects to get a good grade on it.

3 What is the student's opinion of the librarian?

- Ⓐ She did a thorough job.
- Ⓑ She has very little knowledge.
- Ⓒ She was impolite to him.
- Ⓓ She was rather unhelpful.

4 Why does the professor turn down the student's request?

- Ⓐ She believes the student's grade is already high enough.
- Ⓑ She wants the student to challenge himself.
- Ⓒ She knows he can get the information from other sources.
- Ⓓ No other students have complained to her about anything.

5 Listen again to part of the conversation. Then answer the question.
What does the professor imply when she says this: 🎧

- Ⓐ The student needs to read the reserve book on Sir Francis Bacon.
- Ⓑ The test will include some questions on Sir Francis Bacon.
- Ⓒ The student ought to ask her some questions about Sir Francis Bacon.
- Ⓓ The student already knows enough about Sir Francis Bacon.

• *Mastering Question Types*

access	antibody	bothersome	clime
digest	essential	habit	hump
inordinate	metabolic	pesticide	reputation
store	thrive	virulence	weakened
adaptable	application	characteristic	convert
diverse	factor	harsh	immunity
invade	nourishment	prey	require
subcutaneous	tropical	virus	wetland
aggressively	autism	chemical	dam
domestic	grassland	hoof	inject
insulation	oasis	purify	rodent
swiftly	vaccine	wasteland	wild

• *Mastering Topics*

amber	bond	confuse	disrupt
ensnare	fascinate	harden	lifespan
migrate	nocturnal	predator	radar
screech	subspecies	track	web
anchor	chase	consist	distinct
evolve	fossil	instinctive	mammal
mutation	pollen	prehistoric	replenish
secrete	temperate	trap	whine
awareness	colony	crawl	emerge
farfetched	gland	lick	microscope
nectar	potential	protein	resin
struggle	thorax	vibration	wingspan

• *TOEFL Practice Tests*

absorb	aquatic	categorize	concentrate
crustacean	drastic	exploration	glow
immature	larva	metamorphosis	organ
pupa	rigid	smash	tandem
abundant	astonished	chrysalis	consume
depth	emit	filter	gradual
incomplete	literally	molt	precarious
resemblance	shed	strategy	thermal
amphibian	buoyant	complex	crush
dormant	exploit	gelatinous	hormone
internal	marine	nutrient	protrusion
resource	signature	tadpole	undergo

Vocabulary *Review*

📝 Choose the words with the closest meanings to the highlighted words.

1 The conditions were harsh, but the group was able to survive the blizzard.

  (A) unique   (B) encouraging
  (C) severe   (D) outrageous

2 The caterpillar underwent a metamorphosis and became a butterfly.

  (A) change   (B) operation
  (C) arrangement   (D) formation

3 Everyone was astonished by her comments in the meeting.

  (A) upset   (B) bothered
  (C) pleased   (D) stunned

4 The sun emits a huge amount of energy at all times.

  (A) sends up   (B) sends in
  (C) sends out   (D) sends for

5 I am in a precarious position and am not sure what I should do next.

  (A) fortunate   (B) dramatic
  (C) comfortable   (D) sensitive

6 The dog looked confused when it could not find the bone it had just buried.

  (A) hungry   (B) puzzled
  (C) angry   (D) amazed

7 The hunters managed to ensnare several animals during the afternoon.

  (A) shoot   (B) spot
  (C) kill   (D) trap

8 Be sure to purify the water from the stream before you drink it.

  (A) rinse   (B) sanitize
  (C) strain   (D) drain

9 Jason has a reputation as a person that can be trusted with anything.

  (A) name   (B) condition
  (C) knowledge   (D) situation

10 The pipes were anchored to the floor so that they would not be blown away by the wind.

  (A) attached   (B) glued
  (C) cemented   (D) locked

📝 Match the words with the correct definitions.

11 immature   •

12 bothersome   •

13 wasteland   •

14 concentrate   •

15 dam   •

16 buoyant   •

17 distinct   •

18 application   •

19 farfetched   •

20 replenish   •

• (A) to focus on or think intensely about something

• (B) not yet having reached one's stage of maturity

• (C) to block a body of water such as a river or a stream

• (D) highly unlikely

• (E) a use

• (F) to restore or to make new again

• (G) unique; being the only example of something

• (H) very annoying

• (I) an area where nothing can grow or survive

• (J) able to float on the water

Chapter 02   Life Sciences 2 | Conversations

zoology • biology • marine biology • medicine • virology • ecology • biochemistry •
botany • public health

02-016

Listen to part of a lecture in a biology class.

TYPE 1 What aspect of symbiosis does the professor mainly discuss?

   Ⓐ The benefits it provides to both species
   Ⓑ The various relationships that exist in it
   Ⓒ The types of species that engage in it
   Ⓓ The reasons why species make use of it

TYPE 2 What is mutualism?

   Ⓐ A symbiotic relationship that offers advantages to both species
   Ⓑ A type of symbiosis where one species benefits while the other does not
   Ⓒ A parasitic relationship in which the host is killed or harmed by an invader
   Ⓓ A relationship where one of the species suffers no harm from the other

TYPE 3 How does the professor organize the information about symbiosis that she presents to the class?

   Ⓐ By giving the reasons why species would engage in that type of behavior
   Ⓑ By describing it and giving examples of the various forms it assumes
   Ⓒ By comparing it with other types of behavior in the animal kingdom
   Ⓓ By giving examples of it and then explaining what type of symbiosis it is

TYPE 4 Listen again to part of the lecture. Then answer the question.
Why does the professor say this: 🎧

   Ⓐ To criticize the student for his response
   Ⓑ To praise the student for giving a good answer
   Ⓒ To encourage the student to make another attempt
   Ⓓ To politely tell the student his answer is incorrect

Summarizing ▶ Fill in the blanks to complete the summary.

The professor mentions that species sometimes interact with each other, most usually because of food. She says that these interactions are known as _____. She describes three different types of relationships. The first is _____, which involves the parasite causing damage to—or even killing—the host. These relationships often involve to _____. Commensalism is a relationship where both species are fairly unaffected by the relationship. The professor says that _____ have this kind of relationship. And mutualism occurs when both species _____. The cleaner fish and large carnivorous fish have this relationship.

Listen to part of a lecture in a biology class.

02-017

TYPE 5 Why does the professor explain the innate immune system?

    Ⓐ To explain its role in fighting cancer in the body

    Ⓑ To claim that it is the most important part of the body

    Ⓒ To compare it with the immune systems of other animals

    Ⓓ To describe its role in keeping the body healthy

TYPE 6 What is the professor's opinion of T cells?

    Ⓐ They do not have very many vital functions in the body.

    Ⓑ They are of great importance to the body's immune system.

    Ⓒ They are too easily harmed by microbes entering the body.

    Ⓓ They cannot perform as many functions as regular white blood cells.

TYPE 7 Based on the information in the lecture, which part of the immune system do the following statements refer to?

Click in the correct box for each sentence.

	Innate Immune System	Adaptive Immune System
① Develops as the body ages over time		
② Includes the skin and the mucus membranes		
③ Is what the body is born with		
④ Has parts formed in the spleen and the thymus		

TYPE 8 What will the professor probably do next?

    Ⓐ Give the class a short break

    Ⓑ Answer the student's question

    Ⓒ Continue covering the immune system

    Ⓓ Move on to the body's nervous system

Summarizing ▶ Fill in the blanks to complete the summary.

The professor remarks that there are two parts of the body's immune system. The first is ＿＿＿＿＿＿＿＿＿＿, which is what people are born with. It includes ＿＿＿＿＿＿＿＿ that keep harmful microbes out of the body. The second part of it includes special cells such as ＿＿＿＿＿＿＿＿. They work with lymph nodes to trap microbes and to destroy them. The adaptive immune system develops as ＿＿＿＿＿＿＿＿. It forms when the body recognizes past infections and makes antibodies to fight them. It also includes ＿＿＿＿＿＿＿＿, which fight dangerous infections and even attack cancer cells.

02-018

Listen to part of a lecture in a botany class.

TYPE 1   What is the main topic of the lecture?

    Ⓐ The social aspects of drinking coffee

    Ⓑ Various coffee decaffeination processes

    Ⓒ Reasons why people drink decaffeinated coffee

    Ⓓ The most ideal way to decaffeinate coffee

TYPE 2   According to the professor, which of the following occurs in the direct decaffeination method?
Choose 2 answers.

    Ⓐ It takes approximately ten minutes to complete.

    Ⓑ The beans are steamed before chemicals are applied to them.

    Ⓒ Chemicals are applied to water the coffee has been soaked in.

    Ⓓ The process must be repeated several times.

TYPE 3   Why does the professor mention the Roselius method?

    Ⓐ To explain why benzene is no longer used to decaffeinate coffee

    Ⓑ To compare it with direct decaffeination

    Ⓒ To name another way of decaffeinating coffee beans

    Ⓓ To claim that it was the first decaffeination method used

TYPE 4   Listen again to part of the lecture. Then answer the question.
Why does the professor say this: 🎧

    Ⓐ To complain about her morning coffee

    Ⓑ To show some side effects of coffee

    Ⓒ To make a joke about herself

    Ⓓ To note why she has a stuttering problem

Summarizing ▷ Fill in the blanks to complete the summary.

The professor comments that the students _____ because they probably did not
have any coffee in the morning as she did. She then mentions that not all coffee has caffeine since some is
_____ . She notes there are two decaffeination processes: _____ .
Direct decaffeination involves steaming the beans and washing them with chemicals. Indirect decaffeination involves
repeatedly _____ in water to remove the caffeine. She then discusses some other methods of
decaffeination and also explains that drinking coffee is _____ for many people, which is one
reason why coffee is so popular.

02-019

Listen to part of a lecture in a botany class.

TYPE 5   What aspect of the Rafflesia does the professor mainly discuss?

    Ⓐ Its feeding methods

    Ⓑ Its strong smell

    Ⓒ Its pollination methods

    Ⓓ Its unique characteristics

TYPE 6   What can be inferred about the student?

    Ⓐ He is majoring in botany.

    Ⓑ He has never heard of the Rafflesia before.

    Ⓒ He failed to do the homework assignment.

    Ⓓ He wants to speak with the professor after class.

TYPE 7   What can be inferred about the Rafflesia?

    Ⓐ Not everyone considers it a flower.

    Ⓑ Animals often find its scent repulsive.

    Ⓒ Very little research has been conducted on it.

    Ⓓ Its petals can be eaten by some animals.

TYPE 8   Listen again to part of the lecture. Then answer the question.
    What does the professor imply when she says this: 🎧

    Ⓐ Nothing in nature is as strange as the Rafflesia.

    Ⓑ The students will learn about more unusual organisms in later classes.

    Ⓒ She wants the students to be sure to recognize the Rafflesia as a flower.

    Ⓓ She is getting ready to move on to another topic for discussion.

Summarizing ▶ Fill in the blanks to complete the summary.

The professor says the Rafflesia is a rare flower found in the jungles of _____ . It is a parasite, so it grows on a vine, from which it gets its nourishment. Its bloom is a fifteen-pound three-foot-wide flower that _____ . It has the odor of _____ . The reason is that it relies upon flies to pollinate it, so the rotten odor attracts them. When a student argues that the Rafflesia is _____ , she explains why it is. She then states that it is rare because the flowers seldom get pollinated since the male and female Rafflesia often live _____ .

02-020

Listen to part of a conversation between a student and a professor.

TYPE 1 Why does the student visit the professor's office?

    Ⓐ He had made an appointment to see the professor.

    Ⓑ He wants to get an extension on a report due soon.

    Ⓒ He needs some assistance on the topic for his paper.

    Ⓓ He would like the professor to read over his essay.

TYPE 2 According to the professor, how should the student do his assignment?

    Ⓐ By writing a comprehensive biography of the person

    Ⓑ By concentrating on one part of the individual's life

    Ⓒ By comparing the person's life with that of one of his contemporary's

    Ⓓ By interpreting the effects of that person's life on others

TYPE 3 Why does the student mention Winston Churchill?

    Ⓐ To say that he cannot find enough information on him

    Ⓑ To ask if he is an acceptable subject to write about

    Ⓒ To state that he is the topic of the student's report

    Ⓓ To try to get the professor's opinion on his life

TYPE 4 Listen again to part of the conversation. Then answer the question.
What does the professor mean when she says this: 🎧

    Ⓐ The student needs to think harder more often.

    Ⓑ The reason for the student's visit is obvious to her.

    Ⓒ She is much more intelligent than the student is.

    Ⓓ The student has a limited amount of time to speak with her.

Summarizing ▶ Fill in the blanks to complete the summary.

The student wants to talk to the professor about what he says is something important, but she already knows _____ . She tells him that several other students have been in that day to _____ as well. The student wants to write about _____ , but he has too much information on Churchill. The professor tells the student to _____ of his paper. She wants him to choose one part of Churchill's life and then to _____ . That should be all that he writes his paper on.

Listen to part of a conversation between a student and a housing office employee.

02-021

TYPE 5 What are the speakers mainly discussing?

    Ⓐ The cause of some damage in the student's room

    Ⓑ A dispute between the student and his roommate

    Ⓒ The amount of money the student will have to pay

    Ⓓ A report filed by the student's resident assistant

TYPE 6 Who is Eric Shaw?

    Ⓐ The student's resident assistant

    Ⓑ The student's roommate

    Ⓒ The student's advisor

    Ⓓ The student's uncle

TYPE 7 Listen again to part of the conversation. Then answer the question.
What can be inferred about the student when he says this: 🎧

    Ⓐ He thinks the woman's final judgment is fair.

    Ⓑ He wants a complete explanation from the woman.

    Ⓒ He wants his roommate to attend the hearing.

    Ⓓ He believes he should not have to pay for anything.

TYPE 8 What can be inferred about the employee?

    Ⓐ She believes the student acted improperly.

    Ⓑ She is going to fine the student for the problem.

    Ⓒ She has no interest in speaking with the student's roommate.

    Ⓓ She will continue to investigate the matter.

Summarizing ▶ Fill in the blanks to complete the summary.

The student visits _____ to speak with the female employee. She tells him that
according to his resident assistant, there is _____ in his room. She wants to know how
_____. The student mentions that he did nothing wrong. Instead, it was his roommate.
He also notes that he was _____ when the damage was done and that the security
cameras should be able to verify that he was not in the dorm. The woman says that the student may still have to
_____, but she vows to continue investigating.

Listen to part of a lecture in a zoology class.

02-022

--- Bowerbirds ---

| Unique Courtship Ritual: | | Reason for Ritual: |
| | ➡ | Result: |

1   What aspect of the bowerbird does the professor mainly discuss?

Ⓐ How it constructs bowers in the jungle

Ⓑ What the male does in order to attract females

Ⓒ Why it does not get involved in monogamous relationships

Ⓓ Which kinds of objects it adorns its bowers with

2   According to the professor, how do some male bowerbirds get objects for their bowers?

Ⓐ By taking them from other males

Ⓑ By digging them up from the ground

Ⓒ By stealing them from other animals

Ⓓ By collecting them from people's homes

3   Based on the information in the lecture, do the following statements refer to male or female bowerbirds? Click in the correct box for each sentence.

	Male Bowerbird	Female Bowerbird
1 Protects its babies once they are born		
2 Guards its bowers from other birds		
3 Mates with as many bowerbirds as it can		
4 Selects a partner to mate with		

Summarizing ▷ Fill in the blanks to complete the summary.

The professor says that bowerbirds live in New Guinea and Australia. They are unique birds because of _____. The professor notes that male bowerbirds construct elaborate bowers to attempt to attract females. The bowers are often large enough to be _____. They also have many colorful objects that are arranged according to _____. Then, the females examine the bowers and choose a mate. The professor says that males hurriedly mate and then return to their bowers to protect them from _____. The males take no part in raising the chicks. They only mate with as many females as they can.

Listen to part of a lecture in a zoology class.

02-023

How Insects Get Nutrition and Digest It

What Insects Eat:		How Insects Eat:		How Insects Digest Food:
	➡		➡	

---

1 Why does the professor mention mosquitoes' eating habits?

Ⓐ To note the reason why mosquitoes bite animals

Ⓑ To mention that they cannot survive without blood

Ⓒ To give an example of an animal that sucks its food

Ⓓ To explain what allows them to transmit diseases

2 How does the professor organize the information about insects that he presents to the class?

Ⓐ By comparing how several insects consume their food

Ⓑ By noting the kinds of foods that insects can eat

Ⓒ By describing their eating habits and digestive methods

Ⓓ By explaining the differences in the ways they digest their food

3 Listen again to part of the lecture. Then answer the question.
Why does the professor say this: 🎧

Ⓐ To convince the students that he is not joking

Ⓑ To reassure the students that he stated a fact

Ⓒ To apologize for giving the students the wrong number

Ⓓ To ask the students to consider what he just said

Summarizing ▷ Fill in the blanks to complete the summary.

The professor says there are millions of insect species. They get their nutrition in different ways, but most of them digest it similarly. According to the professor, most insects consume either _____ or the nectar of fruit. Other animals, like flies, may feed off of _____. And some, like mosquitoes, may suck blood to get nutrition. Insects will chew or grind their food or else _____ it. As for digesting their food, for most insects, they have _____. After consuming food, the body removes the nutrients, and then the waste matter _____.

Listen to part of a lecture in a biology class.

02-024

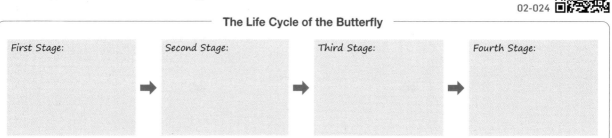

The Life Cycle of the Butterfly

First Stage:

Second Stage:

Third Stage:

Fourth Stage:

1 How is the discussion organized?

Ⓐ By describing the butterfly's life chronologically

Ⓑ By focusing mostly on the butterfly's pupa stage

Ⓒ By asking a question and then answering it

Ⓓ By comparing two butterflies' life cycles with one another

2 What will the professor probably do next?

Ⓐ Describe some butterflies' migration habits

Ⓑ Show some slides of the butterfly's life cycle

Ⓒ Dismiss the class for the rest of the day

Ⓓ Name some butterflies that tend to hibernate

3 Listen again to part of the lecture. Then answer the question.
What does the professor mean when she says this: 🎧

Ⓐ The professor does not know the answer to her question.

Ⓑ The student should be able to answer the question by herself.

Ⓒ The student needs to read the book again.

Ⓓ The student asked a perceptive question.

Summarizing ▶ Fill in the blanks to complete the summary.

The professor talks about _____ of the butterfly. There are four stages. The first is the egg, which lasts for a few days. When the eggs hatch, a caterpillar emerges to live _____ . The caterpillar eats as much as it can. The third stage is the pupa, which is when the caterpillar _____ , or cocoon, in which it stays while it _____ . The fourth stage is the butterfly. During this stage, it mates so that the cycle can begin anew. The professor also mentions that some butterflies that emerge in cold weather will either _____ to warmer areas.

Listen to part of a lecture in a biology class.

02-025

Termites

Physical Characteristics:		Workers:
	➡	Soldiers:
		Reproductives:

1 Why does the professor explain ants' physical characteristics?

Ⓐ To note how all insects share certain physical traits

Ⓑ To focus on the size of their bodies

Ⓒ To answer a student's question about them

Ⓓ To differentiate between them and termites

2 According to the professor, how are soldier termites different from worker termites?

Ⓐ They have wings that they can shed.

Ⓑ They mature more slowly than workers.

Ⓒ They have mandibles while the workers do not.

Ⓓ They have longer lifespans than workers.

3 Listen again to part of the lecture. Then answer the question.
What is the purpose of the student's response?

Ⓐ To boast about getting the answer correct

Ⓑ To indicate she has learned something new

Ⓒ To thank the professor for teaching her

Ⓓ To compliment the professor on his teaching method

Summarizing ▷ Fill in the blanks to complete the summary.

The professor shows some slides of _____ and asks the students which is which. When the students have problems, the professor explains _____ of each. The female student then easily recognizes which picture is the termite. Next, the professor continues to describe _____ of termites. He explains the physical traits of the workers, the soldiers, and the reproductives, which are _____. When the king and the queen form a colony, they mate repeatedly so that the colony can expand. This can go on for years while the queen can lay up to 60,000 eggs over _____ .

Listen to part of a conversation between a student and a professor.

02-026

Office Hours

| Problem 1: | ➡ | Solution 1: |
| Problem 2: | ⬐ ➡ | Solution 2: |

1 Why does the student visit the professor?

Ⓐ To talk with her about a problem he has

Ⓑ To ask her for a letter of recommendation

Ⓒ To receive some help on an application

Ⓓ To get her opinion on an internship possibility

2 What can be inferred about the student?

Ⓐ He prefers waiting until the last minute to do things.

Ⓑ He would rather take a class than work as an intern.

Ⓒ He is not very enthusiastic about the program.

Ⓓ He is going to graduate within a year.

3 What does the professor imply about the student?

Ⓐ His grades in her classes have been high.

Ⓑ He is unqualified for the internship.

Ⓒ He should attend a meeting with her.

Ⓓ He needs to focus on his studies before the semester ends.

Summarizing ▷ Fill in the blanks to complete the summary.

The student visits the professor's office to talk to her about _____ at a company. She asks him why he waited so long to apply, and he says that he found out about it the day before. He states that it is _____ , which is what he really wants to do after he graduates. Then, he asks the professor if she will write _____ for him. The professor agrees even though he needs the letter by _____ . She tells him to pick up his letter the next day around one o'clock and then leaves _____ .

Listen to part of a conversation between a student and an admissions office employee.

02-027

Service Encounter

Problem:

Solutions:

1 What problem does the student have?

Ⓐ She does not remember which office she should go to.

Ⓑ She is unsure where she should meet the student she is hosting.

Ⓒ She does not know where she should take the incoming student.

Ⓓ She is not confident that she can describe the school effectively.

2 According to the man, what should the student do with the incoming high school student?
Choose 2 answers.

Ⓐ Answer every question the student asks her

Ⓑ Be enthusiastic about the university

Ⓒ Show the student some places on campus

Ⓓ Encourage the student to select a major

3 Listen again to part of the conversation. Then answer the question.
What is the purpose of the student's response?

Ⓐ To emphasize how much she likes the school

Ⓑ To prove that she is qualified to host a student

Ⓒ To let the man know that she is a good student

Ⓓ To explain how she got accepted to the school

Summarizing ▷ Fill in the blanks to complete the summary.

The student visits Mr. Sanders in his office. He tells her he is busy because of an upcoming program where _____ come to campus. The student says that is why she is _____ . She does not know what to do with the student. The man tells her to _____ about the school and to try to answer any questions the student has. She should also take the visiting student _____ and show her the department of the subject she thinks she might major in. He emphasizes that the student should make sure the visitor has _____ .

02-028

Listen to part of a lecture in a botany class.

Botany

1   What does the professor mainly discuss?
   (A) The importance of the higher divisions in the plant kingdom
   (B) The work of Carolus Linnaeus
   (C) The use of Latin for the classification of plants
   (D) The classification system of plants

2   Why does the professor explain how to write the scientific name of the coffee plant?
   (A) To emphasize that Carolus Linnaeus gave it its name
   (B) To note the origin of each part of its name
   (C) To remind the students to remember it
   (D) To prove that it was given an improper name

3   According to the professor, what is true about divisions in the plant kingdom?
   Choose 2 answers.
   (A) They include the plant's scientific name.
   (B) They are the third level in the plant kingdom.
   (C) There are a total of twelve of them.
   (D) They are determined by the type of seeds plants have.

4   Why does the professor mention Carolus Linnaeus?

    Ⓐ To state that it was he who gave coffee its scientific name

    Ⓑ To say how long ago he began to work on naming plants

    Ⓒ To credit him with creating the plant classification system

    Ⓓ To claim that he is still important in the field of science today

5   Listen again to part of the lecture. Then answer the question.
    What does the professor imply when she says this: 🎧

    Ⓐ What she will tell the class is not in their textbook.

    Ⓑ She is going to give the class some important information.

    Ⓒ The students need to pay closer attention to her lecture.

    Ⓓ She does not want to repeat the information she is about to say.

6   Listen again to part of the lecture. Then answer the question.
    What can be inferred about the professor when she says this: 🎧

    Ⓐ She recognizes the difficulty of the material she is covering.

    Ⓑ She is going to let the students take a break in a few moments.

    Ⓒ She understands that the students are bored by her lecture.

    Ⓓ She would rather that the students study the material on their own.

Listen to part of a lecture in a marine biology class.

1 What aspect of sharks does the professor mainly discuss?

   (A) Their changes through the process of evolution

   (B) The reasons they are valued for their fins

   (C) Their unique physical abilities

   (D) Their preferred living environment

2 According to the professor, why are sharks such good swimmers?

   (A) They must be in constant motion.

   (B) They begin swimming as soon as they are born.

   (C) Their gills pump enough oxygen to make them strong.

   (D) Their bodies have been designed that way.

3 What is the professor's attitude toward the shark trade?

   (A) It is necessary.

   (B) It should be banned.

   (C) It is regrettable.

   (D) He offers no opinion on it.

4 Based on the information in the lecture, do the statements refer to facts about sharks or speculation about them?
Click in the correct box for each sentence.

	Fact	Speculation
1 Can detect animals in distress in the water		
2 Sometimes sleep on the seafloor		
3 Can turn off part of their brain at times		
4 Do not all have to move continually to breathe		

5 How is the discussion organized?

Ⓐ The professor compares several shark species with one another.

Ⓑ The professor opens and closes by talking about the shark trade.

Ⓒ The professor describes sharks' physical characteristics and gives detailed examples.

Ⓓ The professor mentions some myths about sharks and explains why they are untrue.

6 Listen again to part of the lecture. Then answer the question.
What does the professor imply when he says this: 🎧

Ⓐ Some snakes and spiders are very deadly.

Ⓑ Sharks are less dangerous than certain other animals.

Ⓒ It is completely safe for people to go swimming in the ocean.

Ⓓ Sharks are fairly harmless creatures.

02-030

Listen to part of a conversation between a student and a professor.

1 Why did the professor ask to see the student?

- (A) To find out about his workload in the current semester
- (B) To go over an assignment he submitted recently
- (C) To encourage him to do better in the future
- (D) To ask about some personal issues affecting his work

2 What does the professor say about the student's paper?

- (A) It appears to have been plagiarized.
- (B) It has a number of mistakes in it.
- (C) It was written on an improper topic.
- (D) It is two to three pages too short.

3 What is the professor's opinion of the student's writing ability?

- (A) It is among the best of all her students.
- (B) It is often full of incorrect statements.
- (C) It needs to be improved in style.
- (D) It rarely has any grammatical errors.

4 What will the student probably do next?

- (A) Ask the professor for an extension
- (B) Leave the professor's office
- (C) Attend his next class
- (D) Check out a book from the library

5 Listen again to part of the conversation. Then answer the question.
Why does the student say this: 🎧

- (A) To deny the professor's accusation
- (B) To claim that he is familiar with the text
- (C) To admit to not having thoroughly read the book
- (D) To confess to not having enough time to do his work

• Mastering Question Types

accurate	attach	banned	unisex
chlorophyll	parasite	harmed	brew
mutualism	stimulant	reek	interact
skepticism	avoid	benefit	reproduce
adverse	fungus	host	upset
chronic	survival	refine	bud
specific	bacteria	unaffected	repulsive
affirmative	gill	bloom	virus
extract	pollinator	injured	carnivorous
palpitation	tinker	repetition	misconception

• Mastering Topics

abdomen	anticipate	chrysalis	delve
digestive	elongated	expel	gene
hibernate	intricately	logically	misspeak
replace	saliva	thorax	unsurprisingly
aftermath	beadlike	conceive	devastation
dilemma	enclosure	extract	grind
impregnate	judge	mandible	monogamous
residue	seal	transformation	vicinity
antenna	caste	courtship	differentiate
eggshell	estimated	factor	groom
intelligent	larva	mate	precious
ritual	soil	underside	widespread

• TOEFL Practice Tests

abbreviated	bestow	capitalize	complicated
differ	electromagnetic	fin	habit
lateral	minute	perception	prowl
saltwater	slice	structure	utilize
aeronautically	birthing	cartilage	concise
distress	fatal	freshwater	hail
legendary	moss	pinpoint	recap
seafloor	species	tissue	vine
ail	bush	classification	demonstration
documented	fearsome	genus	indicate
majority	originate	predominantly	reproduction
seed	stature	trunk	weed

📝 Choose the words with the closest meanings to the highlighted words.

1 Fortunately, no one was harmed in the accident.

- (A) disturbed
- (B) bothered
- (C) assaulted
- (D) injured

2 Many wild animals live in the nearby vicinity.

- (A) jungle
- (B) forest
- (C) suburbs
- (D) area

3 The lion is one of the most fearsome creatures on the planet.

- (A) dangerous
- (B) frightening
- (C) troublesome
- (D) vicious

4 Let me recap what happened for those of you who got here late.

- (A) assume
- (B) devise
- (C) review
- (D) remember

5 One of her most precious possessions is an old picture of her parents.

- (A) valuable
- (B) antique
- (C) exquisite
- (D) appropriate

6 That was a good attempt, but your answer was simply not accurate.

- (A) close
- (B) extensive
- (C) responsive
- (D) correct

7 The barometer indicates that it is likely to rain very soon.

- (A) proves
- (B) shows
- (C) assumes
- (D) knows

8 The crowd was estimated to have been more than 1,000 people.

- (A) guaranteed
- (B) guessed
- (C) averaged
- (D) known

9 Some snakebites can be fatal to their victims.

- (A) damaging
- (B) paralyzing
- (C) painful
- (D) lethal

10 Julie suffered a spinal injury when she fell out of the tree.

- (A) back
- (B) leg
- (C) shoulder
- (D) brain

📝 Match the words with the correct definitions.

11 capitalize •

12 extract •

13 mandible •

14 aftermath •

15 concise •

16 misconception •

17 tinker •

18 dilemma •

19 banned •

20 pinpoint •

• (A) to take advantage of an opportunity

• (B) an erroneous thought or opinion about something

• (C) to remove

• (D) to determine the exact location of something

• (E) a type of jaw

• (F) to attempt to adjust

• (G) an event that happens after something has occurred

• (H) not permitted

• (I) a serious problem

• (J) short; terse

Chapter 03   Social Sciences 1 | Conversations

history • archaeology • anthropology • economics • sociology • psychology • education •
geography • political science • linguistics

Mastering Question Types with Lectures | A1

TYPE 1 • Gist-Content   *TYPE 2* • Detail   *TYPE 3* • Understanding Organization   *TYPE 4* • Function of What Is Said

02-031

Listen to part of a lecture in a history class.

TYPE 1   What aspect of shipwrecks does the professor mainly discuss?

    (A) The reasons why they occur

    (B) The number of ships that have sunk

    (C) Some well-known incidents

    (D) Some ways they can be prevented

TYPE 2   According to the professor, what is the most common cause of shipwrecks?

    (A) Rogue waves

    (B) Foul weather

    (C) Warfare

    (D) Human error

TYPE 3   How is the discussion organized?

    (A) By drawing comparisons between the different types of shipwrecks

    (B) By describing natural and then manmade causes of shipwrecks

    (C) By mentioning some shipwrecks and then explaining what caused them

    (D) By explaining how ships in the twentieth century were mostly sunk

TYPE 4   Listen again to part of the lecture. Then answer the question.
What does the professor imply when he says this: 🎧

    (A) Ships will always sink when they lose electricity.

    (B) Even modern ships are capable of being sunk by bad weather.

    (C) A ship that cannot be steered cannot be brought to port.

    (D) The crew often has no control over a ship's fate.

Summarizing ▶   Fill in the blanks to complete the summary.

The professor states that tens of thousands of ships have sunk throughout history. He comments that the most common reason is _____ . In the past, ships' captains and crews had no way of knowing what kind of _____ they were sailing into, so many ships were lost. But even with _____ , bad weather still sinks many ships. The professor mentions that when ships sink in bad weather, it is often due to _____ . Finally, he notes that warfare accounts for many shipwrecks as well. But he also says that crews can _____ and thus cause them to sink.

02-032

Listen to part of a lecture in an archaeology class.

TYPE 5   What aspect of pottery does the professor mainly discuss?

    Ⓐ Its origins around the world

    Ⓑ Its effect on trade in ancient times

    Ⓒ Its importance to archaeologists

    Ⓓ The materials from which it was made

TYPE 6   Listen again to part of the lecture. Then answer the question.

    What can be inferred when the professor says this: 🎧

    Ⓐ The potter's wheel is not relevant to her lecture.

    Ⓑ The pottery industry could not have progressed without the potter's wheel.

    Ⓒ She knows very little about the potter's wheel.

    Ⓓ She will demonstrate how a potter's wheel works in a later class.

TYPE 7   What does the professor imply about pottery shards?

    Ⓐ Many can be recreated into complete pieces of pottery.

    Ⓑ It is possible to determine styles of pottery with them.

    Ⓒ They have a value to archaeologists that they lack to looters.

    Ⓓ The reason they are broken pieces is that they are of low quality.

TYPE 8   What will the professor likely do next?

    Ⓐ She will give the students a quiz to take.

    Ⓑ She will ask the students some questions about her lecture.

    Ⓒ She will read to the students from the textbook.

    Ⓓ She will show the students some pictures.

Summarizing ▶ Fill in the blanks to complete the summary.

The lecturer says that pottery is one of _____ that people learned how to make. She comments that it also helps archaeologists learn about _____. She states that the Chinese invented pottery around 25,000 B.C., and most other cultures were making pottery by _____. She mentions that pottery shards are common at dig sites because they are not valuable to looters. The design and manufacture of pottery often changed, so they can tell archaeologists much about a culture. With pottery and pottery shards, archaeologists can tell _____ they were made and _____ they were made from.

TYPE 1 • Gist-Purpose　　TYPE 2 • Detail　　TYPE 3 • Understanding Organization　　TYPE 4 • Function of What Is Said

02-033

Listen to part of a lecture in a psychology class.

TYPE 1　Why does the professor explain complex decisions?

　Ⓐ To show what their results may be

　Ⓑ To mention the kinds of topics they involve

　Ⓒ To note the best way to make them

　Ⓓ To contrast them with simple decisions

TYPE 2　What are simple decisions?

　Ⓐ Ones that typically have to do with financial matters

　Ⓑ Those concerning minor aspects of people's lives

　Ⓒ Choices that people have to make almost instantly

　Ⓓ Decisions that require input from another individual

TYPE 3　How does the professor organize the information about decisions that she presents to the class?

　Ⓐ She describes how emotions are involved in them.

　Ⓑ She notes some decisions and then explains which type they are.

　Ⓒ She discusses them in the order of their relative ease.

　Ⓓ She talks about them by following along with the book.

TYPE 4　Listen again to part of the lecture. Then answer the question.
　　　　　Why does the professor say this: 🎧

　Ⓐ To say that people will usually fail when they consider their emotions

　Ⓑ To note the difficulty that people have in ignoring their feelings

　Ⓒ To excuse people for the bad decisions that they make

　Ⓓ To give a reason as to why people commonly make certain decisions

Summarizing ▷　Fill in the blanks to complete the summary.

The professor notes that there are both ＿＿＿＿＿＿＿＿＿＿＿＿. Simple decisions are ones that people do all the time and have very little effect on people's lives. They do not require ＿＿＿＿＿＿＿＿＿＿＿, which is unlike complex decisions. These are big choices that often concern things such as ＿＿＿＿＿＿＿＿＿＿, and situations that affect others. These kinds of decisions require a lot of thought because there are often many ＿＿＿＿＿＿＿＿＿＿ involved. The professor says that people solve them in different ways. Some follow their gut while others sleep on the decision. And others approach their decisions in ＿＿＿＿＿＿＿＿＿＿.

02-034

Listen to part of a lecture in an education class.

TYPE 5   What is the main topic of the lecture?

    Ⓐ At which age children should begin to read

    Ⓑ What skills children can learn from reading

    Ⓒ Which genres of books are ideal for children to read

    Ⓓ Why young children ought to read books

TYPE 6   What is the professor's opinion of the *Harry Potter* series?

    Ⓐ It is a work that can benefit children who read it.

    Ⓑ It is something that all young children ought to read.

    Ⓒ It is a work of fiction similar to a fairy tale.

    Ⓓ It was inspired by books written by other authors.

TYPE 7   Based on the information in the lecture, do the following statements refer to ways reading can improve children's skills or enrich their lives?
Click in the correct box for each sentence.

	Improve Skills	Enrich Lives
① Can learn how to state ideas properly		
② Can learn about the world in general		
③ Can learn to think more logically		
④ Can learn many new vocabulary words		

TYPE 8   What can be inferred about the professor?

    Ⓐ He used to read books to his children.

    Ⓑ He is reading the *Harry Potter* series.

    Ⓒ He spends most of his spare time reading.

    Ⓓ He teaches grammar in some classes.

Summarizing ▶ Fill in the blanks to complete the summary.

The professor asks the students about their relationships with books when _____. He then mentions that there are several reasons why it is important for children to read and to be read to. The first is that they gain _____, such as _____ as well as new vocabulary. Reading also can _____ by opening the door of discovery through books. But they can also read to be educated and entertained. And in addition to learning logic _____, they can have their imaginations stimulated by fairy tales and other stories similar to the *Harry Potter* series.

TYPE 1 • Gist-Purpose   TYPE 2 • Detail   TYPE 3 • Understanding Organization   TYPE 4 • Function of What Is Said

02-035

Listen to part of a conversation between a student and a professor.

TYPE 1 Why does the student visit the professor?

Ⓐ To inquire about studying in a foreign country

Ⓑ To ask about the cost involved in studying abroad

Ⓒ To find out where she should spend her next semester

Ⓓ To discuss her need to study more languages

TYPE 2 What does the student say about her Japanese language skills?

Ⓐ They seem to be regressing.

Ⓑ They are not getting any better.

Ⓒ They are improving rapidly.

Ⓓ She speaks with near native fluency.

TYPE 3 Why does the professor mention the study abroad office?

Ⓐ He wants the student to go there next.

Ⓑ It has information on programs in Brazil.

Ⓒ He thinks it can provide the student with some financial information.

Ⓓ It will tell the student about some programs' language requirements.

TYPE 4 Listen again to part of the conversation. Then answer the question.
What is the purpose of the professor's response?

Ⓐ To find out about the student's financial situation

Ⓑ To bring up the high cost of studying elsewhere

Ⓒ To tell the student she should apply for a scholarship

Ⓓ To encourage the student to follow her desire

Summarizing ▶ Fill in the blanks to complete the summary.

The student visits the professor to state that she wants to _____ during her junior year next
year. The professor claims it will be _____, so she should go abroad if she can afford it. He asks
where she wants to go. She says Brazil, but the school lacks _____, so she cannot study there.
He asks about Japan, but she feels her Japanese language skills are not _____. The professor
mentions Mexico since the student is _____. Then, he tells her to go to the study abroad office
for more information.

02-036

Listen to part of a conversation between a student and a Nutrition Department employee.

TYPE 5 What are the speakers mainly discussing?

    Ⓐ How the student should approach others in the dining hall

    Ⓑ What activity the student can do with his club

    Ⓒ Why university students need to have good health

    Ⓓ When the club is going to have its first meeting

TYPE 6 What does the woman suggest that the student do?

    Ⓐ Try to get the cafeteria to serve healthier food

    Ⓑ Copy some of the department's checklists

    Ⓒ Hand out sheets on nutrition to students

    Ⓓ Change his major to nutrition

TYPE 7 What is the woman's attitude toward the student?

    Ⓐ She is happy to speak with him.

    Ⓑ She is impressed with his attitude.

    Ⓒ She is somewhat condescending.

    Ⓓ She is not particularly helpful.

TYPE 8 What will the woman probably do next?

    Ⓐ Talk about how to improve the student's health

    Ⓑ Introduce the student to some professors

    Ⓒ Give the student something

    Ⓓ Make some photocopies

Summarizing ▶ Fill in the blanks to complete the summary.

The student visits _____ to ask for some help. He introduces himself as the new president of the health and nutrition club. The department secretary says she is pleased _____ . The student says he wants to help promote _____ on campus but is not sure what to do, so he asks for some advice. The woman says that the man should be subtle about how he gives other students information. She mentions passing out nutrition checklists _____ . The student thinks that is a good idea, so he asks for _____ .

Mastering Topics with Lectures | B1

Listen to part of a lecture in an anthropology class.

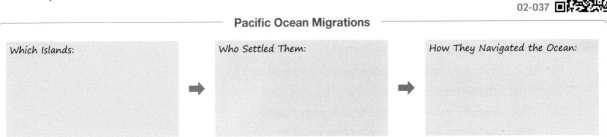

Pacific Ocean Migrations

Which Islands:		Who Settled Them:		How They Navigated the Ocean:

1 What is the lecture mainly about?

Ⓐ How the Pacific islands came to be populated

Ⓑ Why people sailed across the Pacific Ocean

Ⓒ How land can be detected while on the ocean

Ⓓ Why it took so long to populate the Pacific islands

2 How is the discussion organized?

Ⓐ By presenting a problem and then offering a solution

Ⓑ By describing a cause and then explaining its effect

Ⓒ By mentioning a theory and then stating why it is true

Ⓓ By presenting evidence and then disputing its factuality

3 Listen again to part of the lecture. Then answer the question.
What does the professor imply when she says this: 🎧

Ⓐ The ships performed better than some modern-day ones would.

Ⓑ It was unusual for such ships to travel those long distances.

Ⓒ The technology back then was not particularly advanced.

Ⓓ It is highly unlikely that primitive ships actually made those voyages.

Summarizing ▷ Fill in the blanks to complete the summary.

The professor notes that ＿＿＿＿＿＿＿＿ were the last places people inhabited. She mentions that people left China and then populated the various islands. The first people to do this were the Lapita. Later, the Polynesians sailed far to settle islands such as ＿＿＿＿＿＿＿＿. She notes that their ships were primitive, so they relied on their skills as ＿＿＿＿＿＿＿＿. They also knew the stars well so sailed according to them. When searching for land, they tried to spot birds in the sky and ＿＿＿＿＿＿＿＿. They looked for clouds from volcanoes. They also used ＿＿＿＿＿＿＿＿ to sail across the ocean.

Listen to part of a lecture in a psychology class.

02-038

┌─────────────────────── The Human Mind ───────────────────────┐

Perception:　　　　　➡　　Memory:　　　　　➡　　Imagination:

└──┘

1　Why does the professor explain perception?

　　Ⓐ To compare its effects with memory

　　Ⓑ To explain its relevance to imagination

　　Ⓒ To show its relation to the human mind

　　Ⓓ To provide some examples of how it helps people

2　Based on the information in the lecture, which aspects of the human mind do the following statements refer to?

Click in the correct box for each sentence.

	Perception	Memory	Imagination
1 Concerns a person's ability to recall information			
2 May be affected by amnesia			
3 Allows a person to form pictures in his or her head			
4 Affects the way a person regards something			

3　What is the professor's attitude toward the student?

　　Ⓐ It is critical.

　　Ⓑ It is considerate.

　　Ⓒ It is disappointed.

　　Ⓓ It is praising.

Summarizing ▷ Fill in the blanks to complete the summary.

The professor states that _____, and imagination are all parts of the human mind. Perception relates to how people look at and understand information. It can be related to a person's culture, nationality, language, and _____. Memory is the information that people store in their brains and their ability _____. People's memories of the same event can sometimes differ. This is mostly due to _____ of what happened. Imagination consists of _____ that people form. These can be based upon past experiences, or they can be something that a person makes up entirely.

Listen to part of a lecture in a history class.

02-039

The Spice Trade

| Why Use Spices: | First Trade Route: |
| | Second Trade Route: |

1 According to the professor, what is true about the spice trade?
Choose 2 answers.

- Ⓐ It mostly involved salt, pepper, and cinnamon.
- Ⓑ It started sometime around the fifteenth century.
- Ⓒ It cost the Europeans a large amount of money.
- Ⓓ It was done for the sake of the upper classes.

2 How does the professor organize the information about the spice trade that she presents to the class?

- Ⓐ She first explains its cause and then its effects.
- Ⓑ She gives examples of how the trade was carried out.
- Ⓒ She notes some famous traders and the routes they followed.
- Ⓓ She explains some problems involved in the trade.

3 What will the professor probably do next?

- Ⓐ Explain the process involved in cultivating spices
- Ⓑ Hold a discussion on what she has covered so far
- Ⓒ Talk about some European voyages of discovery
- Ⓓ Describe the effects of the spice trade on Venice

Summarizing ▶ Fill in the blanks to complete the summary.

The professor says that the spice trade took place between _____. The spices cost a lot of
money because they were rare and valuable. In the past, people used spices to help _____
of their food and also to preserve their food. Except for salt, spices come from plants and herbs. Pepper,
_____ were commonly traded. When _____ captured Constantinople
in 1453 though, the overland spice trade closed. So the Europeans tried to find _____ to Asia.
They sailed around Africa and also managed to discover the Americas because of the spice trade.

Listen to part of a lecture in a history class.

02-040

┌─────────────── Book Reproduction in the Middle Ages and Renaissance ───────────────┐

Medieval Book Printing:

➡

Renaissance Book Printing:

1 What is the lecture mainly about?
- Ⓐ The duplication of books in Europe
- Ⓑ The effects of the printing press
- Ⓒ The rivalry between monasteries and universities
- Ⓓ The results of copying manuscripts by hand

2 What was the likely outcome of the invention of the printing press?
- Ⓐ The quality of paper improved for the books to be printed on.
- Ⓑ Some universities purchased their own printing presses.
- Ⓒ Monasteries and universities ceased copying books.
- Ⓓ There were no more errors in the books that were printed.

3 Listen again to part of the lecture. Then answer the question.
What does the professor imply when he says this: 🎧
- Ⓐ People were bothered by the many mistakes in hand-copied books.
- Ⓑ Many people welcomed the invention of the printing press.
- Ⓒ It was easier for universities to copy books than for monasteries to do so.
- Ⓓ Books with too many errors in them could not be sold for much money.

Summarizing ▷ Fill in the blanks to complete the summary.

The professor mentions the four primary means of _____ people have used over time. Then, he notes that _____ in the Middle Ages were copied by hand. This was mostly done by monks in monasteries. A scribe would write the words while an illuminator would _____. But this process took a long time, and many mistakes were made. Later, universities started copying books with somewhat better results. Then, in the Renaissance, Johannes Gutenberg invented _____, so most people began to print books this way. Books became _____, and they had much fewer errors in them.

Listen to part of a conversation between a student and a professor.

02-041

---------- **Office Hours** ----------

Professor's Request:

Student's Response 1:

Professor's Explanation:

Students' Response 2:

1 Why did the professor ask to see the student?

   Ⓐ To remind him not to forget an assignment

   Ⓑ To discuss his most recent exam

   Ⓒ To talk to him about his career plans

   Ⓓ To invite him to take part in a contest

2 Why does the professor ask the student about his weekend plans?

   Ⓐ To find out if he can tutor some students

   Ⓑ To see if he can do some repair work

   Ⓒ To determine if he can go on a trip

   Ⓓ To ask if he can meet with a graduate student

3 Listen again to part of the conversation. Then answer the question. What does the student mean when he says this: 🎧

   Ⓐ He does not believe what the professor just told him.

   Ⓑ He is pleased to be going on the trip.

   Ⓒ He thinks that the money being offered is not enough.

   Ⓓ He could not possibly accept the professor's offer.

Summarizing ▷ Fill in the blanks to complete the summary.

The professor tells the student that there is _____ and that she thinks he should take part in it. He wonders why a junior or senior is not invited since he is only a freshman. The professor responds that the student has a knack for _____. He then agrees to go. The professor says the contest will be _____ and the school will pay for everything. The student remarks that he needs to tell his boss at _____ that he cannot work on the weekend. He then states that it is _____ to be selected.

Listen to part of a conversation between a student and a Registrar's office employee.

02-042

Service Encounter

Reason for Visiting:		Result:
Problem:		**Solution:**

1 What does the student need to do?

Ⓐ Finish a class

Ⓑ Pay a bill

Ⓒ Pass a test

Ⓓ Return a book

2 What can be inferred about the student?

Ⓐ He is eager to finish his projects quickly.

Ⓑ He becomes impatient when a situation does not go his way.

Ⓒ He is very thorough when doing something.

Ⓓ He is unlikely to graduate when the semester finishes.

3 Listen again to part of the conversation. Then answer the question.
What is the purpose of the employee's response?

Ⓐ To find out if the conversation is over

Ⓑ To imply that the student should leave his office

Ⓒ To show that he is getting tired of the conversation

Ⓓ To tell the student to ask another question

Summarizing ▷ Fill in the blanks to complete the summary.

The student visits the Registrar's office to make sure that his paperwork _____ is all complete.
The employee takes a look at _____ and says that the student has enough classes to graduate.
He also notes that the student might be able to graduate _____ . The student then gives the
employee his ID so that he can check whether everything is fine. The employee discovers that the student owes
_____ in library fines that he needs to pay. As soon as the student takes care of the fine, he will
be able to _____ .

02-043

Listen to part of a lecture in an economics class.

1 What is the lecture mainly about?

- Ⓐ The methods Carnegie and Rockefeller used to get rich
- Ⓑ American industry in the nineteenth century
- Ⓒ The business activities of two famous industrialists
- Ⓓ The philanthropic actions of some wealthy Americans

2 According to the professor, what kind of businessman was Andrew Carnegie?

- Ⓐ He had a coldblooded attitude.
- Ⓑ He let his underlings do much of his work.
- Ⓒ He mostly trusted his instincts.
- Ⓓ He relied upon his education to guide him.

3 Based on the information in the lecture, do the following statements refer to Andrew Carnegie or John D. Rockefeller?
Click in the correct box for each sentence.

	Andrew Carnegie	John D. Rockefeller
1 Was involved in the oil industry		
2 Was better liked by the public		
3 Made much of his money in steel		
4 May have been the richest man ever		

4 How is the discussion organized?

(A) By comparing and contrasting the lives of two men

(B) By explaining the ultimate uses of the two men's riches

(C) By considering a problem and then presenting a solution

(D) By showing how the two men were products of their time

5 What will the professor probably do next?

(A) Describe the life of another industrialist

(B) Ask the students to submit their term papers

(C) Explore the men's business practices in depth

(D) Offer some criticism of the men's attitudes

6 Listen again to part of the lecture. Then answer the question.
What is the purpose of the professor's response?

(A) To discourage the student from studying Australian history

(B) To indicate his preference for the student's choice

(C) To agree with the student's suggestion

(D) To reject the student's proposal

02-044

Listen to part of a lecture in a child studies class.

Child Studies

1 What aspect of babies does the professor mainly discuss?

   Ⓐ The process by which they develop their skills

   Ⓑ How their motor functions compare with their cognitive abilities

   Ⓒ The importance of making sure they develop naturally

   Ⓓ The dangers that problems like autism pose

2 Why does the professor explain autism?

   Ⓐ To say it could be a reason why a baby fails to develop properly

   Ⓑ To note that it may appear within the baby's first eighteen months

   Ⓒ To mention that it will affect a baby's language skills

   Ⓓ To state that it might happen to babies who are confined to cribs all day

3 According to the professor, what kind of vision do babies have at birth?

   Ⓐ They are unable to see anything.

   Ⓑ They can see only things right in front of them.

   Ⓒ They can make out people's faces.

   Ⓓ They have their entire range of vision.

4 What can be inferred about babies' parents?

    Ⓐ They can help their children develop their skills.

    Ⓑ They must be aware of all of the signs of autism.

    Ⓒ They frequently form bonds with their babies.

    Ⓓ They should teach their babies how to walk.

5 Listen again to part of the lecture. Then answer the question.
Why does the professor say this: 🎧

    Ⓐ To point out something that most people are not aware of

    Ⓑ To advise the students to remember that fact for their exam

    Ⓒ To recommend that the students take note of what she has told them

    Ⓓ To indicate the information she gave is not crucial to the lecture

6 Listen again to part of the lecture. Then answer the question.
What does the professor mean when she says this: 🎧

    Ⓐ Parents need to pay close attention to the progress of their babies.

    Ⓑ Without these standards, it would be impossible to measure a baby's progress.

    Ⓒ The process she describes does not always happen exactly like she said.

    Ⓓ Some babies fail to develop any of the skills that she just mentioned.

02-045

Listen to part of a conversation between a student and a professor.

1   Why does the student visit the professor?

   Ⓐ To invite the professor to her performance
   Ⓑ To inquire about the nature of an exam
   Ⓒ To get answers to some questions on the class material
   Ⓓ To ask about a recent field trip

2   According to the professor, what does the student need to know for the test?
   Choose 2 answers.

   Ⓐ The material covered in the lectures
   Ⓑ The information from the class discussions
   Ⓒ The complete details of their field trips
   Ⓓ The papers the professor gives to the students

3   What is the professor's attitude toward the student?

   Ⓐ He is concerned about her condition.
   Ⓑ He is relaxed while speaking with her.
   Ⓒ He is overbearing in his attitude.
   Ⓓ He is eager to see her do well in his class.

4   Why does the professor mention the student's upcoming performance?

   Ⓐ To show that he is aware of her activities
   Ⓑ To find out when the performance will begin
   Ⓒ To let her know that he will be in attendance
   Ⓓ To say he thinks extracurricular activities are important

5   Listen again to part of the conversation. Then answer the question.
   Why does the professor say this: 🎧

   Ⓐ To compare the student with another one
   Ⓑ To encourage the student to do her best
   Ⓒ To let the student know he talks about her
   Ⓓ To indicate teachers' interest in their good students

• *Mastering Question Types*

accumulate	analyze	broaden	composition
crew	enrich	grammar	iceberg
impending	inspire	looter	mercy
pottery	shard	steer	typhoon
affordable	ancient	capsize	conclusion
earthquake	expose	handle	imaginary
inclement	intuitive	manmade	navigation
reef	sink	tilt	undersea
ammunition	archaeologist	clay	consequence
enhance	forecasting	hurricane	impact
inherent	jewelry	mental	necessitate
rogue	sobering	tsunami	wager

• *Mastering Topics*

absorb	amnesia	conflicting	dispute
eyewitness	illuminator	manuscript	monastery
optical	painstakingly	perception	prevailing
retain	scroll	sense	spoil
account	apprehensive	deposit	disturbing
foreknowledge	illusion	memory	monopoly
outpost	patron	populated	projection
rot	seaway	skyward	tacking
accurate	capacity	descendant	eruption
ignore	imagination	merchant	myriad
overland	pause	preservation	representation
scribe	selective	spice	volcanic

• *TOEFL Practice Tests*

abruptly	babble	billionaire	commercial
coordination	drop	focus	foundation
grasp	kerosene	lubrication	pension
rear	schooling	sibling	trivia
anxious	bear	chiefly	competitor
crib	endeavor	formal	fund
gravity	legacy	mammal	philanthropic
reminder	scrutiny	therapy	vision
autism	benchmark	cognitive	container
dangle	enterprise	fortune	glimpse
ironically	limited	ongoing	profit
roll	sense	track	workforce

Vocabulary *Review*

📝 Choose the words with the closest meanings to the highlighted words.

1 Her patron provides her with a yearly stipend so that she can paint full time.

    (A) professor   (B) guardian

    (C) client   (D) sponsor

2 The businessman was able to accumulate a large amount of money.

    (A) amass   (B) spend

    (C) save   (D) invest

3 The witness got a glimpse of the thief, so she described him to the police.

    (A) opinion   (B) look

    (C) profile   (D) feeling

4 The consequences of his actions were mostly negative.

    (A) causes   (B) opinions

    (C) results   (D) thoughts

5 The company chiefly manufactures electronics, but it also makes some other goods.

    (A) consistently   (B) typically

    (C) primarily   (D) fundamentally

6 The student disputed the answer with the teacher, but the teacher did not change his mind.

    (A) rejected   (B) argued

    (C) explained   (D) considered

7 Some looters took advantage of the power outage and robbed several stores.

    (A) beggars   (B) felons

    (C) merchants   (D) thieves

8 We endeavor to do our best in everything that we do.

    (A) want   (B) pretend

    (C) attempt   (D) desire

9 You look a little apprehensive; why don't you try to calm down a bit?

    (A) nervous   (B) upset

    (C) frustrated   (D) disappointed

10 Everyone was wary of the impending storm, so they decided to go inside.

    (A) approaching   (B) devastating

    (C) forming   (D) tropical

📝 Match the words with the correct definitions.

11 absorb   •

12 archaeologist   •

13 gravity   •

14 perception   •

15 eyewitness   •

16 typhoon   •

17 fortune   •

18 sibling   •

19 shard   •

20 abruptly   •

• (A) a small piece that has usually been broken

• (B) great wealth; good luck

• (C) the force that causes all things to attract one another

• (D) someone who sees something happen in person

• (E) to soak up

• (F) someone who studies civilizations from the past

• (G) suddenly

• (H) a tropical storm similar to a hurricane

• (I) a brother or sister

• (J) the way someone looks at or considers something

Part

B

Chapter 04 Social Sciences 2 | Conversations

history • archaeology • anthropology • economics • sociology • psychology • education •
geography • political science • linguistics

02-046

Listen to part of a lecture in a marketing class.

TYPE 1   What is the lecture mainly about?

    (A) Some reasons why companies try to establish brand names

    (B) The importance of creating logos for a company's products

    (C) The need to ensure that customers stay loyal to a brand

    (D) Some of the most famous logos in the commercial world

TYPE 2   According to the professor, what happens when a company establishes brand loyalty with its customers?

    (A) People engage in word-of-mouth advertising for the company.

    (B) People are willing only to buy products from that company.

    (C) People do not mind paying high prices for its products.

    (D) People more easily recognize the company's logo or other symbols.

TYPE 3   How is the discussion organized?

    (A) The professor covers the material by going over a recent case study.

    (B) The professor asks questions that lead the students into the topic of the lecture.

    (C) The professor conducts a class discussion to get students' opinions on the subject.

    (D) The professor recites information that can be found in the students' textbook.

TYPE 4   Why does the professor ask the students about the checkmark?

    (A) He wants to prove the importance of logos to them.

    (B) He is quizzing the students on their knowledge.

    (C) He would like their opinion of that particular logo.

    (D) He is interested in their reactions upon seeing the logo.

Summarizing ▶ Fill in the blanks to complete the summary.

The professor asks his students about the products they purchase. When one answers, he claims that is the reason why companies want _____ . He notes that companies want to inspire _____ because that will make customers purchase _____ . He then asks about a particular logo, and a student correctly identifies it. He returns to brand names, and he mentions that having a famous _____ product makes customers more likely to purchase other items, especially new ones, that a company sells. Customers often believe that quality in one product means all of the company's products will have _____ .

Listen to part of a lecture in a history class.

02-047

TYPE 5 What aspect of castles does the professor mainly discuss?

Ⓐ The cost and amount of time involved in building them

Ⓑ The reasons that they were popular during medieval times

Ⓒ The various types of defenses that they featured

Ⓓ The methods that were used to construct them in the past

TYPE 6 What is the professor's attitude toward the front gates of castles?

Ⓐ They were not particularly strong.

Ⓑ They should not have been made of stone.

Ⓒ They needed to be made more thickly.

Ⓓ They were typically poorly constructed.

TYPE 7 Based on the information in the lecture, do the following sentences refer to castle gatehouses or baileys?
Click in the correct box for each sentence.

	Castle Gatehouses	Baileys
⬚1 They served as places for people to get together at various events.		
⬚2 They often featured murder holes that were used to attack invaders.		
⬚3 They were places where attackers were led to get shot by arrows.		
⬚4 They contained a portcullis that was made with metal.		

TYPE 8 What can be inferred about castles?

Ⓐ They could hold thousands of people at a time.

Ⓑ They cost too much money for most people to build.

Ⓒ They often took one or two decades to construct.

Ⓓ They were easy to defeat with gunpowder weapons.

Summarizing ▷ Fill in the blanks to complete the summary.

The professor discusses castles and says their two purposes were to protect the people in them and to serve as _____. The professor describes castle fortifications, starting with moats. These were large ditches around the castle walls. A drawbridge was used to _____, and it led to the front gate. By the front gate was _____, which had many defensive fortifications. The bailey was a _____ where people others gathered. Inside the castle walls was the keep, which was where the lord and his family lived. The introduction of _____ led people to stop building castles.

TYPE 1 • Gist-Purpose   *TYPE 2* • Detail   *TYPE 3* • Understanding Organization   *TYPE 4* • Function of What Is Said

02-048

Listen to part of a lecture in an anthropology class.

TYPE 1 What aspect of nomads does the professor mainly discuss?

    (A) Where the majority of them live today

    (B) How certain nomads differ from one another

    (C) Why early nomads chose that lifestyle

    (D) When nomadic lifestyles mostly came to an end

TYPE 2 According to the professor, what made pastoral nomads live that kind of lifestyle?

    (A) They needed to collect food in order to survive.

    (B) They followed their domesticated animals as they looked for food.

    (C) They desired to live their lives away from urban centers.

    (D) They moved around in order to find employment.

TYPE 3 How does the professor organize the information about nomads that he presents to the class?

    (A) By comparing the nomadic lifestyle with the urban lifestyle

    (B) By presenting a problem and then offering a solution to it

    (C) By explaining the reasons why nomads live wandering lives

    (D) By noting the cause of the nomadic lifestyle as well as its effects

TYPE 4 Listen again to part of the lecture. Then answer the question.
Why does the professor say this: 🎧

    (A) To introduce the next topic he wishes to discuss

    (B) To provide evidence that supports his theory

    (C) To prove that his opinion is the one that is correct

    (D) To express his disagreement with some academics

Summarizing ▷ Fill in the blanks to complete the summary.

The professor begins with a description of _____ and then says that humans lived this way
for most of their history. The first nomadic lifestyle he describes is _____ type of nomad.
These nomads followed animals as they migrated and collected food that they found. The next type is the pastoral
nomad. These nomads emerged after humans learned to _____. They followed their own
herds as they foraged for food. _____ is the last one he describes. These include modern-day
nomads. These nomads wander about looking for employment in various places. Some claim these wanderers are
_____, but the professor feels differently.

02-049

Listen to part of a lecture in a political science class.

TYPE 5 What is the main topic of the lecture?

    Ⓐ The process that led to the forming of governments

    Ⓑ The need to establish governed societies

    Ⓒ The Founding Fathers and the American Revolution

    Ⓓ John Locke and the social contract

TYPE 6 What is the professor's opinion of John Locke?

    Ⓐ She considers him a revolutionary thinker.

    Ⓑ She admires his thoughts on politics.

    Ⓒ She likes him more than the Founding Fathers.

    Ⓓ She believes he is one of history's most important philosophers.

TYPE 7 What can be inferred about the Founding Fathers?

    Ⓐ They used Locke's philosophy to justify rebellion.

    Ⓑ They improved upon Locke's political philosophy.

    Ⓒ They disregarded some of Locke's political opinions.

    Ⓓ They used more violence than Locke had advocated when they rebelled.

TYPE 8 Listen again to part of the lecture. Then answer the question.
    What does the professor imply when she says this: 🎧

    Ⓐ One must think about the past when considering the present.

    Ⓑ Some of Locke's ideas were too extreme for people in his time.

    Ⓒ The notion of the divine right of kings has been discredited.

    Ⓓ The students should not apply modern thinking to the past.

Summarizing ▶ **Fill in the blanks to complete the summary.**

The professor says that, at first, there were no governments, and people lived in _____ .
However, eventually, people began giving up some liberties to come together and to establish governments. This
formed _____ in which both people and the government had rights and responsibilities. She
then talks about John Locke and his work _____ . The first treatise refutes the notion of the
divine right of kings. The second says that when a government abuses its trust, the people have the right and the
responsibility to revoke _____ . _____ relied on Locke's philosophy to
justify rebelling against Britain.

TYPE 1 • Gist-Purpose   *TYPE 2* • Detail   *TYPE 3* • Understanding Organization   *TYPE 4* • Function of What Is Said

02-050

Listen to part of a conversation between a student and a professor.

TYPE 1 Why does the student visit the professor?

Ⓐ To complain about another one of his professors

Ⓑ To seek some advice from the professor

Ⓒ To borrow a book that the professor has

Ⓓ To attend a meeting with the professor

TYPE 2 What kind of project is the student working on?

Ⓐ A book report

Ⓑ A computer design

Ⓒ A design project

Ⓓ An essay on architecture

TYPE 3 Why does the student mention Professor Martin?

Ⓐ To let the professor know who recommended that the student visit him

Ⓑ To tell the professor that he enjoys taking her class very much

Ⓒ To help the professor recall a conversation they had earlier in the week

Ⓓ To get the professor to be more eager to offer him some assistance

TYPE 4 Listen again to part of the conversation. Then answer the question.
What can be inferred from the professor's response to the student?

Ⓐ It is nearing time for the professor to retire.

Ⓑ The student's problem is not a challenge for the professor.

Ⓒ The student should be quiet and let the professor explain the solution.

Ⓓ The professor is uninterested in the student's question.

Summarizing ▷ Fill in the blanks to complete the summary.

The student visits the professor in his office and introduces himself. He tells the professor that
_____ —Professor Martin—told him to visit the professor to talk about
_____ . The professor says he has been expecting the student. The student shows the professor
_____ that he has been designing, and the professor recognizes the problem right away. He will
not tell the student what to do since it is the student's project, but he _____ a book that he says
should provide some answers for the student. The student then asks the professor for _____ .

02-051

Listen to part of a conversation between a student and a student services employee.

TYPE 5   What problem does the man have?

(A) He needs to reserve some equipment for a presentation.

(B) He cannot remember where he left his nametag.

(C) He has to get a booth for the exhibition that is going on.

(D) He has to rehearse the presentation that he will be giving.

TYPE 6   Why will the woman not allow the student to use the entrance?

(A) He is not a registered employee at the university.

(B) He does not have the required identification with him.

(C) Students may not use that door under any circumstances.

(D) No one should use that door when someone is giving a presentation.

TYPE 7   Listen again to part of the conversation. Then answer the question.
What can be inferred about the student when he says this: 🎧

(A) He is interested in doing the woman's job.

(B) He would like to speak with the woman's manager.

(C) He is not upset with the woman at all.

(D) He would like to keep talking with the woman.

TYPE 8   What will the student probably do next?

(A) Return to his booth

(B) Apply for a new ID card

(C) Talk to the manager

(D) Borrow a projector

Summarizing ▷ Fill in the blanks to complete the summary.

The student wants to enter a door, but the woman will not allow him to. She says he needs
to gain access. The student responds that he left his nametag at _____. The woman says she
would like to let the man through, but she has to _____. The student then asks the woman
how to _____. He is giving a presentation the next day, so he wants to show some slides.
The woman notes that it may be difficult to do. She tells him to go and get his nametag and then she will talk to
_____ about the projector.

Listen to part of a lecture in an anthropology class.

02-052

The Neolithic Age

Farming:

Pottery:

Civilization:

---

1 Why does the professor explain pottery?

  (A) To say that it was invented after humans learned how to farm the land

  (B) To give the years when it was developed in various parts of the world

  (C) To note that it was a solution to the problem of grain preservation

  (D) To state that the Chinese were among the first to make pottery

2 According to the professor, what happened around 12,000 B.C.?

  (A) Humans first domesticated the dog.

  (B) People learned how to grow crops.

  (C) The first permanent establishments were founded.

  (D) Goats, cattle, and chickens were domesticated.

3 What will the professor probably do next?

  (A) Encourage the students to discuss the lecture material

  (B) Show some pictures of primitive pottery

  (C) Mention the grains that farmers first cultivated

  (D) Discuss the creation of early civilizations

Summarizing ▶ Fill in the blanks to complete the summary.

The professor begins talking about _____ . He notes that there were _____ that happened during this time that influenced people. The first is that humans learned how to _____ . This enabled them to stop living nomadic lives. The second is that humans learned how to _____ . They needed to do this in order to store the surplus grain that they had harvested. Finally, the third reason was that humans began to _____ . They settled down in villages and communities, and from there they began to grow into tribes and nations.

Listen to part of a lecture in a political science class.

- 02-053

Bureaucracies

What They Are:		First Characteristic:
	➡	
		Second Characteristic:

1 How is the discussion organized?

- Ⓐ By explaining bureaucracies and then describing their primary features
- Ⓑ By discussing the strengths and weaknesses of government bureaucracies
- Ⓒ By relying upon students' questions to determine the course of the lecture
- Ⓓ By comparing and contrasting different kinds of bureaucracies

2 Listen again to part of the lecture. Then answer the question.
What does the professor imply when he says this: 🎧

- Ⓐ He is pleased that he has their attention.
- Ⓑ He was not intentionally being funny.
- Ⓒ He does not want any more interruptions.
- Ⓓ He finds the government to be inefficient.

3 Listen again to part of the lecture. Then answer the question.
What does the professor mean when he says this: 🎧

- Ⓐ He wants more students to participate in class.
- Ⓑ The student needs to pay more attention.
- Ⓒ He was expecting a student to ask him that question.
- Ⓓ The student has asked a good question.

Summarizing ▷ Fill in the blanks to complete the summary.

The professor says he wants to _____, but a student first asks him to explain exactly what they are. The professor says that they are basically large _____ who are often found in government organizations. Then, the professor describes their _____. The first is that they make things more efficient because each worker has _____ that he or she is trained for. The second characteristic is that _____ apply to everyone. He notes, however, that there are times when people do not always follow these rules and behave in an illegal manner.

Listen to part of a lecture in a history class.

02-054

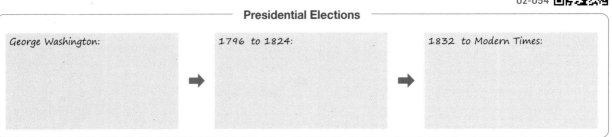

Presidential Elections

George Washington:	1796 to 1824:	1832 to Modern Times:

1 What is the lecture mainly about?

Ⓐ Why people such as George Washington disliked political parties

Ⓑ What the effects of political conventions have been

Ⓒ How presidential candidates have been selected historically

Ⓓ How modern-day presidential candidates are chosen

2 Based on the information in the lecture, do the following sentences refer to the causes or the effects of the creation of political parties?
Click in the correct box for each sentence.

	Cause	Effect
① People developed differing political beliefs.		
② Delegates were needed to win the nomination.		
③ People began to attend political conventions.		
④ The presidential nominating procedure was easily controlled.		

3 Listen again to part of the lecture. Then answer the question.
What does the professor imply when he says this: 🎧

Ⓐ Washington was successfully able to unite the country by ignoring political parties.

Ⓑ There was a lot of bloodshed during the American Revolution.

Ⓒ Washington faced opposition to the revolution by people living in America.

Ⓓ The colonists were mostly pleased when they gained their independence.

Summarizing ▶ Fill in the blanks to complete the summary.

The professor tells the class that he wants to describe the presidential candidate selection process since they are
in .... He then asks a student what political party .... belonged
to. The student responds that Washington did not have one. The professor notes that Washington was against
..........................., but once he stopped serving as president, political parties gained prominence. The two
major parties were .... parties. But in 1824, the House of Representative had to decide on
the president, so the parties ...., which are still used today. Delegates are chosen from every
state, and they choose their party's presidential candidate.

Listen to part of a lecture in a history class.

02-055

─── **Thomas Jefferson and Architecture** ───

Jefferson's Influences:		Jefferson's Buildings:
	➡	

1 What is the lecture mainly about?
- Ⓐ A comparison of the homes designed by Thomas Jefferson
- Ⓑ The influence of Andrea Palladio on Thomas Jefferson
- Ⓒ The reason why Thomas Jefferson became an architect
- Ⓓ Some of the buildings designed by Thomas Jefferson

2 According to the professor, what was a major influence on the design of Monticello?
- Ⓐ Ancient Roman villas
- Ⓑ The Roman Pantheon
- Ⓒ The architecture in Paris
- Ⓓ Andrea Palladio

3 Why does the professor mention *Four Books on Architecture*?
- Ⓐ To say it was the first book of architecture that Jefferson read
- Ⓑ To state the name of the author of the book
- Ⓒ To emphasize its importance on Jefferson's work
- Ⓓ To explain some of the ideas contained in the book

Summarizing ▷ Fill in the blanks to complete the summary.

The professor mentions some of Thomas Jefferson's accomplishments, but then she claims that Jefferson loved
_____ most of all. In early America, there were no _____, and buildings
were poor copies of European styles. Jefferson read *Four Books on Architecture* by Andrea Palladio and was greatly
influenced by it. He also learned much about architecture when he spent five years in _____.
This affected the design of _____, which is very famous today. Jefferson also designed the
capitol building in Virginia, many of the buildings at _____, and Poplar Forest, one of his most
unique designs.

Mastering Topics with Conversations | B5

Listen to part of a conversation between a student and a professor.

02-056

Office Hours

Student's Problem:

Teaching Assistant's Solution:

Professor's Solution:

1 Why does the student visit the professor?

- Ⓐ To discuss her grade in his class
- Ⓑ To complain about her teaching assistant
- Ⓒ To talk about the content of her discussion
- Ⓓ To receive another assignment from the professor

2 What does the professor offer to do for the student?

- Ⓐ Speak with her teaching assistant
- Ⓑ Give her a new project to do
- Ⓒ Let her take the midterm exam again
- Ⓓ Excuse her from taking the final exam

3 Listen again to part of the conversation. Then answer the question.
What does the student imply when she says this: 🎧

- Ⓐ Her teaching assistant is unconcerned with the student's problem.
- Ⓑ She wants the professor to talk to her teaching assistant.
- Ⓒ She thinks her teaching assistant is being unfair to her.
- Ⓓ There is more than one teaching assistant in the class.

Summarizing ▷ Fill in the blanks to complete the summary.

The student visits the professor's office, introduces herself, and says she is taking one of his classes. She then states she wants to talk about _____, which surprises the professor since the semester still has six weeks left. She explains that she missed _____, which is worth twenty percent of her grade, because she was sick. But her teaching assistant is going to give her _____. She shows the professor that she got a ninety-five on the midterm exam despite _____ of classes. He agrees to give her _____ and tells her to visit the departmental secretary the next day.

Listen to part of a conversation between a student and an admissions office employee.

02-057

Service Encounter

Reason for Visiting:		Result:
Problem:		Solution:

1 What problem does the student have?
- Ⓐ Adjusting to her new school is difficult for her.
- Ⓑ She often gets in arguments with her roommate.
- Ⓒ She is having trouble studying in her room.
- Ⓓ Her dorm room is not big enough to accommodate her.

2 What does the student imply about her roommate?
- Ⓐ She is inconsiderate.
- Ⓑ Her grades are poor.
- Ⓒ She has too many friends.
- Ⓓ She comes from a wealthy family.

3 Listen again to part of the conversation. Then answer the question.
What does the student imply when she says this: 🎧
- Ⓐ She gets very good grades.
- Ⓑ She is involved in no extracurricular activities.
- Ⓒ She is attending the school on a scholarship.
- Ⓓ She does not have any friends at school.

Summarizing ▷ Fill in the blanks to complete the summary.

The student visits the student housing office to complain about _____. She says that, because of her roommate, she needs a single dormitory room. The employee asks for more information. The student mentions that _____ to the school so could not choose her roommate. And the roommate she has now never studies and always has friends _____. This means that she cannot study, which is the only activity that she does. The employee tells her it is _____ to give her a single, so she should study at the library. He then promises to help her try to get a new room for _____.

Listen to part of a lecture in an economics class.

02-058

Economics

1   What is the main topic of the lecture?

    Ⓐ The factors involved in the purchases people make

    Ⓑ The importance of age and word of mouth in buying products

    Ⓒ The desire for companies to have consumers with brand loyalty

    Ⓓ The need to rank the reasons why people buy certain things

2   According to the professor, which of the following factors influences what a person buys?
Choose 2 answers.

    Ⓐ Recommendations from others

    Ⓑ Discounts on the items' prices

    Ⓒ The type of job a person has

    Ⓓ The place a person comes from

3   How is the discussion organized?

    Ⓐ The professor contrasts the various reasons with one another.

    Ⓑ The professor ranks the factors in order of importance.

    Ⓒ The professor explains the importance of several factors.

    Ⓓ The professor seeks input from the students on the subject matter.

4   Based on the information in the lecture, do the following sentences about purchases people make refer to a person's happiness or word of mouth?
Click in the correct box for each sentence.

	Happiness	Word of Mouth
1 A friend makes a suggestion to watch a movie.		
2 A person feels he must own something.		
3 A person hears from others about the quality of a product.		
4 A person feels good about making a purchase.		

5   Listen again to part of the lecture. Then answer the question.
Why does the professor say this: 🎧

A He has run out of topics to cover.

B He wants to stress the importance of the next topic.

C He is going to dismiss the class soon.

D He wants the class to pay close attention.

6   Listen again to part of the lecture. Then answer the question.
What does the professor imply when he says this: 🎧

A The student is only partially correct.

B He will describe many important factors.

C The student gave the answer he had expected.

D He needs to discuss some more details now.

Listen to part of a lecture in a history class.

02-059

1 What aspect of railways does the professor mainly discuss?

- Ⓐ The goods and the people they carry
- Ⓑ The transcontinental railway
- Ⓒ The difficulty involved in building them
- Ⓓ Their effect on the United States

2 Why does the professor explain the Pacific Railway Act of 1862?

- Ⓐ To note a piece of legislation supported by Abraham Lincoln
- Ⓑ To state what caused the transcontinental railway to be built
- Ⓒ To show how it positively affected the American economy
- Ⓓ To mention the two companies which were founded by its passing

3 What is the professor's attitude toward oceangoing ships?

- Ⓐ They were less important than railroads.
- Ⓑ They helped open the world to travel.
- Ⓒ They permitted the discovery of America.
- Ⓓ They were necessary to transport goods to South America.

4   Why does the professor mention the population figures for Nebraska and California?

    Ⓐ To prove how influential the transcontinental railway was

    Ⓑ To justify the high cost of constructing the transcontinental railway

    Ⓒ To compare the populations of those states to one another

    Ⓓ To show how their populations increased faster than other states' did

5   Listen again to part of the lecture. Then answer the question.

    Why does the professor say this: 🎧

    Ⓐ To stress that the students need to know the history of this period

    Ⓑ To indicate she will discuss events occurring before the railway's construction

    Ⓒ To encourage the students to recall what they read on this topic

    Ⓓ To imply that she has much to say on this particular subject

6   Listen again to part of the lecture. Then answer the question.

    What does the professor imply when she says this: 🎧

    Ⓐ The railway workers often had to battle Native Americans.

    Ⓑ The construction of the railway took more time than it should have.

    Ⓒ There was little reason at the time to build the railway.

    Ⓓ Many people protested the railway's construction.

02-060

Listen to part of a conversation between a student and a student housing office employee.

1 Why does the student visit the student housing office?

Ⓐ To ask for a new number to select housing

Ⓑ To choose a single room for the next semester

Ⓒ To find out how to get a single room next semester

Ⓓ To inquire about off-campus living arrangements

2 According to the woman, what is the purpose of the school's buddy system?

Ⓐ It ensures that all students have friends on campus.

Ⓑ It permits friends to select rooms with one another.

Ⓒ It enables students to share the cost of their housing.

Ⓓ It grants students the right to live in off-campus housing.

3 Why does the student mention his friend with the high number?

Ⓐ To propose a solution to his problem

Ⓑ To explain why he cannot live off campus

Ⓒ To ask if he can exchange numbers with the student

Ⓓ To find out how the buddy system works

4 Listen again to part of the conversation. Then answer the question.
Why does the student say this: 🎧

Ⓐ To show his frustration

Ⓑ To make a rebuke

Ⓒ To agree with the woman

Ⓓ To lighten the mood

5 Listen again to part of the conversation. Then answer the question.
What can be inferred about the woman when she says this: 🎧

Ⓐ She believes there is a problem with the selection system.

Ⓑ She enjoys teasing the student about what happened.

Ⓒ She sympathizes with the student's unfortunate situation.

Ⓓ She has received visits from other students with similar complaints.

• Mastering Question Types

absolutism	breach	cede	clothe
divine	gap	hunter-gatherer	lifestyle
outlandish	permanent	refund	replacement
sociologist	strive	tolerant	trust
arrow	brilliant	chaos	cohesive
exhausted	gunpowder	inspire	loyalty
pastoral	persuasive	refutation	reputation
stability	sturdily	tradesman	unknown
brand	catapult	checkmark	contract
fortification	herd	itinerant	medieval
peripatetic	promote	reliable	revoke
storm	tame	treatise	urban

• Mastering Topics

adhere	agriculture	bureaucracy	delegate
exempt	glean	historically	integral
norm	originate	pottery	profound
runner-up	skylight	statesman	supervision
affiliation	arguably	candidate	despise
foremost	grain	idyllic	landscape
octagonal	pit	precision	prompt
seminal	specialist	stead	surplus
advent	backtrack	cultivate	elector
found	harvest	inadequate	minimum
official	politician	procedure	recognizable
shy	split	strict	vary

• TOEFL Practice Tests

afford	attached	boon	clunker
convenient	domestication	exploit	five-star
influential	interestingly	luxury	oceangoing
press	railway	resort	statistic
ambitious	blue-collar	carelessly	colossal
decade	ease	dictate	fixed
inroads	interruption	nag	passenger
prime	reap	rural	venture
apt	bold	cargo	compatible
delay	expenditure	firsthand	fortune
insistence	intricacy	note	penetrate
profoundly	recommend	settlement	vice versa

✑ Choose the words with the closest meanings to the highlighted words.

1 I do not have the statistics in front of me, but I can send you the calculations later.

Ⓐ theories   Ⓑ numbers

Ⓒ additions   Ⓓ estimates

2 Sara made a colossal mistake that got her in a lot of trouble.

Ⓐ careless   Ⓑ naive

Ⓒ inappropriate   Ⓓ huge

3 Richard is designing a unique octagonal home for a client.

Ⓐ six-sided   Ⓑ seven-sided

Ⓒ eight-sided   Ⓓ nine-sided

4 That idea is brilliant; I am positive it will work if we try it.

Ⓐ ingenious   Ⓑ potential

Ⓒ magnanimous   Ⓓ noble

5 A prime component of the company's marketing strategy is TV advertising.

Ⓐ major   Ⓑ unique

Ⓒ possible   Ⓓ original

6 The speaker made an extremely profound point that people had to consider.

Ⓐ creative   Ⓑ deep

Ⓒ imaginary   Ⓓ outrageous

7 If you keep up the good work, you will develop an excellent reputation.

Ⓐ career   Ⓑ resume

Ⓒ consideration   Ⓓ name

8 Do you know where that idea originated from?

Ⓐ came   Ⓑ organized

Ⓒ transferred   Ⓓ returned

9 He enjoys living life as a nomad so that he can go wherever he wants.

Ⓐ dissident   Ⓑ refugee

Ⓒ wanderer   Ⓓ beggar

10 John dictated to the workers exactly what he wanted them to do.

Ⓐ requested to   Ⓑ ordered

Ⓒ asked   Ⓓ convinced

✑ Match the words with the correct definitions.

11 catapult •   •Ⓐ a device that can hurl objects through the air

12 cultivate •   •Ⓑ to hand over or give to another

13 fund •   •Ⓒ able to travel on the ocean

14 exhausted •   •Ⓓ to grow or raise, usually referring to crops

15 surplus •   •Ⓔ to pay for

16 persuasive •   •Ⓕ a luxury hotel

17 oceangoing •   •Ⓖ to dislike or hate very much

18 cede •   •Ⓗ convincing

19 resort •   •Ⓘ completely used

20 despise •   •Ⓙ an overabundance of something

Chapter 05   **Physical Sciences 1** | **Conversations**

astronomy • physics • chemistry • geology • environmental science • meteorology •
mineralogy • astrophysics • geophysics • physical chemistry

02-061

Listen to part of a lecture in a physics class.

TYPE 1   What is the lecture mainly about?

    (A) The visible colors of light

    (B) Infrared and ultraviolet light

    (C) Black and white

    (D) The uses of a prism

TYPE 2   What does the professor say about the color black?

    (A) It has relatively short wavelengths.

    (B) It is the absence of all color.

    (C) It has fairly long wavelengths.

    (D) It is a combination of all colors.

TYPE 3   Why does the professor mention Sir Isaac Newton?

    (A) To serve as an introduction to his discussion of the prism

    (B) To claim that he was the first person to name the colors of visible light

    (C) To explain his role in discovering the wavelengths of light

    (D) To talk about the research that he conducted on light

TYPE 4   Listen again to part of the lecture. Then answer the question.

    Why does the professor say this: 🎧

    (A) To go over the definition of a term again

    (B) To make sure the students know how to spell a word

    (C) To indicate they will be tested on a word

    (D) To emphasize the importance of a term

Summarizing ▷   Fill in the blanks to complete the summary.

The professor says he will talk about _____. He states that it is light with wavelengths between _____ light. According to the professor, the eye's retina simply registers individual wavelengths as different colors. He then mentions _____ and his work with prisms, which can divide light into all of its different colors. He notes that colors close to infrared have _____ while those close to ultraviolet have short wavelengths. He briefly mentions that rainbows can split light like a prism. He finally notes that white is a combination of all colors while black is the _____.

02-062

Listen to part of a lecture in a geology class.

TYPE 5 What is the main topic of the lecture?

(A) The upper layers of the Earth

(B) The asthenosphere

(C) The Moho Discontinuity

(D) The theory of plate tectonics

TYPE 6 What is the professor's attitude toward Andrija Mohorovicic?

(A) The professor thinks his work is unimportant because it cannot be proven.

(B) The professor believes he did invaluable work on the asthenosphere.

(C) The professor considers him a person whose work should be studied.

(D) The professor claims that he was a person who was ahead of his time.

TYPE 7 What can be inferred about the upper mantle in places above the oceans?

(A) It is at its most rigid there.

(B) It is around ten times thicker than the crust.

(C) It has a fairly static Moho Discontinuity.

(D) It is more susceptible to continental drift there.

TYPE 8 What comparison does the professor make between the lithosphere and the asthenosphere?

(A) He describes how the composition of both differs.

(B) He explains the differences in their thickness.

(C) He notes how they are different in their firmness.

(D) He talks about how they respond to plate tectonics.

Summarizing ▷ Fill in the blanks to complete the summary.

The professor describes the different layers of the Earth. He notes that _____ together are called
the lithosphere because they are the Earth's solid part. He then describes the thickness of the lithosphere in various
places. He states that the scientist Andrija Mohorovicic theorized the existence of the _____ ,
which runs between the crust and upper mantle. He stresses that it is only a theory and _____ .
Then he proceeds to talk about the asthenosphere, which lies beneath the lithosphere. Less rigid than the lithosphere,
the asthenosphere enables the plates in the lithosphere to move, which makes _____ change
places.

TYPE 1 • Gist-Purpose *TYPE 2* • Detail *TYPE 3* • Understanding Organization *TYPE 4* • Function of What Is Said

02-063

Listen to part of a lecture in an environmental science class.

TYPE 1 Why does the professor explain the use of algae as a biofuel?

Ⓐ To compare its value with soybeans

Ⓑ To state where it can be harvested

Ⓒ To show how it is more efficient than corn

Ⓓ To mention its potential usefulness

TYPE 2 According to the professor, why are some people against the use of biofuels?

Ⓐ The infrastructure is not set up to accommodate them.

Ⓑ They feel that it costs too much to justify producing.

Ⓒ There are not enough cars that can use biofuels now.

Ⓓ They do not want to make energy from sources of food.

TYPE 3 How is the discussion organized?

Ⓐ By defining biofuels and explaining where they can come from

Ⓑ By comparing and contrasting biofuels with fossil fuels

Ⓒ By noting the amount of fuel that can be created from each energy source

Ⓓ By explaining how scientists are trying to develop more biofuels

TYPE 4 Listen again to part of the lecture. Then answer the question.
What does the student imply when he says this: 🎧

Ⓐ He wants the professor to talk about some other biofuels.

Ⓑ More research on biofuels needs to be done immediately.

Ⓒ He cannot understand why biofuels are not used regularly.

Ⓓ He is against the usage of fossil fuels as energy sources.

Summarizing ▷ Fill in the blanks to complete the summary.

The professor talks about the need to find ＿＿＿＿＿＿＿＿＿ because fossil fuels are nonrenewable. He claims that biofuels, which come from ＿＿＿＿＿＿＿＿＿, are a potential energy source. Some that are used to make energy are corn, sugarcane, soybeans, and canola. They produce fewer ＿＿＿＿＿ than fossil fuels. When asked why biofuels are not more common, the professor states that many people do not want to ＿＿＿＿＿＿＿＿＿ to produce as fuel. In addition, not enough biofuel is being produced, it is expensive, and it might not reduce carbon emissions. He then says that alga is ＿＿＿＿＿＿＿＿＿ of biofuel, but more research remains to be done on it.

02-064

Listen to part of a lecture in a meteorology class.

TYPE 5 What aspect of monsoons is the lecture mainly about?

Ⓐ Where they usually appear

Ⓑ How they are created

Ⓒ When they drop large amounts of rain

Ⓓ How people make use of them

TYPE 6 Listen again to part of the lecture. Then answer the question.
What does the professor mean when she says this: 🎧

Ⓐ The students need to continue taking notes.

Ⓑ She welcomes any questions that the students have.

Ⓒ The material she is covering is complicated.

Ⓓ She is ready to move on to another topic.

TYPE 7 What can be inferred about rice?

Ⓐ Rice plants grow well in lots of water.

Ⓑ It is grown more than any other crop in India.

Ⓒ It will not grow in areas with cold weather.

Ⓓ It usually ripens during the summer months.

TYPE 8 What will the professor probably do next?

Ⓐ Explain the damage monsoon floods can do

Ⓑ Assign the students some homework

Ⓒ Start talking about another weather phenomenon

Ⓓ Describe some more benefits of monsoons

Summarizing ▷ Fill in the blanks to complete the summary.

Monsoons are heavy winds and rains that occur seasonally in many parts of the world. Because of the
way both _____ absorb heat, moisture from the ocean comes on land and then
_____ . The rain can last for many days and _____ in a lot of places. In
India, because of the _____ , the monsoons can drop an extreme amount of rain. The professor
says it seems that people would dislike monsoons, but in fact, people like them for many reasons. The rains provide
relief _____ and help crops grow.

TYPE 1 • Gist-Purpose   *TYPE 2* • Detail   *TYPE 3* • Understanding Organization   *TYPE 4* • Function of What Is Said

02-065

Listen to part of a conversation between a student and a professor.

TYPE 1 Why does the student visit the professor?

    (A) To discuss a job offer he had previously mentioned

    (B) To talk about dropping a class that she is taking

    (C) To receive his comments on a paper she wrote

    (D) To get some hints about an upcoming exam

TYPE 2 What does the professor indicate about his class?

    (A) It requires students to complete a class project.

    (B) It has many freshmen and sophomores in it.

    (C) It has a lab that all students must enroll in.

    (D) It is an elementary class in the Astronomy Department.

TYPE 3 Why does the professor mention the previous test?

    (A) To discuss the complaints students had about it

    (B) To state he has not graded all of them

    (C) To say that many students did poorly on it

    (D) To comment that nobody in the class got an A

TYPE 4 Why does the professor ask the student about tutoring?

    (A) He wants her to assist some of the students in the class.

    (B) He believes the student should hire a tutor for herself.

    (C) He thinks the student should apply to become a tutor.

    (D) He knows that students can make good money by tutoring.

Summarizing ▶ Fill in the blanks to complete the summary.

The professor says that _____ the student wrote is good but that she should make a few changes to it. He then talks to the student about his class. He mentions that many _____ are taking his advanced astronomy class. He remarks that _____ on the recent test were poor, but they cannot drop the class now. He would therefore like the student to work _____. The student states that she has never tutored before. However, she agrees to help and informs the professor that she can help on _____ evenings.

02-066

Listen to part of a conversation between a student and a librarian.

TYPE 5   What problem does the student have?

    Ⓐ He is having trouble finding a book.

    Ⓑ He is failing one of his classes.

    Ⓒ The book he wants is checked out.

    Ⓓ He cannot do one of his homework assignments.

TYPE 6   What class is the student not doing well in?

    Ⓐ Computer science

    Ⓑ Biology

    Ⓒ Physics

    Ⓓ Astronomy

TYPE 7   What is the librarian's attitude toward the student?

    Ⓐ He is nonchalant.

    Ⓑ He is sympathetic.

    Ⓒ He is inconsiderate.

    Ⓓ He is overly helpful.

TYPE 8   Listen again to part of the conversation. Then answer the question.
What does the student imply when he says this: 🎧

    Ⓐ He has enough money with him now.

    Ⓑ He is going to purchase the book.

    Ⓒ He will see if he can do without the book.

    Ⓓ He will try to borrow the book from a friend.

Summarizing ▷ Fill in the blanks to complete the summary.

The student tells _____ he is looking for a book on the computer system, but he cannot find it.
The librarian asks for _____ and looks it up himself. When he cannot find it, he asks the student
for the author's name. Upon hearing the name, the librarian realizes the library _____ .
The student is upset because he needs the book for a class he is having trouble with. The librarian then states that
the student can _____ at the school bookstore for under _____ , and the
student implies that he will go and purchase it.

Listen to part of a lecture in a geology class.

02-067

Limestone

Limestone Characteristics:	Why It Forms Caves:
	What It Forms From:
	How It Is Used:

1 Why does the professor mention calcium carbonate?

Ⓐ To explain why limestone is so susceptible to erosion

Ⓑ To state why limestone is found in certain locations

Ⓒ To mention what causes limestone to have different colors

Ⓓ To note what limestone is mostly comprised of

2 What can be inferred about the TAG area?

Ⓐ It covers a large amount of land.

Ⓑ It was once located underwater.

Ⓒ It has more caves than anywhere else in the world.

Ⓓ It is a geological unstable area.

3 Listen again to part of the lecture. Then answer the question.
What does the professor mean when he says this: 🎧

Ⓐ He has not formed an opinion about what he just mentioned.

Ⓑ He would like to hear some of the students' opinions on that matter.

Ⓒ It is possible that the information will have to be reevaluated.

Ⓓ The information he just discussed has not been verified yet.

Summarizing ▷ Fill in the blanks to complete the summary.

The professor mentions that the TAG area has many _____ . He then notes why areas with a lot of limestone tend to have caves in them. He states that most limestone is comprised of _____ , which originally formed from dead animals millions of years ago. He also notes the different colors limestone may be. He claims that many areas with large amounts of limestone were once _____ . The professor says that limestone is used to make buildings and _____ . However, because it is not very hard, some buildings made from limestone get worn down due to _____ .

Listen to part of a lecture in a physics class.

02-068

Solar Power

| Solar Power: | → | Advantages: |
| | | Disadvantages: |

1   Why does the professor explain solar cells?

(A) To show how they create electricity

(B) To talk about their inefficiency

(C) To mention the year they were invented

(D) To note some ways to improve them

2   What does the professor say about the advantages of using solar power?

(A) It takes a short time to set up the solar panels.

(B) It provides savings to people over the long term.

(C) It can be utilized in a large number of places.

(D) It can produce electricity at any time of the day.

3   Listen again to part of the lecture. Then answer the question.
What does the professor imply when she says this: 🎧

(A) The students need to read their textbook more carefully.

(B) The students need to be prepared when they come to class.

(C) The students should take a look at the diagram.

(D) The students should always do their assigned reading.

Summarizing ▷ Fill in the blanks to complete the summary.

The professor notes when _____ were first created. She explains how they work and tells the students to look at a diagram in _____ . She says solar cells are placed on _____ , which are aimed at the sun. She claims that solar power cannot be used to provide an entire country's energy needs and states it accounts for less than one percent of the U.S.'s energy. She says that one advantage of solar power is that it is renewable. It can also provide _____ energy savings. As for disadvantages, it cannot be used on cloudy days or _____ . The panels are also somewhat inefficient.

02-069

Listen to part of a lecture in a geology class.

Diamonds

Black Diamonds:

➡

Nanodiamonds:

---

1 What is the lecture mainly about?

Ⓐ The uses of diamonds in medicine

Ⓑ The value of some rare diamonds

Ⓒ Two unique types of diamonds

Ⓓ The origins of black diamonds and nanodiamonds

2 Based on the information in the lecture, do the following statements refer to black diamonds or nanodiamonds?

Click in the correct box for each sentence.

	Black Diamonds	Nanodiamonds
① May be of future value to medical doctors		
② Are only found in two places on the Earth		
③ May have extraterrestrial origins		
④ Can be formed through human actions		

3 What can be inferred about the professor's thoughts on black diamonds?

Ⓐ He believes the prevailing theory on their origins.

Ⓑ He is not convinced that they are extremely rare.

Ⓒ He thinks there are substances harder than they are.

Ⓓ He feels they are not as old as some people believe.

Summarizing ▶ Fill in the blanks to complete the summary.

The professor claims that black diamonds and nanodiamonds are _____. Black diamonds are found in only two places. One is in Africa, and the other is in _____. They are also around four billion years old. He claims that they may have _____ and explains why people believe that. As for nanodiamonds, these can be made by humans by using explosives. He describes how this process occurs. He then mentions that nanodiamonds may have some use in the _____. However, this is not yet the case. Perhaps they will be used _____ in the future.

Listen to part of a lecture in an astronomy class.

02-070

—— Galaxies and Their Formation ——

The Sizes of Galaxies:

➡

The Shapes of Galaxies:

1 According to the professor, what does the black hole at the center of a galaxy do?

Ⓐ It prevents the galaxy from colliding with another one.

Ⓑ It determines the size of the galaxy.

Ⓒ It maintains the equilibrium of the galaxy.

Ⓓ It permits the galaxy to move through space.

2 Based on the information in the lecture, which kind of galaxy do the following statements refer to?
Click in the correct box for each sentence.

	Elliptical Galaxy	Spiral Galaxy	Barred-Spiral Galaxy
1 May be almost spherical in appearance			
2 Has extremely long arms			
3 May spin like a disk			
4 Has a bar-shaped center			

3 What can be inferred about the Milky Way?

Ⓐ It is older than most other galaxies.

Ⓑ It is smaller than a spiral galaxy.

Ⓒ It is a dwarf elliptical galaxy.

Ⓓ It is a medium-sized galaxy.

Summarizing ▷ Fill in the blanks to complete the summary.

According to the lecturer, _____ proved there were other galaxies in 1924. Now astronomers have seen enough other galaxies to classify them according to _____ . There are dwarf elliptical galaxies, spiral galaxies, and giant elliptical galaxies. She explains their characteristics. Galaxies also have different shapes. There are elliptical galaxies, _____ , and barred-spiral galaxies, all of which she then compares and contrasts. She mentions how galaxies were first formed and why they all are believed to have a massive _____ in their center. Finally, she notes that galaxies move and that some _____ each other.

Listen to part of a conversation between a student and a professor.

02-071

Office Hours

Reason for Visiting:	Result:
Problem:	Solution:

1 Why does the student visit the professor?

- Ⓐ To change her status in the professor's class
- Ⓑ To ask for help interpreting some poems
- Ⓒ To see if the professor can enroll her in the class
- Ⓓ To discuss her extracurricular activities with the professor

2 What is the professor's attitude toward the student?

- Ⓐ She is eager to accommodate the student's request.
- Ⓑ She is complimentary toward the student.
- Ⓒ She is discouraged by the student's numerous activities.
- Ⓓ She is disappointed in the student's performance.

3 Listen again to part of the conversation. Then answer the question.
What is the purpose of the student's response?

- Ⓐ To note her pleasure
- Ⓑ To express doubt
- Ⓒ To show her disagreement
- Ⓓ To accept the compliment

Summarizing ▶ Fill in the blanks to complete the summary.

The student visits the professor's office to talk. The professor thinks the student is there to discuss some poems, but the student says she has come to ＿＿＿＿＿＿＿＿＿＿＿. She explains that she is too busy with all of her ＿＿＿＿＿＿＿＿＿ and needs to focus on her major classes ＿＿＿＿＿＿＿＿＿＿＿. The professor expresses her disappointment because the student makes good contributions and writes excellent poems. When she tries to convince the student to ＿＿＿＿＿＿＿＿＿＿, the student says that is not possible. The professor agrees to let her drop the class and invites the student to ＿＿＿＿＿＿＿＿＿ anytime she wants.

Listen to part of a conversation between a student and a resident assistant.

02-072

Service Encounter

Problem:		Solution:
	➡	
Student's Reaction:	↖	Student's Decision:
	➡	

---

1 What are the speakers mainly discussing?

Ⓐ The student's newest electrical appliance

Ⓑ The punishment the student is going to receive

Ⓒ The student's violation of a school regulation

Ⓓ The student's need to live in another dormitory

2 According to the resident assistant, why are refrigerators not permitted in the dormitory?

Ⓐ The dormitory's electrical system cannot handle the power required.

Ⓑ It would be unfair to the other students who cannot afford to buy one.

Ⓒ The school does not want students to keep food and drinks in their rooms.

Ⓓ The extra electricity used would cost the school too much money.

3 What does the resident assistant imply about the student's situation?

Ⓐ He should have been more cognizant of the rules.

Ⓑ He has no sympathy for the student.

Ⓒ He wants to make an exception for the student.

Ⓓ He understands how the student feels.

Summarizing ▷ Fill in the blanks to complete the summary.

The student tells _____ about the refrigerator he just got. The resident assistant tells the student that refrigerators are not allowed in the dormitory and that he needs to _____ . The student wants to know what his punishment will be if he refuses. He learns he could be fined or _____ student housing. Then the resident assistant offers to drive the student to a place _____ to store the refrigerator. The student asks why refrigerators are not allowed in the dormitory, and the resident assistant says it is due to _____ in the building, which is old.

Listen to part of a lecture in a chemistry class.

02-073

1   What is the main topic of the lecture?
   Ⓐ The best kinds of chemical dating methods
   Ⓑ The difference between carbon-14 dating and potassium-argon dating
   Ⓒ Some methods that scientists use to date old objects
   Ⓓ Which kinds of objects can have their dates ascertained

2   Why does the professor explain carbon-14 dating?
   Ⓐ To describe the most common type of dating method
   Ⓑ To point out its numerous limitations
   Ⓒ To note what kind of materials cannot be dated with it
   Ⓓ To mention which carbon isotope is radioactive

3   According to the professor, how can researchers determine the date of an object by using nonchemical methods?
   Choose 2 answers.
   Ⓐ By consulting pictures in ancient texts
   Ⓑ By comparing linguistic peculiarities
   Ⓒ By noting manufacturing techniques
   Ⓓ By examining the materials used

4 How does the professor organize the information about ascertaining prehistoric objects' dates that she presents to the class?

Ⓐ By mentioning the methods in the order that they were discovered

Ⓑ By discussing the effects that dating methods have on their subjects

Ⓒ By establishing a problem and then showing its solution

Ⓓ By describing two methods that are frequently used

5 Based on the information in the lecture, do the following sentences refer to the carbon-14 dating method or the potassium-argon dating method?

Click in the correct box for each sentence.

	Carbon-14 Dating Method	Potassium-Argon Dating Method
1 It is only correct to within around forty years.		
2 It is used for dating organic material.		
3 It is useful for volcanic rocks.		
4 It can date something back 4.5 billion years.		

6 What will the professor probably do next?

Ⓐ Discuss another type of dating method used

Ⓑ Begin comparing the carbon-14 and potassium-argon dating methods

Ⓒ Let the students take a short break

Ⓓ Talk about how fossils are formed

02-074

Listen to part of a lecture in a geology class.

Geology

1   What aspect of deserts does the professor mainly discuss?

    Ⓐ Their locations around the world

    Ⓑ The geological features found in many deserts

    Ⓒ The various reasons why they may form

    Ⓓ The meteorological effects on deserts

2   According to the professor, what is a unique feature of the Namib Desert?

    Ⓐ It is located in Antarctica.

    Ⓑ It is a coastal desert.

    Ⓒ The rain-shadow effect formed it.

    Ⓓ It is a manmade desert.

3   What is the professor's opinion of the Atacama Desert?

    Ⓐ He finds it to be a typical coastal desert.

    Ⓑ He is amazed by its lack of precipitation.

    Ⓒ He is saddened that it is a manmade desert.

    Ⓓ He feels it has some interesting geological features.

4   Why does the professor mention Antarctica?

  (A) To say that it is the world's coldest desert

  (B) To answer a student's question about it

  (C) To stress how there are many types of deserts

  (D) To show how much annual precipitation it gets

5   Based on the information in the lecture, do the following statements refer to deserts found in central or coastal regions?
Click in the correct box for each sentence.

	Central Regions	Coastal Regions
1 Are formed because of ocean currents		
2 Can form due to the rain-shadow effect		
3 May be located next to mountain ranges		
4 Often receive very little precipitation		

6   Listen again to part of the lecture. Then answer the question.
What does the professor imply when he says this: 🎧

  (A) He does not consider Antarctica a real desert.

  (B) There is no more need to talk about Antarctica.

  (C) He will discuss Antarctica later in the class.

  (D) Antarctica is the world's most unusual desert.

02-075

Listen to part of a conversation between a student and a professor.

1   Why does the student visit the professor?
   Ⓐ To complain about another professor whose class she is taking
   Ⓑ To ask to borrow some of the professor's research materials
   Ⓒ To request assistance on a paper in the professor's class
   Ⓓ To get some help on one of her school assignments

2   What does the professor give the student?
   Ⓐ His email address
   Ⓑ A book
   Ⓒ A paper he wrote
   Ⓓ An essay

3   What is the student's opinion of Professor Eagleton?
   Ⓐ She feels that his class is too difficult.
   Ⓑ She appreciates how helpful he is.
   Ⓒ She believes he is uncaring about his students.
   Ⓓ She thinks he is not an effective lecturer.

4   What can be inferred about Professor Miller?
   Ⓐ He is willing to provide direct assistance to the student.
   Ⓑ He is a low-ranking member in his department.
   Ⓒ He is mostly interested in studying ancient history.
   Ⓓ He has been employed at the university for a short time.

5   Listen again to part of the conversation. Then answer the question.
   Why does the professor say this: 🎧
   Ⓐ To tell the student to remain seated
   Ⓑ To indicate that he has changed his mind
   Ⓒ To give him some more time to consider the situation
   Ⓓ To convince the student not to leave

• Mastering Question Types

absence	asthenosphere	boundary	characterize
dispersion	float	harvest	layer
moisture	organic	prism	represent
spectrum	structure	tectonics	transform
absorb	biodiesel	breeze	cohesive
electromagnetic	flood	infrared	lithosphere
monsoon	phenomenon	rainbow	retina
split	sugarcane	theoretical	undersea
alternative	blow	carbon	continental
emission	geologist	landmass	mantle
omit	presence	release	rigid
starch	switch	thickness	ultraviolet

• Mastering Topics

acidic	asteroid	cancerous	converter
diagram	elliptical	frame	granite
imperfection	inefficient	marble	oxide
reef	seep	spacecraft	spiral
adjacent	byproduct	cement	coral
downstream	extraterrestrial	galaxy	gravity
impurity	invasive	mortar	photovoltaic
sandstone	shell	speculation	susceptible
alluvial	calcite	consequence	delta
dwarf	falter	gemstone	halo
indirect	limestone	nanotechnology	polish
sedimentary	silicon	spelunking	synthetic

• TOEFL Practice Tests

analyze	artifact	circumstance	coastline
dune	evaporate	flux	goldmine
limited	manmade	odd	prehistoric
rain-shadow	storm	topsoil	unstable
argon	ascertain	classify	decay
erode	excavated	formation	half-life
livestock	master	potassium	prevailing
shimmer	sway	trace	uranium
arid	buried	clear	deforest
erupt	extensive	frigid	humanoid
lush	nonradioactive	precipitation	primitive
shipwreck	system	trapped	vegetation

📝 Choose the words with the closest meanings to the highlighted words.

1 There is a lot of moisture in the air right now; it looks like it is going to rain.

    Ⓐ wetness   Ⓑ tension

    Ⓒ coolness   Ⓓ heat

2 The plan seemed ideal, but it had one imperfection in it.

    Ⓐ flaw   Ⓑ revision

    Ⓒ concern   Ⓓ advantage

3 That is a manmade lake created by the construction of a dam downstream.

    Ⓐ residential   Ⓑ extensive

    Ⓒ artificial   Ⓓ deep

4 Dr. Meyers omitted an important step while doing the experiment.

    Ⓐ covered   Ⓑ explained

    Ⓒ improved   Ⓓ forgot

5 The detonation was so loud that it was heard several miles away.

    Ⓐ explosion   Ⓑ crash

    Ⓒ accident   Ⓓ launch

6 We were not able to ascertain the exact ingredients of the formula.

    Ⓐ duplicate   Ⓑ imitate

    Ⓒ acquire   Ⓓ determine

7 Julie's diamond ring often shimmers when the sun is shining brightly.

    Ⓐ burns   Ⓑ sparkles

    Ⓒ reflects   Ⓓ displays

8 There is very little precipitation in this area during summer.

    Ⓐ humidity   Ⓑ sunlight

    Ⓒ cloudiness   Ⓓ rain

9 Jason enjoys going spelunking with his friends every once in a while.

    Ⓐ hiking   Ⓑ skydiving

    Ⓒ caving   Ⓓ swimming

10 How would you characterize his performance during his presentation?

    Ⓐ discuss   Ⓑ describe

    Ⓒ explain   Ⓓ infer

📝 Match the words with the correct definitions.

11 extraterrestrial   •

12 boundary   •

13 consequence   •

14 shipwreck   •

15 transform   •

16 erupt   •

17 decay   •

18 nanotechnology •

19 utterly   •

20 harvest   •

• Ⓐ a result of an action

• Ⓑ completely; entirely

• Ⓒ to change or alter something

• Ⓓ to explode

• Ⓔ not of the Earth; alien

• Ⓕ the undersea wreckage of a sunken ship

• Ⓖ to gather crops from the fields

• Ⓗ to rot

• Ⓘ a limit

• Ⓙ technology dealing with extremely small artificial

Chapter 06 Physical Sciences 2 | Conversations

astronomy • physics • chemistry • geology • environmental science • meteorology • mineralogy • astrophysics • geophysics • physical chemistry

02-076

Listen to part of a lecture in an astronomy class.

TYPE 1 What is the lecture mainly about?

    (A) How the atmosphere affects light from stars

    (B) Why stars twinkle but planets do not

    (C) What makes celestial objects twinkle

    (D) When stars and planets twinkle the most

TYPE 2 According to the professor, why do planets sometimes appear to twinkle?

    (A) There is turbulence in the atmosphere.

    (B) They appear very low on the horizon.

    (C) They reflect enough of the sun's light.

    (D) There is hot air beneath some cool air.

TYPE 3 Why does the professor discuss the planets?

    (A) To prove that all objects in space twinkle

    (B) To compare the way they twinkle with the stars

    (C) To emphasize their closeness to the Earth

    (D) To mention the difference between reflection and refraction

TYPE 4 Listen again to part of the lecture. Then answer the question.
What does the professor imply when he says this: 🎧

    (A) He will only spell that word once for the class.

    (B) He expects the students to remember the definition.

    (C) The spelling of that term is important to know.

    (D) He will not test the students on that term.

Summarizing ▷ Fill in the blanks to complete the summary.

The professor asks the students if stars really do twinkle. A student responds that they do, and he thinks it has something to do with _____. The professor tells the student he is correct. The professor then describes the event known as _____. Because the light from stars must move through the _____ of the atmosphere, it appears to move. The reason is refraction. The movement of air causes the light _____ in many directions. This causes the twinkling effect. The professor then claims that planets twinkle, but it is hard to detect this except when there is _____.

02-077

Listen to part of a lecture in an astronomy class.

TYPE 5 What aspect of supernovae does the professor mainly discuss?

  Ⓐ The types of stars that can cause them

  Ⓑ The possibility of them becoming black holes

  Ⓒ Their brightness when seen from the Earth

  Ⓓ The ways in which they can form

TYPE 6 Listen again to part of the lecture. Then answer the question.
What does the professor mean when she says this: 🎧

  Ⓐ She wants the students to calculate the amount of energy emitted.

  Ⓑ The students must realize how much energy supernovae release.

  Ⓒ There is nothing in the galaxy more powerful than a supernova.

  Ⓓ She misspoke and needs to think about what she just said.

TYPE 7 Based on the information in the lecture, do the following statements refer to type 1 or type 2 supernovae?
Click in the correct box for each sentence.

	Type 1 Supernovae	Type 2 Supernovae
① May happen to stars much larger than the sun		
② Are caused by the implosion of a star		
③ Form from the remnants of white dwarves		
④ Can form when the exploding star takes gases from a nearby star		

TYPE 8 What will the professor probably do next?

  Ⓐ Describe the formation of the solar system

  Ⓑ Talk about the creation of black holes

  Ⓒ Name some of the more famous supernovae

  Ⓓ Show the class some pictures of supernovae

Summarizing ▶ Fill in the blanks to complete the summary.

The professor states that supernovae are some of the most .... in the galaxy and that they release huge amounts of energy. She says there are both type 1 and type 2 supernovae. Type 1 form from .... She explains how exploding white dwarves can take gases from nearby stars to help them explode and become supernovae. As for type 2 supernovae, they form from stars .... times larger than the sun. She then explains the process by which they explode. She mentions that some supernovae can be seen .... Some are so bright that they can even be seen ....

TYPE 1 • Gist-Content   *TYPE 2* • Detail   *TYPE 3* • Understanding Organization   *TYPE 4* • Function of What Is Said

02-078

Listen to part of a lecture in a geology class.

TYPE 1 What is the main topic of the lecture?

Ⓐ Various rocks and where they can be found

Ⓑ The formation of two different kinds of rocks

Ⓒ A comparison of sedimentary and metamorphic rocks

Ⓓ The three major types of rocks

TYPE 2 What are extrusive igneous rocks?

Ⓐ Rocks that are created by cooling magma deep underground

Ⓑ Rock that are made from particles eroded from other rocks

Ⓒ Rocks that are formed from lava on the surface

Ⓓ Rocks that are made from minerals dissolved in water

TYPE 3 Why does the professor mention coal?

Ⓐ To point out where it can usually be found

Ⓑ To name a type of organic sedimentary rock

Ⓒ To talk about the different various of it

Ⓓ To describe the process that can create il

TYPE 4 Why does the professor tell the students about erosion?

Ⓐ To claim that it can change the shapes of some igneous rocks

Ⓑ To compare how it forms both igneous and sedimentary rocks

Ⓒ To talk about how it can affect metamorphic rocks

Ⓓ To explain its role in the creation of sedimentary rocks

Summarizing ▷ Fill in the blanks to complete the summary.

The professor says there are three main types of rocks: igneous, sedimentary, and metamorphic rocks. He says that igneous rocks are formed from _____ deep inside the Earth. Some rocks form underground while others form _____ . _____ of both types makes these rocks different from one another. The professor says that many extrusive igneous rocks, such as pumice, obsidian, and basalt, are found _____ . He then discusses sedimentary rocks. He says they form when _____ accumulates and is then turned into rocks. He mentions clastic, chemical, and organic sedimentary rocks.

02-079

Listen to part of a lecture in a geology class.

TYPE 5 Why does the professor explain stalactites and stalagmites?

    Ⓐ To state the difference between them

    Ⓑ To respond to a student's inquiry

    Ⓒ To point out a unique aspect of some caves

    Ⓓ To mention how they are formed

TYPE 6 Listen again to part of the lecture. Then answer the question.
What can be inferred about the professor when she says this: 🎧

    Ⓐ She enjoys caving in her free time.

    Ⓑ She is planning a trip to a cave soon.

    Ⓒ She has visited this kind of cave before.

    Ⓓ She regrets not going on a previous trip to a cave.

TYPE 7 Based on the information in the lecture, which type of cave formation do the following statements refer to?
Click in the correct box for each sentence.

	The Underground Eroding of Rock	The Action of the Sea	The Aboveground Eroding of Rock
① Can occur because of sand or ice			
② May happen in areas with limestone			
③ May result in the formation of stalactites			
④ Can create beautiful caves			

TYPE 8 What will the professor probably do next?

    Ⓐ Assign the students some homework

    Ⓑ Explain the process of cave formation in mountains

    Ⓒ Let the students take a short break

    Ⓓ Describe another way caves are formed

Summarizing ▷ Fill in the blanks to complete the summary.

The professor mentions there are ＿＿＿＿＿＿ that caves may form. The first is that they are formed underground in ＿＿＿＿＿＿ such as limestone. Acid in water erodes the rocks, which creates caves. These caves often have ＿＿＿＿＿＿ in them. The next type of cave is formed by the actions of the sea or ocean. Hard or soft rock ＿＿＿＿＿＿ gets worn away and can create caves that look beautiful. ＿＿＿＿＿＿ aboveground can make caves in mountains and in other places. This can happen over a long period of time or can happen fairly quickly with ice.

02-080

Listen to part of a conversation between a student and a professor.

TYPE 1   Why does the student visit the professor?

Ⓐ To ask the professor to test him on his language skills

Ⓑ To get some advice on a course he would like to take

Ⓒ To find out why he is unqualified for a certain course

Ⓓ To talk to the professor about his family history

TYPE 2   Why does the student feel he is qualified in the Russian language?

Ⓐ He has already finished Russian three and four.

Ⓑ He is currently enrolled in an advanced Russian class.

Ⓒ He has studied a lot of colloquial Russian.

Ⓓ He learned Russian when he lived in Moscow.

TYPE 3   Why does the student mention his time in junior high school?

Ⓐ To let the professor know he has traveled internationally

Ⓑ To answer the professor's question about his language skills

Ⓒ To confirm he has studied Russian in a formal environment

Ⓓ To reminisce about his days living in another country

TYPE 4   Listen again to part of the conversation. Then answer the question.
What is the purpose of the student's response?

Ⓐ To express his disappointment with the professor's opinion

Ⓑ To confirm what the professor has just told him

Ⓒ To acknowledge his agreement with the professor

Ⓓ To indicate what he plans to do about his schoolwork

Summarizing ▷ **Fill in the blanks to complete the summary.**

The student thanks the professor for being ＿＿＿＿＿＿＿＿＿＿, and the professor responds that he is just
doing his job. Then the student mentions he is thinking of taking an advanced ＿＿＿＿＿＿＿＿ the next
semester. The professor says that is a good choice, but then they talk about the student's ＿＿＿＿＿＿＿＿.
The student lived in Russia for two years, but that was during ＿＿＿＿＿＿＿＿. The professor tells the
student he should take a Russian language class first and take the drama class later. The student is disappointed, but
the professor says that the student, a sophomore, has ＿＿＿＿＿＿＿＿ to take the class.

02-081

Listen to part of a conversation between a student and a housing office employee.

TYPE **5** What are the speakers mainly discussing?

- Ⓐ Why the student's key does not work in her room
- Ⓑ How often the school makes mistakes concerning dormitory rooms
- Ⓒ What the student needs to do to get a missing chair
- Ⓓ Which forms the student has to fill out for the man

TYPE **6** Where did the student go before she visited the man?

- Ⓐ The dormitory's administration office
- Ⓑ The student activities center
- Ⓒ Her dormitory room
- Ⓓ The housing office

TYPE **7** What is the man's attitude toward the student?

- Ⓐ He is frustrated by her problem.
- Ⓑ He treats her with impatience.
- Ⓒ He is quite friendly toward her.
- Ⓓ He has little time to deal with her.

TYPE **8** Listen again to part of the conversation. Then answer the question.
What does the student imply when she says this: 🎧

- Ⓐ She had expected to have to do more.
- Ⓑ She does not want to fill out another form.
- Ⓒ She is eager to get a chair for her room.
- Ⓓ She does not believe what the man just told her.

Summarizing ▶ Fill in the blanks to complete the summary.

The employee tells the student that if she fills out a form, she can _____ in twenty-four hours.
The student says she is not there for a key, and the employee apologizes. He says that many students have been
asking for new keys. The student says that her dorm is _____ . She shows some paperwork she
filled out, and the employee gives her _____ . Once she does that, the school will bring her a
chair by _____ . The student seems pleased by this response.

Listen to part of a lecture in an environmental science class.

02-082

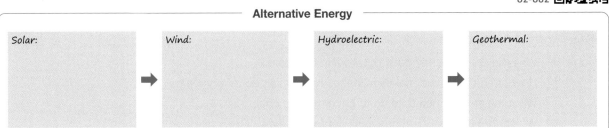

Alternative Energy

| Solar: | | Wind: | | Hydroelectric: | | Geothermal: |

1 Why does the professor explain geothermal energy?

   Ⓐ To claim it is the most efficient type of alternative energy

   Ⓑ To describe one form of alternative energy

   Ⓒ To compare it with hydroelectric power

   Ⓓ To mention which country uses it the most

2 How does the professor organize the information about alternative energy that she presents to the class?

   Ⓐ By comparing how some kinds of alternative energy are used

   Ⓑ By naming and explaining several different kinds of it

   Ⓒ By describing some future uses of many kinds of it

   Ⓓ By listing the types of energy according to their importance

3 What can be inferred about wind power?

   Ⓐ It cannot be created in some places.

   Ⓑ It is commonly used in the agriculture industry.

   Ⓒ It is the least expensive form of alternative energy.

   Ⓓ It is used more often than solar power.

Summarizing ▷ Fill in the blanks to complete the summary.

The professor begins by asking for a definition of _____, which a student provides. She notes that the important word is renewable. Then, she begins by discussing several types of alternative energy. She first talks about solar power and says it is becoming more common. Next, she covers wind power and notes that while people in the past used windmills, _____. After that is hydroelectric power, which comes from water. Finally, she describes geothermal energy, which uses heat from _____ to create electricity. She notes that volcanic places, such as Iceland, can often _____.

Listen to part of a lecture in a geology class.

02-083

The Formation of the Continents

Continental Drift:

How Earth Once Looked:

Evidence for the Theory:

Plate Tectonics:

1 What is the lecture mainly about?
- Ⓐ The life of Alfred Wegener
- Ⓑ Plate tectonics
- Ⓒ The composition of the Earth
- Ⓓ The theory of continental drift

2 What is subduction?
- Ⓐ The colliding of two plates that results in one going under the other
- Ⓑ The fusing together of two plates to create a new mountain range
- Ⓒ The sideways movement of two plates, which causes an earthquake
- Ⓓ The moving away from each other of two tectonic plates

3 Listen again to part of the lecture. Then answer the question.
What does the professor imply when he says this: 🎧
- Ⓐ Scientists refused to read any works written by Wegener.
- Ⓑ People were interested in learning more about Wegener's ideas.
- Ⓒ Many people did not believe in the theory of continental drift.
- Ⓓ There was no way for Wegener to prove that he was correct.

Summarizing ▷ Fill in the blanks to complete the summary.

The professor says that the land on the Earth was once one big continent called Pangaea. This comes from a theory
_____ . He called the theory continental drift. He believed the continents slowly moved across
the face of the planet. At first, he was ridiculed, but later evidence proved that _____ .
This evidence was found _____ and in mineral specimens. Wegener's ideas led to
_____ , which helps explain how earthquakes happen, how volcanoes form, and
_____ . The professor then describes the various movements of plates that result in these
events.

Listen to part of a lecture in an astronomy class.

02-084

--- Life on Mars ---

What Is Necessary for Life to Exist:	Similarities between Earth and Mars:

➡

1 What does the professor imply about the student's answer?

Ⓐ The student has given some thought to it.

Ⓑ The student needs to be more specific.

Ⓒ It could use some improvement.

Ⓓ It was entirely unoriginal.

2 What will the professor probably do next?

Ⓐ Name some other places in the solar system where life may exist

Ⓑ Show the students some evidence against life existing elsewhere

Ⓒ Have the students begin giving their class presentations

Ⓓ Describe some possible life forms that might exist on Mars

3 Listen again to part of the lecture. Then answer the question.
Why does the professor say this: 🎧

Ⓐ To acknowledge she does not believe in aliens

Ⓑ To quote a passage from the students' textbook

Ⓒ To indicate what the topic of her lecture is

Ⓓ To ask the students their thoughts on extraterrestrials

Summarizing ▶ Fill in the blanks to complete the summary.

The professor mentions that people .... often focus on Mars. A student says that he thinks Mars likely had some life in the past or maybe even does today. The professor then explains what would be needed for .... to exist elsewhere. It includes a rocky planet with .... Water and complex organic compounds are also necessary. She then mentions how .... Their temperatures are similar, and they both have an atmosphere. Mars's is thinner, but it may not have been like that in the past. They both also have water ....

Listen to part of a lecture in a geology class.

02-085

┌─ **Petroleum** ─────────────────────────────────────┐

Formation of Petroleum:		Dead Oil:
	➡	
		Live Oil:

└──┘

1 What aspect of petroleum does the professor mainly discuss?

Ⓐ What it is used for

Ⓑ Where it is found

Ⓒ How it is created

Ⓓ Why it is important

2 Why does the professor mention sea creatures and plants?

Ⓐ To explain from what petroleum was created

Ⓑ To indicate whether dead oil or live oil will be made

Ⓒ To name some impurities sometimes found in petroleum

Ⓓ To say that they are transformed into sedimentary rocks

3 Based on the information in the lecture, do the following statements refer to dead oil or live oil?
Click in the correct box for each sentence.

	Dead Oil	Live Oil
① Can be dangerous when handled		
② Includes tar and asphalt		
③ Has no gases in it		
④ Contains some dissolved gases		

Summarizing ▷ Fill in the blanks to complete the summary.

The lecturer starts by noting _____ for transportation as well as in manufacturing. He then gives a definition of petroleum and says that it can be found in _____ . He says that its solid form is tar to respond to a student's question. He then describes the process by which decaying organic matter was converted into petroleum through _____ millions of years ago. Because it comes from organic matter, that is why it is _____ . He also says petroleum is nonrenewable. He then describes the difference between _____ .

Listen to part of a conversation between a student and a professor.

02-086

┌─────────────────────────────── Office Hours ───────────────────────────────┐

Reason for Visiting:

➡

Result:

↙

Problem:

➡

Solution:

└───┘

1 Why does the student visit the professor?

Ⓐ She would like to submit her report to the professor.

Ⓑ She needs to find out how to complete her assignment.

Ⓒ She wants to make an appointment to visit a preschool.

Ⓓ She is responding to the professor's request for more information.

2 According to the professor, what must the student do on her project?
Choose 2 answers.

Ⓐ Provide a complete bibliography

Ⓑ Observe some young children

Ⓒ Interview some preschool children

Ⓓ Analyze the information she collects

3 What can be inferred about the student?

Ⓐ She gets poor grades in most of her classes.

Ⓑ She is determined to do well on the project.

Ⓒ She does not pay attention in class very often.

Ⓓ She is reluctant to ask others for assistance.

Summarizing ▷ Fill in the blanks to complete the summary.

The student wants to _____ with the professor, who says it is due in three weeks and
mentions she hopes _____ . The student says she has not begun it because she is unclear
on how _____ the development of children. The professor says that she mentioned what
to do in a previous class. Then, she explains that the student needs to visit _____ and
make arrangements to visit a local preschool or other place with children. The professor notes that the student will
_____ , but she can still do well on the project.

Listen to part of a conversation between a student and a student center employee.

02-087

Service Encounter

Reason for Visiting:	Result:

Student's Reaction:	Result:

1 What is the student's attitude toward the woman?

(A) He is very courteous.

(B) He is somewhat shy.

(C) He is open minded.

(D) He is eager to please her.

2 What can be inferred about the student?

(A) He has met the woman previously.

(B) He is attending school on a scholarship.

(C) He accepts the woman's job offer.

(D) He is willing to accept a lower salary.

3 Listen again to part of the conversation. Then answer the question.
What is the purpose of the man's response?

(A) To encourage the woman to continue speaking

(B) To admit he will stop looking for a job there

(C) To say that he does not know about the job

(D) To ask the woman to give him some assistance

Summarizing ▶ Fill in the blanks to complete the summary.

The student visits the student center to _____, but the woman does not know what he is talking about. He says that there is a position available to work in the game room. He knows about it because a friend who _____ told him about it. The woman says she is not sure, but she looks for some information about the job. She discovers the student is _____ and that one is available. Then, she says that she has _____, so he can have the job if he wants it. The student _____.

02-088

Listen to part of a lecture in a geology class.

1 What is the main topic of the lecture?

  Ⓐ How extinction level events sometimes occur

  Ⓑ How Tambora changed the world's weather

  Ⓒ How volcanoes can affect the environment

  Ⓓ How the Yellowstone supervolcano devastated the world

2 Why does the professor explain the effects of the Tambora eruption?

  Ⓐ To state how many people it killed

  Ⓑ To note its global consequences

  Ⓒ To compare it with the Krakatoa eruption

  Ⓓ To explain what caused it to erupt

3 Based on the information in the lecture, do the following sentences refer to the Tambora or the Krakatoa eruptions?
Click in the correct box for each sentence.

	Tambora	Krakatoa
① It resulted in "the year without a summer."		
② It created tsunamis that killed many.		
③ The sky appeared red for years afterward.		
④ Most of the deaths it caused were indirect.		

4   What does the professor imply about the asteroid that hit the Earth around sixty-five million years ago?

      (A)   Some of the dinosaurs managed to survive it.

      (B)   It destroyed the physical surface of the planet.

      (C)   It led to the beginning of a mini-ice age.

      (D)   It failed to kill some forms of vegetation on the Earth.

5   Listen again to part of the lecture. Then answer the question.
Why does the professor say this: 🎧

      (A)   She is confirming that many people saw the tsunamis in England.

      (B)   She would like to stress that the tsunamis were deadlier than the eruption.

      (C)   She wants the students to know that the reports may not be true.

      (D)   She is emphasizing that even England was affected by Krakatoa.

6   Listen again to part of the lecture. Then answer the question.
What can be inferred about the student when he says this: 🎧

      (A)   He is not sympathetic to the people's suffering.

      (B)   He does not believe volcanoes can be that destructive.

      (C)   He would like to hear more about Krakatoa.

      (D)   He doubts what the professor just told the class.

Listen to part of a lecture in an astronomy class.

02-089

Astronomy

1   What is the lecture mainly about?

   Ⓐ Descriptions of the objects that comprise the solar system

   Ⓑ A comparison of dwarf planets with classical planets

   Ⓒ A recap of the astronomical conference held in 2006

   Ⓓ The reasons Pluto is no longer considered a classical planet

2   Why does the professor explain Pluto's orbit?

   Ⓐ To focus on how irregular it is

   Ⓑ To mention that it is closer to the sun than Neptune is now

   Ⓒ To contrast its orbit with that of Ceres

   Ⓓ To state why it is so elliptical

3   According to the professor, which of the following characteristics does a dwarf planet have?
Choose 2 answers.

   Ⓐ It can be the moon of another planet.

   Ⓑ It must be nearly spherical in shape.

   Ⓒ It does not follow a standard orbit.

   Ⓓ It must be located in the Kuiper Belt.

4   Why does the professor mention the Kuiper Belt?

(A) To state that Eris and Ceres both orbit the sun from it

(B) To emphasize how big it is in comparison with the solar system

(C) To state where a number of celestial bodies orbit the sun

(D) To claim that more research needs to be conducted on it

5   What comparison does the professor make between Eris and Mercury?

(A) Their orbits

(B) Their sizes

(C) Their locations

(D) Their designations

6   Listen again to part of the lecture. Then answer the question.
What does the professor imply when he says this: 🎧

(A) He wishes the conference had not settled matters so abruptly.

(B) He has not made up his mind on what constitutes a dwarf planet.

(C) He agrees with those who dispute the results of the conference.

(D) He believes the decision the conference made was correct.

Listen to part of a conversation between a student and a student activities center employee.

02-090

1   What are the speakers mainly discussing?

  (A) How to hold an election for a club's officials

  (B) How to register a club with the school

  (C) How to get financial assistance for new clubs

  (D) How to sign up new members for a club

2   What is the student's role in the debate club?

  (A) He is the lead debater.

  (B) He is the acting secretary.

  (C) He is an officer in the club.

  (D) He is the club's sponsor.

3   What is the employee's opinion of Professor Apulu?

  (A) He has heard that the professor is a good lecturer.

  (B) He says the professor is active in student affairs.

  (C) He believes the professor will be an adequate advisor.

  (D) He thinks very highly of the professor.

4   What will the student probably do next?

  (A) Give the employee a writing utensil

  (B) Read over some photocopies

  (C) Complete some application forms

  (D) File a request for some grant money

5   Listen again to part of the conversation. Then answer the question.
     What can be inferred from the student's response to the employee?

  (A) He considers the employee a good friend.

  (B) He is acting in an amiable manner.

  (C) He does not want to offend the employee.

  (D) He will do anything necessary to help the club.

• *Mastering Question Types*

acidic	bend	chunk	crack
evaporation	germinate	implode	multilayered
peak	phenomenon	refraction	shallow
stalactite	stretch	succumb	turbulent
anomaly	blink	cliff	depression
feces	glacier	midst	oasis
percolate	random	refresh	shimmer
stalagmite	stumble	supernova	twinkle
aqueduct	byproduct	collapse	diver
fuse	horizon	mitigate	overhead
permeable	reflection	scintillation	shine
stratosphere	subtype	troposphere	wondrous

• *Mastering Topics*

asphalt	backtrack	controversial	dissolve
drown	foothold	grid	iceberg
mineral	pollutant	rotation	speculate
tar	toothpaste	unearth	waterfall
assert	blade	convergent	divergent
evidence	geothermal	hydrocarbon	jigsaw puzzle
myriad	pump	sector	squeeze
tectonics	turbine	vent	wheat
atop	comparable	disruption	drift
float	greenhouse	hydroelectric	magma
petroleum	reduce	specimen	subduction
theorize	ultimate	viscous	windmill

• *TOEFL Practice Tests*

annihilation	carnivore	constitute	diameter
downgrade	dwell	firecracker	geyser
hurl	intense	misnomer	orbit
pronounced	satellite	stipulation	veracity
astronomical	classical	darken	dire
drastically	elliptical	foresight	horrific
imminent	irregularity	moniker	prediction
regrettably	spark	tsunami	well-defined
bleak	classify	debate	dominant
dwarf	famine	generate	hot spring
indirect	misconception	nuclear	probe
relegate	starvation	undoubtedly	yield

Vocabulary *Review*

📝 Choose the words with the closest meanings to the highlighted words.

1 Would you care to speculate on what is going to happen?

(A) ask   (B) determine
(C) identify   (D) guess

2 The meeting was very turbulent, but all of the problems finally got solved.

(A) chaotic   (B) swift
(C) aggressive   (D) extensive

3 I am not sure what constitutes an effective presentation.

(A) determines   (B) comprises
(C) formulates   (D) regards

4 Why are you walking with such a pronounced limp?

(A) obvious   (B) painful
(C) excessive   (D) minor

5 The light in the distance appears to be blinking.

(A) glowing   (B) shining
(C) dimming   (D) twinkling

6 That rocket is going to take the satellite into outer space.

(A) shuttle   (B) space station
(C) probe   (D) missile

7 The annihilation of the city during the war shocked everyone.

(A) surrender   (B) behavior
(C) destruction   (D) agenda

8 This is undoubtedly the same problem I had trouble with the last time.

(A) definitely   (B) possibly
(C) perhaps   (D) considerably

9 We need to find a way to reduce the amount of money we spend.

(A) monitor   (B) lessen
(C) consider   (D) budget

10 The plane drastically changed its elevation when it suddenly encountered turbulence.

(A) diabolically   (B) distractedly
(C) disparately   (D) dramatically

📝 Match the words with the correct definitions.

11 controversial •

12 unearth •

13 cliff •

14 orbit •

15 sector •

16 supernova •

17 carnivore •

18 evidence •

19 prediction •

20 random •

• (A) following no particular order

• (B) an area or region

• (C) disputed

• (D) an exploding star

• (E) an animal that eats meat

• (F) the steep face of a mountain or rock

• (G) to circle, as in a planet going around a star

• (H) proof of something

• (I) a guess about a future event

• (J) to dig up

Chapter 07 **Arts 1 | Conversations**

city planning • art history • literature • music • industrial design • visual arts • crafts • architecture • film • photography

02-091

Listen to part of a lecture in an art history class.

TYPE 1 What is the lecture mainly about?

    Ⓐ The function women served in early art

    Ⓑ The first appearance of female painters

    Ⓒ Painting during the Renaissance

    Ⓓ The style of the *Mona Lisa*

TYPE 2 According to the professor, what happened after Leonardo da Vinci painted the *Mona Lisa*?

    Ⓐ Women started painting their own pictures.

    Ⓑ Modeling became a more respected position.

    Ⓒ More artists began imitating his style.

    Ⓓ Portraits of men increased in popularity.

TYPE 3 How is the discussion organized?

    Ⓐ The professor covers the material as it is presented in the textbook.

    Ⓑ The professor provides an analysis of several Renaissance paintings.

    Ⓒ The professor shows multiple slides to provide visual stimulation.

    Ⓓ The professor asks questions to get input from the students.

TYPE 4 Listen again to part of the lecture. Then answer the question.
    What does the professor imply when he says this: 🎧

    Ⓐ Western artists were better at portrait painting than those from other cultures.

    Ⓑ The Western world was influenced by artists from other cultures.

    Ⓒ Artists in other cultures had previously painted women from the front.

    Ⓓ The professor is only familiar with Western art and not with art from other cultures.

Summarizing ▶ Fill in the blanks to complete the summary.

The professor begins by saying that women have not had a long role in the world of art as artists. However, he does note that they were used _____ . He then shows them a picture of the *Mona Lisa* and notes that Leonardo da Vinci did something _____ . The professor says that Leonardo was the first Western artist to paint _____ and not in profile. He says the reason had to do with the _____ . Then, he notes that because the *Mona Lisa* became popular, other artists began to _____ .

02-092

Listen to part of a lecture in an art history class.

TYPE 5 What is the lecture mainly about?

ⓐ The Hudson River School

ⓑ The Naturalist Art Movement

ⓒ The Romantic Age

ⓓ William Bliss Baker

TYPE 6 What can be inferred about the professor?

ⓐ She knows very little about the Hudson River School.

ⓑ She does not like answering questions during class.

ⓒ She prefers Naturalist art to Romantic art.

ⓓ She sometimes paints in the Naturalist style.

TYPE 7 Based on the information in the lecture, do the following statements refer to the Hudson River School artists or William Bliss Baker?
Click in the correct box for each sentence.

	The Hudson River School Artists	William Bliss Baker
1 Depicted scenes as they actually were		
2 Worked in the Naturalist style		
3 Painted *Fallen Monarchs*		
4 Created works that were idealized		

TYPE 8 Listen again to part of the lecture. Then answer the question.
What does the professor imply when she says this: 🎧

ⓐ The Atlantic Ocean prevented some ideas from spreading quickly.

ⓑ She is knowledgeable about both the United States and Europe.

ⓒ It was not only Americans who were interested in science.

ⓓ An equal number of scientific discoveries were made in Europe and America.

Summarizing ▶ Fill in the blanks to complete the summary.

The professor states that Naturalism began during _____ . Artists began trying to create paintings that showed their subjects _____ . It went out of style but then became popular again in the nineteenth century. One reason for its renewed popularity was that it was _____ .
It was also based on science and realism, which were important in that century. A student asks about _____ , but the professor says they painted in the Romantic style. She says William Bliss Baker was a Naturalist. She talks about his paintings and how _____ .

TYPE 1 • Gist-Content   *TYPE 2* • Detail   *TYPE 3* • Understanding Organization   *TYPE 4* • Function of What Is Said

02-093

Listen to part of a lecture in a theater class.

TYPE 1   What aspect of Greek theater does the professor mainly discuss?

    Ⓐ The early innovations made to the plays

    Ⓑ Some of the most important playwrights

    Ⓒ The differences between tragedies and comedies

    Ⓓ The role of Aeschylus in influencing early theater

TYPE 2   Which play did Euripides write?

    Ⓐ *Oedipus the King*

    Ⓑ *The Birds*

    Ⓒ *Oresteia*

    Ⓓ *The Trojan Women*

TYPE 3   How does the professor organize the information about ancient Greek playwrights that he presents to the class?

    Ⓐ By discussing aspects of their most famous plays

    Ⓑ By providing a short biography of each one

    Ⓒ By comparing the methods that each one used

    Ⓓ By noting the influence of each of their innovations

TYPE 4   Listen again to part of the lecture. Then answer the question.

    Why does the professor say this: 🎧

    Ⓐ To emphasize a point she just made

    Ⓑ To tell the students she made an error

    Ⓒ To clear up a misunderstanding

    Ⓓ To let the students know the topic of the lecture

Summarizing ▷   Fill in the blanks to complete the summary.

The professor tells the students he wants to give them some biographies of a few important
_____ . He says that many works have been lost over the course of time. However, some
of the plays of four important men still survive. The first is Aeschylus. He added _____ and
authored the *Oresteia*. Sophocles added a third actor to the stage and wrote _____ . Euripides
focused on _____ instead of only writing about the gods and kings. And Aristophanes was
_____ since those were some of the plays that he wrote.

Listen to part of a lecture in an art history class.

TYPE 5   Why does the professor explain the role of literacy in the Middle Ages?

- Ⓐ So that the importance of people listening to Bible stories can be emphasized
- Ⓑ So that she can mention why people built so many religious institutions
- Ⓒ So that she can explain why she is not showing any illuminated manuscripts
- Ⓓ So that she can stress the importance of visual stimulus for people back then

TYPE 6   What is the professor's opinion of stained glass?

- Ⓐ She likes the way that it looks.
- Ⓑ She feels it is a waste of money.
- Ⓒ She thinks it could be improved.
- Ⓓ She prefers only to look at it in person.

TYPE 7   Based on the information in the lecture, do the following statements refer to Lorsch Abbey or Saint-Chapelle?
Click in the correct box for each sentence.

	Lorsch Abbey	Saint-Chapelle
1 Has scenes from the entire Bible in its stained glass		
2 Looks as if it is made totally of stained glass		
3 Had the oldest extant stained glass found there		
4 Was the personal church of a French king		

TYPE 8   Listen again to part of the lecture. Then answer the question.
What does the professor imply when she says this: 🎧

- Ⓐ She is amazed whenever she looks at the picture.
- Ⓑ The students should try to visit the place on their own.
- Ⓒ She has visited Saint-Chapelle before.
- Ⓓ She prefers stained glass to other forms of art.

Summarizing ▷   Fill in the blanks to complete the summary.

The professor begins by telling the students that stained-glass windows became popular in Europe around _____ . The oldest surviving stained glass comes from _____ and was made in the tenth century. She tells the students that stained glass showed Biblical scenes and that most of it was found in _____ . In addition, since most people could not read, they needed visual stimulation. She shows them some pictures of _____ and says that upon entering, it seems as if the entire building is _____ . She then says that she can explain how stained glass is made in another lecture if the students are interested.

TYPE 1 • Gist-Purpose   *TYPE 2* • Detail   *TYPE 3* • Understanding Organization   *TYPE 4* • Function of What Is Said

02-095

Listen to part of a conversation between a student and a professor.

TYPE 1   Why does the student visit the professor?

Ⓐ To ask him about the upcoming conference

Ⓑ To find out how to register for the conference

Ⓒ To show him something she made for a conference

Ⓓ To speak with him about some environmental issues

TYPE 2   What is the professor's role at the upcoming conference?

Ⓐ He is one of the advisors for it.

Ⓑ He is in charge of it.

Ⓒ He is the keynote speaker.

Ⓓ He is the faculty sponsor.

TYPE 3   Why does the student mention the upcoming conference?

Ⓐ To explain why she made her poster

Ⓑ To show her interest in environmental affairs

Ⓒ To let the professor know she is aware of campus events

Ⓓ To ask the professor for some tickets to it

TYPE 4   Listen again to part of the conversation. Then answer the question.
What is the purpose of the professor's response?

Ⓐ To agree with the student

Ⓑ To tell the student to be more modest

Ⓒ To compliment the student

Ⓓ To indicate his failure to understand

Summarizing ▶ Fill in the blanks to complete the summary.

The student visits the professor to show him a poster she made for an _____. He tells the student that he is the co-chair of the event, which surprises her. Then, she shows him a poster that she made to encourage people to _____ since they are bad for the environment. She asks him what he thinks of it, and he responds that _____. He then tells the student that he is impressed by the poster and would like to _____. The student is pleased that he is going to do that.

Listen to part of a conversation between a student and an Art History Department employee.

02-096

TYPE 5   What are the speakers mainly discussing?

Ⓐ The teaching style of a new professor

Ⓑ A piece of machinery the student needs

Ⓒ The best way to borrow some equipment

Ⓓ A broken computer in a classroom

TYPE 6   What does the employee tell the student to do?

Ⓐ Take a training course on how to use a computer system

Ⓑ Sign her name on an application form

Ⓒ Pick up an item in a professor's office

Ⓓ Remind the professor to return a borrowed it

TYPE 7   Listen again to part of the conversation. Then answer the question.

What can be inferred about the employee when he says this: 🎧

Ⓐ He is not having a particularly good day.

Ⓑ He has spoken with the student in the past.

Ⓒ He is too busy to speak with the student now.

Ⓓ He works in the office together with the student.

TYPE 8   What can be inferred about the student?

Ⓐ She is getting a major in Art History.

Ⓑ She has taken class with Professor Davidson before.

Ⓒ She has her next class in a different building.

Ⓓ She will take some equipment to a classroom.

Summarizing ▶ Fill in the blanks to complete the summary.

The student visits the Art History Department office and asks the employee there if she can borrow a slide projector for a class. The employee is surprised because he expects professors to _____ in their classrooms. The student agrees but adds that _____ requested it. The employee responds that the professor is new, is not _____, and only has slides. He tells the student that there is only _____ left, and he lets her borrow it. He then reminds the student to tell the professor to _____ to the office after class.

Listen to part of a lecture in an art history class.

02-097

Parchment

Reason Was First Made:

➡

Material Is Made From:

Advantages:

Disadvantages:

---

1 In the lecture, the professor describes a number of facts about parchment. Indicate whether each of the following statements is a fact about parchment.
Click in the correct box for each sentence.

	Fact	Not a Fact
1 Was first made from the skins of calves		
2 Can be erased and then reused		
3 Was developed during the Middle Ages		
4 Cost more to make than did papyrus		

2 Why does the professor discuss modern technology?

- Ⓐ To say it has made people more interested in parchment nowadays
- Ⓑ To note why parchment is no longer in use
- Ⓒ To explain why people use it to examine ancient parchments
- Ⓓ To mention a better way of erasing parchment than by scraping it

3 Listen again to part of the lecture. Then answer the question.
Why does the professor say this: 🎧

- Ⓐ To indicate that what he is saying is important
- Ⓑ To acknowledge that he believes history is boring
- Ⓒ To tell the students the history lesson will not last long
- Ⓓ To admit he is uncertain about the facts surrounding this story

Summarizing ▶ Fill in the blanks to complete the summary.

The professor begins by talking about how the Egyptians developed papyrus to write on around 3000 B.C. He states that the Egyptian pharaoh refused to _____ to the king of Pergamon around 150 B.C. since both were competing to create _____ . The king's people then developed parchment. They used _____ to write on. It was effective but expensive. People later used goatskins and calfskins, which are _____ . Parchment was used until around the 1400s. Modern technology now lets people read texts that had been written, erased, and then written over, so it is possible that many lost texts may _____ .

Listen to part of a lecture in a music class.

02-098

Throat-Singing

Characteristics:		Tuva Style:
	➡	Inuit Style:

1   What aspect of throat-singing does the professor mainly discuss?

Ⓐ What it sounds like when performed

Ⓑ Where the best throat-singers live

Ⓒ How it is performed by different people

Ⓓ When it developed into a musical genre

2   Why does the professor mention bagpipes?

Ⓐ To name an instrument with a sound similar to that of throat-singing

Ⓑ To claim that throat-singing is as difficult as playing that instrument

Ⓒ To say that they sometimes accompany throat-singers

Ⓓ To explain how they can be integrated into the songs of throat-singers

3   Based on the information in the lecture, do the following statements refer to Tuva or Inuit throat-singing? Click in the correct box for each sentence.

	Tuva Throat-Singing	Inuit Throat-Singing
1 Often involves multiple performers		
2 Is typically performed only by men		
3 Can make two or more pitches simultaneously		
4 Relies upon short, sharp breaths		

Summarizing ▷ Fill in the blanks to complete the summary.

The professor asks the students if they know anything about throat-singing. One student says she saw a .... recently. The professor says that throat-singing developed in Central Asia as people tried to imitate .... in the wild. At first, only men did it, but now .... The Tuva people do a lot of throat-singing. They can create .... at the same time and sometimes accompany their singing with music. The Inuit also do throat-singing. Women typically do it in .... Their style of throat-singing differs from the Tuva's.

Listen to part of a lecture in a literature class.

02-099

Medieval French Poetry

Chansons:

Romances:

1 Why does the professor explain *The Song of Roland*?

  Ⓐ To state that it was changed many times

  Ⓑ To describe it as a story about King Arthur's knight

  Ⓒ To note both its fame and content

  Ⓓ To compare it with some other chansons

2 According to the professor, what was the contribution of French romance writers to the stories about King Arthur?

  Ⓐ They added many new stories to the Arthur legend.

  Ⓑ They wrote about people other than King Arthur in their tales.

  Ⓒ They included Sir Thomas Mallory's *The Death of Arthur*.

  Ⓓ They were the first to mention the Knights of the Round Table.

3 What can be inferred about some knights that went on crusades?

  Ⓐ They were the authors of some *chansons de geste*.

  Ⓑ They were familiar with Sir Thomas Mallory's works.

  Ⓒ Their adventures became the subjects of medieval romances.

  Ⓓ They were inspired to do so because of chansons.

Summarizing ▶ Fill in the blanks to complete the summary.

The professor mentions that chansons and romances were both popular in medieval France. The most famous kind of chanson was the *chanson de geste*, which is a "_____." These chansons often focused on _____. *The Song of Roland*, which concerned one of Charlemagne's warriors, was the most famous chanson. Romances may have been influenced by chansons, or they may _____. There is still a debate on that topic. Romances were often either about _____. Those that were about Britain usually focused on stories about King Arthur and _____.

Listen to part of a lecture in a performing arts class.

02-100

Vaudeville

Characteristics:

→ Tony Pastor:

B.F. Keith:

Sound Movies:

1 What is the main topic of the lecture?

Ⓐ Nineteenth-century American entertainment

Ⓑ A comparison between vaudeville and motion pictures

Ⓒ People important to the vaudeville era

Ⓓ The rise and fall of vaudeville

2 What was the role of B.F. Keith in vaudeville?

Ⓐ He sponsored the first vaudeville show.

Ⓑ He was a vaudeville performer who switched to movies.

Ⓒ He assisted vaudeville acts in going on tour.

Ⓓ He was the leader of a troupe of vaudeville performers.

3 What is the professor's attitude toward vaudeville?

Ⓐ She says it was not a family affair.

Ⓑ She believes it was very entertaining.

Ⓒ She claims it was too bawdy for her.

Ⓓ She considers its humor to be rather dated.

Summarizing ▷ Fill in the blanks to complete the summary.

The lecturer notes that vaudeville had a number of different acts and resembled a variety show. She mentions that _____ in the nineteenth century was for men only and involved alcohol. But in 1881, Tony Pastor put on _____, which was a family-oriented affair. Vaudeville quickly became popular. Later, B.F. Keith began purchasing or building _____ and started the vaudeville circuit, where entertainers went _____ to perform. With the advent of movies, which were often _____, vaudeville began to lose popularity. Finally, when movies with sound came out and the Great Depression began, vaudeville essentially ended.

Listen to part of a conversation between a student and a professor.

02-101

Office Hours

Reason for Visiting:	Result:

➡

↖

Problem:	Solution:

➡

1 Why does the student visit the professor?

Ⓐ To ask him to sign a form

Ⓑ To enroll in his class

Ⓒ To discuss a homework assignment

Ⓓ To go over the last lesson

2 What can be inferred about the student?

Ⓐ She will sign up for the class.

Ⓑ She will take extra lessons with the professor.

Ⓒ She will continue taking the class.

Ⓓ She will find a tutor to assist her.

3 Listen again to part of the conversation. Then answer the question.
What is the purpose of the student's response?

Ⓐ To agree with the professor

Ⓑ To point out a fact to the professor

Ⓒ To complain to the professor

Ⓓ To make a joke with the professor

Summarizing ▷ Fill in the blanks to complete the summary.

The student tells the professor that she is taking his Greek philosophy class but wants to _____ .
He asks why, and she responds that she was very confused in yesterday's class, which was
_____ . The professor asks for more information, and she states that she had never heard of
_____ he had mentioned and that she did not know any of the terms. He says he covered a
lot to give the students an overview of what _____ . He asks the student to stay in class a little
longer because _____ . She agrees to do so.

Listen to part of a conversation between a student and a laboratory assistant.

02-102

Service Encounter

Reason for Visiting:	➡	Result:
Student's Question:	↙ ➡	Result:

1 What does the laboratory assistant say about Professor Peters?

  Ⓐ His specialty is shellfish.

  Ⓑ He runs two labs in the department.

  Ⓒ He is the assistant's advisor.

  Ⓓ He is the head of the department.

2 What will the student probably do next?

  Ⓐ Visit the Biology Department office

  Ⓑ Start cleaning the fish tanks

  Ⓒ Set up a meeting with Professor Miller

  Ⓓ Continue speaking with the laboratory assistant

3 Listen again to part of the conversation. Then answer the question.
What does the laboratory assistant mean when he says this: 🎧

  Ⓐ He would like to trade positions with the student.

  Ⓑ The student is most likely qualified for the job.

  Ⓒ The student should speak with Professor Peters.

  Ⓓ The job is not really worth doing.

Summarizing ▶ Fill in the blanks to complete the summary.

The student visits the laboratory, and the assistant mentions that she is _____. The student
then says that she is not in a class but is looking for a professor. She wants to speak with Professor Miller about
_____. The assistant says that Professor Peters, not Professor Miller, knows about shellfish.
The student then asks about _____ in the building. She wants to work there so that she can
meet more people in her major and _____. The assistant says that there is a job available
and that the student should apply for it.

Listen to part of a lecture in an art history class.

02-103

Art History

1 What aspect of glass does the professor mainly discuss?

Ⓐ Its manufacture during ancient times

Ⓑ The countries that once traded for it

Ⓒ The manner in which colored glass was made

Ⓓ The places in the ancient world where it was manufactured

2 Why does the professor explain the debate about Mesopotamia and Egypt?

Ⓐ To state his opinion on which side he believes is correct

Ⓑ To give the dates when each place is known to have begun making glass

Ⓒ To discuss the uncertainty over where glass was first made

Ⓓ To explain why he does not accept the arguments from either side

3 According to the professor, what can give glass color?

Ⓐ Quartz

Ⓑ Lime

Ⓒ Salt

Ⓓ Cobalt

4 What does the professor imply about the Syrian glassmakers?

    Ⓐ They may have been the first people to make glass.

    Ⓑ They produced glass superior to that made by the Egyptians.

    Ⓒ They were taught how to manufacture glass by the Mesopotamians.

    Ⓓ They refused to show the Egyptians how to make glass.

5 Listen again to part of the lecture. Then answer the question.
What is the purpose of the professor's response?

    Ⓐ To claim that he is unsure of the student's opinion

    Ⓑ To acknowledge that the student may be correct

    Ⓒ To admit that the student's idea needs more researching

    Ⓓ To refute the student's argument

6 Listen again to part of the lecture. Then answer the question.
What does the professor mean when he says this: 🎧

    Ⓐ He has lost some of his lecture notes.

    Ⓑ He wants to get back to giving his lecture.

    Ⓒ He would like the students not to interrupt him.

    Ⓓ He forgot where he was supposed to go.

02-104

Listen to part of a lecture in a literature class.

1 What is the main topic of the lecture?

Ⓐ How directors can improve the quality of science-fiction movies and TV shows

Ⓑ What some of the more famous science-fiction stories are

Ⓒ Why science-fiction literature gets changed when it is adapted for movies or TV

Ⓓ How science-fiction literature, movies, and TV programs are different

2 According to the professor, what is the most limiting factor for science-fiction movies?

Ⓐ Their inability to attract quality actors

Ⓑ The short time they have to tell their stories

Ⓒ The decreasing sizes of their budgets

Ⓓ Their unwillingness to discuss technical matters

3 Why does the professor mention *Dune*?

Ⓐ To say that the movie is very different from the novel

Ⓑ To compare its film adaptation with that of *Starship Troopers*

Ⓒ To claim that it is one of his favorite science-fiction novels

Ⓓ To give an example of a book that explains advanced technology

4   Based on the information in the lecture, do the following statements refer to science-fiction works of literature or science fiction movies?
Click in the correct box for each sentence.

	Science-Fiction Works of Literature	Science-Fiction Movies
1 Require people to accept advancements on faith		
2 Frequently focus on human emotions		
3 Provide detailed descriptions of technology		
4 Are more concerned with making money		

5   Listen again to part of the lecture. Then answer the question.
Why does the professor say this: 🎧

Ⓐ To inform the students of his familiarity with the topic

Ⓑ To state that he remembers the literature he read as a child

Ⓒ To tell the students about his life as a young child

Ⓓ To argue that he knows more about science fiction than the students

6   Listen again to part of the lecture. Then answer the question.
What can be inferred about the professor when he says this: 🎧

Ⓐ He hopes that science-fiction movies will soon improve in quality.

Ⓑ He believes the students should avoid watching current science-fiction movies.

Ⓒ It has been several years since he has seen a science-fiction movie.

Ⓓ He prefers reading science fiction to watching science-fiction movies.

02-105

Listen to part of a conversation between a student and a professor.

1 What are the speakers mainly discussing?
- Ⓐ The adjustments to university life the student must make
- Ⓑ The professor's experiences as a student
- Ⓒ The need for the student to improve her grades
- Ⓓ The student's thoughts on her future major

2 Why did the professor ask to speak with the student?
- Ⓐ To find out what her last semester's grades were
- Ⓑ To discuss her plans to become a journalism major
- Ⓒ To check on her progress at the university
- Ⓓ To learn why the student is thinking of transferring

3 What can be inferred about the student?
- Ⓐ She is undecided about her academic major.
- Ⓑ She comes from a fairly small town.
- Ⓒ She needs good grades to keep her scholarship.
- Ⓓ She likes having the professor as her advisor.

4 Listen again to part of the conversation. Then answer the question.
What is the purpose of the student's response?
- Ⓐ To make an attempt at humor
- Ⓑ To express her happiness
- Ⓒ To show her wariness
- Ⓓ To defend her actions

5 Listen again to part of the conversation. Then answer the question.
What can be inferred about the professor when he says this: 🎧
- Ⓐ He is impatient for the student to make up her mind.
- Ⓑ He wants the student to enjoy her class.
- Ⓒ He thinks the student chose her classes well.
- Ⓓ He studied his major because he enjoyed it.

• Mastering Question Types

biography	consciously	divine	inappropriate
inkling	interact	memorize	mistaken
morph	oxide	playwright	precede
protagonist	stage	strive	venture
breathtaking	countless	frontal	incomplete
innovator	literacy	metallic	molten
motivation	phenomenal	portrait	profile
psychological	stained	tragedy	vernacular
cathedral	depiction	idealistic	influential
inspiration	manuscript	misspeak	monastery
novel	pictorial	pose	prolific
revenge	stimulus	triumphant	vogue

• Mastering Topics

analyze	burlesque	chivalry	coffin
exhalation	forerunner	heroic	howl
infertile	mimic	oral	predate
simultaneously	superstition	theft	vellum
bawdy	chanson	circuit	communal
exotic	guttural	heyday	illiterate
inhalation	minstrel	parchment	pumice
spiritual	tablet	variation	vocalization
bubble	chant	clergy	exceed
folk	heritage	honor	inevitable
loyalty	nobleman	pickle	sheepskin
steppe	text	vaudeville	warrior

• TOEFL Practice Tests

adaptation	bronze	cerebral	craftsman
depth	device	impurity	hyperspace
interstellar	novelization	pharaoh	powder
reveal	storyline	technology	uncover
artisan	calcium	circular	cram
descendant	exacting	glassmaker	ingot
jewelry	ongoing	plausible	reference
science fiction	surmise	thoughtful	vessel
beloved	ceramic	container	crush
detract	excavate	humanity	insight
millennium	perfume	plot	reheat
script	tackle	time machine	warp

Vocabulary *Review*

Choose the words with the closest meanings to the highlighted words.

1 The land was so infertile that nothing would grow on it.

(A) dry   (B) barren
(C) rocky   (D) acidic

2 The ancient manuscript fell apart as soon as he touched it.

(A) jewel   (B) text
(C) painting   (D) sculpture

3 I spent a phenomenal amount of time working on that project.

(A) potential   (B) minor
(C) virtual   (D) incredible

4 This is a communal lounge that all employees are permitted to use.

(A) shared   (B) comfortable
(C) sizable   (D) private

5 Be careful with that ceramic; it is extremely fragile.

(A) device   (B) glass
(C) pottery   (D) mirror

6 Her ideas were overly idealistic and could not possibly be successful.

(A) naive   (B) distorted
(C) improper   (D) complicated

7 The book's plot is somewhat complicated, but everything works out in the end.

(A) theme   (B) narration
(C) character   (D) storyline

8 In American history, George Washington predates Abraham Lincoln.

(A) comes from   (B) comes to
(C) comes before   (D) comes with

9 What you just said is plausible; now we have to make sure it can happen.

(A) possible   (B) logical
(C) inexpensive   (D) acceptable

10 The triumphant general returned to his homeland as a hero.

(A) avenging   (B) promoted
(C) ingenious   (D) victorious

Match the words with the correct definitions.

11 artisan •

12 literacy •

13 warrior •

14 coffin •

15 excavate •

16 biography •

17 pharaoh •

18 inhalation •

19 detract •

20 protagonist •

• (A) the container in which a person is buried

• (B) a great fighter or soldier

• (C) the ability to read

• (D) a work of literature about a person's life

• (E) a craftsman, often one with great skill

• (F) an ancient king of Egypt

• (G) the hero in a work of literature

• (H) to take away from the value of something

• (I) to dig up; to unearth

• (J) the breathing in of air

Chapter 08   **Arts 2** | **Conversations**

art • art history • literature • music • musicology • theater • performing arts •
architecture • film • dance

02-106

Listen to part of a lecture in an architecture class.

TYPE 1 What aspect of the Leaning Tower of Pisa does the professor mainly discuss?

(A) Its construction

(B) Its history

(C) Its repairs

(D) Its architects

TYPE 2 According to the professor, what is the reason the tower originally began to lean?

(A) The weight of the bells put too much pressure on the tower.

(B) There were not enough counterweights to keep it from tilting.

(C) Its thin foundation was constructed on top of unstable soil.

(D) The concrete used on the tower sank beneath the soil.

TYPE 3 Why does the professor mention Benito Mussolini?

(A) To name the original designer of the building

(B) To talk about a failed attempt to right the tower

(C) To explain how the tower was finally completed

(D) To compliment his work on the tower

TYPE 4 Listen again to part of the lecture. Then answer the question.
What does the professor imply when he says this: 🎧

(A) The project leader was incompetent.

(B) Not enough money was spent to fix the tower.

(C) The new construction made the tower look strange.

(D) The tower should not have been built higher than six floors.

Summarizing ▶ Fill in the blanks to complete the summary.

The professor begins by noting that not all mistakes can be erased and that some are _____
for everyone to see. He is referring to the Leaning Tower of Pisa. He then describes its construction. According
to him, _____ and the soil it was built on made it start to lean. Construction stopped, but
when it resumed again, it _____ as it was built higher. People made many attempts to
_____ , but they all failed. Some, like Benito Mussolini's attempt in the twentieth century, made it
worse. Recently, it has been stabilized, so visitors are _____ .

02-107

Listen to part of a lecture in a literature class.

TYPE **5**   What is the main topic of the lecture?

Ⓐ The works of Mark Twain

Ⓑ A comparison of Mark Twain and Rebecca Harding Davis

Ⓒ The writing styles of two Realist authors

Ⓓ Social issues in the United States after the Civil War

TYPE **6**   Listen again to part of the lecture. Then answer the question.
What does the professor mean when he says this: 🎧

Ⓐ Mark Twain had his own individual style.

Ⓑ No one wrote as well as Mark Twain did during his lifetime.

Ⓒ Mark Twain wrote dialog effectively.

Ⓓ Reading Mark Twain's works requires great effort.

TYPE **7**   Based on the information in the lecture, do the following statements refer to Rebecca Harding Davis or Mark Twain?
Click in the correct box for each sentence.

	Rebecca Harding Davis	Mark Twain
1 Wrote under an assumed name		
2 Wrote a book about political corruption		
3 Tried to assist deprived groups of people		
4 Was one of America's greatest writers		

TYPE **8**   What does the professor imply about his class?

Ⓐ The students will have to read some poems.

Ⓑ It will focus on twentieth century works.

Ⓒ It will involve the study of Realist authors.

Ⓓ It requires the students to make presentations.

Summarizing ▷   Fill in the blanks to complete the summary.

The professor notes that the U.S. went through _____ after the Civil War. Literature in this period also changed. He mentions that the style of writing called Realism lasted from 1865 to 1910. Two of its greatest writers were Rebecca Harding Davis and _____. Davis tried to help underprivileged groups of people and often wrote about the _____. This included slavery and political corruption. Mark Twain wrote two very famous books: _____. He tried to write the same way that people speak, so it can make his books difficult. Still, he is recognized as _____.

Mastering Question Types with Lectures | A2

TYPE 1 • Gist-Content *TYPE 2* • Detail *TYPE 3* • Understanding Organization *TYPE 4* • Function of What Is Said

Listen to part of a lecture in an art history class.

02-108

TYPE 1 What is the lecture mainly about?

    Ⓐ The life and work of Cezanne

    Ⓑ The Impressionist paintings of Cezanne

    Ⓒ Cezanne and his early years

    Ⓓ The influences on Cezanne's work

TYPE 2 According to the professor, what is characteristic of Cezanne's work?
Choose 2 answers.

    Ⓐ Heavy brushstrokes

    Ⓑ Dark colors

    Ⓒ Complex scenes

    Ⓓ Pictures of people

TYPE 3 Why does the professor mention Cubism?

    Ⓐ To name some of the Cubist works Cezanne painted

    Ⓑ To discuss Cezanne's effect on that genre

    Ⓒ To compare Cezanne's Cubist works with his Impressionist ones

    Ⓓ To say that he turned Picasso to Cubism

TYPE 4 Listen again to part of the lecture. Then answer the question.
Why does the professor say this: 🎧

    Ⓐ To explain how Cezanne had enough time to paint

    Ⓑ To show why Cezanne had very few friends

    Ⓒ To emphasize Cezanne's reclusive nature

    Ⓓ To mention a theory about why Cezanne disliked fame

Summarizing ▷ Fill in the blanks to complete the summary.

The professor begins with a biography of Paul Cezanne. She describes his life and notes that
_____ and had few friends. He also endured much rejection early in his career and was very
reclusive. Cezanne painted landscapes, portraits, self-portraits, bathers, and still lifes. He used bright colors, heavy
brushstrokes, and _____. He was often accused of making simple work, but he focused more
on the process than _____. He painted in the Impressionist style, but his work changed in the
last years of his life. He began painting _____ and is often considered the father of Cubism.

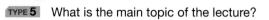

02-109

Listen to part of a lecture in a music class.

TYPE 5 What is the main topic of the lecture?

  Ⓐ Classical music composers

  Ⓑ Popular music forms in the Classical Period

  Ⓒ Some characteristics of the Classical Period

  Ⓓ The changes made during the Classical Period

TYPE 6 What is the professor's opinion of classical music?

  Ⓐ It is better than modern music.

  Ⓑ It sounds best with violins.

  Ⓒ Symphonies are its ideal form.

  Ⓓ Not enough people attend classical music performances.

TYPE 7 Based on the information in the lecture, which form of music do the following sentences refer to? Click in the correct box for each sentence.

	Sonata	Chamber Music	Symphony
1 It made frequent use of the violin.			
2 It was based on homophonic sound.			
3 It had four separate movements.			
4 It utilized the ABA form.			

TYPE 8 What does the professor imply about string quartets?

  Ⓐ They were more popular than sonatas.

  Ⓑ They required more musicians than symphonies.

  Ⓒ They were dominated by the violin.

  Ⓓ They lasted longer than sonatas.

Summarizing ▷ Fill in the blanks to complete the summary.

The professor claims that few people these days listen to classical music. He then states that classical music covers _____, but he only wants to focus on the Classical Period, which was _____. The Classical Period lasted from around 1750 to 1820. It had music that was _____, and structured. Balance was what the composers of this period strived for. The three main forms of music were _____, and symphonies. There were also many composers, like Mozart, Haydn, and Beethoven, who lived during this time and became _____ from their work.

02-110

Listen to part of a conversation between a student and a professor.

TYPE 1   Why does the student visit the professor?

- Ⓐ To find out how to become a stagehand
- Ⓑ To ask to be allowed to act in the upcoming play
- Ⓒ To tell the professor about his recent issues
- Ⓓ To talk about the auditions for a school play

TYPE 2   According to the student, why was he unable to try out for the play?

- Ⓐ He was taking care of some business out of town.
- Ⓑ He was not aware of when he should have done that.
- Ⓒ He was busy studying for his exams.
- Ⓓ He was not interested in the play until now.

TYPE 3   Why does the professor explain the role of a stagehand?

- Ⓐ To offer the student a paid position on her staff
- Ⓑ To answer the student's question concerning that matter
- Ⓒ To say what the student could do to help with the play
- Ⓓ To tell the student she thinks that is the role best suited for him

TYPE 4   Why does the student tell the professor that he has some family problems?

- Ⓐ To mention why he forgot about their appointment
- Ⓑ To try to gain some sympathy from her
- Ⓒ To say why his performance has suffered recently
- Ⓓ To explain why he missed the auditions

Summarizing ▶   Fill in the blanks to complete the summary.

The student visits the professor to talk about _____ . The professor says that they were held last week. The student acknowledges that he knows that but says he was dealing with _____ , so he could not attend them. The professor says she would like to help him, but _____ have been filled. She will not make an exception for him either, but she offers him a job as a stagehand to help with _____ . The student agrees and says that he would like to be _____ in some manner.

02-111

Listen to part of a conversation between a student and a student services employee.

TYPE **5**   What are the speakers mainly discussing?

Ⓐ The student's performance with the student orchestra

Ⓑ How the student can protest a fine he received

Ⓒ A ticket that the student got

Ⓓ Where the student can park his car

TYPE **6**   Where was the student's car parked when he got a ticket?

Ⓐ In front of the student services building

Ⓑ At the school's auditorium

Ⓒ Near the library

Ⓓ In the student parking lot

TYPE **7**   Listen again to part of the conversation. Then answer the question.
What does the woman mean when she says this: 🎧

Ⓐ She wants the student to leave her office.

Ⓑ She would like to take the student's order.

Ⓒ Her office does not take credit cards.

Ⓓ The student still has to pay the fine.

TYPE **8**   What can be inferred about the student?

Ⓐ He is going to stop parking at the school.

Ⓑ He is displeased to have gotten a ticket.

Ⓒ He cannot afford to pay the fine.

Ⓓ He would like to continue speaking with the woman.

Summarizing ▷ Fill in the blanks to complete the summary.

The student asks to speak with ＿＿＿＿＿＿＿＿＿＿＿ , who is the woman. The student is upset about a ticket
he got and would like to protest it. The woman says he probably got it because he has ＿＿＿＿＿＿＿＿＿＿＿ ,
but the student says he has one. Then, the woman suggests he was parked ＿＿＿＿＿＿＿＿＿＿＿ , which is
not allowed, but the student says he left earlier than that. When she looks at the ticket, she realizes that the student
had taken up ＿＿＿＿＿＿＿＿＿＿＿ when he parked, so he was ticketed. Then, she tells the student that he still
＿＿＿＿＿＿＿＿＿＿＿ .

02-112

Listen to part of a lecture in an art class.

Illustrations

Characteristics:

➡ Illustrations as Art:

Computer-Generated Illustrations as Art:

---

1 What aspect of illustrations does the professor mainly discuss?

Ⓐ Their status in the world of art

Ⓑ Their relationship with pop art

Ⓒ Their creation by computers

Ⓓ Their early history

2 What resulted from the invention of photography?

Ⓐ People began to lose interest in illustrations.

Ⓑ Illustrations entered a golden age.

Ⓒ Illustrations were used less often in newspapers.

Ⓓ People learned how to reproduce illustrations in color.

3 Why does the professor mention Norman Rockwell?

Ⓐ To compare his work with Andy Warhol's

Ⓑ To say that he was an illustrator

Ⓒ To credit him with making colored illustrations

Ⓓ To point out that he made computer-generated illustrations

Summarizing ▶ Fill in the blanks to complete the summary.

The professor states he wants to know whether _____ . He then describes what illustrations are made with. He notes that cave art drawings were illustrations, _____ had illustrations, and many newspapers also had illustrations. Photography's invention caused illustrations to be _____ , but they were still popular in the nineteenth and twentieth centuries. A student says that illustrations are not classic art but are _____ , and the professor agrees. He says that _____ should also be considered art despite being made by computers.

Listen to part of a lecture in an art history class.

02-113

Ateliers

Characteristics:

➡️

Paris:

Techniques:

---

1 What aspect of ateliers does the professor mainly discuss?

    Ⓐ The types of methods most students learned at them

    Ⓑ Why students preferred learning at them than at universities

    Ⓒ How they were used to provide instruction to students

    Ⓓ The reasons that they lost popularity in the twentieth century

2 According to the professor, what did novice students in ateliers do in their first year?
Choose 2 answers.

    Ⓐ They learned how to make forms in correct proportions.

    Ⓑ They learned how to paint still-life objects.

    Ⓒ They learned how to draw with charcoal.

    Ⓓ They learned how to sculpt with various materials.

3 Why does the professor mention Leon Bonnat?

    Ⓐ To claim he ran the biggest atelier in Paris

    Ⓑ To describe the manner in which he taught

    Ⓒ To compare his work with that of his students

    Ⓓ To name some of his most famous works

Summarizing ▶ Fill in the blanks to complete the summary.

Ateliers were art studios modeled on medieval guilds. A master artist took in apprentices and trained them to become artists or art teachers. Most students studied for around _____. At first, they drew with _____, but as they learned more skills, they could paint and sculpt. Students often used the _____. This taught them to paint objects with the _____. While this method restricted skills and imaginations, it provided students with a good foundation in art methods. Some ateliers gave students more freedom. For instance, _____ taught many styles and encouraged students to use their imaginations.

Listen to part of a lecture in an art history class.

02-114

Apprentices

Apprentices:		Initial Tasks:
	➡	
		Later Tasks:

1 What is the professor's attitude toward apprentices?

Ⓐ They were often abused by their masters.

Ⓑ They did not learn quickly enough.

Ⓒ They served a useful purpose.

Ⓓ They were only good for making their masters money.

2 What does the professor imply about master painters?

Ⓐ Most were reluctant to see their apprentices graduate.

Ⓑ Some of them refused to take any apprentices at all.

Ⓒ Those with many apprentices earned a lot of money.

Ⓓ The best master painters had no time to train apprentices.

3 Listen again to part of the lecture. Then answer the question.
Why does the professor say this: 🎧

Ⓐ To show that even Leonardo da Vinci had to work as an apprentice

Ⓑ To tell a humorous story about Leonardo da Vinci

Ⓒ To let the class know that she enjoys telling stories

Ⓓ To indicate the incident probably did not happen

Summarizing ▷ Fill in the blanks to complete the summary.

The professor mentions that Renaissance artists did whatever _____ of them. These could be any number of tasks. Since they were often very busy, they required apprentices. These were young boys between the ages of _____ who trained with the master for around twelve years. Their parents had to pay tuition for them to _____ . They started out just like cleaning and preparing paint, but as they learned, they got to do more involved work. This included actually _____ . Some, like Leonardo da Vinci, eventually became better than their masters.

Listen to part of a lecture in an architecture class.

02-115

Art Deco

Characteristics:

Influences:

Notable Art Deco Examples:

---

1 Why does the professor explain the Roaring Twenties?

Ⓐ To mention its relationship with Art Deco

Ⓑ To compare that period's effect on other art forms

Ⓒ To say that Art Deco ended during that period

Ⓓ To describe some of the changes made during that period

2 According to the professor, what was an influence on Art Deco?

Ⓐ African artwork

Ⓑ Modern European designs

Ⓒ Ancient Greek styles

Ⓓ Impressionist works

3 What is the professor's opinion of Art Deco?

Ⓐ He finds it too overwrought.

Ⓑ He is highly appreciative of it.

Ⓒ He thinks it is exceedingly flashy.

Ⓓ He believes it is extremely influential.

Summarizing ▷ Fill in the blanks to complete the summary.

The professor shows some slides and asks the students to _____ . A student says it is Art Deco but cannot explain _____ . The professor says that Art Deco was popular in _____ . It was first highly functional and then evolved to be decorative. It was _____ . It resembled the Roaring Twenties and the attitudes that people in this time period shared. The professor says both the Roaring Twenties and Art Deco _____ . He mentions that many different cultures influenced it as well. Then, he names some buildings and places that employ the Art Deco style.

Listen to part of a conversation between a student and a professor.

02-116

Office Hours

Reason to See Student:	Result:
Request:	Result:

1 Why does the professor ask to see the student?

(A) To discuss the term paper the student just submitted

(B) To tell the student about a change she has to make

(C) To encourage the student to do some more research

(D) To ask why the student failed to follow directions

2 Why does the professor tell the student about his past students?

(A) To make it clear that he has been using the same topics for fifteen years

(B) To show how long he has been teaching the same class

(C) To indicate that the student will not get special treatment

(D) To request that the student work as hard as his other students did

3 What can be inferred about the professor?

(A) He is going to retire from teaching soon.

(B) He does not accept input from his students.

(C) He encourages the students to participate in class.

(D) He gives numerous homework assignments.

Summarizing ▶ Fill in the blanks to complete the summary.

The professor asks the student to come in and speak with him. He says that _____ that he saw the student. He wants to speak with the student about _____. The professor says it is a good abstract, but the student cannot use it. The student asks why. The professor responds that it is not on the list of _____. The student asks for the professor to _____, but the professor refuses. He says that the student should _____ by the time the class meets again.

Listen to part of a conversation between a student and a librarian.

02-117

Service Encounter

Problem:	➡	Solution:
Student's Question:	⬉ ➡	Result:

1 According to the librarian, why is the library not putting books on the shelf quickly these days?
   Ⓐ The student employees are slow workers.
   Ⓑ There are not enough people working there.
   Ⓒ The students are putting books in the wrong places.
   Ⓓ The head librarian is currently out on sick leave.

2 What will the student probably do next?
   Ⓐ Continue looking for the book
   Ⓑ Try to find a different book
   Ⓒ Speak with Mrs. Richardson
   Ⓓ Leave the library

3 Listen again to part of the conversation. Then answer the question.
   What can be inferred about the librarian when he says this: 🎧
   Ⓐ He has no more suggestions for the student.
   Ⓑ He thinks the student should give up her search.
   Ⓒ He is tired of speaking with the student.
   Ⓓ The student needs to try harder.

Summarizing ▷ Fill in the blanks to complete the summary.

The student asks the librarian about a book. She mentions it is listed as available, but _____. The librarian says another student is probably reading it in the library. She asks when it _____. The librarian states that they normally put books back on the shelf quickly, but the library is _____. After that, she changes topics and asks about getting _____. The librarian says that some jobs are available and that she should speak with Mrs. Richardson. The student asks _____, and the librarian points it out to her.

Listen to part of a lecture in an art class.

02-118

1   What aspect of frescoes does the professor mainly discuss?

    Ⓐ Buon and secco frescoes

    Ⓑ The type Michelangelo made

    Ⓒ Their advantages and disadvantages

    Ⓓ The manner in which they are made

2   Why does the professor explain how Michelangelo painted the Sistine Chapel?

    Ⓐ To mention how long it took

    Ⓑ To admit that Michelangelo got assistance

    Ⓒ To impress the students with Michelangelo's brilliance

    Ⓓ To note how difficult it was

3   According to the professor, what did Michelangelo do sometimes before working on the Sistine Chapel?

    Ⓐ He mixed his own paints.

    Ⓑ He attached the plaster himself.

    Ⓒ He erected the scaffolding.

    Ⓓ He looked at sketches he had made.

4   How does the professor organize the information about frescoes that he presents to the class?

    Ⓐ By talking about the history of frescoes in chronological order

    Ⓑ By explaining the various features of two different types of frescoes

    Ⓒ By describing how to make a fresco from start to finish

    Ⓓ By comparing and contrasting the ways in which people paint frescoes

5   Based on the information in the lecture, do the following statements refer to buon frescoes or secco frescoes?

Click in the correct box for each sentence.

	Buon Fresco	Secco Fresco
① May start to flake after some time		
② Results in the paint bonding with the plaster		
③ May take a long time to complete		
④ Is used to cover up mistakes that are made		

6   Listen again to part of the lecture. Then answer the question.
What does the professor imply when he says this: 🎧

    Ⓐ Few artists make frescoes nowadays.

    Ⓑ Modern paints are better than those used in the past.

    Ⓒ He has rarely experienced the problem he just described.

    Ⓓ People had problems making frescoes in the past.

Listen to part of a lecture in a film class.

02-119

Special Effects

1   What is the main topic of the lecture?
   Ⓐ Special effects used in the past
   Ⓑ The most believable special effects
   Ⓒ The history of special effects
   Ⓓ Stop-motion photography and Claymation

2   According to the professor, what do physical effects require nowadays?
   Ⓐ Claymation characters
   Ⓑ Stuntmen
   Ⓒ Miniatures
   Ⓓ Read projection

3   How is the discussion organized?
   Ⓐ By explaining how special effects have improved over the years
   Ⓑ By naming some movies and explaining the effects used in them
   Ⓒ By describing several different types of special effects
   Ⓓ By comparing modern special effects with earlier ones

4 Based on the information in the lecture, do the following statements refer to stop-motion photography or miniatures?

Click in the correct box for each sentence.

	Stop-Motion Photography	Miniature
1 Is a very meticulous process to film		
2 Was used in some *Godzilla* movies		
3 Often looks like it is not real		
4 Makes use of very small-scale models		

5 Listen again to part of the lecture. Then answer the question.
Why does the professor say this: 🎧

   Ⓐ To ask the students for their opinions

   Ⓑ To retract his previous statement

   Ⓒ To say that he will speak more clearly

   Ⓓ To repeat what he just said

6 Listen again to part of the lecture. Then answer the question.
What does the professor imply when he says this: 🎧

   Ⓐ *Star Wars* used advanced special effects when it was filmed.

   Ⓑ The effects used in *Star Wars* were expensive.

   Ⓒ Miniatures were used in the filming of *Star Wars*.

   Ⓓ He enjoys talking about science-fiction movies.

02-120

Listen to part of a conversation between a student and a professor.

1 Why does the student visit the professor?

   Ⓐ She wants to discuss her performance on the test.

   Ⓑ She does not understand her homework assignment.

   Ⓒ She has some questions about the lecture material.

   Ⓓ She has a complaint about something in the class.

2 According to the professor, how can art historians identify what certain cave paintings are pictures of?

   Ⓐ By consulting historical texts

   Ⓑ By making educated guesses

   Ⓒ By comparing them with other drawings

   Ⓓ By looking at drawings that are very clear

3 What will the student probably do next?

   Ⓐ Leave the professor's office

   Ⓑ Go to her next class

   Ⓒ Ask the professor another question

   Ⓓ Submit her paper to the professor

4 Listen again to part of the conversation. Then answer the question.
   Why does the student say this: 🎧

   Ⓐ To agree with the professor

   Ⓑ To bring up another point

   Ⓒ To admit the professor's reasoning is better than hers

   Ⓓ To respond to a question

5 Listen again to part of the conversation. Then answer the question.
   What does the professor mean when he says this: 🎧

   Ⓐ The student has just offered a valuable insight.

   Ⓑ She would like the student to speak more in class.

   Ⓒ The student ought to sign up for her class.

   Ⓓ She is pleased with the student's decision.

• Mastering Question Types

accurate	brooding	chord	conform
corruption	display	foundation	geometrical
intend	melodic	orchestra	quartet
rejection	societal	strum	tilt
belfry	brushstroke	circumstance	contemporary
dense	downward	futile	harmonize
leaning	misguided	pen	reclusive
resume	stabilize	stylistic	tumultuous
biographical	burden	compensate	counterweight
dismal	extraordinary	generation	inherit
mechanics	musicologist	proponent	recognize
slavery	structure	terminate	urbanize

• Mastering Topics

accuracy	altarpiece	astute	carve
commission	dramatic	goldmine	illustration
influence	neoclassical	prehistory	proliferation
rear	sophistication	surpass	vow
advertisement	apocryphal	austerity	charcoal
decorative	encompass	grandeur	impetus
mass-market	ornamental	prime	prolific
renew	stoicism	tuition	widespread
aerodynamics	apprentice	avant-garde	coincidentally
distorted	engrave	heroism	incompetent
mural	pigment	progress	qualify
sketch	streamlined	veneration	woodcut

• TOEFL Practice Tests

adhesive	beforehand	ceiling	damp
explosion	fresco	gunfire	limited
meticulous	mortar	plaster	reappear
scaffolding	shoot	stuntman	visible
agent	border	chemically	deteriorate
expulsion	fuse	harden	locale
miniature	moviemaking	property	resin
scale	specialist	trick	warship
background	bullet	Claymation	drawback
flake	grid	leisure	masterpiece
mold	operator	pyrotechnic	rough
scenery	stop-motion	tromp	yolk

Vocabulary *Review*

📝 Choose the words with the closest meanings to the highlighted words.

1 The council commissioned the construction of two new buildings.

    (A) ordered   (B) financed

    (C) asked about   (D) requested

2 That man is a contemporary artist and is still painting today.

    (A) famous   (B) renowned

    (C) extraordinary   (D) modern

3 The veneration the priest's followers felt for him was quite obvious.

    (A) duties   (B) adoration

    (C) abhorrence   (D) consideration

4 Be careful when carving with that knife; it is very sharp.

    (A) chopping   (B) mincing

    (C) honing   (D) cutting

5 The situation in the colony is clearly beginning to deteriorate.

    (A) stabilize   (B) progress

    (C) worsen   (D) manifest

6 The CEO made many accurate statements during the conference.

    (A) proper   (B) correct

    (C) sophisticated   (D) appropriate

7 Can you give me a rough idea of what exactly you would like to do?

    (A) descriptive   (B) basic

    (C) coherent   (D) permanent

8 This topic encompasses a wide range of subjects.

    (A) reveals   (B) excludes

    (C) covers   (D) exceeds

9 When is he going to pen his next novel?

    (A) write   (B) publish

    (C) edit   (D) proofread

10 Do not tromp all over the flowers; you are going to crush them.

    (A) run   (B) jump

    (C) play   (D) stomp

📝 Match the words with the correct definitions.

11 apprentice •   • (A) a person who is training for a job

12 specialist •   • (B) to advance

13 foundation •   • (C) smart; clever; prudent

14 progress •   • (D) a supporter

15 adhesive •   • (E) an agent like glue that attaches objects to one another

16 astute •   • (F) a great work of art, literature, or something similar

17 proponent •   • (G) the base of something such as a house or building

18 masterpiece •   • (H) to raise, like a baby

19 rear •   • (I) a group of four

20 quartet •   • (J) an expert

Part

C

Experiencing the TOEFL iBT Actual Tests

CONTINUE   VOLUME

Listening Section Directions

03-01

This section measures your ability to understand conversations and lectures in English.

The listening section is divided into separately timed parts. In each part you will listen to 1 conversation and 1 or 2 lectures. You will hear each conversation or lecture only **one** time.

After each conversation or lecture, you will answer some questions about it. The questions typically ask about the main idea and supporting details. Some questions ask about a speaker's purpose or attitude. Answer the questions based on what is stated or implied by the speakers.

You may take notes while you listen. You may use your notes to help you answer the questions. Your notes will not be scored.

If you need to change the volume while you listen, click on **Volume** at the top of the screen.

For some questions, you will see this icon: 🎧 This means that you will hear, but not see, part of the question.

Some of the questions have special directions. These directions appear in a gray box on the screen.

Most questions are worth 1 point. If a question is worth more than 1 point, it will have special directions that indicate how many points you can receive.

A clock at the top of the screen will show you how much time is remaining. The clock will not count down while you are listening. The clock will count down only while you are answering the questions.

Set A

Listening Directions

03-02

In this part, you will listen to 1 conversation and 2 lectures.

You must answer each question. After you answer, click on **Next**. Then click on **OK** to confirm your answer and go on to the next question. After you click on **OK**, you cannot return to previous questions.

You may now begin this part of the Listening section. You will have **10 minutes** to answer the questions.

Click on **Continue** to go on.

03-03

1 Why does the student visit the professor?

   Ⓐ To discuss a change she would like to make

   Ⓑ To talk about some problems in her flute class

   Ⓒ To get permission to take an upper-level class

   Ⓓ To complain about a grade she just received

2 What does the professor say about the class the student is taking?

   Ⓐ Fewer than fifteen students are enrolled in it.

   Ⓑ Only juniors and seniors are eligible to take it.

   Ⓒ It is a class designed for graduate students.

   Ⓓ The average grade in the class is an A–.

3 Why does the professor tell the student about the exceptions made for the course in the past?

   Ⓐ To tell the student how long he has been at the school

   Ⓑ To convince her not to be discouraged by her grade

   Ⓒ To emphasize how accomplished the student really is

   Ⓓ To ask her to continue taking the class and not to drop it

4 What can be inferred about the student?

   Ⓐ She will wait before making a decision.

   Ⓑ She will ask another professor for advice.

   Ⓒ She will drop the class she is struggling in.

   Ⓓ She will go ahead with her original plan.

5 Listen again to part of the conversation. Then answer the question.
   What does the professor mean when he says this: 🎧

   Ⓐ The student needs to stop being so shy.

   Ⓑ The student must stop wasting the professor's time.

   Ⓒ The student needs to think before she speaks.

   Ⓓ The student should be honest with the professor.

03-04

Physiology

6   What is the lecture mainly about?

     Ⓐ The skeletal system and its role in the body

     Ⓑ The functions of the muscles in the heart

     Ⓒ The parts of the body that control movement

     Ⓓ The body's digestive system

7   What does the professor say about the heart?

     Ⓐ It is the center of the body's muscular system.

     Ⓑ It is attached to the body by tendons.

     Ⓒ It must continue beating for the body to survive.

     Ⓓ It contains both skeletal and smooth muscles.

8   Based on the information in the lecture, do the following statements refer to skeletal muscles or smooth muscles?
     Click in the correct box for each sentence.

	Skeletal Muscles	Smooth Muscles
① Are comprised of muscle fibers		
② Depend on the spinal cord to function properly		
③ Are not controlled through voluntary means		
④ May be found in the stomach and blood vessels		

9   What will the professor probably do next?

     Ⓐ Give the students their lab assignment

     Ⓑ Start talking about the heart

     Ⓒ Answer some more questions

     Ⓓ Describe smooth muscles in more detail

10   Listen again to part of the lecture. Then answer the question.
     Why does the professor say this: 🎧

     Ⓐ To explain her throat irritation

     Ⓑ To complain about the weather

     Ⓒ To show how weather can affect the body

     Ⓓ To indicate her desire for some water

11   Listen again to part of the lecture. Then answer the question.
     What can be inferred about the professor when she says this: 🎧

     Ⓐ She dislikes the idleness of young people.

     Ⓑ She is comfortable using the Internet.

     Ⓒ She has muscles that are well developed.

     Ⓓ She spends little time watching television.

03-05

12 What aspect of petroleum does the professor mainly discuss?

Ⓐ Its formation

Ⓑ Its recovery

Ⓒ Its manifestations

Ⓓ Its locations

13 Why does the professor explain a hydrocarbon trap?

Ⓐ To describe the process by which kerogen becomes petroleum

Ⓑ To mention why petroleum is only found in some locations

Ⓒ To note one of the conditions necessary for creating petroleum

Ⓓ To show how some vegetation decayed and then formed petroleum

14 According to the professor, what did type 3 kerogen primarily form?

Ⓐ Liquid gas

Ⓑ Coal

Ⓒ Methane

Ⓓ Natural gas

15 How is the discussion organized?

Ⓐ By the asking and answering of questions from the students

Ⓑ By the presentation of information in a straightforward manner

Ⓒ By the quoting of extensive passages from the textbook

Ⓓ By the explaining of why the topic was chosen

16 What does the professor imply about bitumen sands?

Ⓐ They are found trapped under a layer of impermeable rock.

Ⓑ They have only been located in places in Canada at this time.

Ⓒ They are typically found in abundance near coastal or desert areas.

Ⓓ Extracting oil from them may be economically feasible in the future.

17 Listen again to part of the lecture. Then answer the question.
What does the professor mean when he says this: 🎧

Ⓐ The students will be tested on the day's lecture material.

Ⓑ He will provide lecture notes for the students after class.

Ⓒ The students had better study hard for their upcoming test.

Ⓓ The students are not taking good enough notes in class.

Set B

Listening Directions

03-06

In this part, you will listen to 1 conversation and 1 lecture.

You must answer each question. After you answer, click on **Next**. Then click on **OK** to confirm your answer and go on to the next question. After you click on **OK**, you cannot return to previous questions.

You may now begin this part of the Listening section. You will have **7 minutes** to answer the questions.

Click on **Continue** to go on.

03-07

1   What problem does the student have?

   Ⓐ Her application for a scholarship was declined.

   Ⓑ A class she wants to take is not offered.

   Ⓒ She is doing poorly in one of her classes.

   Ⓓ She cannot fit a class into next semester's schedule.

2   What is the student's attitude toward Professor Monroe?

   Ⓐ She believes his exams were quite difficult.

   Ⓑ She did not learn much in the class she took with him.

   Ⓒ She considers him the top teacher in his department.

   Ⓓ She thinks he was very good at lecturing.

3   What is one of Professor Monroe's interests?

   Ⓐ Medieval Europe

   Ⓑ Egyptian archaeology

   Ⓒ Roman history

   Ⓓ Ancient Greece

4   What can be inferred about the professor?

   Ⓐ He has a strong interest in ancient Egypt.

   Ⓑ He is a member of the History Department.

   Ⓒ He has done some work in archaeology in the past.

   Ⓓ He is meeting the student for the first time.

5   What will the professor probably do next?

   Ⓐ Meet Professor Monroe in person

   Ⓑ Visit the departmental office

   Ⓒ Have lunch with a colleague

   Ⓓ Make a telephone call

03-08

6 Why does the professor explain the props used in Greek theater?

    Ⓐ To mention their roles in relation to that of the chorus

    Ⓑ To indicate when they were first utilized in dramatic performances

    Ⓒ To claim that they added to the authenticity of the play

    Ⓓ To show how the actors conveyed emotions to the audience

7 According to the professor, what was the role of the chorus in Greek theater?
Choose 2 answers.

    Ⓐ It sometimes went on stage to interact with the actors.

    Ⓑ It stood for the citizens of the area where the play was set.

    Ⓒ It provided the audience with information that it needed.

    Ⓓ It repeated the actors' lines during the intermission periods.

8 What is the professor's opinion of Greek theater?

    Ⓐ It was highly influential on other forms of theater.

    Ⓑ It would have been better had women been allowed to act.

    Ⓒ It excelled at tragedy but was inferior at comedy.

    Ⓓ It was improved by the actors' use of masks.

9 How does the professor organize the information about amphitheaters that she presents to the class?

    Ⓐ She shows some pictures and then describes them in detail.

    Ⓑ She explains the process by which they were constructed.

    Ⓒ She goes into detail on how the sites for them were chosen.

    Ⓓ She talks about a famous amphitheater and some performances held there.

10 Listen again to part of the lecture. Then answer the question.
What does the professor mean when she says this: 🎧

    Ⓐ The actors were not paid enough money then.

    Ⓑ The actors had more difficult roles than the chorus.

    Ⓒ The actors' abilities were rather impressive.

    Ⓓ The actors' roles were fairly uncomplicated.

11 Listen again to part of the lecture. Then answer the question.
What does the professor imply when she says this: 🎧

    Ⓐ All Greek dramatic performances had a hero that fought a villain.

    Ⓑ The role of the villain was the one desired by most actors.

    Ⓒ The two main characters were often not on stage at the same time.

    Ⓓ The lack of competent actors meant that some had to play dual roles.

CONTINUE   VOLUME

Listening Section Directions

03-09

This section measures your ability to understand conversations and lectures in English.

The listening section is divided into separately timed parts. In each part you will listen to 1 conversation and 1 or 2 lectures. You will hear each conversation or lecture only **one** time.

After each conversation or lecture, you will answer some questions about it. The questions typically ask about the main idea and supporting details. Some questions ask about a speaker's purpose or attitude. Answer the questions based on what is stated or implied by the speakers.

You may take notes while you listen. You may use your notes to help you answer the questions. Your notes will not be scored.

If you need to change the volume while you listen, click on **Volume** at the top of the screen.

For some questions, you will see this icon: 🎧 This means that you will hear, but not see, part of the question.

Some of the questions have special directions. These directions appear in a gray box on the screen.

Most questions are worth 1 point. If a question is worth more than 1 point, it will have special directions that indicate how many points you can receive.

A clock at the top of the screen will show you how much time is remaining. The clock will not count down while you are listening. The clock will count down only while you are answering the questions.

Set A

Listening Directions

03-10

In this part, you will listen to 1 conversation and 1 lecture.

You must answer each question. After you answer, click on **Next**. Then click on **OK** to confirm your answer and go on to the next question. After you click on **OK**, you cannot return to previous questions.

You may now begin this part of the Listening section. You will have **7 minutes** to answer the questions.

Click on **Continue** to go on.

03-11

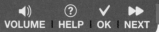

1   What are the speakers mainly discussing?

   Ⓐ The student's desire to transfer elsewhere

   Ⓑ The student's need to get involved in school activities

   Ⓒ The student's failure to adjust to school

   Ⓓ The student's poor performance in her classes

2   Why did the student ask to see the man?

   Ⓐ Her advisor recommended she speak with the man.

   Ⓑ She was told to go there by her roommate.

   Ⓒ Her classmates made the appointment for her.

   Ⓓ Her family members requested that she do so.

3   What does the student say about her hometown?

   Ⓐ She is from New York City.

   Ⓑ It is fairly small.

   Ⓒ She lives in a suburb.

   Ⓓ It has 25,000 people.

4   What will the student probably do next?

   Ⓐ Try out for the school's orchestra

   Ⓑ Check out the school's website

   Ⓒ Speak with the conductor of the orchestra

   Ⓓ Schedule another meeting with the counselor

5   Listen again to part of the conversation. Then answer the question.
   What is the purpose of the student's response?

   Ⓐ To thank the man for his compliment

   Ⓑ To acknowledge her skill on the violin

   Ⓒ To disregard what the man said

   Ⓓ To claim she has no current interest in music

03-12

6   What is the lecture mainly about?

  Ⓐ The similarities between Earth and Titan
  Ⓑ The recent unmanned missions to Titan
  Ⓒ The possibility of life existing on Titan
  Ⓓ The physical characteristics of Titan

7   According to the professor, why did astronomers once believe that Titan was larger than Ganymede?

  Ⓐ Scientists had not photographed the planet until recently.
  Ⓑ The methane clouds obscured the size of the moon.
  Ⓒ Ganymede appeared smaller than it is in reality.
  Ⓓ Titan's thick atmosphere gave it that appearance.

8   Why does the professor mention methane?

  Ⓐ To say that it is found in its liquid form in Titan's lakes
  Ⓑ To describe an integral component of Titan's atmosphere
  Ⓒ To compare the amounts of methane and ethane on Titan
  Ⓓ To state that Titan undergoes periodic methane showers

9   Based on the information in the lecture, do the following statements refer to facts or speculation about Titan?
    Click in the correct box for each sentence.

	Fact	Speculation
☐1 It is capable of supporting life.		
☐2 It has geographical features like those on the Earth.		
☐3 Most of its atmosphere is nitrogen.		
☐4 Methane oceans on the surface make its atmosphere so dense.		

10 Listen again to part of the lecture. Then answer the question.
    Why does the professor say this: 🎧

  Ⓐ To announce a discovery she recently made
  Ⓑ To confirm that she has no opinion on the matter
  Ⓒ To identify which theory she subscribes to
  Ⓓ To question the opinions of some astronomers

11 Listen again to part of the lecture. Then answer the question.
    What can be inferred about the student when he says this: 🎧

  Ⓐ He is surprised by the professor's comment.
  Ⓑ He would like the professor to continue her lecture.
  Ⓒ He is familiar with the *Cassini-Huygens* probes.
  Ⓓ He keeps up to date on astronomical matters.

Set B

Listening Directions

03-13

In this part, you will listen to 1 conversation and 2 lecture.

You must answer each question. After you answer, click on **Next**. Then click on **OK** to confirm your answer and go on to the next question. After you click on **OK**, you cannot return to previous questions.

You may now begin this part of the Listening section. You will have **10 minutes** to answer the questions.

Click on **Continue** to go on.

03-14

1   Why does the student visit the professor?

    Ⓐ To ask about a report she was recently assigned

    Ⓑ To talk about the upcoming final exam

    Ⓒ To discuss her performance in a class discussion

    Ⓓ To complain about a low grade she received

2   Why does the professor explain what the student wrote about cells?

    Ⓐ To justify the way he graded the student's exam

    Ⓑ To tell the student how wrong her answer was

    Ⓒ To show why the student needs to pay closer attention in class

    Ⓓ To say that she knows very little about cell reproduction

3   What does the professor imply about the student's recent performance?

    Ⓐ It was one of the worst performances in the class.

    Ⓑ It proved that she did not understand the material.

    Ⓒ It could have easily received a lower score.

    Ⓓ It cost her the chance to get an A in the class.

4   What can be inferred about the student?

    Ⓐ She is eager to do her extra assignment.

    Ⓑ She is unsatisfied with the professor's decision.

    Ⓒ She will study very hard in the future.

    Ⓓ She is not capable of doing well in the class.

5   Listen again to part of the conversation. Then answer the question.
    Why does the student say this: ∩

    Ⓐ She disagrees with the professor's decision.

    Ⓑ She is indicating that she has another idea.

    Ⓒ She has given up on convincing the professor of her opinion.

    Ⓓ She wants the professor to consider her first proposal.

03-15

Marine Biology

6   What is the lecture mainly about?

   Ⓐ Different types of plankton and their characteristics

   Ⓑ Plankton and their importance to the food chain

   Ⓒ The role of plankton in the global ecosystem

   Ⓓ Plankton and the animals that usually consume them

7   How does the professor organize the information about plankton that he presents to the class?

   Ⓐ By focusing on the benefits that plankton provides

   Ⓑ By explaining why plankton is considered a keystone species

   Ⓒ By lecturing on how plankton can create their own food

   Ⓓ By separately discussing two main types of plankton

8   What comparison does the professor make between phytoplankton and zooplankton?

   Ⓐ What temperatures each type prefers

   Ⓑ Where each type is usually found

   Ⓒ How large each type is

   Ⓓ How each type helps the ocean

9   How do zooplankton move?

   Ⓐ By using their feelers to swim

   Ⓑ By being carried by tides and currents

   Ⓒ By moving forward and backward

   Ⓓ By traveling upward and downward

10 What will the students probably do next?

   Ⓐ Think about a problem the professor suggested

   Ⓑ Submit their midterm papers to the professor

   Ⓒ Provide feedback to one another

   Ⓓ Ask the professor some questions about the lecture

11 Listen again to part of the lecture. Then answer the question.
    Why does the professor say this: 🎧

   Ⓐ To correct a mistake the student made

   Ⓑ To tell the student to come up with a better answer

   Ⓒ To advise the student to think again

   Ⓓ To confirm the student's information is right

03-16

12 Why does the professor explain the founding of Venice?

    Ⓐ To show how its founders felt defensive measures were crucial

    Ⓑ To compare the reasons for its location with that of Hong Kong

    Ⓒ To state his belief on what made it become such a great city

    Ⓓ To mention why Venice focused on becoming a naval power

13 According to the professor, what was the reason for the founding of Canberra?

    Ⓐ It was built to help defend the country.

    Ⓑ It was meant to establish some new trade routes.

    Ⓒ It was established due to political issues.

    Ⓓ It was founded to be alongside a railroad line.

14 How does the professor organize the information about the founding of cities that he presents to the class?

    Ⓐ He examines the process by which cities develop and then expand.

    Ⓑ He lists several factors and then covers them individually.

    Ⓒ He compares and contrasts some reasons why people found cities.

    Ⓓ He lists the reasons people found cities in order of their importance.

15 Based on the information in the lecture, were the following cities originally founded for defensive purposes or for trade?

Click in the correct box for each sentences.

	Defensive Purposes	Trade
1 Hong Kong		
2 London		
3 Quebec		
4 Chicago		

16 What will the professor probably do next?

    Ⓐ Show the class some charts on how cities develop

    Ⓑ Stop the class to take a short break

    Ⓒ Continue lecturing on a similar subject

    Ⓓ Request that the students submit their homework

17 Listen again to part of the lecture. Then answer the question.

What can be inferred about the professor when he says this: 🎧

    Ⓐ He believes the students should spend more time studying ancient cultures.

    Ⓑ He finds the layouts of the cities to be somewhat futuristic.

    Ⓒ He is impressed by the planning involved in making these cities.

    Ⓓ He regrets that he cannot cover this topic in more detail at the moment.

Listening Directions

03-17

In this part, you will listen to 1 conversation and 1 lecture.

You must answer each question. After you answer, click on **Next**. Then click on **OK** to confirm your answer and go on to the next question. After you click on **OK**, you cannot return to previous questions.

You may now begin this part of the Listening section. You will have **7 minutes** to answer the questions.

Click on **Continue** to go on.

03-18

1   Why does the student visit the newspaper office?

    Ⓐ To apply for a job as a reporter

    Ⓑ To ask about a recent submission

    Ⓒ To complain about an article that was printed

    Ⓓ To talk about life as a journalist

2   What does the editor say about opinion columnist positions?

    Ⓐ There are not any available right now.

    Ⓑ They are for reporters who get promoted.

    Ⓒ Many students have applied for them.

    Ⓓ They involve submitting two columns a week.

3   What is the editor's attitude toward the student?

    Ⓐ She acts nonchalantly toward him.

    Ⓑ She is critical of his work.

    Ⓒ She is pleased to speak with him.

    Ⓓ She acts nervously around him.

4   Listen again to part of the conversation. Then answer the question.
    What does the editor imply when she says this: 🎧

    Ⓐ She believes the student will make a good editor.

    Ⓑ She wants the student to write for the newspaper.

    Ⓒ She needs the student to rewrite his column first.

    Ⓓ She thinks the student has to improve his writing.

5   Listen again to part of the conversation. Then answer the question.
    What can be inferred from the editor's response to the student?

    Ⓐ She is bothered by what he has told her.

    Ⓑ He has made her a little angry.

    Ⓒ She is shocked by his comment.

    Ⓓ She believes the student is lying.

03-19

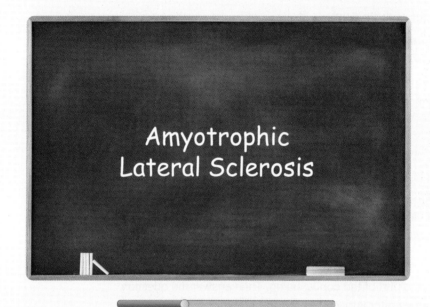

Amyotrophic
Lateral Sclerosis

6   What is the main topic of the lecture?

   Ⓐ How ALS affects the body

   Ⓑ How scientists are researching ALS

   Ⓒ How a cure for ALS will likely be found

   Ⓓ How ALS killed Lou Gehrig

7   What is the professor's attitude toward research on ALS?

   Ⓐ Fewer scientists should be investigating it.

   Ⓑ There is currently not enough funding for it.

   Ⓒ It is something that should be pursued.

   Ⓓ It will probably not lead to a major breakthrough.

8   How is the discussion organized?

   Ⓐ The professor encourages the students to get involved in the class.

   Ⓑ The professor presents the students with a number of facts.

   Ⓒ The professor asks questions and lets the students answer them.

   Ⓓ The professor goes over a handout that he gave to the students.

9   Based on the information in the lecture, do the following statements refer to aspects of ALS that are known or unknown?
   Click in the correct box for each sentence.

	Known	Unknown
1 Its causes		
2 Its types		
3 Its symptoms		
4 Its effects		

10 What can be inferred about Stephen Hawking?

   Ⓐ The care he received was extraordinary.

   Ⓑ He was unable even to blink his eyes.

   Ⓒ He was a supporter of research on ALS.

   Ⓓ He had a slowly progressive form of ALS.

11 Listen again to part of the lecture. Then answer the question.
   What is the purpose of the student's response?

   Ⓐ To prove that he has some knowledge of ALS

   Ⓑ To ask why some ALS patients live longer than others

   Ⓒ To dispute a point the professor just made

   Ⓓ To distinguish Lou Gehrig's occupation from Stephen Hawking's

MEMO

MEMO

MEMO

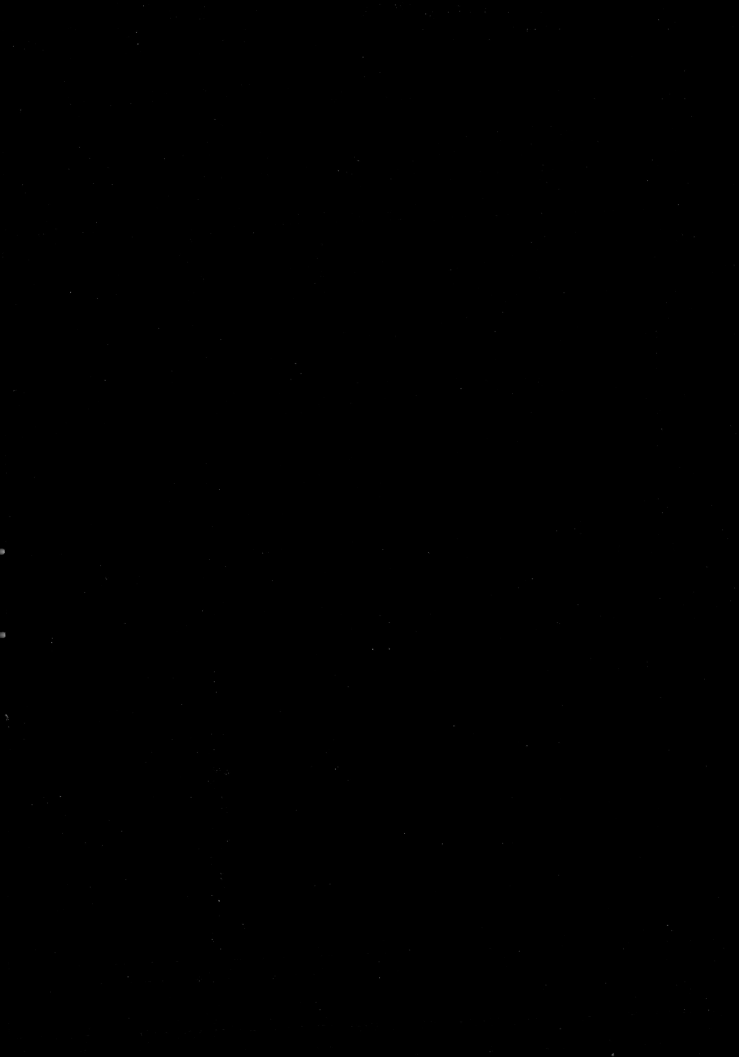

TOEFL MAP Listening

Advanced

New TOEFL® Edition

Answers, Explanations, and Scripts

DARAKWON

TOEFL® MAP Listening

New TOEFL® Edition

Advanced

Answers, Explanations, and Scripts

 DARAKWON

Part B
Building Background Knowledge of TOEFL Topics

Mastering Question Types with Lectures A1   p.32

| TYPES 1–4 |

TYPE 1 Ⓒ   TYPE 2 Ⓓ   TYPE 3 Ⓒ   TYPE 4 Ⓑ

Script 02-001

M Professor: Deserts are, by definition, places which get a bare minimum of water annually. Nevertheless, there are still animals that do not simply live there but which actually thrive in the desert. Can you believe that . . .? Now, we all know that life as we know it requires water . . . so . . . that leaves us with one very important question: How do these animals get the water that they need in order to, well, to survive? Allow me to enlighten you now.

Proving just how adaptable to their environment animals can be, there are actually numerous ways in which they survive in the desert without having easy access to water. The first method is one that's exemplified by an animal with which I'm sure you're all familiar: the camel. Yes, that's right . . . The camel. As you likely know, camels have either one or two humps on their backs. And, no, the humps aren't there to make it easier for people to ride on their backs. Instead, they store food and water in the form of fat for the camel. That enables camels to go an inordinate period of time . . . up to fifty days in some cases . . . without drinking any water. So please be sure to note that the humps store fat, not water. All right? Oh, the Gila monster is another animal that stores fat in its body to use as water. Of course, it doesn't have a hump. Instead, it stores fat in its tail.

⁴Additionally, you may have noticed that camels can move swiftly but, uh, only when the urge strikes them, which, admittedly, isn't often. This speed enables them to live in the desert as well since they're, uh, able to move quickly across the land from one water source to another. Remember . . . deserts do have water sources. We typically call them oases. However, they're few and far between, and only the swiftest of animals can travel back and forth between them without dying of thirst. That ability is something that lets other large mammals, like hyenas, jackals, and even ostriches, live in deserts. Yes, don't act so surprised . . . We commonly think of ostriches as living on the grasslands of Africa, but they are actually highly adaptable animals and have no problem living in the desert as well. And their speed is essential. Without it, they'd have trouble getting to water sources.

Now, here's another interesting way some animals get water in the desert . . . They make it in their own bodies. What do I mean . . .? The kangaroo rat, which lives in North American deserts, creates something called metabolic water. In other words, when its stomach is digesting food, it converts the food to water. Pretty neat, huh . . .? Kangaroo rats actually never have to drink water. If you offered one some, it simply wouldn't drink it. It doesn't need to. And they aren't unique animals either. Many desert animals get their water from their prey. This is particularly true of cold-blooded animals like snakes and lizards. Their bodies convert the prey they capture and eat into water, which enables them to survive.

TYPE 1   [Gist-Content Question]

The professor talks about several different ways in which animals manage to survive in the desert without water.

TYPE 2   [Detail Question]

The professor compares the two by stating that camels store fat in their humps while Gila monsters store fat in their tails.

TYPE 3   [Understanding Organization Question]

About the kangaroo rat, the professor states, "The kangaroo rat, which lives in North American deserts, creates something called metabolic water," and then he proceeds to explain how this happens.

TYPE 4   [Understanding Function Question]

When the professor notes that the urge to move swiftly does not often strike camels, he is indicating that camels do not usually like to run.

Summarizing ▶

The professor explains what deserts are and then asks how some animals can live there when water is so scarce. He states that animals adapt to the desert in many ways. He notes that some animals can go long periods of time without water. The camel is one such creature. He then says another adaptation is the animal's ability to move quickly from one oasis to another. Camels, hyenas, and ostriches can all do this. Finally, some animals, like kangaroo rats, create metabolic water. This means they never have to drink water since they make it from the food they eat.

| TYPES 5–8 |

TYPE 5 Ⓑ   TYPE 6 Ⓓ

TYPE 7 Biodiversity: ③   Water Purification: ②, ④
Preventing Flooding: ①   TYPE 8 Ⓑ

W Professor: Let's take a look at the next slide. Here we go . . . Now, who can tell me what this animal is called?

M Student: It's a beaver. We've got a mating pair that lives on some land on my family's farm.

W: Well done, James. And out of curiosity, what does your family think of the beavers?

M: That's a good question . . . They're always busy damming up the stream, which can be somewhat, er, annoying, but they also do a lot of good for us and the other animals that live around the farm. I don't mean the domestic animals; I'm referring to the, uh, the wild animals.

W: A perfect answer. As a matter of fact, beavers have something of an undeserved bad reputation. Part of it, of course, has to do with them being rodents. But many people find the beavers' habit of damming up streams and creeks to be incredibly bothersome. I'm here to tell you differently today . . . Beavers are actually a keystone species and are integral to their environment. That's why it's a shame so many of them have been hunted for their pelts.

Now, what exactly is a keystone species? Anyone . . .? Okay, I guess none of you has gotten that far in your reading yet. Okay, so what is a keystone species? Well, it's an animal crucial to the biosphere in which it lives. In other words, in one way or another, it alters or affects its biosphere so much that, without its presence, the environment would look very different and would negatively affect many animals. The elephant is one example of a keystone species. And the beaver is another. What does the beaver do? Well, it does three things . . . Let's see . . . First, it contributes to the biodiversity of its region. Next, it helps purify the water in the area in which it lives. And third, it helps prevent flooding.

Let's look at its effect on, uh, biodiversity. As James told us, beavers make dams. And they typically build their dams on creeks and streams in low-lying valleys. This contributes to the making of wetlands as the stream gets backed up, and this creates ponds or small lakes. Naturally, the presence of abundant water attracts animals. Mammals like deer, bears, and rabbits are attracted. Fish, naturally, thrive, especially since the waters are full of food sources. This, in turn, attracts turtles, frogs and other amphibians, and birds. In fact, many wetlands are so diverse in life that they're comparable to tropical rainforests. Now, as for purifying the water, well, again, beavers' dams are directly responsible. Here's a picture of one . . . Not bad, huh? First, the dams eventually collect several feet of silt, which keeps it out of the water supply downstream. In addition, many pesticides in the water get broken down while they're in the wetlands created by the beavers.

Finally, beavers' dams slow down the flow of water, so, during spring, when the snow is melting and heavy rains are often falling, the dams keep the water levels in streams and creeks down. This prevents flooding, which helps both animals as well as humans. Any questions so far?

TYPE 5 [Gist-Content Question]

The professor notes that beavers are keystone species and then describes how they can affect the environment in which they live.

TYPE 6 [Understanding Attitude Question]

The student states, "They're always busy damming up the stream, which can be somewhat, er, annoying, but they also do a lot of good for us and the other animals that live around the farm." So while he can find them annoying, he thinks they are generally beneficial.

TYPE 7 [Connecting Content Question]

According to the professor, beavers contribute to biodiversity by attracting new animals to the wetlands they create. They contribute to water purification when their dams keep silt out of the water and when pesticides in the water get broken down in the wetlands their dams have created. And they contribute to preventing flooding when their dams keep the water level low.

TYPE 8 [Making Inferences Question]

The professor states that a keystone species "alters or affects its biosphere so much that, without its presence, the environment would look very different and would negatively affect many animals." She therefore implies that keystone species are necessary to maintain the existing state of an ecosystem.

Summarizing ▶

The professor begins by showing a slide of an animal and asking the students to identify it. A student says it is a beaver and that beavers are somewhat helpful despite their damming up streams and creeks. The professor agrees and then calls beavers a keystone species. According to her, beavers greatly affect their environment in three ways. The dams create wetlands, so many animals live in them. This creates a great amount of biological diversity. The dams also help to purify the water that flows downstream. And the dams help prevent flooding in the spring when water levels begin to rise.

| TYPES 1-4 |

TYPE 1 (A)   TYPE 2 (A), (D)

TYPE 3 (A)   TYPE 4 (C)

Script 02-003

M Professor: I'd like to continue our talk on how various animals adapt to their environments. However, now we're departing the rainforests and moving on to much colder climes. In fact, we're going to examine an animal that lives in some of the coldest places on the planet. This animal survives in the Arctic Circle in the frozen wastelands of Russia, Canada, and Alaska. I'm talking about . . . reindeer.

First, let's talk about what they are. As their name implies, reindeer, commonly known as caribou, are members of the deer family. Both males and females have antlers, and females can grow to be almost 400 pounds while males can get up to, oh, about 650 pounds. Pretty impressive, isn't it? But . . . How do they get to be so big in such a harsh environment? **⁴Oh, and don't be mistaken . . .** Reindeer thrive in the cold. There are an estimated eight million reindeer on the Earth . . . Yes, that's right. Eight million. Of course, some are raised on farms, but many of them live in the wild.

How do they manage to survive? As you might guess, there are several factors involved. And they start from birth. Female reindeer typically give birth in either will be, uh, slightly warmer and that some of the snow will have melted. This means the babies will have an easier time adapting to the environment and won't immediately be subjected to harsh weather that could kill them soon after birth. The babies themselves are highly active after birth, constantly moving from place to place to feed. This movement helps keep them warm and thus lets them survive to adulthood.

As I mentioned a moment ago, reindeer weigh several hundred pounds. Well, much of that weight is taken up by, er, subcutaneous fat. What does this do . . .? A couple of things. First, naturally, it provides another layer of, uh, shall we say, insulation, for the reindeer, which, along with the reindeer's coarse hair, helps protect it from the cold. Additionally, in the lean winter months, the reindeer can convert the fat into nourishment, which enables them to remain alive when there's little food to be found. This subcutaneous fat is often what reindeer survive upon during the winter months. Naturally, they lose a tremendous amount of weight during winter and must begin extensive feeding in spring to build up their weight again.

Finally, reindeer's physical characteristics enable them to adapt to their environment. Here are just two examples. First, their hooves are actually quite adaptable. In summer, they soften so that it's easier for them to walk on the ground. However, in the winter months, their hooves get smaller and essentially harden so that plodding through the snow is easier. Many reindeer also have shorter legs than other members of the deer family. Having shorter legs means they have less body surface to be heated in the winter. This, in turn, lets them preserve some of that subcutaneous fat we just talked about.

TYPE 1 [Gist-Content Question]

During the lecture, the professor mostly talks about how reindeer manage to adapt to the frigid environment.

TYPE 2 [Detail Question]

According to the lecture, reindeer give birth in spring because "the babies will have an easier time adapting to the environment and won't immediately be subjected to harsh weather that could kill them soon after birth. The babies themselves are highly active after birth, constantly moving from place to place to feed. This movement helps keep them warm and thus lets them survive to adulthood."

TYPE 3 [Understanding Organization Question]

The professor begins the lecture by noting some of the reindeer's characteristics, and then he focuses on how they are able to survive in cold weather.

TYPE 4 [Understanding Function Question]

When the professor states, "Oh, and don't be mistaken," he is getting ready to make an important point about reindeer, which he does when he mentions that there are eight million reindeer on the Earth despite the fact that they live in very cold areas.

Summarizing ▶

The professor's lecture begins with him describing the physical characteristics of the reindeer and noting where they live. Afterward, the professor states that it must be difficult to survive in the harsh, cold environment, so he explains how reindeer adapt to the cold. They give birth in the spring, so their babies can slowly get used to the cold weather. They also regularly stay active to keep themselves warm. Their bodies have much subcutaneous fat, which they rely upon for heat and nourishment in the winter. Finally, their hooves and the length of their legs help them during cold weather.

| TYPES 5-8 |

TYPE 5 (D)   TYPE 6 (C)

TYPE 7 Inactive Vaccines: [2], [3]   Active Vaccines: [1], [4]

TYPE 8 (A)

W Professor: Okay, everyone, settle down. Break time's over . . . If there aren't any questions . . . okay, then I'd like to continue my lecture. I want to discuss vaccines now. In particular, I shall focus on what they do and the two major types of vaccines. Yes? Question?

M Student: I read in the paper about how some parents don't want to give their children vaccines because they, uh, they cause autism and can even give the person the virus. Is that true?

W: Well, there's no direct connection with autism as far as I know. However, it's possible, in some cases, for a person to catch a virus when given the vaccine. But let me get to that in a minute, okay, Tom?

M: Sure, Professor Carey.

W: Thanks. Okay . . . Now, what is a vaccine? Well, essentially, it's something that is composed of either a dead or weakened part of a virus and which is injected into a body and then provides that body—either human or animal—with immunity to the disease. Wow, that was a mouthful. Okay, let me go a little slower. Basically, a vaccine injects part of a virus into a body. Then, the body's immune system recognizes the virus as harmful and tries to kill it. What the body does is create antibodies for that particular virus. These antibodies learn how to attack the virus, so, in the future, if the virus tries to . . . uh, shall we say, invade the body, the antibodies will kill it, thereby, uh, keeping the body safe and sound. Thus, the body has immunity to that particular virus.

There are two major types of vaccines. They are inactive and active vaccines. Let me describe inactive vaccines first. These vaccines use a dead part of the virus. It has been killed either by chemicals or the application of heat. This makes inactive vaccines safe simply because there's no way the virus injected in the body can, um, infect it. However, there's a drawback to this particular type of vaccine. Does anyone know what it is . . .? No . . .? Okay, well, because the virus in the vaccine is dead, the body's immune system responds to it rather, er, weakly. This means the antibodies created in the body are only good for a temporary period. This could be a couple of years, or it could be up to ten or eleven years. That's why, if you travel internationally, you have to get cholera or plague vaccinations every decade or so.

Active vaccines, on the other hand, use viruses that have been weakened in their virulence. They're still alive, yet they aren't powerful. These, as you may have guessed, require just one boost—one shot, that is—for the patient's entire life because the body responds to these vaccines quite aggressively. However, as Tom indicated, sometimes patients given active vaccines catch the virus itself and aren't immunized to it. That's unfortunate, but it does happen . . . a

very small percentage of the time, mind you, so by no means should they be banned like some people have proposed. Measles and mumps are two viruses that have active vaccinations . . . Now, let me talk about a third type of vaccine that's sometimes used.

TYPE 5 [Gist-Content Question]

The professor mostly talks about what vaccines do and the different types of vaccines that exist.

TYPE 6 [Understanding Attitude Question]

When talking about live vaccines, the professor states, "By no means should they be banned like some people have proposed." This indicates that she believes live vaccines are useful.

TYPE 7 [Connecting Content Question]

According to the lecture, inactive vaccines need to be given to a person every few years, and the virus in them has been killed. As for active vaccines, the virus in them has been weakened, and a person taking one of them may actually get the virus that he or she is being vaccinated against.

TYPE 8 [Making Inferences Question]

At the end of her lecture, the professor states, "Now, let me talk about a third type of vaccine that's sometimes used."

Summarizing ▶

The professor tells the students she wants to talk about vaccines. A student asks about vaccines causing autism, but the professor states she believes that does not happen. Then, she explains how vaccines give the body immunity from certain viruses. She also mentions that there are two types of vaccines: inactive and active ones. Inactive vaccines use dead virus material but must be renewed every few years. Active vaccines use live virus material, so a body only needs to be boosted once. However, active vaccines may sometimes not work properly and might give the person the virus instead of preventing it.

Mastering Question Types with Conversations A3

p.36

| TYPES 1–4 |

TYPE 1 (D) **TYPE 2** (C) **TYPE 3** (C) **TYPE 4** (A)

Script 02-005

M Student: Excuse me, but are you, um, the person I should speak with about dormitory rooms?

W Housing Office Employee: Possibly . . . Why don't

you tell me what you're here for, and then I can let you know if you're in the right place?

M: Sure. I'm here to, uh, change rooms.

W: Well, you can speak to me about that, but I don't think it's going to do you any good.

M: Huh? What do you mean?

W: You need a clear reason why you want to move. That's what I mean. You just can't move because you want to.

M: Oh, I wasn't aware of that.

W: By any chance, are you a new student here?

M: Yeah, I just transferred here this semester. But I'm a junior.

W: Ah . . . that would explain why you don't know. Here, I've got a brochure that explains some of the housing rules . . . Why don't you take this and read through it?

M: Uh, okay. Thanks. But I really need to change rooms.

W: ⁴How come?

M: Well, I'm in a single room, and . . .

W: You want to move out of a single? Most students want to move into those. **What's up with that?**

M: To be honest, the room is too expensive for me to pay for. I can't afford it . . . I'm already working two part-time jobs as it is, and my parents haven't been able to send me any more money ever since my dad's business started going badly. My tenure here is in jeopardy if I can't move somewhere cheaper.

W: Hmm . . . In that case, you might actually qualify for a move.

M: Really? That would be great! I'd love to move into a double . . . or even a triple . . . if it would help me save just a few dollars.

W: Here, fill out this application form, and I'll see . . . uh, I'll see what I can do for you. Sit down over there to do it, and give it back to me when you're done. I think I'll be able to arrange something for you.

TYPE 1 [Gist-Purpose Question]

The student says, "I'm here to, uh, change rooms."

TYPE 2 [Detail Question]

The woman wants the student to fill out the form so that she can then try to help him get another room.

TYPE 3 [Understanding Organization Question]

The student mentions, "My parents haven't been able to send me any more money ever since my dad's business started going badly," so he is explaining why he does not have enough money to pay for his current room.

TYPE 4 [Understanding Function Question]

When the woman asks, "What's up with that?" she is trying to understand why the student wants to move out of a single.

Summarizing ▶

A student visits the university's housing office to inquire about changing dormitory rooms. The housing employee says that he needs a clear reason for wanting to move, or the school will not permit it. The student responds that he is in a single room but cannot afford it, so he would like to move into a double or triple room. The employee is surprised by his response but indicates that she can probably accommodate his request. She gives the student a form to fill out to request a room change.

| TYPES 5–8 |

TYPE 5 Ⓑ   TYPE 6 Ⓒ   TYPE 7 Ⓐ   TYPE 8 Ⓓ

Script 02-006

M Professor: Good morning, Wanda. I didn't realize you were waiting outside my office. Come on in and have a seat, please . . . So, uh, what can I do for you this morning?

W Student: Good morning, Professor Barkley. Actually, I just arrived a minute ago, so it's no big deal.

M: That's a relief. I would have hated for you to waste your time standing around.

W: So, um, I want to speak about our class project. You know, uh, the one you mentioned on the first day of class.

M: The class project? Well, it's not due until the last week of the semester, and we just started school this week. I don't think I've ever had someone speak with me about it this early.

W: Normally I wouldn't, but my idea might require a lot of time, so that's why I'm here now.

M: I'm intrigued. Okay. Tell me what you're thinking of doing, please.

W: I'd like to do my project on grafting.

M: Ah . . . It's definitely a good thing you came here now then.

W: That's what I thought.

M: Do you have any particular plants in mind?

W: I'm planning to graft some branches onto plumeria trees.

M: Hmm . . . Are you aware that plumerias grow in the tropics? We got snow the other day, so I'm not sure they'll do well here.

W: Oh, don't worry about that. I have an apartment off campus, and I have a few plumerias in pots. I put them close to windows so they get plenty of sunlight, but they don't get exposed to cold air.

M: That sounds like it would work. Have you grafted any plants before?

W: No, I haven't, but I've read about it. Supposedly, it's not too hard to graft branches onto plumerias, but it can take a couple of months to find out if the graft is effective and if the tree accepts the new branch. So I thought I would get your approval first and then get started.

M: Yes, yes, you have my approval. I think it's a wonderful topic. You're my first student to ask about doing grafting for the botany class project, so I'm looking forward to seeing the results.

W: Wonderful. Thank you so much, sir. I'll keep detailed notes and take pictures so that I can chronicle how the process goes.

TYPE 5 [Gist-Content Question]

The student and the professor are mostly discussing a class assignment that the student must complete.

TYPE 6 [Detail Question]

The professor tells the student, "Are you aware that plumerias grow in the tropics?"

TYPE 7 [Understanding Attitude Question]

The professor remarks, "Yes, yes, you have my approval. I think it's a wonderful topic. You're my first student to ask about doing grafting for the botany class project, so I'm looking forward to seeing the results."

TYPE 8 [Making Inferences Question]

The professor first states, "The class project? Well, it's not due until the last week of the semester, and we just started school this week. I don't think I've ever had someone speak with me about it this early." The student responds by saying, "Normally I wouldn't, but my idea might require a lot of time, so that's why I'm here now." So it can be inferred that the student does not like to delay work she must do.

Summarizing ▶

The professor invites the student to come in to his office and apologizes for making her wait outside. The student responds that she wants to discuss the class project. The professor is surprised because it is the first week of class, and the project is due the last week of the semester. The student says she wants to graft plumerias, so it might take a long time. The professor mentions that they are tropical plants, but the student grows them in pots indoors. The professor supports the student's idea and says that he is interested in seeing the results.

Mastering Topics with Lectures B1 p.38

1 (B) 2 (D) 3 (A)

Script & Graphic Organizer 02-007

M Professor: Amber is a glassy-looking fossil of plant resin that formed millions of years ago. Although people often see amber as a gemstone, it is not . . . I repeat, not . . . a stone. Amber formed from plant resin, a liquid-like substance found in the leafy parts of plants, usually trees. The resin was secreted and then hardened. Over time, it fossilized and became amber. Fossil resin consists mainly of hydrogen and carbon atoms that make hexagonal rings. Bonds occur between the rings, which make the fossil amber, uh, hard. Amber has been sought and traded since ancient times and is commonly used in jewelry.

W Student: Where is amber usually found, sir?

M: It's found in a wide number of areas, but the most valuable amber comes from the Dominican Republic and the Baltic coastal regions of Lithuania and Russia, most notably the Kaliningrad area. In fact, for whatever, uh, reason, almost . . . um, 90% of the world's best amber is found near Kaliningrad.

Now, amber's unique nature has made it important for the study of prehistoric life forms. Occasionally, in the far past, when the amber was still in a gel-like state, an insect or other life form got stuck on it and died. When the amber hardened and fossilized, the animals were trapped inside the amber. Please note that many other things, including plants and pieces of wood, got trapped as well. Objects trapped in amber are called amber inclusions.

W: Isn't that how they made dinosaurs in the movie *Jurassic Park*? I mean . . . uh, from blood found in mosquitoes in amber.

M: ³Well, that movie may have taken a few liberties with the science involved. Let me see . . . Okay, yes, mosquitoes did exist millions of years ago and may have sucked the blood of dinosaurs, **but actually to use this blood and its DNA to create cloned dinosaurs is rather, uh . . . shall we say . . . farfetched.** The idea does, however, come from real tests done by real scientists. In 1992, a team of American scientists initially believed they had extracted DNA from a weevil found in some amber 125 million years old. Unfortunately, subsequent tests done by others concluded that they didn't actually extract DNA . . . Instead, they got mutations of DNA. In many cases, inside the amber, there's no extant part of the ancient insect or object. Instead, there's merely a hollowed-out mold left by whatever was, well, once there. Of course, many completely intact insects and plant matter have been found in amber. From these trapped objects, we can discover many things about ancient life.

Most creatures discovered in amber aren't exactly like those alive today. Therefore, these preserved animals can show how modern creatures have developed or evolved. The most commonly found animals encased in amber are mosquitoes, ants, bees, spiders, and lizards. Most trapped animals are very small and must be examined with microscopes. That should give you an idea as to how small some insects once were.

Here's something interesting for you . . . In 2006, an American scientist discovered an ancient species of bee inside a piece of amber from Myanmar. The bee is only three millimeters long and shares some features with modern bees. The scientist believed it was 100 million years old and may have had the ability to spread pollen. This may explain why a rapid expansion of flower-like plants occurred during that time. Remember . . . we studied that in last week's lecture? I hope that you all were paying attention at that time . . . Anyway, pollen attached itself to the legs of ancient bees, and as they flew around, it then dropped off and helped spread plants to other regions.

Amber Fossils

Fossilization Process:	Modern-Day Uses:
Forms from plant resin	Can study fossilized insects, life forms, plants, and wood
Is secreted by plants	Can learn about ancient life
Traps insects or other life forms	Can be used as jewelry
Hardens over time	

1 [Gist-Content Question]

During the lecture, the professor mainly discusses various life forms that were trapped in amber.

2 [Understanding Organization Question]

When the professor brings up bees, he says, "Remember . . . we studied that in last week's lecture? I hope that you all were paying attention at that time . . . Anyway, pollen attached itself to the legs of ancient bees, and as they flew around, it then dropped off and helped spread plants to other regions." He is thus explaining the basis of a theory that he had previously spoken about.

3 [Understanding Attitude Question]

When the professor says that the notion of creating cloned dinosaurs from blood and DNA is "farfetched," he means that this DNA cannot be used to clone dinosaurs.

The professor describes amber's characteristics and notes how it forms and that people use it as jewelry. He then mentions where it is commonly found and states that it is important to the study of prehistoric animals. A student asks about cloning dinosaurs from the blood of animals in amber, but the professor claims that is impossible. He mentions that DNA has been extracted from some amber-encased animals though. The professor claims much can be learned about past and present animals by examining creatures in amber, and he states how studying a bee in amber might explain something that happened 100 million years ago.

Mastering Topics with Lectures B2   p.39

1 Ⓑ   2 Myth: 1, 2, 3 Asia: 4   3 Ⓐ

Script & Graphic Organizer 02-008

W Professor: Let's move on to the only true mammal that can fly: the bat. These nocturnal creatures have been mentioned in folklore and myths for many centuries. There are more than 1,000 types of bats, which represent almost a quarter of all mammal species. They range in size from very large . . . with a wingspan greater than six feet . . . to very small with some as tiny as an inch long. Bats live in almost every climate on the Earth, excluding, naturally, the poles and extreme desert conditions. Their diets vary by species. Most—almost three-quarters of them in fact—eat insects regularly. Others, like the flying fox bat, eat fruit. And some bats merely suck the nectar of various fruits. There are a few bats that eat small animals and fish.

M Student: Aren't there some bats that suck blood like vampires?

W: Um . . . you do realize vampires are legendary creatures, right? Anyway . . . yes, there are the so-called vampire bats that live in South America. These bats drink the blood of large mammals, typically cattle and horses, at night. They use their teeth to make a small cut in the animal, and then they, well, well they lick its blood. But they don't suck it. Although there are some documented cases of them attacking people, these are rare. Most bats are nocturnal, meaning they are more active at night than during the daytime. Many of the myths surrounding vampires and their supposed connections to bats developed from their nighttime activity.

Bats' lifespans vary from species to species, and the longest recorded lifespan for one is thirty years. That's quite a long time in case you're curious. They typically live in dark places, such as, um, caves, trees, and buildings. ³Some bats prefer to live alone while others form colonies consisting of thousands of members.

The largest bat colony ever discovered was in a cave in Texas, where it is estimated that up to twenty million bats may have been living. **Yes, that number's correct by the way. That's a lot of bats.** In temperate climates where the winters are long, some bat species migrate to warmer areas while others go into hibernation.

What else do you need to know . . .? Okay, most bats have their babies, called pups, in the spring. Some have a gestation period of forty days whereas others' gestation periods can last for up to six months. As a general rule, the bigger the bat, the longer the gestation period. They usually have a litter of only one baby at a time although two is possible. The babies are small and pink and must typically be cared for until about a month before they mature. Male bats usually take, uh, no part in raising young bats. The young bat pups are about a quarter the size of their mother, and the mothers group together to raise them in maternity colonies. The pups suckle milk from their mothers, like all other mammals do.

Finally, bats are well known for having an ability that is similar to radar. They have poor eyesight in darkness, which is, you know, surprising considering they're nocturnal. Instead of eyesight, they depend on echoes from their high-pitched screeching to judge where objects are, what their size is, and whether they are moving or not. Bats use a very highly refined sense of hearing to do these things. The other unique thing about bats is that they can, well, fly. Bats have no feathers. Their wings are, in reality, their hands. The five fingers of a bat's hand-like appendage are covered in a thin membrane of skin, which gives them the power of flight.

The Characteristics of Bats

General Information:	Life Spans:
Only mammals that can fly	Can live up to thirty years
Are more than 1,000 species	
Live almost everywhere	Pups:
Have various diets	Females raise their young and suckle them
	Special Ability:
	Use something like radar to see

1   [Understanding Organization Question]

Throughout the lecture, the professor focuses on the various physical characteristics of bats.

2   [Connection Content Question]

According to the lecture, it is a myth that bats suck the blood of their victims. As for facts, bats have poor eyesight, tend to live in large groups, and have sometimes attacked people.

3   [Making Inferences Question]

When the professor says, "Yes, that number's correct by the way," she is implying that she thinks some students might not believe that what she just said is true.

Summarizing ▶

The professor mentions that there are many myths and folktales about bats. She then notes where they live and some bat species' eating habits. In response to a question about bats sucking blood, the professor claims that some bats lick blood but that they do not suck the blood of animals. This is where their connection to vampires in mythology occurs. The lecture then continues by noting how bats raise their young. The professor concludes by commenting that bats have poor eyesight, so they use a kind of radar in order to guide their flight and to find various objects.

Mastering Topics with Lectures B3   p.40

1 Ⓐ   2 Ⓒ   3 United States: ①, ③, ④ Asia: ②

Script & Graphic Organizer 02-009

M Professor: Have you ever heard a high-pitched whine outside when it's really hot . . .? That's the sound of the cicada. There are over 2,500 species of them. Most live in Asia and Australia. They're found in tropical and warmer temperate climates. I'd like to direct your attention to the screen now . . . where I'll show you some photos of adult cicadas. As you can see . . . here . . . their wings are typically longer than their bodies, and their eyes are set wide apart. Most cicadas are fewer than five centimeters long, but some can be as long as fifteen centimeters.

The unusual noise that people associate with cicadas is made by the males. They have two drum-like membranes on their thorax that can vibrate to produce the high-pitched sound. Take a look at this slide here . . . Each species makes a different sound, many of which have been recorded and analyzed. Experts believe that the noise is used to attract females and that the males of each species have a special sound they use only for females. Typically, a male begins his mating song at the hottest time of the day. This song has another use though . . . The noise can also scare away predators like birds. Some studies have proved that the cicada's noise confuses birds and disrupts their ability to communicate and to hunt in groups.

Cicadas' life cycles vary depending on the species, but they all have some things in common. After mating, the female finds a tree or plant and makes a space in its twigs or leaves. Then, she deposits her eggs in the space. When the eggs hatch, the emerging nymphs fall to the ground. The nymphs, uh, burrow deep into the ground and remain there for many years. Most cicadas stay underground from two to five years before emerging. While underground, they survive on the juices of plant roots, which enable them to grow. They even shed their outer skin as they get bigger while under the ground. Finally, they emerge and crawl up a tree or plant. That's when they shed their last layer of nymph skin and then become full-grown adult cicadas. Their lives are now quite short . . . only a couple of weeks or a month at most . . . and they must mate during this time.

In the United States, there are several types of cicadas, but two are more common than the others. The first is sometimes called the dog-day cicada since it emerges in the heat of late summer in, uh, around July and August. The other is the one that seems to fascinate people the most because of its unusually long lifecycle. The Magicicada species lives in the eastern United States. There are, um, two distinct subspecies, one living in northern states and the other in southern states. The northern cicadas remain underground for seventeen years while the southern ones stay below for thirteen years. There are different colonies of cicadas throughout the country, and they're all on different time schedules. Experts and amateur cicada enthusiasts call these different colonies "broods." They've tracked many broods so precisely that they can accurately estimate when they'll next emerge from underground.

What's unique to the Magicicada species is that the adults emerge at the same time after being underground for however many years. This is actually atypical of cicadas. Most colonies see some, yet not all, cicadas emerging at the same time. Most experts believe they emerge in such large numbers to ensure their survival in the face of predators. With such extensive periods between emergences, birds should fail to develop an instinctive awareness of when they will emerge. After all, birds might instinctively increase their populations if a Magicicada pattern were deduced, thereby greatly reducing the size of some broods.

Cicadas and Their Life Cycles

General Information:	Life Cycles:	Dog-Day Cicada:
2,500 species	Live underground for several years	Dog-day cicada emerges in summer in U.S.
Live in tropical and warm climates	Then come aboveground to mate	
Are often fewer than 5cm long		Magicicada:
		Magicicada has two groups in the U.S.
		One stays under for 17 years and the other for 13

1 [Gist-Content Question]

The majority of the lecture is spent describing the lifestyles of different cicadas.

2 [Detail Question]

The professor states, "While underground, they survive on the juices of plant roots, which enable them to grow."

3 [Connecting Content Question]

According to the lecture, cicadas in the United States have longer-than-average life cycles, belong to the Magicicada family, and emerge from underground at times known to people. As for cicadas in Asia, they often live in tropical climates.

Summarizing ▶

The professor comments on the number of cicada species and where on the Earth they primarily live. He describes how cicadas make their distinct noise and notes that it is believed to be a mating song. He describes some common characteristics of cicadas, particularly the fact that they live underground for several years. He then mentions the two most prevalent species in America and explains what makes one of them, the Magicicada, so unique. According to the professor, the Magicicada spends a long period of time underground and then emerges in enormous numbers.

Mastering Topics with Lectures B4 p.41

Script & Graphic Organizer 02-010

M Professor: One of the more fascinating things about spiders is the webs they spin. Most spiders have this ability. A spider web is a form of silk produced from a spider's glands. Scientists have discovered six . . . uh, no. I misspoke. I mean seven . . . yes, seven different types of web glands, but a spider doesn't have all seven types. Most have anywhere from four to six web glands as well as external spinnerets that shoot the silk. The silk spiders produce is remarkable in many aspects. First of all, it's quite strong and, for its size, is stronger than steel. Second, most spiders can spin two types of silk: sticky and non-sticky silk. Both are used to make webs. The non-sticky parts are what the spider crawls along while the sticky parts are those that catch prey.

The web's main purpose is to catch prey, usually insects. Using webs to obtain food is both good and bad for the spider. By using a web, the spider saves energy since it doesn't have to chase its prey. On the contrary, prey often comes to the spider. However, creating a web requires a lot of energy, specifically protein, and spiders can run out of silk if they don't feed and drink water. Therefore, a spider takes a chance by spinning an intricate web to catch prey. If successful and an insect is captured, the spider can replenish its protein and silk supplies. If the web fails or is damaged, then the spider has expended an enormous amount of energy for, well, no gain. Spiders often eat their webs if they cannot catch any prey. Why . . .? Well, in this way, they can regain some lost protein.

The orb web, which is flat in the vertical plane and typically has a rounded shape, is the most common type of web. A spider begins its web with an anchor line. This is typically a horizontal strand of silk anchored between two fixed points—like a tree or leaf branches, walls, or virtually anything that's available. This first strand, or anchor line, is doubled and sometimes tripled, thereby giving it extra strength. The spider then drops from the middle of the first fixed strand and attaches a vertical strand, pulling down the top horizontal strand until a Y shape is formed. From this Y-shaped frame, the spider builds its web, making both sticky and non-sticky sections. The spider typically moves along the non-sticky parts. While most spiders don't get stuck on their webs, this sometimes happens, which ensnares the spiders themselves.

Once the web is complete, the spider waits for prey. Some wait on the side, remain hidden, and keep parts of their bodies on the web. This lets them feel the vibrations of a struggling insect that has gotten caught on the web. Other spiders stay in the center of the web. Spiders sometimes even decorate their webs. These decorations can be formed from silk, the remains of dead insects, or other matter, like twigs or small pieces of plants. No one has yet ascertained the exact purpose of these decorations. One theory is that they're used to make the web more visible to birds and other large creatures that could accidentally destroy the web. Another theory is that they make the spider—particularly those that lie in the center of the web—appear bigger than they really are. This could possibly scare off large predators.

W Student: But wouldn't that also scare away potential prey?

M: Yes, that's possible and would seem to defeat the purpose of the web. As I've stated, no one knows what the decorations are for.

Spider Webs

How It Makes Its Web:	How It Uses Its Web:
Uses silk from its body	Captures prey like insects with the sticky part of the web
Makes sticky and non-sticky parts	
Requires much energy to spin its web	Unique Feature of Some Webs:
	May have decorations made from insects, silk, or twigs

1 [Detail Question]

The professor says that the decorations "can be formed from silk, the remains of dead insects, or other matter, like twigs or small pieces of plants."

2 [Understanding Attitude Question]

Concerning spider webs, the professor mentions, "One of the more fascinating things about spiders is the webs they spin," which indicates that he finds spider webs to be interesting.

3 [Understanding Organization Question]

About orb webs, the professor notes, "The orb web, which is flat in the vertical plane and typically has a rounded shape, is the most common type of web."

Summarizing ▶

The professor begins by describing spider silk and saying that there are seven types, yet no one spider can spin all seven. He notes the strength of spider silk and the fact that it can be a sticky or non-sticky web. He mentions how spiders use webs to catch prey, which they must do since spinning a web expends much energy. He describes orb webs and the process by which spiders weave sticky and non-sticky webs to create them. He then mentions how spiders decorate their webs in different ways but comments that no one knows exactly why they do so.

Mastering Topics with Conversations B5 p.42

1 (B)   2 (A)   3 (A)

Script & Graphic Organizer 02-011

W Student: Pardon me, but is your name Ryan Walker?

M Student Center Employee: Yes, I'm Ryan. Can I, uh, can I help you with something?

W: My name's Kate Burgess, and I was told to speak with you about getting a job at the student center. My friend Anne Parkins works here as a cashier, and she told me you're looking for employees.

M: [3]Anne recommended you? She's one of my best

workers.

W: I'll be sure to tell her you said that.

M: Be my guest . . . Anyway, yes, we are looking to hire some more students . . . In fact, I've got some openings I'd love to, uh, fill . . . First, I need someone to work behind the counter taking orders from students. What do you think?

W: That sounds great. I did some similar work in my hometown during summer vacation.

M: That's promising. Then I wouldn't have to train you too much. Let me see . . . The job calls for you to work the morning shift on Monday, Tuesday, and Friday, and then . . . What's the matter? You're not a morning person?

W: No, no, it's, uh . . . it's not that. I actually get up before six most days. It's just . . . well, I have class on both Tuesday and Friday morning.

M: Hmm, that won't work then.

W: Do you have any other jobs available? I could really use a job.

M: Hmm . . . I need a floor manager. Basically, you'd be responsible for making sure the tables are cleared off, there are no spilled drinks on the floor . . . that kind of thing.

W: Those were some of my responsibilities at my summer job. I just hope these hours fit my schedule. When are the shifts?

M: Right now . . . Um, the only slots available are Monday afternoon and . . . oh, no . . . Friday morning. I know you can't do Friday . . . What about Monday?

W: I've got a three-hour seminar then. And there's no way I can change it to another time since Monday is the only day it's being offered.

M: It looks like I'm not going to be able to help you. Sorry . . . You seem like a nice young lady.

W: Do you have any suggestions? What do you think that I ought to do?

M: Try the coffee shop on the third floor.

W: What's up there?

M: I know it's hiring. Maybe something there will fit your schedule. I'll call Mary there and let her know you're coming. And I'll put in a good word for you as well.

W: Thanks. I appreciate that.

Service Encounter

Problem:	Solution:
Student: Is looking for a part-time job at the student center	*Employer: Needs someone to work the morning shift and to work as a floor manager*

---

1 [Gist-Purpose Question]

The student tells the employee, "I was told to speak with you about getting a job at the student center."

2 [Understanding Function Question]

The man mentions the coffee shop because he knows they are hiring, and he thinks that the student should apply for a job there.

3 [Understanding Attitude Question]

When the man says, "Be my guest," he is giving his consent to what the woman says she is going to do.

Summarizing ▶

A woman goes to the student center to apply for a job. The employee mentions that he is currently hiring and tells the student about a job and its hours. The student can do the job, but the hours do not match her schedule. Then, the employee describes another job that is currently available, but the woman's schedule again is not a good match for the job. The employee then recommends that the woman go to the coffee shop and apply for a job there. He says that he will put in a good word for her with the manager.

Mastering Topics with Conversations B6   p.43

1   **2**   **3**

Script & Graphic Organizer 02-012

W1 Student: Professor Jenkins, do you have a minute? I'd really like to chat if you aren't doing anything right now.

W2 Professor: Sure, Lisa. Come on in and have a seat . . . You said in class you wanted to talk to me about something . . . So, uh, what's up?

W1: Um, you see, it's, uh, it's about the seminar you're teaching this semester.

W2: Ah, yes . . . You've signed up for it, haven't you?

W1: Well, yes, I have, but there's kind of a problem . . .

W2: Oh? What is it?

W1: You know I'm majoring in both French and Economics, right? My Economics advisor, Professor Giovanni, arranged an internship for me, and, well, uh, unfortunately . . . it happens to be at the exact same time as your seminar class.

W2: Well, that's a shame. I was looking forward to having you in my class again this semester.

W1: Yeah, and I was looking forward to taking it. But the problem is that I really need to take that seminar to graduate next semester. Or . . . wait a minute . . . You remember that class I took last year when I was in the study abroad program in Paris, don't you? Could I count that class as my seminar in lieu of taking yours?

W2: [3]No . . . I don't think that would work. That class and mine cover completely different topics, so it wouldn't be right to let you count it as a graduation credit. You'll have to come up with something else.

W1: Hmm . . . Is there any way I could take the class online?

W2: Excuse me? What do you mean?

W1: Well . . . you know, um, since you, uh, post the class notes on the website, what if I just read the notes instead of attending class but, er, still write the papers and take the tests? Yeah . . . that would work . . . wouldn't it?

W2: Unfortunately, no. Remember, a crucial aspect of seminars is the discussions that go on in them. I'll only lecture for half the class. The rest will be discussions involving the students.

W1: Oh, I see.

W2: And those discussions will be a big part of your grade, too.

W1: Okay . . . I understand. It wouldn't be fair to the other students in that case.

W2: Sorry, Lisa . . . I'd love to help you out, but I can't.

W1: What do you think I should do?

W2: Why don't you try to reschedule your internship for another time? Then you could take my class and get your internship done . . . Try looking into that.

W1: Okay. I'll find Professor Giovanni and see what he thinks.

Office Hours

Problem:	Solution:
Student: Has a conflict with professor's seminar and internship she is doing	Professor: Insists that student has to attend seminar since discussions are important

1 [Gist-Purpose Question]

The student goes to speak with the professor to try to solve her school and internship conflict by coming up with a special arrangement for the class she is taking with the professor.

2 [Detail Question]

The student says that her internship "happens to be at the exact same time as your seminar class." Then, she notes, "The problem is that I really need to take that seminar to graduate next semester."

3 [Understanding Function Question]

When the professor asks the student what she means, it can be inferred that the professor has never considered the solution that the student has just mentioned.

Summarizing ▶

A student visits a professor to talk about a seminar. The student says she has an internship at the same time as the seminar, but she really wants to take the class. Then, she suggests that she not attend the class but do all the work for the class. The professor disagrees. The student wonders if a class she took abroad could substitute for the seminar, but the professor claims the two classes are different. The professor suggests that the student change the time of the internship, and the student agrees to speak with her professor about doing that.

TOEFL Practice Tests C1

p.44

1 Ⓓ   2 Ⓐ   3 Simple Metamorphosis: ③, ④
Complex Metamorphosis: ①, ②   4 Ⓒ   5 Ⓑ
6 Ⓒ

Script 02-013

M1 Professor: Now, if there aren't any more questions . . . why don't we move on to metamorphosis, which is the process by which some living beings change from an immature stage to become mature adults? This process is most often seen in insects . . . yet may also happen with some amphibians, shellfish, and, uh, crustaceans. Today, however, we're only going to concentrate on the process as it applies to insect life. We'll discuss metamorphosis in other animals in our next class. Okay? With insects, there are two ways metamorphosis occurs . . . The first is simple metamorphosis—sometimes called incomplete metamorphosis—in which the insect undergoes some changes from its immature form to its mature form. However, there aren't too many, uh, shall we say, drastic differences in the insects in these stages. The second is a more complex form of metamorphosis. Here, the insect in its mature stage may bear no resemblance whatsoever to itself when it was in its immature stage.

First, let me talk about, um, simple metamorphosis. This has a scientific name which you should know . . . It's hemimetabolism. Spell it like it sounds . . . There are three stages in simple metamorphosis: the egg, the nymph, and the adult. Excuse me . . . Now, the egg is just what it sounds like. It's, uh, an egg from which the insect hatches. Upon doing so, it goes straight to the nymph stage. The nymph closely resembles the adult in appearance, but it lacks size and sometimes, um, certain other, er, features. For example . . . with grasshoppers, nymphs don't have wings and can't fly like adult grasshoppers can. With frogs and toads, in their nymph stage, they're called tadpoles and aren't amphibious yet. They live in the water and are unable to venture onto the land. Only when they advance to the adult stage are they able to depart from their aquatic homes.

[6]The change from the immature nymph stage to the adult stage in simple metamorphosis is gradual, and there's nothing dramatic to distinguish immature insects from mature ones. There is, however, something that we call, um . . . molting, which occurs with some insects. **You already ought to be familiar with this term.** The insects shed a layer of outer skin or covering as they grow in size. Then, the outer layer grows hard again, only to be shed anew once the insect gets bigger. After each stage of molting, the insect is called an instar . . . That's I-N-S-T-A-R . . . As the insect molts and each instar appears, there are obvious changes, such as, er, an increased number of body segments and the possible addition of wings.

M2 Student: What about complex metamorphosis?

M1: Yes, I was just about to cover that. In more complex metamorphosis, there are some, let's say . . . dramatic changes that take place. Thus, there are very distinct stages of development. The most common example, of course, is the caterpillar, which changes into the butterfly. Complex metamorphosis also has a scientific name . . . holometabolism . . . Insects that make use of complex metamorphosis typically go through four stages.

Here they are . . . First are eggs, then larva, next pupa, and finally adults. The caterpillar is a larva. [5]It constantly consumes plant leaves to grow to the size necessary for it to continue to the pupa stage. It doesn't mate, lay eggs, or do anything but eat. That must be nice, huh? **I'm sure some of you might find that an appealing lifestyle.** Anyway, the pupa stage is also called the chrysalis stage. Once the caterpillar is large enough, it seeks a place to anchor itself for the pupa stage. This is typically the underside of a leaf. Once anchored, the caterpillar is covered with a hardened outer shell and becomes dormant. Some species can move if they sense a predator nearby, but most are immobile until the adult emerges. Inside the shell, however, dramatic changes are taking place. For example, the ugly little caterpillar is changing into a beautiful butterfly. Finally, when the pupa stage ends, the insect splits the hard shell of its cocoon and emerges as a fully . . . a fully grown adult.

All these actions are controlled by hormones in the insects. Additionally, the time for each stage of an insect's life cycle varies from species to species. Some butterflies have short pupa stages—as short as a few weeks—while others remain in the pupa stage for months. This is especially true for species in temperate climates with colder winters. Almost all insects that undergo complex metamorphosis cannot reproduce until they reach the adult stage, and they don't grow any larger upon reaching this stage. Most experts consider metamorphosis a successful strategy for insect survival. As larvae or nymphs, they can exploit certain food resources. After becoming adults, flying insects can move to new areas to take advantage of different food sources. Now, let's look at some slides so that I can show you the differences between the various stages.

1 [Gist-Content Question]

The professor talks about both simple and complex metamorphosis throughout the lecture.

2 [Detail Question]

A caterpillar is a butterfly in its larva stage.

3 [Connecting Content Question]

According to the lecture, simple metamorphosis involves a slow change from the nymph to the adult change, and some insects molt and change while they are instars. As for complex metamorphosis, it involves four different stages, and the result is that the insects look very different when they reach their adult stage.

4 [Understanding Organization Question]

During the lecture, the professor describes the two types of metamorphosis, and he also gives examples of some insects that go through each type of metamorphosis.

5 [Understanding Function Question]

The professor is making a joke when he says, "I'm sure some of you might find that an appealing lifestyle."

6 [Understanding Attitude Question]

When the professor says, "You already ought to be familiar with this term," it can be inferred that he assumes his students understand what he is talking about.

TOEFL Practice Tests C2 p.46

1 (B)   2 (B)   3 (A)   4 (A)   5 (B)   6 (D)

Script 02-014

W Professor: The deepest parts of the ocean lie more than 35,000 feet beneath the surface. That's deeper than Mount Everest is high by over a mile. At such depths, you'd expect there to be no life, wouldn't you . . .? In such extreme cold, dark, and pressure, how, after all, can anything exist . . .? [6]**Yet, phenomenally, life does exist in the ocean depths.** Scientists on explorations to these deep areas were astonished to find life down there. Of course, it's not abundant, and it lives an extremely precarious existence, yet life can still be found at the greatest ocean depths.

The ocean depths are categorized in several ways. Some terms refer to the depth of the ocean and the amount of light it receives while other terms refer to the temperature. The deepest parts of the ocean are the abyssal zone, which starts around 4,000 meters below the surface, and the hadal zone, which is only found in deep ocean floor trenches and can go as deep as . . . as 10,000 meters. As for temperature, the most important term to remember is thermocline. This is the depth where, as the ocean gets even deeper, the temperatures suddenly record tremendous decreases. Most of the ocean's heat is in the top 200 meters, where sunlight filters through the water. The thermocline can change with different conditions and climates, but it's generally in the one- to two-hundred-meter depth range.

For the longest time, no one believed there could be life in waters deeper than a few thousand meters and certainly not in the abyssal or hadal zones. Almost all life needs both a source of oxygen and food. How do life forms at the bottom of the oceans get both . . .? First, oxygen in the water comes from photosynthesis that occurs in microscopic plants on the water's surface. The oxygen then filters down through the water. When it reaches the hadal zone, the deepest part of the ocean, it may already be centuries old. As for food, plant matter cannot grow on the ocean floors since there's no light. Instead, life on the ocean floor lives off of what is called marine snow. These are food particles that slowly fall to the ocean depths from the upper layers of the ocean. Among these particles are the remains of dead fish.

The second issue concerning how life survives is the freezing cold temperatures and the crushing pressure down below. At the bottom of the ocean, the water temperature hovers around, oh, zero to three degrees Celsius, which is about, uh . . . uh, thirty-five degrees Fahrenheit. The pressure there is over a thousand times greater than the pressure on the surface and can crush almost anything like a hammer smashing an egg. One of the main reasons why life can survive in such conditions is that it has adapted. How, you may ask . . .? Well, certain fish have adapted their internal organs to adjust to the great pressure so that they aren't crushed by the extreme pressure. Most fish use air and internal gases to remain buoyant. The fish of the deep use liquids of a biological nature to counteract the pressure. They are also more gelatinous and don't have rigid skeletal structures that could collapse under the pressure. Interestingly, if these fish are brought to the surface, the extreme change in pressure, uh, well, it often kills them instantly.

Another reason life exists at such depths is the existence of thermal vents in the ocean floor. These are places, typically near areas of volcanic activity, where heated water shoots out from cracks in the floor. These thermal vents heat the ocean water, and life forms, er, form around them. Species of shrimp, clams, and tubeworms have all been spotted near thermal vents at extreme depths. Organisms at the lower end of the food chain consume various bacteria that come from the vents, and then higher-order creatures consume them and so on, establishing a complex micro-ecosystem on the ocean floor. Many animals actually thrive in the super-heated water; thus, little colonies of life exist around the thermal vents.

Other life forms have adapted in different ways to the ocean depths. Most have larger-than-normal eyes, and some can even emit light. The anglerfish, for example, has a long protrusion on its head that emits a glowing light. This attracts prey, so the anglerfish then attacks and consumes the curious fish. Other fish have developed feelers, which can reach out and feel for prey. As for mating, some deep-sea fish have developed chemical signatures that allow them to find a mate in the inky darkness. One strange custom is that used by male anglerfish. When he finds a female, he, er, locks on to her with his lips and never lets go. Thus, they literally mate for life. The male subsequently absorbs nutrients from her body as they travel in tandem. What an interesting way to live, don't you think?

1   [Gist-Content Question]

During the lecture, the professor primarily describes some of the creatures that live deep in the ocean.

2   [Gist-Purpose Question]

After mentioning marine snow, the professor states that it is "food particles that slowly fall to the ocean depths from the upper layers of the ocean. Among these particles are the remains of dead fish." This explains how creatures living deep in the ocean get food.

3   [Connecting Content Question]

The professor notes how far down in the water both zones reach.

4   [Understanding Organization Question]

When the professor mentions thermal vents, she then describes how the parts of the ocean near them have their own mini-ecosystems that are thriving with life.

5   [Making Inferences Question]

When talking about the anglerfish, the professor states, "One strange custom is that used by male anglerfish. When he finds a female, he, er, locks on to her with his lips and never lets go. Thus, they literally mate for life."

6   [Understanding Attitude Question]

The professor's use of the word "phenomenally" means that she finds it surprising that anything can live at the bottom of the ocean.

TOEFL Practice Tests C3

p.48

1 Ⓓ   2 Ⓒ   3 Ⓓ   4 Ⓒ   5 Ⓑ

Script 02-015

M Student: Professor Thagard, I've got something, um, I really need to chat with you about.

W Professor: Sure. What can I do for you, uh . . .

M: David. David Reynolds . . . I'm in your History 202 class.

W: Ah, yes . . . Mr. Reynolds. You always sit in the front row, right? I'm generally awful with names, but I never forget a face.

M: Yes, ma'am. Thanks for noticing.

W: Okay . . . so what's so urgent that you need to talk to me about? Is it about next week's term paper?

M: Uh, no. That paper is going quite well . . . As a matter of fact, I'm almost finished . . . However, I have a question about something else. It's about this Friday's test. You know, the one on Britain in the sixteenth and seventeenth centuries.

W: I hope you've been studying hard for it. It's never an easy one.

M: ⁵Oh, I've been studying for it day and night, but there's something of a problem . . . I went to the, uh, library to check out that book on Sir Francis Bacon you put on reserve.

W: Ah, yes, good thinking. **You'll need to know all about him for the test if you know what I mean.**

M: Er, uh, yes. Well . . . um, the book's not there . . . And neither are the pictures of Bacon you put on reserve.

W: What do you mean . . . "It's not there"?

M: That's exactly what I mean . . . It's not in the library. The woman at the reserve desk couldn't find the material. She wasn't, er, particularly useful either, to put it diplomatically. Actually, she barely even looked for any of the things I asked for, and then she just told me to talk to you.

W: Well, I'll have to go have a chat with her then.

M: Okay, then, um, what I was wondering was, uh, if it would be all right if you, uh, you know, delayed the test for a week or so?

W: Why would I do that?

M: Er . . . I get the impression that there are going to be a lot of questions about Bacon on the test, but if the reserve book is missing, there's no way we can learn as much about him as we should.

W: Well, I must admit that you make a compelling argument . . .

M: Thank you, Professor Thagard. I knew that you'd see things my way if I just got a chance to speak with you.

W: But I'm sorry to say that I must disagree with you . . . You see, while that book is important and Bacon himself is most assuredly important, the library has a plethora of books on Bacon in its holdings.

M: Pardon me? I don't get what you're trying to say.

W: Mr. Reynolds . . . try checking out another book on Bacon. Remember that my class isn't a seminar, so you don't need to know everything about Bacon's life. Any number of books in the library's collection will tell you everything you need to know about him for this test.

M: Ah, yes, I think I understand now.

W: Good . . . Now why don't we both go to the library? You can check out a book on Bacon—I'll give you the titles of some good ones on the way there—and I'm going to chat with the librarian . . . Oh, and the test is still on for Friday.

M: Yes, ma'am. Thanks a lot.

1 [Gist-Purpose Question]

After the student explains the problem, he asks, "What I was wondering was, uh, if it would be all right if you, uh, you know, delayed the test for a week or so?"

2 [Detail Question]

When the professor asks the student if he wants to talk about his term paper, he responds that he does not and that he has actually almost finished writing it.

3 [Understanding Attitude Question]

When talking about the librarian, the student comments, "She wasn't, er, particularly useful either, to put it diplomatically," which shows that he feels the librarian was not helpful.

4 [Detail Question]

The professor says that there are many books available on Sir Francis Bacon, so she turns his request down because he can get the necessary information about Bacon from some other sources.

5 [Understanding Attitude Question]

When the professor states, "If you know what I mean," she is hinting to the student that the test will have some questions about Sir Francis Bacon.

1	C	2	A	3	D	4	C	5	D
6	B	7	D	8	B	9	A	10	A
11	B	12	H	13	I	14	A	15	C
16	J	17	G	18	E	19	D	20	F

Chapter **02** | Life Sciences 2 · Conversations

Mastering Question Types with Lectures A1   p.52

| TYPES 1–4 |

TYPE **1**   B   TYPE **2**   A   TYPE **3**   B   TYPE **4**   D

Script **02-016**

W Professor: When animals belonging to different species interact, it almost always involves food. Why? Well, think about it. Every animal needs food to ensure its survival. These food interactions can occur in several ways. They can, um . . . let's see . . . they can involve two species competing for the same food supply. They could also involve one species trying to eat another while the other tries to, er, avoid getting eaten. We call that the predator-prey relationship. Most interactions between animals are brief in nature, yet there are many cases where two species actually live together for long periods of time. When this occurs, it's called symbiosis. ⁴Do any of you know anything about symbiotic relationships . . .? Yes?

M Student: I believe that's when both species benefit from the relationship.

W: Hmm . . . **You're close but not quite on target.** To be a little more accurate, in symbiotic relationships, at least one member of the pair must benefit from the relationship. What you just defined is a special condition of symbiosis called mutualism. We'll get to that in just a second, and then I'll explain how symbiosis and mutualism differ.

Now, let's return, uh, to symbiosis. There are several types of symbiotic relationships. Let me give you a couple. One of the members in the relationship could be injured or harmed by the other. This is known as parasitism. Or, both species could be relatively unaffected by the relationship, which is called commensalism. Finally, both members could gain some kind of a, uh, a benefit from the relationship. That's mutualism, which I just mentioned. Okay, now let's talk about each of them in slightly more detail. First, let's examine parasitic relationships. In these, a parasite

typically lives in its host for a brief period of time before moving on to somewhere else. Now, when it moves, the reason could be because it killed the host, but that's not always the case. Of course, when parasites don't kill their hosts, they tend to cause some kind of a chronic infection in it. Not good, huh? Any number of bacteria and viruses establish parasitic relationships with humans and animals.

As for commensalism, it's best defined by an example. I'm sure you've all heard of the remora, right . . .? Uh, no? Okay, well, you know there are certain fish that can attach themselves to sharks then, don't you . . .? Right. I see heads nodding now. Well, that's a remora. It attaches itself to a shark, and then, when the shark feeds, it eats the leftovers. Meanwhile, it doesn't harm the shark, which therefore leaves the remora alone.

Now, the third and final example of symbiosis is mutualism. As I stated, in this relationship, both species somehow benefit. Many plants and fungi have these kinds of relationships. What else . . .? Hmm . . . In the ocean, there are many examples. Here's one. There's an animal called the cleaner fish. That's what it does: It cleans. To do so, it enters the mouth and gills of large carnivorous species and cleans them by eating the bits of food stuck in the mouth and gills. The carnivores recognize what the fish is doing, so they don't make a snack out of the cleaner fish. That's not exactly a job I'd want to have, but it does wind up benefitting both species in a classic example of mutualism.

TYPE **1**   [Gist-Content Question]

Throughout the lecture, the professor describes the various types of symbiotic relationships that organisms can have with one another.

TYPE **2**   [Detail Question]

According to the professor, in mutualism, "Both species somehow benefit."

TYPE **3**   [Understanding Organization Question]

During her lecture, the professor explains what symbiosis is, and then she describes some of the forms in which it can occur in nature.

TYPE **4**   [Understanding Function Question]

When the professor says that the student is "not quite on target," she is telling the student that his answer is incorrect, but she is being polite about it.

Summarizing ▶

The professor mentions that species sometimes interact with each other, most usually because of food. She says that these interactions are known as symbiotic relationships. She describes three different types of relationships. The first is a parasitic relationship, which involves the parasite causing damage to—or even killing—the host. These relationships often involve to bacteria or viruses. Commensalism is a relationship where both species are fairly unaffected by the relationship. The professor says that sharks and remoras have this kind of relationship. And mutualism occurs when both species gain from the relationship. The cleaner fish and large carnivorous fish have this relationship.

| TYPES 5–8 |

TYPE 5 ⓓ   TYPE 6 ⓑ

TYPE 7 Innate Immune System: ②, ③ Adaptive Immune System: ①, ④   TYPE 8 ⓒ

Script 02-017

W Professor: When the human body is attacked by microbes such as viruses and bacteria, the body's immune system fights to prevent serious infection and illness. The immune system is comprised of various organs and cells, some of which we're born with and others which we acquire as we become older. The ones we're born with are called the innate immune system, and the ones that develop as we age are called the adaptive immune system.

The innate immune system consists of natural barriers to infection that everyone is born with. These include, uh, the skin and the mucus membranes that lie inside the nose, the lungs, and the digestive system. These initial barriers are capable of stopping many harmful microbes from entering sensitive areas in the body. Sometimes, however, microbes get past these barriers and enter the body. For example, if you cut your skin, microbes can enter the cut and cause an infection. Additionally, colds and flu viruses can enter the nose, the throat, and the lungs to infect your body. That's when the second part of the innate system takes action.

Special cells called white blood cells are the primary component of the second level of the innate immune system. White blood cells are also known as lymphocytes or leukocytes. They're mainly made in bone marrow and constantly move through the body through the lymphatic system. This system consists of tubelike vessels connected to small structures known as lymph nodes. Lymph nodes trap microbes to prevent the body from becoming ill. As they do this job, white blood cells race through the body in search of infections. Then, they trap microbes and destroy these harmful organisms. You should also know that white blood cells flow along a river of colorless fluid called lymph, which goes to every part of the body.

As we grow and get exposed to various microbes, the body recognizes them from previous encounters, knows they are dangerous, and attacks them at once. This is the adaptive immune system. The body recognizes past infections and creates measures to defeat them by creating antibodies, which are special cells, proteins, and chemicals that attack intruders. The main problem is that each antibody created is only useful for a specific microbe. So when a new and, um, unknown microbe enters the body, the body may require time to develop a defense against it. We've seen this happen many times in history. You know, uh, a new infection arises, and many people die before their bodies can develop effective responses.

M Student: Are white blood cells and antibodies only formed in the bone marrow?

W: No, not only there. Special white blood cells and antibodies can be formed in the spleen. Additionally, the thymus, another organ which is located in the chest just in front of the heart, is crucial to developing special white blood cells that we call T cells. T cells start their lives in bone marrow but must travel to the thymus to become fully grown and mature. Once that happens, they begin searching for infections. Just so you know, T cells are like the, uh, the superheroes of the immune system since they go to war with the most dangerous infections and even attack cancer cells. So you definitely want a healthy supply of T cells in your body. Here, uh, let me show you a short video of how T cells operate. I think you'll find it interesting.

TYPE 5 [Gist-Purpose Question]

The professor describes the role of the innate immune system in keeping the body healthy.

TYPE 6 [Understanding Attitude Question]

During her lecture, the professor tells the students, "Just so you know, T cells are like the, uh, the superheroes of the immune system since they go to war with the most dangerous infections and even attack cancer cells. So you definitely want a healthy supply of T cells in your body." She clearly believes that T cells are of great importance to the body's immune system.

TYPE 7 [Connecting Content Question]

According to the professor, the innate immune system includes the skin and the mucus membranes and is what the body is born with. As for the adaptive immune system, it develops as the body ages over time and has parts formed in the spleen and the thymus.

TYPE 8 [Making Inferences Question]

At the end of the lecture, the professor says, "Here, uh, let me show you a short video of how T cells operate. I think you'll find it interesting." She will therefore probably continue covering the immune system with the students.

The professor remarks that there are two parts of the body's immune system. The first is the innate immune system, which is what people are born with. It includes skin and mucus membranes that keep harmful microbes out of the body. The second part of it includes special cells such as white blood cells. They work with lymph nodes to trap microbes and to destroy them. The adaptive immune system develops as the body grows. It forms when the body recognizes past infections and makes antibodies to fight them. It also includes T cells, which fight dangerous infections and even attack cancer cells.

Mastering Question Types with Lectures A2   p.54

| TYPES 1–4 |

| TYPE 1 | B | | TYPE 2 | A , B |
| TYPE 3 | C | | TYPE 4 | C |

Script 02-018

W Professor: It sure looks like we've got lots of sleepyheads here this morning. I guess you didn't drop by the campus center for some coffee before class like I did. Or perhaps you did, but you went for some decaffeinated brew instead. Personally, I don't see the point of drinking coffee with no caffeine, but some people enjoy it . . . I guess. Anyway, what I'd like to cover now is how caffeine is actually extracted from coffee beans.

There are . . . and you may be surprised to hear this . . . several processes that can be used, and all of them have been, er, let's say . . . tinkered with and refined over the years. First, let me stress that the decaffeination process is rather, uh, delicate, since coffee contains almost 400 different substances . . . yeah, all in one little bean . . . so removing the caffeine without affecting anything else in the bean can be somewhat difficult. 4Overall, there are two primary methods of decaffeination: direct decaffeination, which utilizes chemicals, and indirect decaffeination, which uses w-w-w-water. **Whoa, looks like I had a little too much caffeine this morning.**

The most common chemicals used in direct decaffeination are methylene chloride and ethyl acetate. The beans are steamed and then washed with one of those chemicals for, oh, about ten minutes or so, to remove the caffeine. And, uh, that's it. Simple, huh? As for indirect decaffeination, it also uses chemicals in part of the process, but they aren't applied directly to the beans, hence the name indirect decaffeination. Here's what happens: The beans are soaked in water, and then the coffee-flavored water has the caffeine in it removed by the same chemicals utilized in the direct method. After several repetitions of this process, the beans have

no more caffeine in them, yet they retain all of their other properties.

While these two are the most common processes, there are many other methods that will also do the trick. For example, there's one method that uses carbon dioxide in a high-pressure environment to remove the caffeine. Another, called the Roselius method, was actually one of the first caffeine-extraction methods used. However, because it employs the chemical benzene, it was later banned due to possible health issues.

Now, I want to go back to the first point I made . . . Why would anyone want to, you know, drink decaffeinated coffee? After all, most people enjoy coffee because it's a stimulant. So it can help them wake up in the morning, concentrate better, and be more energetic throughout the day. Well, some people, unfortunately, have adverse reactions to coffee. Their bodies simply can't handle the caffeine. For instance, they may start shaking, speak very rapidly, get heart palpitations or upset stomachs, or suffer from other side effects.

You might think that these people should just avoid coffee or anything caffeinated. But there are two reasons why they might not wish to do so. First, they enjoy the taste and smell of coffee. Second, drinking coffee, as I'm sure most of you well know, is a very social activity. It's been that way for centuries. So drinking decaffeinated coffee lets people enjoy the benefits of coffee without suffering any ill effects.

TYPE 1   [Gist-Content Question]

Throughout her lecture, the professor describes several ways in which coffee can be decaffeinated.

TYPE 2   [Detail Question]

Concerning direct decaffeination, the professor states, "The beans are steamed and then washed with one of those chemicals for, oh, about ten minutes or so, to remove the caffeine."

TYPE 3   [Understanding Organization Question]

When the professor mentions the Roselius method, she is simply telling the students another way that coffee beans can be decaffeinated.

TYPE 4   [Understanding Function Question]

When the professor stutters and then makes a comment about having had too much caffeine in the morning, she is making a joke about how she just stumbled over her words.

Summarizing ▶

The professor comments that the students look sleepy because they probably did not have any coffee in the morning as she did. She then mentions that not all coffee has caffeine since some is decaffeinated. She notes there are two decaffeination processes: direct and indirect. Direct decaffeination involves steaming the beans and washing them with chemicals. Indirect decaffeination involves repeatedly soaking the beans in water to remove the caffeine. She then discusses some other methods of decaffeination and also explains that drinking coffee is a very social event for many people, which is one reason why coffee is so popular.

| TYPES 5–8 |

TYPE 5 (D)   TYPE 6 (C)   TYPE 7 (A)   TYPE 8 (B)

Script 02-019

W Professor: Have any of you ever heard of the Rafflesia flower? No hands? Okay, that's not too surprising, but after today's lecture, you'll be able to answer that question in the affirmative. The Rafflesia is a parasitic plant found only in Southeast Asia, specifically on the islands of Sumatra, Java, and Malaysia, where the climate is always warm and humid, which is exactly the kind of weather the Rafflesia needs. There are also only . . . um . . . sixteen known species of this plant.

This rare flower is visible only when it's ready to reproduce. Before that, it appears as a tiny bud on the outside of the Tetrastigma vine, to which it has attached itself . . . remember that it's a parasite . . . and that's how it obtains nourishment and survives. Since it has no roots, leaves, or stems and contains no chlorophyll, which would let it perform photosynthesis and nourish itself, it must attach itself to the outside of the vine's roots or stem in order to survive. It takes anywhere from nine months to one year for the bud to bloom and to develop into something that resembles a, er, a cabbage.

When it blooms, it can produce a flower that's three feet across and weighs up to fifteen pounds . . . Yes, fifteen pounds. Imagine that. Now, here's why the Rafflesia is so famous. While it's in bloom, the flower has a repulsive odor similar to that of rotting meat. Gross, huh? But there's a reason for this . . . The odor attracts flies, beetles, and other insects, which pollinate the plant. If it didn't smell so bad, it wouldn't, uh, attract any pollinators; therefore, over time, it evolved to reek like that. And pollinating the flower is crucial since it only blooms for less than a week. After that, its five or six petals blacken, and the flower withers. Yes, Samuel. Question?

M Student: Why is it considered a flower if it smells so bad? I thought flowers all smelled nice. The shape and size sound weird, too. From your description, I'd never consider the Rafflesia a flower.

W: That's a good question, but you're making a common misconception. There's nothing that requires flowers to smell nice or to have a certain shape or size. Look at the definition of "flower" in your books on page fourteen . . . You should have read this as part of your homework. ⁸It simply reads that it's a plant, right? No characteristics are identified. **Please remember, everyone, that nature is full of many things we consider strange or weird, as Samuel puts it, and the Rafflesia is one of the many I intend to teach you about.**

Now, let's continue . . . The Rafflesia rarely gets pollinated. As I just stated, one reason is that it blooms for a short period of time. It also lacks a specific flowering season. Finally, while the plants are unisex, in general, plants of the same sex grow near one another while plants of the other sex grow somewhere far away. And female Rafflesia flowers are quite rare. So for pollination to occur, an insect or other organism must visit the flowers of both sexes. Now you should be starting to understand why it's such a rare flower.

TYPE 5 [Gist-Content Question]

The professor mostly discusses the characteristics of the Rafflesia that make it unique.

TYPE 6 [Understanding Attitude Question]

When telling the student that the Rafflesia really is a flower, the professor states, "Look at the definition of 'flower' in your books on page fourteen . . . You should have read this as part of your homework." Since the student was not aware that the Rafflesia is a flower, it can be inferred that he did not do his homework assignment.

TYPE 7 [Connecting Content Question]

When the student indicates that he does not believe the Rafflesia is a flower, it can be inferred that not everyone considers it to be a flower.

TYPE 8 [Making Inferences Question]

When the professor talks about nature being full of strange things and then says, "The Rafflesia is one of the many I intend to teach you about," she is implying that the students will learn about more strange or weird organisms in her class.

Summarizing ▶

The professor says the Rafflesia is a rare flower found in the jungles of Southeast Asia. It is a parasite, so it grows on a vine, from which it gets its nourishment. Its bloom is a fifteen-pound three-foot-wide flower that smells awful. It has the odor of rotting meat. The reason is that it relies upon flies to pollinate it, so the rotten odor attracts them. When a student argues that the Rafflesia is not a flower, she explains why it is. She then states that it is rare because the flowers seldom get pollinated since the male and female Rafflesia often live far from one another.

Mastering Question Types with Conversations A3

p.56

| TYPES 1–4 |

TYPE 1 ⒸC   TYPE 2 ⒷB   TYPE 3 ⒸC   TYPE 4 ⒷB

Script 02-020

M Student: Professor Watkins, I know you're not having office hours right now, but I'd really like to speak with you. It's, uh, quite urgent.

W Professor: Oh, don't be so dramatic, Mark. Come in, and tell me what's up.

M: Phew. Thanks a lot, Professor.

W: Okay, so . . . what's going on with your paper?

M: H-H-How did you know that's what I wanted to talk about?

W: ⁴I wasn't born yesterday, Mark. Let's see . . . It's due in three days, and I've already had five other students here this morning to talk about it. **It doesn't take a genius to figure out that's what you're here for, too.**

M: Oh . . . Right. Okay, yeah. That's what I need to speak about.

W: Go on.

M: Well, I decided to write my report on Winston Churchill. So, uh, I looked up some information about him on the Internet . . . but, uh, there's just so much.

W: That shouldn't be too surprising. He was, after all, one of the most influential people of the twentieth century. You could spend your whole life reading books about him and never get through them all.

M: Oh . . . I, um, hadn't realized that.

W: Okay, so what do you want to write about him?

M: Well, I'd been planning to write about his life, but there's, uh, there's just too much stuff.

W: Okay. Stop. You're going about this wrongly.

M: Er . . . What exactly do you mean, ma'am?

W: I mean that you need to limit the scope of your paper. Choose one aspect of his life, and write about that one thing. And don't just give me a bio. Interpret the events in his life. Tell me what they mean to you.

M: Okay. That clears things up. I hadn't considered that. I guess I'd better get back to the library and start doing some research now.

W: Great. I look forward to reading your paper.

TYPE 1 [Gist-Purpose Question]

The student visits the professor to get some help in determining about what he should write his paper.

TYPE 2 [Detail Question]

The professor tells the student, "I mean that you need to limit the scope of your paper. Choose one aspect of his life, and write about that one thing."

TYPE 3 [Understanding Organization Question]

The student brings up Winston Churchill to tell the professor that it is Churchill about whom he plans to write his paper.

TYPE 4 [Understanding Function Question]

When the professor makes her comment about the student, she means that it is apparent to her why the student has come to her office.

Summarizing ▶

The student wants to talk to the professor about what he says is something important, but she already knows what he wants to discuss. She tells him that several other students have been in that day to discuss their paper as well. The student wants to write about Winston Churchill, but he has too much information on Churchill. The professor tells the student to narrow the scope of his paper. She wants him to choose one part of Churchill's life and then to interpret those events. That should be all that he writes his paper on.

| TYPES 5–8 |

TYPE 5 ⒶA   TYPE 6 ⒷB   TYPE 7 ⒹD   TYPE 8 ⒹD

Script 02-021

M Student: Er, hello. My name is Peter Saks. I was told by my resident assistant that I needed to report to you.

W Housing Office Employee: Ah, yes, Mr. Saks. Why don't you sit down, please?

M: Sure. Um, is everything all right?

W: I'm afraid not. You see, Mr. Saks, your RA reported that there's some damaged furniture in your room caused by you. Let me see . . . According to this, one of your chairs was broken . . . And there are some holes in the wall of your room. What do you have to say about that?

M: Well . . .

W: What on earth have you been doing in that room?

M: Actually, I've got to be honest with you . . . I didn't do it.

W: Then who, may I ask, is the responsible party?

M: My roommate, ma'am.

W: Are you sure? That's a pretty big accusation to be throwing out. According to your RA, you were responsible.

M: No, no. That's not true. Glen—my RA—he's a good guy, but he has no clue what happened.

W: Then how about filling me in on the details, please?

M: Well, I-I-I was out for the entire evening when it happened. I stayed at my uncle's house two nights ago. When I went to my room yesterday, it was a mess. My roommate . . . Eric Shaw . . . He, uh, he must have done something while I was gone.

W: Okay, I'll need to speak with Mr. Shaw. Your RA never mentioned him in the report.

M: That's strange. I don't know why he didn't. But I have an alibi. I can get you my uncle's contact information. And I'm sure the security cameras have pictures of me leaving the building and returning the next day.

W: ⁷Okay, but if Mr. Shaw doesn't confess to causing the damage, you're still going to be partially responsible for paying for everything.

M: How is that possible?

W: Well. . . Those are the rules, Mr. Saks. And let me remind you that you agreed to them upon signing your contract and deciding to live in the dormitory. But I'll do my best to get to the bottom of this mystery.

TYPE 5 [Gist-Content Question]

The student and the employee are mostly discussing how the student's dormitory room suffered some damage.

TYPE 6 [Detail Question]

Eric Shaw is the student's roommate.

TYPE 7 [Understanding Attitude Question]

When the student asks, "How is that possible?" in response to the woman's comment that he still might be partially responsible for paying for the damage to the room, he is implying that he believes he should not have to pay for the damage since he did not cause it.

TYPE 8 [Making Inferences Question]

When the employee promises, "But I'll do my best to get to the bottom of this mystery," it can be inferred that she is going to continue trying to determine exactly what happened.

Summarizing ▶

The student visits the housing office to speak with the female employee. She tells him that according to his resident assistant, there is a large amount of damage in his room. She wants to know how the damage occurred. The student mentions that he did nothing wrong. Instead, it was his roommate. He also notes that he was visiting his uncle's house when the damage was done and that the security cameras should be able to verify that he was not in the dorm. The woman says that the student may still have to pay for some of the damages, but she vows to continue investigating.

Mastering Topics with Lectures B1   p.58

1 Ⓑ   2 Ⓐ   3 Male Bowerbird: ②, ③   Female Bowerbird: ①, ④

Script & Graphic Organizer 02-022

W Professor: Okay, enough of that topic. We're running out of time, and I want to cover one more animal before class ends . . . Now, I'd like to discuss one of the most unique members of the bird kingdom. I'm referring to the bowerbird. This small bird is native to New Guinea and parts of Australia and is remarkable for its unique courtship rituals. The male seeks to attract as many females as possible to impregnate and thereby pass on his genes. To do this, bowerbird males create elaborate structures that researchers call, logically enough, bowers. In fact, some who've seen these bowers consider them the animal kingdom's most elaborate structures.

Take, for example, famed bird expert and author Jared Diamond's discovery of one bower in New Guinea. While walking through the jungle one day, he stumbled upon what he thought was a human-made hut. It was circular, eight feet wide, and four feet high with a small opening for a door. In fact, what he found was one of the largest bowers ever recorded. The hut was intricately woven and strong. In front of and inside it were hundreds of objects of various colors. Each was grouped according to its color—blue, red, purple, yellow, black, white, and so on. Some objects were rocks, some were parts of plants, some were fungi, and some were manmade objects. The male bowerbird had, had expended a great amount of effort to build it and was now waiting for females to judge him on his work. Here's a picture of a bower . . . Impressive, isn't it? Go ahead and pass it around . . . Interestingly, male bowerbirds take no part in building a nest or raising, feeding, and protecting their young. Their sole purposes are to build bowers and to mate.

As for the females, well, they move from bower to bower and examine them. What do they look for? Well, how well they're built and how elaborate they are. Then, they choose their mates based upon the bowers. Why? It all comes down to natural selection. Females are seeking the strongest, most intelligent males that can provide them with the largest number of strong offspring that can survive. They instinctively sense that a male that can both build an elaborate bower and protect it is the ideal mate for them. Oh, did I say protect . . .? Here, allow me to explain. You see, male bowerbirds have to protect their bowers since other males are constantly trying to steal items from them. After all, why go out and find everything you need for your bower when the bird next door has all the stuff you need?

So the female picks a mate, and they go off to, uh, mate, but now the male bowerbird has a dilemma. You see, he certainly has no interest in a monogamous relationship with the female no matter how, um, attractive she may be. Why? Well, male bowerbirds don't mate for life. They aren't even monogamous for a day. Unfortunately for a mating bowerbird, while in the process of mating, other males might steal his precious possessions or pick apart his beautiful bower. So the male mates as quickly as possible and then returns to his bower, where he repairs it or replaces missing objects if necessary. Then, he waits around for another female to pick him out of the crowd again. When that happens, he's got to hurry back to his bower once again to protect it. As you can see, this is a never-ending cycle for the bowerbird. And this should also probably make clear why males play no role in the lives of their young other than conceiving them.

Bowerbirds

Unique Courtship Ritual:	Reason for Ritual:
Males create elaborate bowers in jungles to impress females	Males hope to get chosen by females
Bowers appear to be large huts and are decorated with colorful items	Result: Males mate with as many females as possible

1 [Gist-Content Question]

By mostly speaking about bowers and how and why male bowerbirds erect them, the professor is lecturing about what male bowerbirds do to attract females.

2 [Detail Question]

The professor mentions, "Male bowerbirds have to protect their bowers since other males are constantly trying to steal items from them."

3 [Connecting Content Question]

According to the lecture, male bowerbirds guard their bowers from other males and mate with as many females as possible. As for female bowerbirds, they protect and take care of their newborn babies, and they are also the ones that select which bowerbird they will mate with.

Summarizing ▶

The professor says that bowerbirds live in New Guinea and Australia. They are unique birds because of their courtship rituals. The professor notes that male bowerbirds construct elaborate bowers to attempt to attract females. The bowers are often large enough to be human dwellings. They also have many colorful objects that are arranged according to their colors. Then, the females examine the bowers and choose a mate. The professor says that males hurriedly mate and then return to their bowers to protect them from other bowerbirds. The males take no part in raising the chicks. They only mate with as many females as they can.

Mastering Topics with Lectures B2   p.59

1 ⓒ   2 ⓒ   3 ⓑ

Script & Graphic Organizer 02-023

M Professor: [3] Insects are the most numerous creatures on the planet. And if estimates are correct, there may be as many as ten million or more species of insects . . . **No, I did not misspeak either.** Like all living things, insects need nutrition, and they get it in the form of food. Most insects' food comes from consuming plants or nectar whereas other insects consume dead animals. Some have also adapted so that they eat human food whether it's fresh or not. While insects get their nutrition in various ways, they all have similar digestive systems.

By far, most insects consume plants and their various parts, including leaves, stems, roots, and sap. Insects can cause great destruction to plants, which may sometimes result in widespread devastation. For example, the boll weevil attacks cotton plants, and locusts consume virtually any plant in their path. There's a picture of the aftermath of a locust swarm's arrival in a field in your book. It's not a pretty sight. Farmers resort to insecticides to protect their crops, yet these aren't always effective. Okay, back to eating . . . Other insects, such as honeybees, suck nectar from flowers and transport it to their hives, where it's used to feed the colony. Ants act similarly by transporting food to their underground colonies. Additionally, some ant species have an unusual relationship with aphids, another insect species. The ants provide the aphids with protection from predators while the aphids allow the ants to suck the sweet nectar that the aphids produce.

When animals die in the wild, their carcasses are frequently consumed by insects. Flies lay eggs on dead animals, and the maggots that subsequently hatch devour the dead animal's flesh. Some insects, like the mosquito, thrive on human and animal blood. The mosquito is considered one of history's, uh, deadliest creatures because it spreads diseases like malaria to humans. In fact, here's an interesting, um, fact . . . More people may have died because of mosquitoes than have died in all the wars ever fought. Think about that for a minute . . . Finally, there are insects like the cockroach, which will eat almost anything, and is attracted to human food. If you have cockroaches in your house, it's a sure sign that food residue on the floor or counters is attracting them.

Now, what about how they eat their food? Well, insects have two basic types of mouths. There are those that grab, chew, and grind food and those that suck or sponge food. Each species has adapted its mouth to the type of food it eats. Mosquitoes, of course, suck their food. Ants, on the other hand, grab, grind, and chew their food.

Despite their differences in diets and how they eat their food, almost all insects digest their food similarly. Like humans, they have complete digestive systems. This means that food goes in one end and waste products come out the other. A tube-like enclosure, the alimentary canal, goes from the insect's mouth to its anus. This is where food is digested. When food first enters an insect's mouth, it's subjected to the first stage of digestion, where it's combined with saliva. The mouth moves the food around and mixes it with saliva to soften it. Then, the food passes into the alimentary canal, which is divided into three sections: the foregut, the midgut, and the hindgut.

The main purposes of the foregut are to break down food particles even more and to pass them on to the midgut. The midgut is the main section where food is broken down and nutrients are absorbed. From here, the remaining food passes into the hindgut, which is where the colon, the rectum, and the anus are located. The final nutrients are extracted from the food, and the waste is then expelled from the insect's body. Of course, some insects may digest their food in slightly varying ways, but, with few exceptions, this basic digestive structure can be found in all insects.

How Insects Get Nutrition and Digest It

What Insects Eat:	How Insects Eat:	How Insects Digest Food:
Insects may consume food like plants and nectar or parts of dead or living animals	They may grab, chew, and grind their food, or they may suck or sponge their food	They have complete digestive systems that remove nutrients from food and get rid of waste

1 [Understanding Organization Question]

When describing the mouths that insects have, the professor mentions, "Mosquitoes, of course, suck their food."

2 [Understanding Organization Question]

During his lecture, the professor focuses first on the eating habits of various insects and then goes on to describe how they digest the food that they consume.

3 [Understanding Function Question]

When the professor says, "No, I did not misspeak either," he makes that comment because the number he gave is so high that the students might need to be reassured that he was speaking the truth and did not make a mistake.

Summarizing ▶

The professor says there are millions of insect species. They get their nutrition in different ways, but most of them digest it similarly. According to the professor, most insects consume either vegetation such as plants or the nectar of fruit. Other animals, like flies, may feed off of decaying animal matter. And some, like mosquitoes, may suck blood to get nutrition. Insects will chew or grind their food or else suck or sponge it. As for digesting their food, for most insects, they have complete digestive systems. After consuming food, the body removes the nutrients, and then the waste matter leaves through the anus.

Mastering Topics with Lectures B3 p.60

1 Ⓐ   2 Ⓐ   3 Ⓓ

Script & Graphic Organizer 02-024

W1 Professor: As I just mentioned, there are four distinct stages in the growth process of the butterfly. All four are integral to it, so I'm going to go into detail on them. Now, naturally, once a butterfly mates, it lays eggs. The egg is the first stage. Typically, butterflies lay their eggs on leaves or stems. They may lay single eggs or large groups of them. Oh, and keep in mind that there are around 28,000 known species of butterflies, each of which lays eggs with their own distinctive sizes, shapes, and colors. As a general rule, it only takes a few days for the eggs to hatch.

What emerges from the egg is the caterpillar, which is the second stage. Keep in mind though, that the scientific name for it is the larva. Caterpillar is just what most people call it. Anyway, the larva has one goal in life: to eat. As soon as it hatches, it typically devours the eggshell and then gets to work on the leaf or stem where it was laid. This was actually the butterfly's intention when it laid its eggs: to provide a ready food source for its young. Anyway, as the larva eats more and more, it, uh, gets bigger of course. [3]Like people who eat too much and have to purchase new clothes, the larva outgrows its skin, which it has to shed in a process called molting.

W2 Student: Professor Morris, does the larva molt once or more often than that?

W1: That's a shrewd query, Mary, and one I don't often get in an introductory class like this. Actually, depending on the species, the larva will molt anywhere from three to ten times. When it molts for the final time, its new skin becomes a hard shell called the chrysalis, which is better known as the . . . Yes, you guessed it: the cocoon. This is the third stage, called the pupa. Inside its cocoon, the larva is protected while its body undergoes the transformation that turns it into a butterfly. Okay, I think I can anticipate your next question . . . How long does that take, right? Well . . . it could be anywhere from a couple of weeks to a few months. Some species spend the entire winter in this form and emerge only in the spring. Basically, it depends on the species.

The fourth and final stage begins when the caterpillar, er, larva, becomes the beautiful butterfly. Basically, the chrysalis breaks open, and a butterfly emerges. After a brief period of time . . . during which its wings fully develop . . . it then flies off in search of a mate to start the cycle once again. This is something that butterflies often need to do quickly. The reason is that, while many species can actually survive for around ten to eleven months in the wild, they typically live for only about two to fourteen days once they emerge from their cocoon. There are a number of factors involved. Let me think . . . Predators are the main one of course. The weather is another. There are others, but I won't get into them right now.

So those are the butterfly's four stages of life. But what does it do in the final stage? Well, those that come out of their cocoons in warm weather will search for a mate in the immediate vicinity. However, keep in mind that butterflies are cold-blooded creatures. They can't even fly unless their body temperature is about eighty-six degrees Fahrenheit. So those that emerge in cold weather have two options: hibernate or migrate. A few species hibernate by finding a sheltered place— a pile of leaves, the underside of a log, a crack in a wall, or some other comfortable place. Then, their body secretes a chemical that keeps them from freezing until the weather warms up, which is when they awake. However, most butterflies migrate rather than hibernate.

The Life Cycle of the Butterfly

First Stage:	Second Stage:	Third Stage:	Fourth Stage:
Butterfly hatches from egg	Larva (caterpillar) eats as much as possible	It undergoes metamorphosis in the chrysalis	It emerges as an adult butterfly

1 [Understanding Organization Question]

The professor goes over the stages in the butterfly's life according to how they take place chronologically.

2 [Making Inferences Question]

The lecture ends with the professor noting that some butterflies may either migrate or hibernate. She then says that more migrate, so it is likely that she will go into more detail on some butterflies' migration habits.

3 [Understanding Attitude Question]

The professor notes that the student made a "shrewd query" and then comments that she does not usually get a question like that in an introductory class, so she is telling the student that she asked a perceptive question.

Summarizing ▶

The professor talks about the life cycle of the butterfly. There are four stages. The first is the egg, which lasts for a few days. When the eggs hatch, a caterpillar emerges to live the larva stage. The caterpillar eats as much as it can. The third stage is the pupa, which is when the caterpillar forms a chrysalis, or cocoon, in which it stays while it undergoes a metamorphosis. The fourth stage is the butterfly. During this stage, it mates so that the cycle can begin anew. The professor also mentions that some butterflies that emerge in cold weather will either hibernate or migrate to warmer areas.

Mastering Topics with Lectures B4　　　p.61

1 Ⓓ　**2** Ⓒ　**3** Ⓑ

Script & Graphic Organizer 02-025

M1 Professor: Take a look at this slide here . . . Okay, who can tell me which is the termite and which is the flying ant? Jason?

M2 Student: It's definitely the one on the right.

M1: Ann?

W Student: I disagree. I think it's the insect on the left.

M1: Well, at first glance, it's actually quite hard to tell them apart. So I think I can understand why you two don't agree on which is which. I tell you what . . . Let me describe some of their physical characteristics, and then we should be able to differentiate between termites and flying ants. First, a termite's body is basically straight, and it has beadlike antennae whereas an ant's body is elbowed or, um, bent. Notice that both termites and ants have two pairs of wings. However, both sets of a termite's wings are virtually of equal length and size. On the other hand, an ant's wings are unequal in size as their front wings are much larger than their hind wings. The final main physical difference between the two is the waist, which connects the abdomen to the chest, or, as it's known in scientific circles, the thorax . . . Yes, you need to remember that term and use it as well. I don't want to see anyone writing about a termite's chest. Okay? ³Anyway, a termite has a very broad waist while that of the ant is quite narrow.

W: Now that you've pointed out the differences, it's so simple to tell them apart. **My answer was just a lucky guess, but I'll be able to give an educated response from now on.**

M1: In that case, I already consider this lecture a success . . . Now that I've taught you how to tell the difference between winged ants and termites, I'd like to delve into the study of termites a little more deeply if you don't mind. Termites actually have a caste system and live in colonies. First, let's do their caste. There are three distinct castes in all termite colonies. They are the workers, the soldiers, and the winged reproductives, which are more commonly known as the king and queen. Unsurprisingly, the workers comprise the greatest number of termites in any colony by far. White, soft-bodied, wingless, and blind, they care for the eggs, build and maintain the tunnels, find food, and, uh, feed and groom the members of the other castes. They mature within a year of being hatched and live anywhere from three to five years.

As for the soldiers, they have one job . . . Naturally, it's the defense of the colony. They have the same physical characteristics as the workers, but they also possess enormously elongated hard heads that have two jaws—otherwise known as mandibles—which they use as weapons against predators or invaders. They also mature within a year of hatching and can live for up to five years assuming, of course, that they don't fall in battle.

Last are the king and queen, which are responsible for reproducing and ensuring the colony's growth and survival. When a king and queen find a place to establish a new colony, they land on the ground and shed their wings. Their colonies, by the way, will always be located somewhere near wood. Anyway, they dig a hole in the soil, seal it, and then proceed to mate. Soon afterward, the queen starts laying eggs, which hatch after a gestation period of, oh, say around fifty to sixty days. A queen may live for twenty-five years and can lay up to 60,000 eggs in her lifetime. Talk about being busy! The king, meanwhile, only lives for around a decade or so. During this time, he continually mates with the queen to increase the size of the colony.

Termites

Physical Characteristics:	Workers:
Straight bodies	Take care of colony's needs
Beadlike antennae	
Two pairs of wings	Soldiers:
Broad waists	Protect the colony
	Reproductives:
	King and queen create more termites

1 [Gist-Purpose Question]

The professor shows a picture of a termite and a flying ant and asks the students to tell him which one is which, but they are unable to do so. Then, he talks about their physical characteristics so that the students will be able to tell them apart.

2 [Detail Question]

In speaking about soldier termites, the professor states, "They have the same physical characteristics as the workers, but they also possess enormously elongated hard heads that have two jaws—otherwise known as mandibles—which they use as weapons against predators or invaders."

3 [Understanding Function Question]

When the student says, "I'll be able to give an educated response from now on," she is saying that she has learned something new and has now been educated.

Summarizing ▶

The professor shows some slides of flying ants and termites and asks the students which is which. When the students have problems, the professor explains the physical characteristics of each. The female student then easily recognizes which picture is the termite. Next, the professor continues to describe the caste system of termites. He explains the physical traits of the workers, the soldiers, and the reproductives, which are the king and queen. When the king and the queen form a colony, they mate repeatedly so that the colony can expand. This can go on for years while the queen can lay up to 60,000 eggs over twenty-five years.

Mastering Topics with Conversations B5   p.62

1   2   3

Script & Graphic Organizer 02-026

M Student: Knock, knock.

W Professor: Oh, hi there, Matt. Can I do something for

you?

M: Well, if you don't mind, I've got something I'd really like to speak with you about.

W: Okay, I've got a few minutes before I have to attend a staff meeting. But until the meeting begins, I'm all yours. What's on your mind?

M: Um, I just found out about this internship program that the Omega Corporation is sponsoring this summer.

W: This summer? But, uh, isn't it a little, well, a little too late to be applying for an internship right now? I mean, we've only got two weeks until the semester is over.

M: Er, yeah, I suppose I could have applied a little earlier, but . . .

W: But what?

M: Well, to be honest, I just found out about this internship program yesterday. One of my friends told me about it.

W: And what makes it so appealing if I may ask?

M: It's in the company's computer software division. That's what I really, really want to do when I get out of here next year. I mean, I've always wanted to write software, so, uh, getting this internship would most likely help me get a leg up on the competition. You know what I'm saying?

W: That's most assuredly true, Matt. But what makes you think you can get in by applying so late?

M: According to the advertisement, the company is still accepting applications until next week. It's on a rolling basis, so the various departments might have already filled every position, but I bet there are at least a few left. And it's not like my grades are bad or anything. I mean, uh, I've made the Dean's List every semester I've been here.

W: That is true. Okay, go for it. The worst that can happen is that you get turned down. So, uh, what do you want me to do?

M: Oh, right . . . Well, I'd like for you to write me a letter of recommendation, please. I'm supposed to turn two in to them. Professor Dorcas is writing the other.

W: And when would you like to have this letter, Matt?

M: Um . . . Tomorrow?

W: Okay, I can do that. I wouldn't normally do this on such short notice, but you have been a model student in all of my classes.

M: Oh, thank you so much, ma'am. I truly appreciate it.

W: Stop by tomorrow around one, and I'll have it ready for you. Oh, I've got to run. It's time for my meeting.

M: Thanks, Professor Stuart. See you tomorrow.

Office Hours

Problem 1:	Solution 1:
Just found out about an appealing internship program	Will apply for the program despite being late
Problem 2:	Solution 2:
Needs a letter of recommendation from the professor	Will write letter of recommendation by one o'clock tomorrow

1 [Gist-Purpose Question]

The student needs a letter of recommendation from the professor, and although he asks for it near the end of the conversation, that is the reason he goes to see the professor.

2 [Understanding Attitude Question]

When the student says, "That's what I really, really want to do when I get out of here next year," it can be inferred that he is going to graduate in one year's time.

3 [Making Inferences Question]

The professor tells the student, "You have been a model student in all of my classes," which implies that his grades have been high in the classes that he has taken with her.

Summarizing ▶

The student visits the professor's office to talk to her about an internship at a company. She asks him why he waited so long to apply, and he says that he found out about it the day before. He states that it is a computer position, which is what he really wants to do after he graduates. Then, he asks the professor if she will write a letter of recommendation for him. The professor agrees even though he needs the letter by the next day. She tells him to pick up his letter the next day around one o'clock and then leaves for a meeting.

Mastering Topics with Conversations B6 p.63

1 Ⓒ **2** Ⓑ, Ⓒ **3** Ⓐ

Script & Graphic Organizer 02-027

W Student: Pardon me, but are you Mr. Sanders?

M Admissions Office Employee: Yes, that's me. Is there something I can do for you, miss? As you can see, I'm a little busy right now.

W: Oh, well . . . If I'm troubling you, I, uh, I guess I could come back another time. It's just that your door was open and . . .

M: No, no. I'm sorry. Have a seat, please. I apologize. I'm just having a busy day. Things are kind of hectic around here these days. We're preparing to host a lot of high school students this weekend. They're all thinking about attending school here, so it seems like I've got a million things to do before they start arriving . . . But enough about me. What can I do for you?

W: Actually, I'm here about the high school student program.

M: How so?

W: I'm going to be hosting a student in my room.

M: Excellent. Thanks so much for your involvement in the program . . . Oh, well, in that case, you can find out who your guest is going to be from the RA in your dorm.

W: Oh, no. Pardon me. That's not what I'm here to find out.

M: Then what do you need to know?

W: Well, uh, what am I supposed to do with my student? I asked my RA, but she was kind of, uh, clueless. So the woman out front told me to come back here to speak to you.

M: ³Okay, well, first, you need to have a positive attitude. You do like attending this school, don't you?

W: Totally! **I was an early-decision student here.**

M: Excellent. Then just be positive about the school. Try to answer as many questions as you can when your guest asks you things.

W: What if I don't know the answers to some questions?

M: Be honest. Tell her you don't know. Then either find out the answer or tell her how she can find out.

W: That makes sense. What else?

M: Hmm . . . Try taking her around campus. Find out what she's, you know, what she's thinking of majoring in. Make sure to show her around that department.

W: Okay. I can do that.

M: And make sure she sits in on a couple of classes to see what the college educational experience is like. But most of all, just make sure your guest has a good time and comes away with a positive impression of our school.

W: I can do that. Thanks so much, Mr. Sanders.

Service Encounter

Problem:	Solutions:
Student will host a visitor but is not sure what she should do for her guest	Have a positive attitude; Answer questions; Show the visitor around campus; Make sure the visitor has a good time

1 [Gist-Content Question]

The student does not know where on campus she should take the incoming student.

2 [Detail Question]

The man tells the student to "just be positive about the school" and to "try taking her around campus."

3 [Understanding Function Question]

When the student notes that she was an early-decision student, she is telling the man that the school was her first choice and that she really likes it there.

Summarizing ▶

The student visits Mr. Sanders in his office. He tells her he is busy because of an upcoming program where high school students come to campus. The student says that is why she is visiting him. She does not know what to do with the student. The man tells her to be enthusiastic about the school and to try to answer any questions the student has. She should also take the visiting student around campus and show her the department of the subject she thinks she might major in. He emphasizes that the student should make sure the visitor has a good time.

TOEFL Practice Tests C1
p.64

1 Ⓓ **2** Ⓑ **3** Ⓒ, Ⓓ **4** Ⓒ **5** Ⓑ
6 Ⓐ

Script 02-028

W Professor: Plants are some of the planet's most diverse organisms. And like we do with most things, people try to name plants in a way that makes them fit into our understanding of the world. Of course, we utilize common names like, um, tree, bush, flower, grass, weed, and moss, all of which describe large groups of plants in general. More specifically, though, we have names that we use to describe certain plants within these groups. So we have apple trees, rose bushes, daffodils, lilacs, and so on. But even these names aren't perfect since the common names used for some plants may differ from country to country or even from region to region. That's why botanists use a scientific classification of plants: to prevent confusion.

First, plants have been given their own kingdom as opposed to the animal kingdom. Within the plant kingdom, the next level is called a division, of which there are twelve. ⁵What's next . . .? All right . . . **Get ready to take notes . . .** Divisions are divided into classes, which are divided into orders, which are divided into families and then into genus and species. Got it? Let me recap.

To be more concise, we have kingdom, division, class, order, family, genus, and species. All plants have their own scientific name, which is expressed in Latin and has two parts: the genus and the species. It was Carolus Linnaeus, a Swedish botanist, who created this system in the eighteenth century with his book *The Species of Plants*. It was published, uh, in 1753, but don't worry about that. His system has undergone some changes over the years, but as a whole, his work still heavily influences the modern-day classification of plants.

Let me show you how it works. Let's take the, uh . . . the . . . the coffee plant will do for this demonstration. Its scientific name is *Coffea arabica L*. Let me write that on the board here . . . Please note how I write it. The first word is capitalized while the second isn't, and the third part is the letter L. This letter indicates it was Linnaeus himself who created the name. Other botanists who have named plants may also have their name abbreviated at the end of a plant's scientific name. That's not always the case though. Okay, back to the coffee plant. Typically, the first word—the genus— is a noun that describes some aspect of the plant. It could be its color, smell, size, or something else. The second word—the species—indicates something about the plant's origin or some other, uh, more specific characteristic. In the eighteenth century, it was believed that coffee had originated in Arabia, hence the name Linnaeus bestowed upon it. Of course, we now know it really hails from Ethiopia, but no one's bothered to change the name.

Let's return to the higher divisions of the plant kingdom now. It can get a little complicated, so I'll try to simplify things as much as I can. Firstly, remember that there are twelve divisions. These divisions are divided according to a plant's tissue structure, seed structure, and stature, or height. Tissue structure itself is divided into two parts: vascular and nonvascular. Vascular plants comprise the vast majority . . . Oh, what are they? They're plants with leaves, stems, and root systems. Nonvascular are the opposite, like, er, mosses. That is, they have no leaves, stems, or root systems.

Next, plants are divided according to the nature of their seeds, of which there are pardon me . . . there are three types: spore producers, naked seeds, and covered seeds. Spore producers, as their name implies, lack seeds. Instead, they release spores that blow in the wind and land in new spots, where they grow. Mosses and several fern species are spore producers. Plants with naked seeds are called gymnosperms . . . It's in your books. Look it up . . . They usually have cones and no flowers. As you may have guessed, naked seed plants include spruce, pine, and fir trees. Covered seed plants have their seeds covered in some way. [6]This is typically done inside fruit or shells. They're called angiosperms. Virtually all flowering plants are angiosperms. **These can be divided into two types,**

but I won't get into them since I can see a few of you have glazed looks in your eyes.

Remember when I said that plants are also characterized by their stature? At the bottom are the mosses, which hug rocks and tree trunks. From there, we move up to low-growing grasses, flowers, and bushes. Then there are trees of various levels and vines, which can grow to surprisingly great heights so long as they, uh, they have something to support them like, you know, a tree or a building. Okay. That's basically how we classify plants. It does seem a little complicated, but it's really helpful once you understand the system.

1 [Gist-Content Question]

During her lecture, the professor describes how the classification system of plants works.

2 [Gist-Purpose Question]

When the professor explains all three parts of the name of the coffee plant, she is describing where each part of the name comes from.

3 [Detail Question]

During the lecture, the professor states that "the next level is called a division, of which there are twelve" and also mentions that "plants are divided according to the nature of their seeds."

4 [Understanding Organization Question]

The professor says, "It was Carolus Linnaeus, a Swedish botanist, who created this system in the eighteenth century with his book *The Species of Plants*."

5 [Understanding Function Question]

When the professor tells the students to take notes, it can be inferred that she wants them to remember what she is about to say, so she is going to give them some important information.

6 [Understanding Attitude Question]

When the professor notes that she will not cover something because sees some students with glazed looks in their eyes, she is letting them know that she realizes the difficulty level of what she is talking about. When a person gets a glazed look in his or her eyes, it often means that the person does not comprehend what he or she is listening to, which explains the reason why the professor makes her statement.

TOEFL Practice Tests C2

p.66

| 1 Ⓒ | 2 Ⓓ | 3 Ⓒ | 4 Fact: ①, ④ Speculation: ②, ③ | 5 Ⓒ | 6 Ⓑ |

M Professor: When people hear the word "shark," almost automatically, visions of a fearsome man-eating sea creature often come to mind. That's the public perception of sharks, which is based on movies, books, and the heavy media attention paid to every shark attack on humans. [6]In actuality though, there are fewer than fifty attacks on people each year, and on average, only four . . . four of them are fatal. Talk about a low number. **Many more people are killed by snakes and spiders, you know.** Unfortunately, millions of sharks are killed by humans every year, mostly because their fins are considered a delicacy in China and other Asian countries.

In today's lecture, first, I'd like to speak about the shark's physical characteristics and habits. Then, we'll look at some individual sharks in detail. There are over 400 species of sharks. Some of the better-known ones are the great white, the tiger, the mako, the hammerhead, the bull, the whale, and the blue shark. Sharks are among the oldest creatures on the Earth with the fossil record showing that they were around more than 400 million years ago. Fortunately, modern sharks are considerably smaller than the monsters that prowled the oceans back then. While they are predominantly saltwater fish, a few species, most notably the bull shark, are known to live in freshwater lakes and river deltas. Sharks can be found in all of the world's oceans, but most prefer the warm waters found in tropical regions. Most sharks live around twenty years on average, but some, like the whale shark, can live for up to a century.

Sharks' bodies are streamlined and well adapted to the water, making them powerful swimmers. Millions of years of evolution will do that after all. Their skin is covered with a tooth-like surface that enhances their swimming ability by reducing drag. It's like they're aeronautically designed—except for the water, not the air. Interestingly, there is a myth that sharks must continually move, or they, uh, they won't be able to breathe. Okay, it's only part myth. It's true for some species, but many have the ability to pump water through their gills even while resting.

W Student: Do sharks sleep, Professor Brody?

M: Hmm . . . There are documented cases of some sharks . . . nurse sharks I believe . . . sleeping on the seafloor. But there's some disagreement about this since their eyes were open at the time, so it's not known if they were sleeping or not. I would say they weren't, but others disagree with me. Some experts think sharks sleep by, uh, turning off part of their brain to let them sleep, but no one really knows for sure.

Now, how about their senses? Sharks are legendary for their ability to pinpoint prey in the water at great distances. How . . .? They have a highly developed sense of smell. That's how. They can detect minute drops of blood in the water from miles away, which is why you shouldn't go swimming if you've got an open cut anywhere on your body. It's like you're inviting a shark to visit. Anyway, sharks also have lateral lines running the length of their bodies. These lines allow them to sense when something in the water is moving, splashing, or generally acting like it's, er, in distress. Finally, sharks can detect the electromagnetic presence of living things . . . Yeah, that is pretty cool. Some experts believe this ability is unparalleled in the animal kingdom. So by using all three of these abilities, sharks can find and home in on their prey. As for what they eat, most feed on fish while a few species eat plankton. Some sharks are known to attack squid and crustaceans as well. Sharks may hunt alone or in groups. Now that is something I would definitely not want to be in the water for.

What about reproduction? Well, males mate with females of course. After that, it starts to vary. Some species lay eggs internally while others reproduce through birthing in a manner similar to mammals, which they most assuredly are not. Additionally, other species lay eggs that remain inside the female until the babies are hatched. The number of young given birth to ranges from two to dozens. In some species, those that hatch first eat their brothers and sisters that have not yet emerged from their eggs. Most sharks are born fully developed, so they have no need for parental care and are left alone either to survive or perish.

Despite being formidable predators, sharks have met another predator stronger than they are: man. Humans are the biggest danger facing sharks today. Many that are caught by fisherman simply have their fins sliced off and are then dumped back into the ocean, where they die since they can't swim without their fins. Additionally, some claim that shark cartilage has medicinal benefits, so some people seek it to cure whatever is ailing them despite most doctors' protestations that shark cartilage is ineffective at curing anything. But with millions of dollars to be made from the shark trade, it is unlikely that humans will cease killing sharks in great numbers anytime soon.

1 [Gist-Content Question]

During much of the lecture, the professor describes some of the abilities that sharks have that make them different from other animals.

2 [Detail Question]

The professor explains, "Sharks' bodies are streamlined and well adapted to the water, making them powerful swimmers. Millions of years of evolution will do that after all. Their skin is covered with a tooth-like surface that enhances their swimming ability by reducing drag. It's like they're aeronautically designed—except for the water, not the air."

3 [Understanding Attitude Question]

About the shark trade, the professor states, "Unfortunately, millions of sharks are killed by humans every year, mostly because their fins are considered a delicacy in China and other Asian countries."

4 [Connecting Content Question]

According to the lecture, the facts about sharks are that they can tell when other animals in the water are suffering distress and that all of them do not have to move continually in order to breathe. As for speculation, sharks may sometimes sleep on the bottom of the ocean, and they may be able to turn off part of their brain on occasion.

5 [Understanding Organization Question]

During the lecture, the professor notes the physical characteristics of sharks and then goes into detail while describing them.

6 [Understanding Function Question]

When the professor mentions that snakes and spiders kill more people than sharks, he is implying that sharks are not as dangerous as some other animals are.

TOEFL Practice Tests C3

p.68

1 (B) **2** (B) **3** (A) **4** (B) **5** (C)

Script 02-030

W Professor: Charles, thanks for coming in when I asked . . . I've been going over the paper that you submitted to me last week.

M Student: Ah, yes, Professor Haber. So, what did you think of my writing? Is my paper okay?

W: Well . . . As always, your writing is quite excellent. You truly have a way with words that I rarely see in someone so young. It's quite impressive.

M: Thank you.

W: But . . . I must confess that I've found several . . . problems with your essay, and I haven't even finished going over it yet. I still have, um, two or three pages, I believe, which I need to look at.

M: Problems? Like what?

W: Well, to begin with, you got several of the facts wrong in your paper. That's rather unlike you. I've got your paper right here . . . Let me give you an example . . . Take a look here . . . See?

M: Um, I'm not exactly sure what I'm supposed to be looking at, Professor. Would you mind explaining to me

what you're referring to, please?

W: Sure. Okay, your essay was on *Jane Eyre*, right?

M: Yes.

W: Well, right here, you wrote . . . And I quote . . . "It was when Jayne was working as the governess at Gateshead Hall that she met the man who was to become her husband."

M: Uh, sure. What's wrong with that?

W: Well, Jane never worked at Gateshead Hall. That's where she lived in her early years. She was most definitely not the governess there. Nor did she meet her future husband there . . . [5]I don't want to do this, but I simply have to ask . . . Charles, did you read the book?

M: Well, um, I . . . **I guess you could say that I skipped over a few parts.**

W: What on earth would possess you to write a report about a book you merely skimmed through?

M: Um . . . I just . . . Well, I have simply been overwhelmed by all my schoolwork this semester, so it's been hard for me to keep up with my studies.

W: What exactly do you mean? You're not taking any extra classes, are you?

M: Actually, I'm taking a heavier workload than normal. I've also got a part-time job that I do on the weekend. Both of those are really causing me to fall behind on my coursework.

W: Well, I understand that you're busy, but that's still no excuse for turning in a paper for something that you clearly, uh, clearly have no knowledge of.

M: So, uh, what was I supposed to do?

W: You could have asked me for an extension. I do grant them, you know.

M: Actually, um, that thought never even occurred to me. I've never once turned in any assignment late, so I never realized that, uh, you know, you could get an extension.

W: Well, you may need to do that in the future, Charles . . . Okay, I tell you what . . . Here, take your paper back. Now, go and read *Jane Eyre*. Completely this time. Then, rewrite your paper. I want it on my desk a week from today.

M: Seriously?

W: Yes, seriously. Now, go on and get out of here. You've got some reading to do.

1 [Gist-Purpose Question]

The professor says that she wanted to see the student because she found some problems in the paper that he just turned in to her.

2 [Detail Question]

About the student's paper, the professor mentions, "Well, to begin with, you got several of the facts wrong in your paper."

3 [Understanding Attitude Question]

About the student, the professor states, "As always, your writing is quite excellent. You truly have a way with words that I rarely see in someone so young. It's quite impressive."

4 [Making Inferences Question]

At the end of the conversation, the professor tells the student, "Now, go on and get out of here. You've got some reading to do." It can therefore be assumed that the student will leave the professor's office since she told him to go.

5 [Understanding Function Question]

When the student confesses that he "skipped over a few parts," he is admitting that he failed to make a thorough reading of the book.

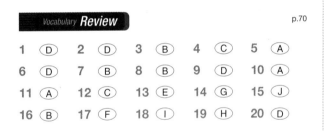

Vocabulary **Review**   p.70

1 Ⓓ	2 Ⓓ	3 Ⓑ	4 Ⓒ	5 Ⓐ
6 Ⓓ	7 Ⓑ	8 Ⓑ	9 Ⓓ	10 Ⓐ
11 Ⓐ	12 Ⓒ	13 Ⓔ	14 Ⓖ	15 Ⓙ
16 Ⓑ	17 Ⓕ	18 Ⓘ	19 Ⓗ	20 Ⓓ

Chapter **03** | Social Sciences **1** · Conversations

Mastering Question Types with Lectures A1   p.72

| TYPES 1–4 |

TYPE **1** Ⓐ   TYPE **2** Ⓑ   TYPE **3** Ⓑ   TYPE **4** Ⓓ

Script 02-031

M Professor: Around the world, there are literally . . . and I mean that in the true sense of the word . . . literally tens of thousands of ships lying at the bottom of the oceans and seas. The reasons they sank are many, but they can all be divided into natural and manmade causes. The natural causes are mostly weather related, you know, storms or perhaps tsunamis that resulted from undersea earthquakes. The manmade causes include warfare, improper navigation, poor handling that led to collisions with rocks, reefs, and icebergs, and

poor loading that led to the capsizing of the vessels. Yeah, being at sea is not exactly safe, is it?

Throughout history, the vast majority of ships sank because they encountered bad weather. Prior to the twentieth century, weather reporting services were scant, and once ships were at sea, no one could communicate to warn them of impending bad weather. Captains and crews knew the signs of a coming storm through years of experience, yet it was difficult for sailing ships to avoid, er, inclement weather. Even today, with modern weather forecasting, communications, navigation aids, and propeller-driven ships, bad weather still sinks numerous ships each year.

In bad weather, ships most commonly sink either by capsizing or flooding. Capsizing in bad weather without first flooding is rare and only occurs when there are extremely high waves such as those that occur in hurricanes or typhoons. Oh, yeah, there are rogue waves that might be thirty-or-so meters high. They can sink a ship instantly, but, uh, but they're, well, uncommon . . . Thank goodness. Note that ships have an inherent stability that makes them return to an upright position when they're struck by waves, but when they tilt a certain angle from the upright position, they can lose this stability and suddenly capsize. [4]More commonly, however, a ship will flood first as waves break the hatches and windows and seawater enters the ship. **If water short-circuits the electrical system and the engine stops, most modern vessels are at the mercy of the sea since they're, uh, unable to move or steer.** Eventually, the weight of the water will drag the ship under, but it will typically cause the ship to capsize first.

Ships may sink from manmade causes in both war and peacetime. As for warfare, well, there are numerous ways to sink ships. Let's see . . . torpedoing . . . bombing, internal ammunition explosions . . . But let's not dwell on this aspect. Outside of war, the most common way for ships to sink because of people is by being mishandled. This can lead to collisions with obstacles or even other ships. The world's waterways have numerous reefs, rocks, shallow areas, and even icebergs. Countless vessels have collided with them, often because of mistakes by, uh, the crew. The bottom or sides of the ship are ripped, water enters, and the ship, well, goes down. The *Titanic*, of course, is the most famous example of this type of collision, but she was most definitely not the only one. Take a look at the handout I gave you earlier in class. It's got a list of famous ships that have gone down and how many lives were lost when these events happened. It's rather sobering when you think of how many people drowned.

TYPE **1** [Gist-Content Question]

During the lecture, the professor talks about a number of different reasons why shipwrecks happen.

TYPE 2 [Detail Question]

The professor claims, "Throughout history, the vast majority of ships sank because they encountered bad weather."

TYPE 3 [Understanding Organization Question]

During the lecture, the professor first goes over some natural causes of shipwrecks, and then he switches his attention to some of the manmade reasons for them.

TYPE 4 [Understanding Function Question]

When the professor states, "Most modern vessels are at the mercy of the sea," when their engines stop, he is implying that the crew can do nothing to save the ship, so they therefore have no control over its fate.

Summarizing ▷

> The professor states that tens of thousands of ships have sunk throughout history. He comments that the most common reason is <u>bad weather</u>. In the past, ships' captains and crews had no way of knowing what kind of <u>inclement weather</u> they were sailing into, so many ships were lost. But even with <u>modern technology</u>, bad weather still sinks many ships. The professor mentions that when ships sink in bad weather, it is often due to <u>flooding or capsizing</u>. Finally, he notes that warfare accounts for many shipwrecks as well. But he also says that crews can <u>mishandle their ships</u> and thus cause them to sink.

| **TYPES 5–8** |

TYPE 5 Ⓒ   TYPE 6 Ⓐ   TYPE 7 Ⓒ   TYPE 8 Ⓓ

Script 02-032

W Professor: Okay . . . Now that I've got everyone's homework, we need to get started. There's a lot of material for us to cover today. So . . . everyone ready . . .? Good. Let's go back in time and talk about pottery. Why go back in time when there is pottery all around us? Well, pottery is one of the first advanced, uh, products that humans learned to make. It developed in early civilizations at different times and was made by various methods and with all kinds of materials. These facts make pottery rather, um, useful to the study of ancient civilizations. First, what is pottery? Simple. It's an object made of clay that is heated, or fired, to harden it. The first objects made of fired clay date back to around 25,000 B.C.

M Student: Pottery is that old? I never knew that.

W: Well, strictly speaking, these objects weren't pottery but were actually figurines. The first, uh, I guess you could say, uh, real pottery, dates to around 18,000 B.C. It was found in China. Japanese pottery making started around 10,000 B.C., and it began in Mesopotamia

---

around the same time. [6]It was also in Mesopotamia that the potter's wheel was invented. **The potter's wheel made the creation of high-quality pottery possible, but we'll get to how it works another day.** By around, oh, let's say 5000 B.C., pottery had either been independently invented or had spread to most areas in the world where civilizations existed.

Now, how is pottery useful to the study of ancient civilizations? There are many ways. First, it's strong and can last for ages. Literally. Second, it's often found broken and in shards, so it's not particularly valuable, especially to looters. They're more interested in gold, jewelry, and other expensive items that they can pawn off. What that means is that there are lots of pottery shards left at ancient sites, which is a boon for archaeologists. Third, people in all levels of society used it, so archaeologists don't have to confine their studies only to the upper classes. Finally, pottery breaks, so it requires frequent replacing, which necessitates a . . . you guessed it: a pottery industry. A region's pottery industry could have lasted for thousands of years. As time passed, the pottery designs and materials both changed. Studying these changes can provide archaeologists with clues as to how, uh, society itself changed and developed as well.

Now, what can experts do with the shards and intact pottery they find . . .? A couple of things. First, since ancient pottery was heated, it can be easily dated by specialized testing methods. Second, the clay in the pottery can be analyzed, and its composition can tell archaeologists from where it came. Let's say the clay in pottery at one site comes from a place hundreds of kilometers away. What does that indicate . . .? Anyone . . .? No? It tells you that trade was going on between the two regions. Third, the designs of the pottery provide clues to many aspects of society. I'll show some slides in just a bit to show you what I mean . . . Fourth, pottery styles can show how ideas spread in the ancient world. So if a Mesopotamian style pot is found in Egypt hundreds of years later, it may suggest the spread of that style of pottery between the two civilizations.

TYPE 5 [Gist-Content Question]

The professor mostly focuses on why archaeologists are interested in pottery and what they can learn from studying it.

TYPE 6 [Understanding Attitude Question]

When the professor notes that they will go over how the potter's wheel works another day, she is implying that it is irrelevant to her current lecture, which is why she does not need to talk about it.

TYPE 7 [Connecting Content Question]

While talking about pottery, the professor notes, "Second, it's often found broken and in shards, so it's not particularly valuable, especially to looters. They're more interested in gold, jewelry, and other expensive items that they can pawn off. What that means is that there are lots of pottery shards left at ancient sites, which is a boon for archaeologists." It is therefore implied that the shards are important to archaeologists yet have no value to looters.

TYPE 8 [Making Inferences Question]

Near the end of the lecture, the professor states, "I'll show some slides in just a bit to show you what I mean."

Summarizing ▶

> The lecturer says that pottery is one of the first advanced products that people learned how to make. She comments that it also helps archaeologists learn about ancient societies. She states that the Chinese invented pottery around 25,000 B.C., and most other cultures were making pottery by 5,000 B.C. She mentions that pottery shards are common at dig sites because they are not valuable to looters. The design and manufacture of pottery often changed, so they can tell archaeologists much about a culture. With pottery and pottery shards, archaeologists can tell the dates they were made and what kinds of materials they were made from.

Mastering Question Types with Lectures A2 p.74

| TYPES 1–4 |

Script 02-033

W Professor: Every day, people make decisions that can affect their lives and the lives of others. Some are simple while others are complex. Simple choices aren't that hard to point out. They're the minor things we do, you know, each and every day. For example, what to eat for breakfast. You can have cereal, toast, or eggs. Picking one over the others isn't particularly hard to do, nor will it have any long-lasting effects. Other simple choices include, er . . . what clothes to wear, what TV show to watch, what book to read, and who to have lunch with. These choices don't require much in the way of mental gymnastics and, in general, have no dramatic impact on your life. Simple enough, huh?

But . . . Other decisions are more complex. They may involve situations relating to, let's see . . . money, relationships, work, and situations that will affect others. With these decisions, there are more variables involved, and the consequences of a bad decision are more profound. How about money? It commonly requires complex decisions. People have to decide whether or not to purchase a car. Or they need to decide between

---

renting and buying a house. How about the factors involved? Think about renting an apartment, something that many people do. Where should the person live? Is there public transportation nearby? What are the neighbors like? Is the rent affordable? How about the utilities? The questions go on and on and on, don't they? Even more daunting is that other people, such as family members, may be involved in the decisions. If you move, will your spouse and children like the place? How will it affect their lives? Will they suffer emotional distress? Make new friends?

So how do people deal with complex decisions? It seems as though, when faced with a complex decision, they could ask themselves question after question and never get around to making a choice. Well, there are some ways to handle them. The first is the, uh, the gut reaction. What's that? It's just an intuitive feel as to what's good or bad. I'm sure you've experienced this before. You instinctively knew what decision to make. You felt it in your gut. Most of the time, your choice was correct, wasn't it . . .? Of course, some gut decisions are made on the spur on the moment and may result in poor choices. To avoid doing that, some people prefer to sleep on a decision. This gives them time to consider their options, get some rest, and make a decision the next day, when their minds are clearer. This method can also lead to both good and poor decisions.

Others decide to make decisions on complex problems in a more, uh, analytical manner. They weigh the pros and cons, logically examine the issue from all sides, and might even seek advice from others. [4]When people do that, they tend to remove some of the emotional aspect from their decision. Of course, it's hard to completely do this . . . **After all, we're only human and can't help but consider our emotions when making hard choices.**

TYPE 1 [Gist-Purpose Question]

The professor first explains simple decisions, and then she contrasts them by explaining complex decisions.

TYPE 2 [Detail Question]

About simple decisions, the professor states, "Simple choices aren't that hard to point out. They're the minor things we do, you know, each and every day."

TYPE 3 [Understanding Organization Question]

The professor first talks about simple decisions and then moves on to complex decisions. So she goes over decisions according to how easy they are.

TYPE 4 [Understanding Function Question]

When the professor states, "We're only human and can't help but consider our emotions when making hard choices," she is admitting that it is very difficult for people to ignore their feelings when trying to make a decision.

Summarizing ▶

The professor notes that there are both simple and complex decisions. Simple decisions are ones that people do all the time and have very little effect on people's lives. They do not require much thought, which is unlike complex decisions. These are big choices that often concern things such as money, relationships, work, and situations that affect others. These kinds of decisions require a lot of thought because there are often many different factors involved. The professor says that people solve them in different ways. Some follow their gut while others sleep on the decision. And others approach their decisions in an analytical manner.

| TYPES 5–8 |

TYPE 5 Ⓓ   **TYPE 6** Ⓐ

TYPE 7 Improve Skills: ☐1☐, ☐4☐   Enrich Lives: ☐2☐, ☐3☐

TYPE 8 Ⓐ

Script 02-034

M Professor: Let me ask you all a question: How many of you received books as gifts when you were young? Hands up . . . Okay, that's what I'd expected. Almost all of you. And can I assume that someone read to you when you were young . . .? Uh-huh. Well, we've often been told that it's important to read, so we read and are read to. But how often are we told why it's important for us to read from an early age? I'd wager not very often. Well, there are three main reasons. First, books help children develop vital reading skills. Second . . . Oh, excuse me. Second, reading can open new worlds and enrich children's lives. Third, it can enhance children's social skills.

I'm going to go over all of them in detail now. We'll cover the development of vital language skills first. Obviously, you're all here today thanks to your language skills. If you hadn't learned to read and then further developed your, uh, reading skills while growing up, I'd bet that none of you would be here today. Wouldn't you agree . . .? Uh-huh. By learning to read, you've become able to learn about various subjects, and you have the ability to find information about anything you want to know about. To survive in the academic world, one must be able to read. But you don't just learn facts when you read. While reading, you get exposed to correct grammar and phrasing. Not only that, but you are introduced to new vocabulary, which can help both your reading and your oral skills to improve, too. You should see how much my own kids' speaking skills improved at an early age.

The second reason children should read is that their

lives can be enriched by the experience. By knowing how to read, as I just said, people can find out just about anything they would like to know. Reading gives people instant access to all of, well, to all of mankind's accumulated knowledge. It enables people to be able to find out about all the ideas and thoughts of the world's greatest minds. Readers can learn about people and places around the world, thereby broadening their understanding of the world to a more global rather than local level.

In addition, reading can be either fiction or nonfiction, and both are beneficial. Many novels, for instance, are set in other times and places yet are rooted in fact. Reading them provides not only enjoyment but also education. Reading mysteries, for instance . . . uh, mysteries teach the reader to follow clues to their logical conclusions. Even fairy tales or, let's say books like the *Harry Potter* series . . . These create entire new worlds for children, which help stimulate their imaginations. And it's pretty obvious, especially in the case of *Harry Potter*, that children's lives are improved by reading. Look at how many children have been inspired to turn off the TV or computer and start reading because they were interested in experiencing the imaginary world of a teenage wizard. That's what books can do for young people. Okay, let's move on to the third reason now.

TYPE 5   [Gist-Content Question]

During his lecture, the professor mentions that there are three main reasons why children should read or be read to, and he discusses two of them in detail.

TYPE 6   [Understanding Attitude Question]

The professor claims, "And it's pretty obvious, especially in the case of *Harry Potter*, that children's lives are improved by reading."

TYPE 7   [Connecting Content Question]

According to the lecture, learning how to state ideas properly and developing a larger vocabulary are ways that children can improve their skills. Meanwhile, learning about the world and learning to think more logically are two skills that the professor believes can enrich children's lives.

TYPE 8   [Making Inferences Question]

About his children, the professor states, "You should see how much my own kids' speaking skills improved at an early age." Since he is an advocate of reading to children and since his children's speaking skills improved when they were young, it can be inferred that he read to his children in their youth.

The professor asks the students about their relationships with books when they were young. He then mentions that there are several reasons why it is important for children to read and to be read to. The first is that they gain vital language skills, such as proper grammar and phrasing as well as new vocabulary. Reading also can enrich children's lives by opening the door of discovery through books. But they can also read to be educated and entertained. And in addition to learning logic from mysteries, they can have their imaginations stimulated by fairy tales and other stories similar to the *Harry Potter* series.

Mastering Question Types with Conversations A3

p.76

| TYPES 1–4 |

TYPE 1 (A)   TYPE 2 (B)   TYPE 3 (A)   TYPE 4 (D)

Script 02-035

M Professor: So, Jessica, what would you like to speak with me about this afternoon?

W Student: Well, Professor Corinth, as you know, next year's going to be my junior year at this school.

M: Right.

W: And, uh, well, that's when it seems like a lot of students here go to study abroad for a semester or two. I have been thinking of doing the same thing, but I'm not positive if, uh, if I should do it or not.

M: Why wouldn't you? It's a totally fantastic experience that will stay with you for the rest of your life. I wholeheartedly recommend that you go to study abroad somewhere. After all, who knows? It may be the only chance in a long time that you get to study or even travel overseas. You wouldn't want to miss out on it.

W: ⁴Wow. I never knew you felt so passionately about it.

M: I say that if you have the financial wherewithal to make it happen, go.

W: All right. I've made up my mind then. I'll go.

M: Great. Now . . . do you have any particular country in mind?

W: Hmm . . . One of my friends elsewhere did a semester abroad in Brazil, and she said it was amazing there. I thought I could do the same thing.

M: While Brazil is quite nice, they speak Portuguese there, and we don't offer that language at our school. Hmm . . . How about Japan? You're taking classes in that language, aren't you?

W: Well, yes, but I get the feeling that I'm not improving very much in Japanese. Even though I'm taking two

classes in it right now, I'm simply not particularly confident in it.

M: Okay. You speak Spanish as well, don't you?

W: Yes, I'm fluent in that language.

M: How about studying in Mexico? We have a couple of exchange programs with universities there.

W: No way. I had no idea.

M: Totally. Check it out. Visit the study abroad office and ask someone there about it.

W: Thanks. I think I'll go do that right now.

TYPE 1 [Gist-Purpose Question]

Near the beginning of the conversation, the student states, "And, uh, well, that's when it seems like a lot of students here go to study abroad for a semester or two. I have been thinking of doing the same thing, but I'm not positive if, uh, if I should do it or not."

TYPE 2 [Detail Question]

About her Japanese skills, the student mentions, "I get the feeling that I'm not improving very much in Japanese."

TYPE 3 [Understanding Organization Question]

When the professor mentions the study abroad office, he states, "Visit the study abroad office and ask someone there about it." He wants the student to go there to get more information about studying abroad.

TYPE 4 [Understanding Function Question]

When the professor tells the student that she should study abroad if she has the money, he is encouraging her to go ahead and do what she wants to do by studying abroad.

Summarizing ▶

The student visits the professor to state that she wants to study abroad during her junior year next year. The professor claims it will be a fantastic experience, so she should go abroad if she can afford it. He asks where she wants to go. She says Brazil, but the school lacks Portuguese languages classes, so she cannot study there. He asks about Japan, but she feels her Japanese language skills are not improving very much. The professor mentions Mexico since the student is fluent in Spanish. Then, he tells her to go to the study abroad office for more information.

| TYPES 5–8 |

TYPE 5 (B)   TYPE 6 (C)   TYPE 7 (A)   TYPE 8 (C)

M Student: Hello there. I was wondering if you could assist me with something.

W Nutrition Department Employee: I sure hope so. Why don't you tell me what you need, and I'll see what I can do for you?

M: Sounds good . . . My name is James Eagleton, and I'm the president of the school's health and nutrition club.

W: Ah, yes. I've heard about you, but I've never gotten the chance to meet you. It's a pleasure. But, uh, your major isn't nutrition, is it?

M: Er, no. I'm a double major in physics and chemistry. I'm planning to attend medical school in the future. But, uh, that's not really important.

W: Okay, James. What do you need? I'd love to be able to assist you.

M: Thanks. Well, here's the deal. We at the club have been thinking about holding some kind of an event that could, uh, you know, promote good health and nutrition. After all, a lot of the students here aren't in, uh . . . they aren't in the best of shape. I suppose that's a polite way of putting it.

W: I'll say.

M: Anyway, what we are looking for is some advice. I know the Nutrition Department sponsored some events last year, so, um, what I'd really like is some advice.

W: Then you've come to the right place.

M: That's great.

W: First, one thing you should realize is that no one wants to have health and nutrition information shoved in his or her face.

M: What do you mean?

W: Well, people can be sensitive about that. So we try to do some simple, subtle things that will encourage students to start thinking about their health.

M: Okay, I'm with you so far. So what should we do?

W: How about passing out nutrition checklists at the dining halls? The students could take a look at what they're eating and see if it's healthy or not. We did that last year, and it was a big success.

M: Hey, that sounds good. Oh, do, uh, do you have a copy of that checklist?

W: Sure. I've got one right here.

TYPE 5 [Gist-Content Question]

The student and the employee are mostly talking about what kind of activity the student, as the president of the health and nutrition club, should do with his club.

TYPE 6 [Detail Question]

The woman says, "How about passing out nutrition checklists at the dining halls? The students could take a look at what they're eating and see if it's healthy or not. We did that last year, and it was a big success."

TYPE 7 [Understanding Attitude Question]

When the woman meets the man, she states, "Ah, yes. I've heard about you, but I've never gotten the chance to meet you. It's a pleasure."

TYPE 8 [Making Inferences Question]

The student asks for a copy of the checklist, and the woman says that she has a copy of it somewhere, so she is going to give it to him momentarily.

Summarizing ▶

The student visits the Nutrition Department to ask for some help. He introduces himself as the new president of the health and nutrition club. The department secretary says she is pleased to meet him. The student says he wants to help promote good health and nutrition on campus but is not sure what to do, so he asks for some advice. The woman says that the man should be subtle about how he gives other students information. She mentions passing out nutrition checklists in dining halls. The student thinks that is a good idea, so he asks for a copy of the checklist.

Mastering Topics with Lectures B1   p.78

1   2   3

Script & Graphic Organizer 02-037

W Professor: Okay, any more questions . . .? No? Then shall we continue our discussion of human migration . . .? Good. After the Americas were populated with humans . . . that would be sometime after the last ice age, approximately twelve to eighteen thousand years ago, the last places on the Earth to be inhabited were the eastern Pacific islands.

M Student: What about the Arctic and Antarctic? They still aren't really inhabited, are they?

W: Ah, yes. You have a point, but let's ignore those two regions since no one really lives there today. Now, back to our topic of the populating of the Pacific islands . . . The best evidence suggests that humans sailed across the Pacific Ocean first from China to Taiwan. From there, they went to the Philippines, New Guinea, and then to Australia and the Solomon Islands. All this was accomplished by approximately 30,000 B.C. Yeah, they had ships back then. Then, for the longest time, there was no eastward movement. [3]Suddenly, for reasons as yet unexplained, sometime around 1300 B.C., the people that archaeologists call the Lapita . . . that's L-A-P-I-T-A . . . began sailing east from the Solomon Islands. **By 800 B.C., they had reached as far as Fiji, Tonga, and Samoa, which is pretty impressive sailing for primitive ships.**

Again, after these migrations, there was a pause of more than a thousand years. Then, the Lapita's descendants, known today as Polynesians, set sail to explore the vast reaches of the eastern Pacific Ocean. They went north to the Hawaiian Islands, south to New Zealand, and east to the last lonely outpost of the Pacific: Easter Island. The big question is this . . . How did the Lapita first, and the Polynesians later, manage to navigate and sail large, uh, canoes across such huge ocean distances with no compasses or charts? What makes these voyages even more remarkable is that these explorers had no foreknowledge of where the islands were or even if they existed in the first place.

One secret to their success lies in their unique skills as open-ocean navigators. A great deal of evidence suggests that every generation knew the stars and constellations in their area very well and thus effectively used them to navigate the ocean. There were, of course, other, simpler clues. Like what? Well, near land, there would be birds in the sky and branches, leaves, and fruits like coconuts floating in the water. Even from far distances, islands could have been detected by the buildup of clouds over land on a hot day. Additionally, volcanic activity, of which there is quite a lot in the Pacific . . . Remember that Hawaii and many other islands were formed because of volcanic eruptions . . . Anyway, volcanic activity can send massive clouds of steam skyward when lava hits the water and begins to cool. Those clouds could have been sighted from far, far away.

But archaeologists remain puzzled by one issue . . . The prevailing winds in that part of the Pacific do not blow from west to east but from east to west. So, how did they sail eastward? Perhaps they had learned the art of tacking. And they . . . Oh, tacking is the ability to sail into the wind. That's all. Maybe they did that. Unfortunately, no ancient canoes have been excavated, so we can't say that with certainty. There's another possibility though. Perhaps they sailed during an El Nino period. El Nino is a weather phenomenon that occurs in the Pacific every few years and can disrupt weather all over the world. During intense El Nino periods, the winds . . . yeah, you guessed it . . . they blow from west to east in that part of the Pacific. By sailing during these times, the Lapita and the Polynesians would have been able to reach the eastern Pacific quite easily.

Pacific Ocean Migrations

Which Islands:	Who Settled Them:	How They Navigated the Ocean:
First settled in islands around Southeastern Asia and then sailed east to islands as far away as Hawaii and Easter Island	The Lapita were the first to settle the Pacific Islands The Polynesians sailed to other islands after them	They knew the stars and constellations They looked for birds, branches, leaves, and fruit They searched for clouds They used El Nino winds

1   [Gist-Content Question]

During the lecture, the professor describes some ways in which it is believed that the Lapita and the Polynesians managed to sail across the Pacific and populate the various islands in the ocean.

2   [Understanding Organization Question]

At the beginning of the lecture, the professor mentions the problem of trying to figure out how the Pacific islands were settled, and then she spends the rest of the time providing the solution to that problem.

3   [Understanding Function Question]

When the professor comments that it was "impressive sailing for primitive ships," she is implying that at that time, ships did not usually travel long distances such as the Lapita did.

Summarizing ▶

The professor notes that the Pacific islands were the last places people inhabited. She mentions that people left China and then populated the various islands. The first people to do this were the Lapita. Later, the Polynesians sailed far to settle islands such as Hawaii and Easter Island. She notes that their ships were primitive, so they relied on their skills as open-ocean navigators. They also knew the stars well so sailed according to them. When searching for land, they tried to spot birds in the sky and coconuts in the water. They looked for clouds from volcanoes. They also used El Nino winds to sail across the ocean.

Mastering Topics with Lectures B2   p.79

1 Ⓒ   2 Perception: ④ Memory: ①, ②
Imagination: ③   3 Ⓓ

M Professor: Next, I'd like to examine three things related to the human mind: perception, memory, and imagination. They're all different yet somewhat interrelated in that all three have to do with how people view the world around them and the events that take place in their lives.

Perception is related to how people organize and view the large amounts of information their senses absorb on a daily basis. How each person sees and understands this information differs, uh, it differs widely. Some factors influencing perception are culture, nationality, language, and past experiences. Perception can also differ depending upon how others see the reality of a situation. With sight, for example, optical illusions represent a test of a person's perception. You know, one person may see one thing while another sees something completely different. One of the main theories concerning perception is that humans can only understand new things based on their past experiences. For example, imagine two people are walking in a forest. One's happy while the other's apprehensive. While walking, they see a stick on the ground. The second person screams when the first person tries to pick it up. Why? The stick resembles a snake to the second person because he was once almost bitten by one in another forest in the past. The first person lacks this experience and thus has no apprehension.

Memory is also related to people's past experiences. People can store information from the past, retain it for a long time, and recall events from the past. Very often, however, the brain acts like a computer with a limited storage capacity. Memories of important events . . . a wedding day, a sporting event a person took part in or attended, a graduation day . . . are retained while the activities a person did the previous day are hard to recall. Part of the problem with memory is that it isn't always accurate. Two people who experience the same event may have different memories of it. The basic facts . . . you know, the date, time, or weather . . . may be in agreement, but how the events unfolded may be radically different. This is partially connected to people's perception of the events. In this way, perception can affect memory. Police experience this problem all the time. For instance, eyewitnesses to crimes often give conflicting accounts. Odd, huh? There's also something called selective memory, which happens when people block out traumatic events. Some experts believe that's the body's way of protecting itself from recalling disturbing events that could result in emotional and, by extension, physical harm . . . Yes?

W Student: Is that why some people get amnesia?

M: Well, yes, in some cases. But amnesia, which can be partial or total, more frequently results from an injury to the brain and its memory center. But that was a very perceptive question. Now, moving on to imagination . . .

This is the ability to form a mental image of something. It can be something you experienced in the past—and in this way, it's related to memory—or it could be something you've never experienced. One of the primary ways humans use their imagination is when they hear stories. For instance, children listening to their parents read a story have no visual representations of the characters or setting, so they imagine and form mental images instead. As children get older and learn to read, they take this mental image projection to the next step by relating the words on the page to images in their minds. Some words may be familiar. Others may not. In that case, they require a leap of the imagination in that people must create an image in their mind of something that they've never seen or experienced before.

The Human Mind

Perception:	Memory:	Imagination:
How people organize and view the information they receive	The storing, retaining, and recalling of information from people's pasts	The mental images people form of either past experiences or things they have never experienced

1 [Gist-Purpose Question]

During the lecture, the professor mentions three things that are related to the human mind, and perception is one of them.

2 [Connecting Content Question]

According to the lecture, perception affects how people regard something. Memory deals with how a person can recall information, and it can be affected by amnesia, which happens when a person loses all or some of his or her memory. And imagination lets people create various pictures in their heads.

3 [Understanding Attitude Question]

After the student asks her question, the professor states, "But that was a very perceptive question." By listening to the professor's words and tone of voice, it is possible to tell that he is praising her.

Summarizing ▶

The professor states that perception, memory, and imagination are all parts of the human mind. Perception relates to how people look at and understand information. It can be related to a person's culture, nationality, language, and past experiences. Memory is the information that people store in their brains and their ability to recall it. People's memories of the same event can sometimes differ. This is mostly due to their perception of what happened. Imagination consists of the mental images that people form. These can be based upon past experiences, or they can be something that a person makes up entirely.

Mastering Topics with Lectures B3

p.80

1 Ⓒ, Ⓓ   2 Ⓐ   3 Ⓒ

Script 02-039

W Professor: The spice trade between the East . . . by which I mean Asia . . . and Europe is what drove the Europeans to seek an easier route to Asia during the early modern period of, oh, the fifteenth and sixteenth centuries. Of course, they managed to find a water route to Asia by sailing around Africa, and eventually explorers like Columbus sailed west to the New World. So tell me . . . What was it about spices that drove men to sail toward the horizon while not even knowing where they were going . . .? Anyone?

M Student: As far as I know, spices were pretty valuable back then, so people were, uh, they were willing to pay a lot for them. So I guess . . . I guess finding the lands with the spices was worth the risk.

W: That's true. The spice trade was quite lucrative. But what was it that made people think that spices were valuable . . .? Remember that something's value is related to how people perceive it. Okay? Well, spices were valuable because of the Europeans' diets and the technology that existed at that time. Now, first, when I say "Europeans," I'm referring mostly to the rich upper classes. Few members of the middle class could afford spices, and as for peasants, rarely, with the exception of salt, did they ever come close to spices. Now, uh, people used spices like we do today: to make their food taste better. But that wasn't the only reason. Hundreds of years ago, there was no real means to keep food fresh for long periods of time. Salt, the most commonly used and most readily available spice, was often utilized to preserve meat and fish. Dried salted fish, for instance, was good for months and merely had to be soaked in water to make it soft and easy to cook. Centuries ago, since food preservation methods were so primitive, food often spoiled. So people may have used spices to mask the taste of spoiled meat. However, some academics dispute this notion. They claim that no cooks would have wasted valuable spices on rotting meat. But let's consider that this was still possible.

Now, as for the spices themselves, what are they? They come from plants and herbs. All except salt, that is, as it comes from the sea or deposits found in the ground. Now, the herb and plant spices that can be grown vary according to the land and climate. Back then, most of Europe's spices came from Asia, Africa, and the Middle East . . . But mostly from Asia. Since spices were so valued in Europe, the spice trade between East and West began. Pepper was the most common spice, but cinnamon and cloves—as well as many others—were also traded. Italian cities such as Venice controlled much of the spice trade and thus grew quite wealthy. However, when the Ottoman Turks captured Constantinople in the middle of the fifteenth century . . . 1453 to be exact . . . the overland spice trade with East Asia was essentially shut down.

At the same time, fortunately for the Europeans, people started becoming interested in sailing directly to China and India. Men like Vasco de Gama sailed southward around Africa and attempted to reach Asia that way. This opened up a long seaway connecting Europe and Asia. Additionally, men like Christopher Columbus and John Cabot thought that an easier way to get to the Asian spices would be to sail west across the Atlantic. Of course, the Americas were, uh, in the way. But remember that it was the spice trade that drove these early explorers. Men like da Gama, whom we need to cover now, sought riches for themselves and their patrons, who were typically kings or groups of wealthy merchants.

The Spice Trade

Why Use Spices:	First Trade Route:
Make food taste better	Over land from Asia to Europe through Constantinople
Help preserve food	
Mask the taste of spoiled meat	Second Trade Route:
	By water south around Africa all the way to Asia

1 [Detail Question]

According to the lecture, spices were valuable and cost the Europeans a lot of money to purchase. In addition, the professor states, "When I say 'Europeans,' I'm referring mostly to the rich upper classes. Few members of the middle class could afford spices, and as for peasants, rarely, with the exception of salt, did they ever come close to spices."

2 [Understanding Organization Question]

During her lecture, the professor first mentions why the Europeans wanted spices—the cause of the spice trade—and then she goes over some of the results of the spice trade—its effects.

3 [Making Inferences Question]

When talking about the voyages of discovery, the professor states, "Men like da Gama, whom we need to cover now, sought riches for themselves and their patrons, who were typically kings or groups of wealthy merchants." She is therefore indicating that she is going to talk about some of the voyages that the Europeans went on.

The professor says that the spice trade took place between Europe and Asia. The spices cost a lot of money because they were rare and valuable. In the past, people used spices to help improve the taste of their food and also to preserve their food. Except for salt, spices come from plants and herbs. Pepper, cinnamon, and cloves were commonly traded. When the Ottoman Turks captured Constantinople in 1453 though, the overland spice trade closed. So the Europeans tried to find water routes to Asia. They sailed around Africa and also managed to discover the Americas because of the spice trade.

Mastering Topics with Lectures B4

p.81

1 Ⓐ   2 Ⓒ   3 Ⓐ

Script & Graphic Organizer 02-040

M Professor: So that's what you need to study for next week's midterm. Oh, today's lecture will also be on the exam, so please take good notes. Our topic today is mass communication methods in the Middle Ages and Renaissance. But first, we need a little background information . . . Throughout history, there have been four primary means of mass communication. First is the oral tradition, where stories are passed by word of mouth. Second is the writing and copying of manuscripts, which started in ancient times and continued until the late Middle Ages. Third is the printing press, which was invented in the fifteenth century. Fourth is the electronic age of communication, which began in the late nineteenth century and continues even today.

While there was some printing on wooden blocks in the Far East during medieval times in Europe, all book and manuscript copying was done by hand. This was mostly accomplished by monks in monasteries until around the twelfth century or so, which was when more commercial-oriented enterprises entered the book copying and selling business. In their monasteries, monks would painstakingly copy books or manuscripts. There were typically two people who worked on the same project: the scribe and the illuminator. The scribe did the actual writing while the illuminator drew and colored fancy lettering and pictures. The process was incredibly slow, so most monasteries had relatively few books and manuscripts. Oh, what's the difference between the two? Well, books were distinguished by being bound and covered—usually with leather—while manuscripts were a, ah, a more open form that, uh, were usually rolled into scrolls. Both types were copied on parchment, which was made from animal skins.

In some monasteries, one scribe and one illuminator would work on a single copy of a book or manuscript.

Later on, after businesses and guilds took over, they would have a person work on only a single part of the text. He'd copy the same few pages over and over again. Hopefully, he didn't make too many mistakes. This, by the way, was a major problem back then. Anyway, by using this method, more copies could be produced in a shorter period of time. Sound familiar?

W Student: It sounds like an assembly line.

M: [3]How right you are! That's exactly what it resembled. Now, in the twelfth and thirteenth centuries, it became common in Europe to give universities, which were starting to be established, monopolies in book and manuscript copying and selling. **The hope was that they'd produce some uniformity in copying and also cut down on the myriad errors that many books had.** For some time, this practice was effective, and there were even strict laws and codes concerning the book and manuscript trade. However, monasteries and many of the newly created religious orders in this period sought to regain their former position—or to attain it—so they began improving the quality of their work thanks to new laws and the more intense supervision of scribes. Then, along came the printing press, which changed, well, it changed everything.

Now, during the Renaissance, Johannes Gutenberg invented the printing press in Germany around 1439 or 1440, and this marked the beginning of the end of hand copying. By the end of the fifteenth century, it was clear that the printing press had overtaken hand copying. Printing presses were faster and had the ability to make copies that looked similar and had no errors when they were copied . . . Well, that is, unless, of course, an error was made when the type was set. Printing thus became extremely popular with people. Not only did books become abundant, but they also became cheap to buy. By the end of the sixteenth century, printing presses had almost completely taken over the job of copying.

Book Reproduction in the Middle Ages and Renaissance

Medieval Book Printing:	Renaissance Book Printing:
Scribes copied books by hand	Johannes Gutenberg invented printing press
Illuminators drew pictures	Most books copied by machine, not by hand
Monasteries and universities copied books	

1 [Gist-Content Question]

During his lecture, the professor talks about how scribes copied manuscripts and then begins talking about the printing press. Thus, he is going over the duplication of books in Europe.

2 [Connecting Content Question]

The professor states, "By the end of the sixteenth century, printing presses had almost completely taken over the job of copying." It can therefore be assumed that monasteries and universities stopped copying books at this time.

3 [Understanding Function Question]

The professor notes that there were many errors in the books and that people hoped that the fact that universities were in charge of copying books would lead to fewer errors. He therefore implies that people disliked the mistakes in books written by hand.

Summarizing ▶

The professor mentions the four primary means of mass communication people have used over time. Then, he notes that books and manuscripts in the Middle Ages were copied by hand. This was mostly done by monks in monasteries. A scribe would write the words while an illuminator would draw pictures. But this process took a long time, and many mistakes were made. Later, universities started copying books with somewhat better results. Then, in the Renaissance, Johannes Gutenberg invented the printing press, so most people began to print books this way. Books became cheaper and more common, and they had much fewer errors in them.

Mastering Topics with Conversations B5   p.82

1   **2**   **3**

Script & Graphic Organizer 02-041

W Professor: Peter, would you mind stepping into my office for a moment, please? There's something I'd like to discuss with you.

M Student: Sure thing, Professor Partridge.

W: Let me get straight to the point . . . What are you doing next weekend?

M: Um . . . I haven't really thought that far in advance yet. Do you need some more work done on your computer or something? I suppose I have time to drop by for that.

W: Oh, no. It's not that. You see, uh, there's a competition coming up, and I think you'd be perfect for it.

M: A competition? Like sports? You might want to ask someone from the football team in that case. I've never been much of an athlete.

W: Actually, it's a math competition.

M: Math? Er . . . I guess I could do it. I've never been in one before, but I'm willing to give it a try. But why me and not any of the juniors or seniors here? I'm just getting started here. You know, uh, it's just my first

semester at college.

W: That may be true, but you have a knack for solving math problems that I've never seen in anyone at this school before. This competition will basically pit you against other students from various colleges. You'll compete against others to solve questions as quickly as possible.

M: That sounds kind of fun. Sure. I'll do it.

W: Great. I'm glad you can go. We'll be flying to Atlanta on Friday evening.

M: Flying? I don't think I can afford that. That's way out of my price range.

W: Don't worry about a thing. ³The school is sponsoring everything. That means your airfare, lodging, and food will be completely free. The school will even give you 50 dollars a day to spend while you're away.

M: No way!

W: It's true, Peter. I wouldn't make up anything like that. We'll leave on Friday evening and return on Sunday evening.

M: Who is going on the trip?

W: You, me, a graduate student in the Math Department, and Professor Whipple.

M: That sounds great. I'll have to contact my boss at my part-time job and tell him that I can't go in on Saturday, but he should be fine with that. He's very understanding about academic matters.

W: That's wonderful news. I'll have the department secretary confirm everything then. Just be sure to do your best at the contest. I think you have a legitimate chance at winning.

M: Thanks for having confidence in me, Professor. And thanks for selecting me. It's an honor.

Office Hours

Professor's Request:	*Student's Response 1:*
Wants the student to take part in a math competition	*Wonders why the professor doesn't ask a junior or senior to go*
Professor's Explanation:	*Students' Response 2:*
Says that the student has a knack for solving math problems and has a chance to win	*Agrees to participate in the contest*

1 [Gist-Purpose Question]

The professor tells the student, "You see, uh, there's a competition coming up, and I think you'd be perfect for it."

2 [Understanding Function Question]

When the professor asks the student about his weekend plans, she is trying to determine if he can go on a trip to take part in a math competition.

3 [Understanding Attitude Question]

When the student responds, "No way!" he is indicating that he does not believe what the professor just told him is true.

Summarizing ▶

The professor tells the student that there is a math competition and that she thinks he should take part in it. He wonders why a junior or senior is not invited since he is only a freshman. The professor responds that the student has a knack for solving math problems. He then agrees to go. The professor says the contest will be in Atlanta and the school will pay for everything. The student remarks that he needs to tell his boss at his part-time job that he cannot work on the weekend. He then states that it is an honor to be selected.

Mastering Topics with Conversations B6

1 Ⓑ   2 Ⓒ   3 Ⓐ

Script & Graphic Organizer 02-042

M1 Student: Good afternoon. My name's Tom Snyder, and I have an appointment for one thirty. It's a little early, but, uh, do you mind if we start now?

M2 Registrar's Office Employee: Not at all. I was just waiting for you to get here, Tom. Have a seat . . . Now, what can I do for you today?

M1: I'm here to make sure that all of my paperwork for graduation has been taken care of. It seems like there's a lot of, uh, stuff for us to do before we can actually graduate.

M2: That's true. There does seem to be a lot more red tape than usual this year, but that shouldn't pose any problems. At least, I hope not. Why don't you give me your paperwork, and I'll see if everything is . . . is in order?

M1: Sure. Here you are.

M2: Okay. This is your updated transcript, right?

M1: Yes, it's current up to this semester. So I, uh, I have enough credits to graduate, don't I?

M2: Let me see . . . You're an engineer according to this . . . So, uh . . . yes. ³Assuming you don't drop any of your current classes, you will have two more credits than you need in order to graduate.

M1: Okay. That's what I had thought, but I'm glad to

have someone in a position of authority confirm it.

M2: So then . . . If that's everything . . .?

M1: Uh, actually, I'm not sure. I want to make sure there's nothing wrong or nothing else for me to do.

M2: Well, your classes are fine . . . Your grades are good. It looks like you might even graduate with honors if you can pull off a couple of A's this semester. I don't think you've got any problems.

M1: Can you just confirm that for me though? I've got a lot of relatives coming for graduation, and they'd be really disappointed if I didn't get my diploma.

M2: Sure, sure. I see your point. May I see your student ID, please?

M1: ID? Uh, yeah. Hold on. I need to get it out of my wallet . . . Here it is.

M2: This will only take a second for me to . . . Hmm . . .

M1: Hmm? What does that mean? I don't like the sound of that.

M2: It seems you owe the library some money. Five dollars, to be exact. It's some kind of a fine you got three months ago but haven't bothered to pay yet. Is this correct?

M1: Oh, my goodness. I totally forgot about that. I'll head over and pay the fine right now. Uh, is there anything else?

M2: Pay the fine, and you're good to go.

M1: Thanks, sir. I appreciate your time and effort. Have a great day.

Service Encounter

Reason for Visiting:	Result:
Wants to make sure that he can graduate this semester	Student has enough classes to graduate this semester
Problem:	Solution:
Has to pay a five-dollar library fine	Will go to the library and pay the fine

1 [Detail Question]

The student owes the library a five-dollar fine, so he needs to pay a bill.

2 [Understanding Attitude Question]

When the employee tells the student that he has nothing to worry about, the student responds by asking, "Can you just confirm that for me though?" He shows that he is quite thorough when doing something.

3 [Understanding Function Question]

When the employee asks, "If that's everything . . .?" he is trying to find out if the student needs anything else or

Answers, Explanations, and Scripts | 43

if their conversation is finished.

Summarizing ▶

The student visits the Registrar's office to make sure that his paperwork for graduation is all complete. The employee takes a look at his transcript and says that the student has enough classes to graduate. He also notes that the student might be able to graduate with honors. The student then gives the employee his ID so that he can check whether everything is fine. The employee discovers that the student owes five dollars in library fines that he needs to pay. As soon as the student takes care of the fine, he will be able to graduate.

TOEFL Practice Tests C1

1 Ⓒ 2 Ⓐ 3 Andrew Carnegie: ②, ③ John D. Rockefeller: ①, ④ 4 Ⓐ 5 Ⓒ 6 Ⓓ

Script 02-043

M Professor: This is just a reminder to everyone that your paper on the life of an American businessperson is due next Monday. Some of you still have to tell me who you are going to write about, so please fill me in as soon as possible.

W Student: [6]Professor Jackson, can we write about someone who's not American, like, uh, Rupert Murdoch?

M: Actually, I'd like you to stick with Americans. Okay? That's the focus of this class after all. Now, if there are no further questions . . . Let's look at two American businessmen who made their fortunes in the nineteenth century. I'm referring to Andrew Carnegie and John D. Rockefeller. Both became billionaires and left legacies of philanthropic endeavors that haven't been equaled since. Carnegie hailed from Scotland and made his fortune in the steel business while Rockefeller was from the U.S. and became the world's first oil magnate. Both were acknowledged as the richest men in America during their lifetimes.

Let's take a glimpse first at Carnegie. He was what we call a self-made man. He never had a formal education, nor did he come from wealth or status. He came to Pennsylvania with his family in 1848 at the age of, um, thirteen, and he promptly entered the workforce to support his family. He became a telegraph messenger and, later, an operator. In this job, he made many connections that would serve him well throughout his life. He saved part of his money and made wise investments, mostly in the railway industry, which further increased his fortune. Carnegie made the transition to the steel business during the Civil War, and he earned huge profits from supplying war materials

to Union armies. He founded a steel company in 1870 that later became U.S. Steel, the world's largest steel manufacturer. Decades later, Carnegie abruptly retired from business in 1901 and spent the rest of his life establishing foundations, libraries, universities, and other institutions, most of which bear his name even today.

John D. Rockefeller, meanwhile, was the world's first billionaire, and some consider him the wealthiest person in history. Like Carnegie, he gave away much of his fortune in his later years after he retired. Also like Carnegie, he never attended college, and he actually had little schooling beyond what he received as a child. Unlike Carnegie, Rockefeller made his fortune in oil. He, his brother, and several partners got into the oil business in Ohio when it first started becoming a commercial enterprise in the, uh, the 1850s and 1860s. They constructed a refinery near Cleveland during the Civil War. At that time, oil was mainly used for lubrication and for making kerosene for oil lamps. Rockefeller founded Standard Oil, the company that made him most of his riches, in 1870. He was a strict person who barely spent any money, and he ruled his company with an iron will. Through careful planning and, at times, ruthless business practices, twenty-five years later, Standard Oil became the world's largest oil company.

Both Carnegie and Rockefeller, despite their philanthropic activities, came under scrutiny for their business practices. Both were accused of not paying their workers enough and of not sharing their wealth with their employees. These accusations were mostly false as Carnegie established pension funds for his workers, and Rockefeller made many people who worked for him wealthy thanks to the success of his business. Both men, however, were antiunion, and this led to clashes with workers. But most of the animosity toward them came from people's jealousy that they had achieved great wealth. This jealousy fell more on Rockefeller than on Carnegie. Why . . .? Well, for his entire career, Rockefeller was accused of unfair business practices, of pushing aside competitors, and of ruining many of them in the process. Most of these accusations were at least partially true. Under pressure from various public and business interests, the U.S. government went on the offensive against Standard Oil. In 1911, the government called it a monopoly and broke it up. The many oil companies we have today, such as Exxon and Chevron, are the legacy of this breakup.

Today, both men are remembered chiefly for their great wealth and philanthropy. In comparing them, we can note both similarities and differences. Carnegie was the better liked of the two by the public, and by the time he died in 1919, most of his fortune had been given away. Rockefeller lived until he was almost ninety-eight years old and died in 1937. He spent the last forty years of his life in retirement, during which time he also gave away his fortune. Yet it would be safe to say that despite his philanthropy, Rockefeller was hated more than he was loved. Rockefeller often wouldn't stop until he had bought out or crushed a competitor, which gave him a bad reputation. Ironically, some say that Carnegie was really the more ruthless of the two. Let's take a look at some of their deals in detail, and I'll let you decide on that one.

1 [Gist-Content Question]

During the lecture, the professor talks about how Andrew Carnegie and John D. Rockefeller, two Americans, conducted business.

2 [Detail Question]

About Carnegie, the professor states, "Ironically, some say that Carnegie was really the more ruthless of the two." This shows the professor believes that Carnegie had a coldblooded attitude.

3 [Connecting Content Question]

According to the lecture, Andrew Carnegie was more popular with the public and made most of his fortune in the steel industry. As for John D. Rockefeller, he was in the oil industry, and he might have been the richest man of all time.

4 [Understanding Organization Question]

During the lecture, the professor both compares and contrasts Carnegie's and Rockefeller's business activities and lives in general.

5 [Making Inferences Question]

At the end of the lecture, the professor tells the class, "Let's take a look at some of their deals in detail, and I'll let you decide on that one."

6 [Understanding Function Question]

When the professor tells the student to "stick with Americans," he is rejecting her proposal to write her paper on Rupert Murdoch.

TOEFL Practice Tests C2

1 Ⓐ 2 Ⓐ 3 Ⓑ 4 Ⓐ 5 Ⓓ 6 Ⓒ

Script 02-044

W Professor: Among mammals, humans spend the most time rearing their young. Human babies are quite helpless and remain so even after they gain some ability to move and communicate. The process of aging from a baby to a mature adult takes between, oh, fifteen and twenty years, and some, unfortunately, never really seem to become very mature at all. Anyway, what I'd

like to discuss now is the early development of babies, in particular their motor functions and cognitive abilities.

Motor functions involve the use of the muscles to move the limbs around and, eventually, to perform such tasks as walking, picking up objects, feeding, and writing. At first, babies have limited motor functions. Think about it like this: They have spent up to forty weeks floating freely inside their mother's womb, and with the exception of giving kicks and possibly sucking their thumbs, they have no experience whatsoever with movement. That's why they're so helpless at first. The first couple of months after birth, they lie on their back and only move their arms and legs a bit. Parents can often help develop their babies' muscles by helping them move their arms and legs. By the third month after birth, most babies can reach for dangling objects, open and close their hands, grasp small toys, and track movement with their eyes.

By the, uh, the sixth month, babies can roll over by themselves. This, of course, can cause problems, so babies must be constantly watched. Next, they learn to keep their head up and how to crawl, first on their belly and finally on all fours. The next major action, which usually occurs by the eighth month, is, uh, is sitting up without being supported by anything. By the twelfth month, babies can put objects in and out of a container and may take a few steps with someone's assistance. Walking usually doesn't begin until a few months later. Developing motor skills, as you can see, is an ongoing activity for babies and children. Toys and games that involve using the hands and fingers are great ways to help babies develop their motor skills. Later, as children age, toys and games with smaller objects can also improve their ability to pick up things and improve their hand-eye coordination.

Meanwhile . . . at the same time babies are developing their motor skills, they're also developing their cognitive skills. This means they're developing their senses . . . you know, touch, sight, hearing, smell, and taste. They're also learning to speak. When babies are born, they have limited vision. ⁵Actually, here's an interesting fact for you . . . Did you know that the eyes are the only part of the body that don't grow and are the same size at birth and death? **Just a little trivia for you.** Anyway, babies can only see about a foot in front of them when they're born. After one month, they can focus on objects near them and will also respond to bright lights. As for their hearing, they will turn their head toward loud noises and may respond to familiar voices, such as those of their parents or siblings.

Over the next few months, babies begin making different sounds, such as "ah" and "oh," learn to recognize individuals, and smile when they recognize certain people. By their fourth month, babies can move their eyes in a 180-degree arc to follow an object, can make babbling sounds, and can recognize

Answers, Explanations, and Scripts | 45

colors, shapes, and the feel of things. Soon, they are able to see across a room, make more sounds, and recognize anger or happiness in the tone of someone's voice. By the eighth month after their birth, babies have discovered gravity, so they might start dropping objects from a chair or bed just for fun. They also babble continuously, recognize their own name, and may become anxious if someone takes them away from their mother or father. At some point during the next four months, they will say their first word. This is most commonly the word for mother or father. Babies can also recognize themselves in a mirror, will shake their head "no" if they don't want to do something, and can begin to recognize music and make dancing movements when it is played.

⁶**Of course, all of these months are just benchmarks.** Every child is different and naturally develops at different rates. However, if some or all of these actions don't happen within the first eighteen months, there could be certain, uh, issues with the child. For instance, if a child fails to look people in the eye, doesn't track movement, or makes no language sounds, it could be a sign of autism. In addition, children who don't get enough play time or are kept in a crib all day will develop poor motor control and may require massage therapy to overcome this. In all cases, parents need to be aware of how quickly or slowly their children are developing so that proper steps can be taken if there are any issues.

1 [Gist-Content Question]

During her lecture, the professor goes over how babies develop various skills.

2 [Understanding Organization Question]

In bringing up autism, the professor states, "If some or all of these actions don't happen within the first eighteen months, there could be certain, uh, issues with the child. For instance, if a child fails to look people in the eye, doesn't track movement, or makes no language sounds, it could be a sign of autism."

3 [Detail Question]

The professor mentions, "Babies can only see about a foot in front of them when they're born."

4 [Making Inferences Question]

The professor states, "Parents can often help develop their babies' muscles by helping them move their arms and legs," and, "Children who don't get enough play time or are kept in a crib all day will develop poor motor control and may require massage therapy to overcome this." Both sentences imply that parents can help their children become more developed.

5 [Understanding Function Question]

When the professor tells the students that she is giving them some trivia, she is letting them know that the information is not particularly important and that she is just saying something that they might find interesting.

6 [Understanding Attitude Question]

When the professor says that the "months are just benchmarks," she is letting the students know that all of the developments do not happen exactly like she has told them and that there could be some variation in how babies develop. She has merely given them a general outline.

TOEFL Practice Tests C3   p.88

Script 02-045

W Student: If you don't mind, Professor Venarde, I'd like to ask you a couple of questions about our upcoming midterm.

M Professor: Sure, that's no problem at all. What exactly would you like to know about it? I hope you're not planning on asking me for any of the actual questions. I don't think I can give you that much help. The other students might not appreciate it.

W: The thought never even crossed my mind . . . Well, okay. It did cross my mind, but I figured you wouldn't tell me even if I asked you nicely.

M: Good one. Okay. What do you want to know?

W: Well, are we going to be tested only on the material from the book or also from the various field trips we've gone on?

M: Good question . . . I'd say that the majority of the information on the exam will come from the lectures. Not just the book, mind you. You're responsible for everything I talk about in class as well as the handouts I give you each week. As for the field trips . . . Just keep the main reasons why we visited each place in mind, and you'll be fine.

W: Thanks. That's helpful. I'll be sure to review my notes in that case. I'll also have to find all of the handouts that you gave. Okay.

M: So, uh, is there anything else you'd like to know?

W: Er, yes, actually, that is if you don't mind my asking. This is actually the more important question: Is this going to be an essay test or what?

M: Oh, I don't give merely essay tests.

W: All right. That's a relief.

M: Slow down. I'm not finished yet. The test will be

quite comprehensive. So there will be fill-in-the-blank questions, short answers, and yes, a couple of essays for you to answer.

W: Oh . . . I see. I suppose that I'd better get out of here and hit the books. I'm going to have to go over everything at least two more times before I feel like I'm completely ready for the test. Thanks for your help, sir.

M: The pleasure is all mine. Oh, by the way, Molly, good luck with the performance tomorrow.

W: Good luck? Oh, how did you know I'm going to be acting in the school play?

M: I often have lunch with Professor Trout, your advisor. He's told me all about you and your acting ability.

W: [5]Wow, I had no idea that I was the subject of discussion.

M: Yes, we commonly discuss our brightest students. It's a habit many of us have.

W: Oh . . . Thank you, sir. So, uh, will you be in attendance tomorrow evening?

M: Actually, yes, I will. Before you got here, I was getting ready to go over to the student center so that I could purchase a couple of tickets.

W: Wow, that's so cool. I didn't know that faculty attended events like these.

M: I think you'll be surprised tomorrow by the number of faculty members that are in attendance. A lot of the teachers at this school try to be involved in the student activities here. It creates more of a, uh, a feeling of togetherness with the student body.

W: That's great. Well, I hope you enjoy the performance.

M: I'm sure I will. Good luck tomorrow. And good luck on the exam. See you on Friday.

W: Yeah, thanks.

1 [Gist-Purpose Question]

The student asks the professor, "Are we going to be tested only on the material from the book or also from the various field trips we've gone on?" so she is trying to find out what the exam is going to cover.

2 [Detail Question]

The professor tells the student, "The majority of the information on the exam will come from the lectures," and, "You're responsible for everything that I talk about in class as well as the handouts I give you each week."

3 [Understanding Attitude Question]

The professor makes jokes with the student and laughs while talking with her. It shows that he is quite relaxed while the two are having a conversation.

4 [Understanding Organization Question]

When the professor mentions the student's upcoming performance, he is letting her know that he is aware of what activities she is involved in at the school.

5 [Understanding Function Question]

When the professor says that he and other professors often talk about their brightest students, he is indicating that they are interested in the accomplishments of their good students.

1	(D)	2	(A)	3	(B)	4	(C)	5	(C)
6	(B)	7	(D)	8	(C)	9	(A)	10	(A)
11	(E)	12	(F)	13	(C)	14	(J)	15	(D)
16	(H)	17	(B)	18	(I)	19	(A)	20	(G)

Chapter **04** | **Social Sciences 2** · Conversations

Mastering Question Types with Lectures A1   p.92

| TYPES 1–4 |

TYPE **1** (A)   TYPE **2** (C)   TYPE **3** (B)   TYPE **4** (A)

Script 02-046

M1 Professor: I know many of you enjoy shopping, so let's talk about that for a second. When you're at a store and see two products that are the same . . . except that one's made by an unknown company while the other is made by a famous company, which are you most likely to purchase? Gloria?

W Student: Easy! The famous company.

M1: Why is that?

W: Hmm . . . I suppose because I trust that company.

M1: Right there, class, is one of the most persuasive reasons why a company should strive to establish a good brand name. This takes time of course. But once a company has been around and has established a reputation as a producer of reliable products, it will typically . . . no, almost always . . . develop customer loyalty. This means that customers will buy its products since they trust the company. Simply put, the company becomes known for its quality products . . . something that most consumers want . . . and should anything go wrong with the products, the customers know they'll have no trouble getting refunds or replacements.

There's plenty of evidence proving that customers will pay a premium for a good brand-name product and will remain loyal to it. I believe that was the subject of the case studies you were supposed to read for your homework last night, right?

Now, I just mentioned brand names, but . . . what are they? Well, brands are one way that companies differentiate their products from those of other companies. Many times, companies use logos . . . you know, signs or symbols, to help identify their brand-name products. I'm sure you've all seen this symbol here . . . haven't you? Yeah, that's what I thought. What does this checkmark symbol represent? Anyone?

M2 Student: Easy. That's Nike, the shoe company.

M1: Precisely. See how important a simple symbol can be? When you see it, you immediately associate that checkmark with Nike. If you look in your textbooks on page, uh . . . page 103, I believe, you'll see several more logos that, I'm willing to bet, most of you will recognize almost instantly. Okay, but I don't want to get too much into logos quite yet. So, uh, let's go back to brand names.

All right . . . Aside from inspiring customer loyalty, why do companies want to have a famous brand name? For one, it makes it much easier for them to release new products. After all, perhaps you're a loyal customer of a, oh, let's say a shoemaker . . . and you hear that this shoemaking company is going to come out with a . . . hmm . . . a new line of tracksuits. Well, if you're in the market for a tracksuit, you're more likely to buy one of that company's new tracksuits simply because you trust its other products. That's exactly what companies want. In many cases, customers assume that high quality in one product means that every product the company makes will be of the same quality. Of course, that's not necessarily true, and that's something we need to look at right now. Here's a prime example of that.

TYPE 1 [Gist-Content Question]

The professor talks about brand names and discusses why companies want to establish them.

TYPE 2 [Detail Question]

The professor states, "There's plenty of evidence proving that customers will pay a premium for a good brand-name product and will remain loyal to it."

TYPE 3 [Understanding Organization Question]

During the lecture, the professor asks the students questions and then allows them to answer. This helps set up what the professor wants to discuss in class.

TYPE 4 [Understanding Function Question]

After the student tells the professor what the checkmark represents, the professor answers by saying, "See how

important a simple symbol can be?"

Summarizing ▶

The professor asks his students about the products they purchase. When one answers, he claims that is the reason why companies want a good brand name. He notes that companies want to inspire brand loyalty because that will make customers purchase more of their products. He then asks about a particular logo, and a student correctly identifies it. He returns to brand names, and he mentions that having a famous brand-name product makes customers more likely to purchase other items, especially new ones, that a company sells. Customers often believe that quality in one product means all of the company's products will have the same quality.

| **TYPES 5–8** |

| TYPE **5** Ⓒ | | TYPE **6** Ⓐ |
| TYPE **7** Castle Gatehouses: ②, ④ Baileys: ①, ③ |
| TYPE **8** Ⓓ |

Script 02-047

M Professor: During the medieval period in England, which lasted roughly from the ninth century to the fifteenth, there was a great deal of castle building. Castles served both as forts and homes for the wealthy landowners who constructed them. As such, castles had to serve two purposes. They protected the lord, his family, and their servants and also served as places to live.

During times of war, castles acted as defensive fortifications for the occupants and others who lived nearby. To protect people inside, castles had several defensive features. The moat was a primary one. It was a large ditch surrounding the castle on all sides. Its main purpose was to prevent attackers from getting too close to the castle walls so that they could use ladders to climb up the walls or dig beneath the walls to collapse them. A moat could be filled with water or could be dry but feature obstacles such as sharpened stakes inside it. To cross the moat, a drawbridge was used. It was a bridge that could be lowered or raised with a winch.

The drawbridge led to the weakest part of castles, uh, the front gate. It was often the only large opening in a castle's defenses, so attackers naturally tried storming the front gates since it led directly into the castle. To prevent this, many castles had a large, solid gatehouse built of strong stones. Inside the gatehouse were solid wooded doors and often a metal portcullis, which was like the bars in a modern prison cell. Many gatehouses were like tunnels leading into their castles, and inside the tunnel roofs were holes, called murder holes, through which defenders could drop boiling oil or shoot various weapons at attackers.

If attackers got past all these defenses, they entered a wide-open area called the bailey. In peacetime, this area was often the site of games, music festivals, and other forms of entertainment, and it also served as a marketplace for local farmers. However, during battles, the bailey was utilized as an open place where attackers could be led and then arrows fired at them from above by defenders on the walls. These walls, called curtain walls, were very high and surrounded the entire castle. The walls almost always had towers at the corners. Towers could be square shaped, circular, or half-circles. Most towers had narrow arrow slits in their walls so that defenders could fire out while they were protected by the thick stone walls. The tops of the walls were called battlements, and they served as posts for men to fire arrows and to drop stones on attackers below.

Now, uh, in the middle of the castle was usually the central keep or great keep. This was a large, solid structure with many floors and which housed the lord and his family. It had bedrooms, kitchens, dining halls, and other types of rooms. In addition, most castles had a dungeon in the lower part of the keep, where prisoners were kept. Yes? You have a question?

W Student: Yes, sir. Why did people stop building castles?

M: Hmm . . . I guess the main reason was the introduction of gunpowder weapons in the fifteenth century. Cannonballs fired at high velocity could easily knock down castle walls. So, uh, what happened was a trend toward building low-lying solid forts that acted as military bases at strategic points in the country while not being homes for lords and their families.

TYPE 5 [Gist-Content Question]

When talking about castles, the professor mostly focuses on the various types of defenses that they featured to protect their inhabitants from attackers.

TYPE 6 [Understanding Attitude Question]

About the front gates of castles, the professor remarks, "The drawbridge led to the weakest part of castles, uh, the front gate."

TYPE 7 [Connecting Content Question]

According to the lecture, castle gatehouses had murder holes and also contained a portcullis made with metal. As for baileys, there served as places for people to get together at various events and were also places where attackers were led to get shot by arrows.

TYPE 8 [Making Inferences Question]

When asked why people quit building castles, the professor responds, "I guess the main reason was the introduction of gunpowder weapons in the fifteenth

century. Cannonballs fired at high velocity could easily knock down castle walls." It can therefore be inferred that castles were easy to defeat with gunpowder weapons.

Summarizing ▶

The professor discusses castles and says their two purposes were to protect the people in them and to serve as places to live. The professor describes castle fortifications, starting with moats. These were large ditches around the castle walls. A drawbridge was used to cross the moat, and it led to the front gate. By the front gate was the gatehouse, which had many defensive fortifications. The bailey was a wide-open area where people others gathered. Inside the castle walls was the keep, which was where the lord and his family lived. The introduction of gunpowder weapons led people to stop building castles.

Mastering Question Types with Lectures A2   p.94

| TYPES 1–4 |

Script 02-048

M Professor: Nomads are people who have no permanent homes but instead move around from place to place. In fact, that's the one characteristic that nomads all over the world share. Anyway, here are a few facts about them for you . . . Nomads have been around for thousands of years. The nomadic lifestyle was actually how all humans lived prior to the emergence of settled civilizations. Even today, there are still nomads. Surprised to hear that? Some sociologists estimate there are between forty and fifty million nomads scattered around the world today. However, keep in mind that nomads are somewhat, um, rare in industrialized countries.

Why do, or did, people become nomads . . .? I think that question will be easier to answer after we look at the various types of nomads there are. Nomads can pretty much be broken down into three main groups: hunter-gatherers, pastoral nomads, and peripatetic nomads.

Let's look first at the hunter-gatherers, who have been around the longest of all. Hunting and gathering is how humans managed to survive before they discovered agriculture and started cultivating the land. What exactly did these hunter-gatherers do? In most cases, they simply followed herds of wild animals as they migrated from place to place throughout the year. The hunter-gatherers killed the animals for meat and also used their hides to clothe themselves. Oh, let's not forget the gathering part of their name, too. They gathered whatever wild fruits, vegetables, and grains they could find. In some cases, these nomads most likely fed upon the same foods as the animals they were following. It was a simple life, but it worked for them.

Pastoral nomads didn't appear until after people began to domesticate animals. Of course, this happened thousands of years ago, so don't think that pastoral nomads are relatively new because, well, they're not. Anyway, once humans tamed various animals . . . sheep, goats, and cattle, for example . . . they needed to provide their animals with food. In most cases, they merely let their animals wander here and there feeding on the grass or other vegetation that grew naturally. Of course, when the food in one area was exhausted or the temperature changed, the animals, and the nomads . . . don't forget them . . . migrated somewhere else. There have been a number of pastoral nomads throughout history, including, uh, let's see . . . Bedouin Arabs, Huns, Kurds, and Mongols.

Now, the third kind is the peripatetic nomad. Ah, that comes from a Greek word and simply means, uh, itinerant, or wandering. Anyway, you actually see these nomads today, and they're even found in some developed countries. What do they do? Well, unlike the first two kinds of nomads, who move around in search of food, peripatetic nomads move around in search of work. They are often tradesmen who travel together or individually. Gypsies . . . you've heard of them, right? They're nomads. And so are Irish Travelers. Look them up if you want to know more about them. ⁴They're actually quite fascinating. Oh, please keep in mind that some critics argue that these, uh, urban nomads aren't true nomads. **However, I, for one, do not concur with what they think for a couple of reasons.**

TYPE 1 [Gist-Purpose Question]

During his lecture, the professor describes the three different types of nomads and notes how they are different from one another.

TYPE 2 [Detail Question]

The professor states that pastoral nomads wandered because their herds needed food, so they followed their animals wherever they went while looking for food.

TYPE 3 [Understanding Organization Question]

During the lecture, the professor explains the different reasons why nomads wander from place to place.

TYPE 4 [Understanding Function Question]

When the professor says that he does not concur with some other people's opinions, he is stating that he disagrees with what some other individuals say.

Summarizing ▶

The professor begins with a description of the nomadic lifestyle and then says that humans lived this way for most of their history. The first nomadic lifestyle he describes is the hunter-gatherer type of nomad. These nomads followed animals as they migrated and collected food that they found. The next type is the pastoral nomad. These nomads emerged after humans learned to tame animals. They followed their own herds as they foraged for food. The peripatetic nomad is the last one he describes. These include modern-day nomads. These nomads wander about looking for employment in various places. Some claim these wanderers are not real nomads, but the professor feels differently.

| **TYPES 5–8** |

| TYPE 5 D | TYPE 6 B | TYPE 7 A | TYPE 8 D |

Script 02-049

W Professor: Okay, everyone, settle down. Break's over, so we need to start up again. I'd like to cover a couple more topics, and then we're going to have our class discussion in the time remaining. But before we do that, I'd like to go over the notion of the social contract. I'm sure it's something you've all heard about, but perhaps you have, um, problems putting it into words. Well, simply put, the social contract holds that a long time ago in man's earliest years, men lived in what is known as a state of nature. During this time, there were no governments. The security of each individual depended upon his or her physical and mental abilities. However, when the people in a certain area joined together and agreed to make some kind of a government or a union of sorts, then each person surrendered some of his or her personal freedom in order to promote the safety and wellbeing of every individual in that area. This is how governments came into being. People essentially established a social contract whereby they and the government they formed had both rights and responsibilities.

One of the early proponents of the social contract was John Locke, a brilliant English philosopher. Born in 1632, at the end of the seventeenth century, he published the work *Two Treatises of Government* . . . Okay, yes, I know. It has a much longer name, but people commonly refer to it by its shorter, and, may I add, more convenient name. Anyway, Locke's work dealt a blow to political absolutism. ⁸The first treatise . . . there are two. Remember? Okay, the first treatise offers a refutation of the divine right of kings, which is the notion that monarchs get their authority from God. **Yes, that may seem outlandish to modern ears, but it was widely believed in centuries past.**

As for the second treatise, well, it wound up being

the more important one because the theory of politics it set out eventually found its way into American law by way of the Constitution. Yes, the Founding Fathers were deeply influenced by the social contract, but I'm getting ahead of myself again. Okay, so, back to the second treatise. Locke believed that people were naturally tolerant and reasonable yet needed some kind of governing force to help them avoid falling into chaos and other kinds of unpleasant behavior. He also believed that people should be able to go anywhere and do anything they wished. Yet to establish a cohesive society, they needed to form a government, to which they would cede certain rights. Now, here's a really important part: Locke felt that the people's consent to give up power and their consent to be governed were the essential elements of the social contract. He also felt that if the government ever abused the trust given to it by the people, the people had the right—the responsibility even—to revoke the government's power.

I think you can see why this philosophy appealed to the Founding Fathers, can't you? They believed that the British government under King George III was abusing the American colonists, and thus they had the right to do something about it. The direct result of this was the American Revolution.

TYPE 5 [Gist-Content Question]

The professor focuses on discussing both John Locke and the idea of the social contract that Locke was a proponent of.

TYPE 6 [Understanding Attitude Question]

The professor calls Locke "brilliant," and she speaks admiringly of him throughout the lecture, which shows that she admires his work and ideas.

TYPE 7 [Connecting Content Question]

The professor states, "I think you can see why this philosophy appealed to the Founding Fathers, can't you? They believed that the British government under King George III was abusing the American colonists, and thus they had the right to do something about it. The direct result of this was the American Revolution." She thus implies that the Founding Fathers used Locke's philosophical ideas to justify the American Revolution.

TYPE 8 [Making Inferences Question]

When the professor tells the students that the idea seems "outlandish to modern ears," she is implying that they should not use modern standards of thought to judge the past.

Summarizing ▶

The professor says that, at first, there were no

governments, and people lived in a state of nature. However, eventually, people began giving up some liberties to come together and to establish governments. This formed a social contract in which both people and the government had rights and responsibilities. She then talks about John Locke and his work *Two Treatises of Government*. The first treatise refutes the notion of the divine right of kings. The second says that when a government abuses its trust, the people have the right and the responsibility to revoke the government's power. The American Founding Fathers relied on Locke's philosophy to justify rebelling against Britain.

Mastering Question Types with Conversations A3

p.96

| TYPES 1–4 |

TYPE 1 (B)   TYPE 2 (C)   TYPE 3 (A)   TYPE 4 (B)

Script 02-050

M1 Professor: Yes? Is there something I can help you with?

M2 Student: Hello, Professor Gibson. I'm Charles Thomas. I was . . . uh, I was hoping I could borrow a few moments of your time if you're not too busy.

M1: Of course, Charles. Please have a seat. I don't believe we've had the pleasure of meeting.

M2: No, sir. Actually, Professor Martin told me to come here and speak with you about a project I'm doing for her class. I hope you don't mind.

M1: Ah, okay. You're the one she told me about. I've been expecting you for a couple of days.

M2: She told you about me? Cool . . . Okay, well, here's my problem. I'm trying to design a store for an architecture project, but I'm having some problems.

M1: What exactly is the nature of your problem?

M2: Well, uh, do you mind if I show you the plans I've drawn?

M1: ⁴Of course not. Let's take a look. . . Ah, yes. I see. You're having problems with the layout of the floor, aren't you?

M2: Wow. You could tell all that just by looking at my drawing?

M1: Young man, I've been doing this kind of work for thirty years. I'd be a pretty bad professor if I couldn't do that.

M2: Oh, yeah. I see your point . . . So, uh, what do you think I should do? There just isn't enough floor space for the kind of store I'm designing.

M1: Well, I won't tell you what to do. It's your

assignment after all. However, I do think that I can give you a couple of hints.

M2: Excellent.

M1: First, look at some of the designs in this book . . . here. I think you'll get some ideas from it. Just return it to me when you're done.

M2: You're lending me this book? Wow.

M1: I expect to get it back in the same condition you're receiving it though.

M2: No problem, sir. And, uh, what about the second piece of advice?

TYPE 1 [Gist-Purpose Question]

The student has a problem in another class, so his professor in that class recommended that he visit Professor Gibson to get some advice on the project that he is doing.

TYPE 2 [Detail Question]

The student says, "I'm trying to design a store for an architecture project."

TYPE 3 [Understanding Organization Question]

The student mentions Professor Martin because he wants Professor Gibson to know who told him that he should visit the professor to talk about his problem.

TYPE 4 [Understanding Function Question]

When the professor tells the student that he has been doing that sort of work for thirty years, the professor is implying that what the student is doing is not difficult for the professor at all.

Summarizing ▶

The student visits the professor in his office and introduces himself. He tells the professor that another teacher—Professor Martin—told him to visit the professor to talk about a class project. The professor says he has been expecting the student. The student shows the professor some plans that he has been designing, and the professor recognizes the problem right away. He will not tell the student what to do since it is the student's project, but he lends the student a book that he says should provide some answers for the student. The student then asks the professor for some more advice.

| TYPES 5–8 |

| **TYPE 5** Ⓐ | **TYPE 6** Ⓑ | **TYPE 7** Ⓒ | **TYPE 8** Ⓐ |

Script 02-051

W Student Services Employee: I'm sorry, but you

aren't permitted to come back here. Only staff members are allowed to use this entrance.

M Student: Oh, that's all right. I've got a booth at the exhibition. They told me I could come back here whenever I need to.

W: Hmm . . . Well, you don't have a nametag or anything indicating you're taking part in the exhibition, do you?

M: Uh, sorry. I didn't know I was supposed to wear it all the time. I, uh, I left mine back at my booth.

W: Okay, in that case, why don't you go back and get it? Then I'll have no problem letting you in. I really hate to be a stickler for the rules, but my boss wouldn't be very pleased with me if I let any unauthorized people back here.

M: Hey, that's no problem. You're just doing your job.

W: Thanks for understanding. ⁷Not too many people would take this as calmly as you are.

M: Well, to tell you the truth, I've done the same kind of work in the past, and I know what kind of, uh, shall we say, problems, that people can cause . . . Oh, say. I've got a question for you if you don't mind.

W: Go ahead. Shoot.

M: I need to reserve a projector.

W: What for?

M: Well, I'm supposed to be giving a presentation here at the exhibition tomorrow morning, and I was hoping to show some slides during it. So, uh, what do I need to do to make sure I can get one?

W: You need one by tomorrow morning?

M: Yeah . . . Uh, is that, um, going to be a problem?

W: Possibly . . . You shouldn't have waited for so long. They might all be reserved by now.

M: Oh . . . That's not good. What should I do then?

W: Tell you what . . . You go back and get your nametag and ID. When you return here, we'll have a chat with my boss and see if he can help you out.

M: Thanks a lot. I appreciate that.

TYPE 5 [Gist-Content Question]

Near the end of the conversation, the man tells the woman that he needs to reserve a projector because he is giving a presentation the next day and wants to show some slides during it.

TYPE 6 [Detail Question]

According to the woman, the student is not wearing a nametag, so she cannot allow him to go through the door.

TYPE 7 [Understanding Attitude Question]

When the student tells the woman that he has done the same work that she has in the past, he is indicating that he understands she is just doing her job, so he is not upset with her.

TYPE 8 [Making Inferences Question]

At the end of the conversation, the woman tells the student to go back to his booth to get his nametag while she will do something else. The man then thanks her, so it can be assumed that he is going to follow her instructions.

Summarizing ▶

> The student wants to enter a door, but the woman will not allow him to. She says he needs a nametag to gain access. The student responds that he left his nametag at his booth. The woman says she would like to let the man through, but she has to follow the rules. The student then asks the woman how to reserve a projector. He is giving a presentation the next day, so he wants to show some slides. The woman notes that it may be difficult to do. She tells him to go and get his nametag and then she will talk to her boss about the projector.

Mastering Topics with Lectures B1   p.98

Script & Graphic Organizer 02-052

M1 Professor: The Neolithic Age, or as it's sometimes called, the New Stone Age, is what I'd like to discuss now. Keep in mind that, despite happening thousands of years ago, it had quite a, hmm . . . quite a profound effect on human history. Why's that? Well, please allow me to answer my own question. Three key changes occurred during the Neolithic Age. They were the advent of agriculture, the creation of pottery, and the establishment of organized, permanent human settlements. All three were integral to the development of civilization.

M2 Student: Professor Gooden, when exactly was the Neolithic Age? The book wasn't, uh, it wasn't really clear on that.

M1: Well, the reason the book was unclear is that there's some disagreement in academic circles as to when it took place. You see, civilizations entered the Neolithic Age at different times. It basically depended upon when they developed the three things I just mentioned. Anyway, many scholars say it began around 9500 B.C., which is when, in some places, farming began to spread, and they say it ended when metal tools became more prevalent than the stone tools that

characterized this period. Again, it varies from place to place, but I'd say 3000 B.C. is a good place to put the end of the Neolithic Age. By this time, the world's first civilizations—in Mesopotamia and Egypt—had already been founded.

Okay, but let's backtrack to before the Neolithic Age. For tens of thousands of years, humans were nomads who moved around and followed their food sources. Pardon me. Then, around 12,000 B.C., some humans learned how to cultivate the wild grains that grew in the region covering the modern-day countries Syria, Jordan, and Israel. This knowledge spread elsewhere in the Middle East, and, by 9500 B.C., there were a few small towns, which were the first permanent human settlements. Why did people establish towns? Well, mostly because they needed to be near their fields to grow their grain as well as to protect it from those still living nomadic lives. In addition to agriculture, it was during this time that the major farm animals—including cows, sheep, pigs, chickens, goats, and horses—were domesticated. But this happened near the end of the Neolithic Age, not the beginning. Dogs, however, had been domesticated much earlier than this time.

I'm sure you've noticed that as soon as people solve one problem, another seems to rise in its stead. That's exactly what happened once people learned how to grow their own crops. What, you may ask, was the problem? Well, the problem was what to do with the surplus grain. Nomads, it must be remembered, typically consumed whatever food they found or hunted. There was no surplus. But that changed with the advent of farming. When farmers harvested a large crop, they didn't want to leave the grain to rot in the fields. So in some cases, they stored it in underground pits or caves. But these proved to be inadequate. Eventually, human ingenuity won again as people developed pottery to use as a storage device. In the early years of the Neolithic Age, there was no pottery. But archaeologists have found evidence for it in the Middle East dating back to 6500 B.C. Oh, but please remember that pottery had developed in the Far East in China and Japan much earlier, and it may have spread to the Middle East from there.

Anyway, pottery developed, and people used it to store their grain and other foods in. So now we have farming and pottery. What's next? Towns. Cities. Civilization. As people's quality of life improved, they lived longer and had more children. People started developing communities. Small villages were formed, and they turned into towns and cities. Bands became tribes, which, in turn, became nations.

The Neolithic Age

Farming:	Pottery:	Civilization:
Was developed around 12,000 B.C. and began to spread around 9,500 B.C.	Was developed in the Far East first and then spread elsewhere	People began to settle in places to watch over and protect their fields
People learned how to cultivate wild grains	Was needed to store surplus grain that farmers harvested	They started forming communities and villages, and, from this, civilizations began

1 [Gist-Purpose Question]

The professor claims, "Human ingenuity won again as people developed pottery to use as a storage device."

2 [Detail Question]

The professor states, "Then, around 12,000 B.C., some humans learned how to cultivate the wild grains that grew in the region covering the modern-day countries Syria, Jordan, and Israel."

3 [Making Inferences Question]

The lecture ends with the professor saying that people began forming communities, which led to the creation of towns, cities, tribes, and nations, so it is likely that the professor will start speaking about some early civilizations.

Summarizing ▶

The professor begins talking about the Neolithic Age. He notes that there were three key changes that happened during this time that influenced people. The first is that humans learned how to cultivate wild grains. This enabled them to stop living nomadic lives. The second is that humans learned how to make pottery. They needed to do this in order to store the surplus grain that they had harvested. Finally, the third reason was that humans began to develop civilizations. They settled down in villages and communities, and from there they began to grow into tribes and nations.

Mastering Topics with Lectures B2   p.99

1 Ⓐ   2 Ⓑ   3 Ⓓ

Script & Graphic Organizer 02-053

M1 Professor: Good morning, everyone. I'd like to get started right away since we've got a lot of ground to cover. So let's jump right in and start talking about bureaucracies. Yes, Kevin?

M2 Student: ³I know I should know this, but what

exactly is a bureaucracy? I always hear the word but have never gotten an explanation as to, uh, as to what exactly it is.

M1: There's no need to be shy about asking that question, Kevin. That goes for the rest of you, too. Asking questions is how we learn things. I'm actually glad you brought that up so that I can go over bureaucracies before I get too much into the lecture. A bureaucracy is often associated with government, but that's not always the case. That's probably what prompted Kevin to ask his question. Anyway, a bureaucracy is basically a group of officials or administrators who, er, administrate over something. As a general rule, they are noted for both their size and complexity. Bureaucracies typically have many layers, which creates something called red tape. You know, that's what we call all of those forms and applications you have to fill out when you're applying for something or trying to do anything that involves the government. Anyway, there are bureaucracies all the way from the highest levels of government down to the lowest local levels. And today I want to talk about their two major characteristics.

²Their first characteristic is that they're formed with the intent of making all operations move smoothly . . . **No, seriously. Don't laugh.** Okay, I'm sure many of you who've had to deal with the government would disagree with what I just said, but that is what bureaucracies are intended to do. They're supposed to make things more efficient by having specialists work within an organization. Every worker performs a specialized task that calls for a specific level of training and expertise. The result is that trained workers can do their jobs efficiently and with a minimum level of supervision. Of course, such extreme specialization means that these workers are frequently unable to perform jobs that are outside their purview. So long as everyone comes to work and does his or her duties, this isn't a problem. However, if a bureaucrat is away for an extended period of time, that person's work may go undone, which can cause disruptions in the organization. That's where many of people's complaints about bureaucracies originate. Most bureaucrats are simply unable to do even the simplest work if they haven't been trained for it.

Next, the second major characteristic of bureaucracies is that they have strict rules and regulations that are supposed to apply to everyone. The rules are made and then recorded in what's commonly known as standard operating procedures, or SOP for short. These rules are then published in a series of procedural manuals and are made available to all who need or desire them. In order for a bureaucracy to function smoothly, these rules and regulations must be strictly adhered to. Yes?

M2: I don't mean to be picky, but you said that these

rules are "supposed to apply to everyone." Does this mean that sometimes they don't?

M1: Ah, I'm very glad at least one of you was paying close attention and caught that. Yes, you're right. There are often exceptions where the rules aren't applied uniformly. In some cases, they're caused because certain people are taking advantage of the system. This could be bureaucrats themselves, politicians, or others exempting themselves . . . often illegally, I might add . . . from the very rules they were hired to enforce and follow. This, of course, is wrong. Yet there are other cases where not blindly following the rules is the right thing to do.

Bureaucracies

What They Are:	First Characteristic:
Groups of officials who administrate things and are typically found in governments	Should make all operations move smoothly
	Second Characteristic:
	Have strict rules and regulations that apply to everyone

1 [Understanding Organization Question]

The professor first explains what bureaucracies are, and then he proceeds to describe what they are mainly supposed to do.

2 [Understanding Function Question]

The professor tells the students not to laugh because he did not intend to make a joke but was actually being serious.

3 [Understanding Attitude Question]

The professor tells the student not to be shy about asking a question because he wants the student to know that he has asked a good question that deserves an answer.

Summarizing ▶

The professor says he wants to discuss bureaucracies, but a student first asks him to explain exactly what they are. The professor says that they are basically large groups of administrators who are often found in government organizations. Then, the professor describes their two major characteristics. The first is that they make things more efficient because each worker has a specific role that he or she is trained for. The second characteristic is that the rules and regulations apply to everyone. He notes, however, that there are times when people do not always follow these rules and behave in an illegal manner.

Mastering Topics with Lectures B3 p.100

1 Ⓒ   2 Cause: [1]   Effect: [2], [3], [4]   3 Ⓒ

Script & Graphic Organizer 02-054

M Professor: As I hope you're all aware, it's an election year, so I thought I'd cover how American presidential candidates have historically been selected by their parties. Over the years, the process has sometimes changed.

W Student: Thank you so much, Professor Holmes. The primary system is so, uh, confusing at times that I just can't comprehend it.

M: Well, I hope to clear things up for you, but I think we need a brief history lesson first. So why don't you answer a question for me . . . ? Which political party did George Washington belong to?

W: Is that a trick question? To the best of my knowledge, he didn't have a political party.

M: Precisely. When George Washington became president, there were no national political parties in the U.S. Of course, there were political factions even though many people shared common beliefs, but there were no organized national political parties when Washington's presidency started. [3]He personally despised the notion of political associations because he felt they pitted one group of citizens against another. **Since the U.S. had so recently been involved in a revolution, which, let me remind you, not all of the colonists had been in favor of, Washington was more concerned with uniting the people than in highlighting their differences.**

Now, a little background . . . When the Founding Fathers wrote the Constitution, they created four national institutions: the presidency, Congress, the Supreme Court, and the presidential selection system, which was centered on the Electoral College. As you know, it's the Electoral College, not direct voting by the people, that selects the president. At that time, since there were no political parties, when the state electors voted for president, the votes were counted, and the winner was the person who got the majority of the votes. He became president while the runner-up became the vice president.

This meant, if you think about it, that the president and the vice president would probably have many differing beliefs. And this was true in the early years. But the Founding Fathers had assumed that the loser would be able to overcome his differences with the president and would act in the best interests of the country.

Anyway, Washington made it clear he'd only serve two terms, so that meant there'd be a new president in 1796. And that's when political parties began to gain importance. In 1796, the two major national political parties, the Federalist Party and the Democrat-

Republican Party, took control of the nominating procedure. There were few problems in the nominating process in the early years of political parties primarily because in most cases, it was a foregone conclusion who would be each party's nominee. However, the election of 1824 saw multiple candidates, none of whom received a majority, run for office. This directly led to the splitting of the Democrat-Republican Party into the Jeffersonian Democrats, who followed Andrew Jackson, and the Whigs, who were led by Henry Clay. Anyway, in 1824, the presidential election had to be decided by the House of Representatives.

Party leaders didn't want this to happen again, so in 1832, Martin Van Buren proposed the establishment of a party convention. For the convention, large numbers of delegates would be chosen from each state. They would then gather for the convention and work together to select their presidential nominee. And that's basically where we are today. Of course, it's more complicated than that. Individual states hold either a primary or a caucus to award delegates to each presidential candidate. A candidate needs a certain number of delegates to secure the nomination of his or her party. Should no candidate get a majority before the convention, then the candidate will be selected at the convention. However, there's no official way to select a presidential nominee. Both the states and the political parties are free to change what they do. And they have done this in the past, as I'd like to show you.

Presidential Elections

George Washington:	1796 to 1824:	1832 to Modern Times:
Disliked political parties so was not a member of one	Federalist Party and Democrat-Republican Party dominated national politics and controlled the nominating procedures	Political conventions were formed to nominate candidates
Political parties had little importance during his presidency		Delegates were selected in each state, and they choose who will be the party's presidential candidate

1 [Gist-Content Question]

The professor gives a brief history lesson on how American presidential candidates have been selected by political parties since the formation of the United States.

2 [Connecting Content Question]

According to the lecture, a cause of the creation of political parties is that people have different political beliefs. As for their effects, delegates were required to

win the nomination, people started attending political conventions, and the presidential nominating procedure was easily controlled.

3 [Understanding Function Question]

When the professor states that "not all of the colonists had been in favor of" the revolution, he is implying that Washington was opposed by some of the people who were living in the United States because of the revolution.

The professor tells the class that he wants to describe the presidential candidate selection process since they are in an election year. He then asks a student what political party George Washington belonged to. The student responds that Washington did not have one. The professor notes that Washington was against political parties, but once he stopped serving as president, political parties gained prominence. The two major parties were the Federalist and Democrat-Republican parties. But in 1824, the House of Representative had to decide on the president, so the parties established conventions, which are still used today. Delegates are chosen from every state, and they choose their party's presidential candidate.

Mastering Topics with Lectures B4 p.101

1 Ⓓ   2 Ⓓ   3 Ⓒ

Script & Graphic Organizer 02-055

M Professor: While Thomas Jefferson is well known as the writer of the Declaration of Independence and as the third president of the United States, during his lifetime, he was also one of the country's foremost authorities on architecture. Much of his interest in architecture stemmed from his personality as a perfectionist. He also strived to find order and precision in all things, and this led him to architecture. Indeed, although he trained as a lawyer and later became one of the country's greatest statesmen, architecture was arguably his greatest love.

In prerevolutionary America, there was little interest in architecture. Much of this was due to a lack of money. Most people couldn't afford much more than a log cabin or a similar type of simple home, and, in the few towns and cities in the colonies, most buildings were imitations of European styles. There were no schools that trained architects, so most construction was done . . . poorly, in Jefferson's expert opinion . . . based on mere paintings or drawings, not designs, of European homes, churches, and other buildings.

Jefferson first became interested in architecture when

he read the famous work *Four Books on Architecture* written by Andrea Pa-Pa-Palladio. Sorry about that. During his time, the book was considered one of the seminal works on architecture. Palladio . . . There, I got his name right . . . He was from Venice, Italy, and was regarded as one of the masters of sixteenth century Italian architecture. Even to this day, he's still somewhat influential in architectural circles. Much of Palladio's ideas came from ancient Roman architecture, so this too had a profound effect on Jefferson. Around 1767, he began working on his home, called Monticello, in Virginia. It was a place he frequently redesigned as his ideas changed over the years. Today, Monticello is one of the most recognizable buildings in the entire country. Here's a slide of it for you to see . . .

After the American Revolution ended, Jefferson spent five years in Paris, France, from, uh, 1784 to 1789, where he represented America's interests. In his free time, he walked around examining Parisian architecture, and he also made frequent trips through the rest of the country. He gleaned much from his time there. In Paris, for instance, he learned about how skylights could allow natural light to enter a building. Upon returning home, he introduced them to Monticello. Here's a shot of one . . . Nice, huh? And here's another . . . In the south of France, he explored Roman ruins and came to realize just how much Palladio had borrowed from the Romans. When he designed the capitol building in Virginia, as you can see here . . . these ruins would greatly influence the final result.

One of Jefferson's most cherished dreams was to found a university. But he wanted one with no religious affiliation, which was the norm at the time. So he began designing the University of Virginia. Its library, not a church, as was the case at most universities, was its focal point. The other buildings were heavily influenced by Jefferson's Roman tastes. For instance, the library took its shape from the Roman Pantheon, which was a temple used to worship the gods in ancient Rome. Here it is . . .

After these three places, Jefferson's greatest . . . and possibly his most unique architectural achievement . . . was the octagonal home he built in an idyllic landscape setting. He called it Poplar Forest, and he used it as a retreat where he could rest and think. Take a look at it . . . Unsurprisingly, it was based on ancient Roman villas. Now, this is one of my personal favorites, and it's a work of pure genius. So we're going to cover it in detail and then compare it with some actual Roman villas, all right?

Thomas Jefferson and Architecture

Jefferson's Influences:	Jefferson's Buildings:
Four Books on Architecture by Andrea Palladio	Monticello
Ancient Roman architecture	Virginia state capitol
Parisian architecture	University of Virginia
	Poplar Forest

1 [Gist-Content Question]

During the lecture, the professor talks about some of the most famous buildings that were designed by Thomas Jefferson.

2 [Detail Question]

About Monticello, the professor states, "Much of Palladio's ideas came from ancient Roman architecture, so this too had a profound effect on Jefferson. Around 1767, he began working on his home, called Monticello, in Virginia. It was a place he frequently redesigned as his ideas changed over the years. Today, Monticello is one of the most recognizable buildings in the entire country."

3 [Understanding Organization Question]

The professor mentions the book to say that it was what got Jefferson interested in architecture in the first place, so she is noting its importance.

Summarizing ▶

The professor mentions some of Thomas Jefferson's accomplishments, but then she claims that Jefferson loved architecture most of all. In early America, there were no architectural schools, and buildings were poor copies of European styles. Jefferson read *Four Books on Architecture* by Andrea Palladio and was greatly influenced by it. He also learned much about architecture when he spent five years in Paris, France. This affected the design of his home Monticello, which is very famous today. Jefferson also designed the capitol building in Virginia, many of the buildings at the University of Virginia, and Poplar Forest, one of his most unique designs.

Mastering Topics with Conversations B5   p.102

1 Ⓐ   2 Ⓑ   3 Ⓓ

Script & Graphic Organizer 02-056

W Student: Hello, Professor Bianconi. Do you have a minute to speak with me? I see you're having office hours now.

M Professor: Of course. Please come in, uh . . .

W: Nancy. Nancy Perkins. I'm a student in your

Introduction to Political Science class that meets on Monday and Thursday mornings.

M: Ah, yes. Please have a seat, Ms. Perkins. I'm sorry I'm not familiar with your name. It is a big class after all.

W: That's no problem, sir. I don't think that I could remember 200 students either.

M: Anyway, what brings you here this afternoon?

W: It's my final grade, sir.

M: Final grade? Don't you mean midterm grade? After all, there are still six weeks until the semester ends.

W: Uh, no, sir. Actually, I really do mean my final grade.

M: Well, this should be interesting. Would you please care to enlighten me then?

W: Of course. Well, I have a small problem. You see, I missed about three weeks right before the midterm exam because I fell ill. I, uh, actually missed all of my classes in all my subjects.

M: Goodness! Are you feeling better now?

W: Yes, sir. Much better. ³Thanks for asking. So, uh, I missed three weeks' worth of classes with my TA . . . **Her name's Jenny by the way . . .** and one of those classes was the discussion class, which, as you know, counts for twenty percent of our final grade.

M: Ah, yes. I see your point. It would be rather hard, shall we say, to get any kind of decent grade when you get no points for the discussion.

W: Yes, sir. Exactly. So, uh . . . I talked to Jenny about it, but she said I was going to get a zero. She didn't really seem to, er, care about my problem.

M: That's too bad. May I ask how you did on the midterm?

W: Hold on a second. I've got it with me in my bag . . . Ah, here's my test, sir.

M: Goodness! A ninety-five despite missing three weeks of lectures? Very impressive. Okay, first I need to see a doctor's note. Then, I can give you an alternative assignment. I'll have to think of one for you though.

W: When will I know what it is? Should I come back here and speak with you?

M: No, there's no need for you to do that. How about this . . . ? Check with the departmental secretary by the end of the day tomorrow. She'll fill you in on what you need to do to make up for the missed assignment.

W: Thank you so much, sir. You've just made my day.

Office Hours

Student's Problem:	Teaching Assistant's Solution:
Missed a discussion class so needs to get some points for it so that her final grade is not too low	Student will get a zero on the assignment
	Professor's Solution:
	Student can do a makeup assignment that he will give her the next day

1 [Gist-Purpose Question]

When the professor asks the student why she has come, she says, "It's my final grade, sir."

2 [Detail Question]

After the student explains everything, the professor tells her, "I can give you an alternative assignment."

3 [Understanding Function Question]

When the student tells the professor the name of her TA, she implies that there are at least two TAs in the class since the professor would not need to know her name if there were only one.

Summarizing ▶

The student visits the professor's office, introduces herself, and says she is taking one of his classes. She then states she wants to talk about her final grade, which surprises the professor since the semester still has six weeks left. She explains that she missed the discussion class, which is worth twenty percent of her grade, because she was sick. But her teaching assistant is going to give her a zero. She shows the professor that she got a ninety-five on the midterm exam despite missing three weeks of classes. He agrees to give her a makeup assignment and tells her to visit the departmental secretary the next day.

Mastering Topics with Conversations B6   p.103

1   **2**   **3**

Script & Graphic Organizer 02-057

M Admissions Office Employee: Greetings. Is there something I can do for you this morning?

W Student: Uh, I sure hope so. I've got a big problem, and I could really use some assistance.

M: Okay. In that case, why don't you take a seat? Would you like some coffee or something else to drink?

W: Oh, no thanks. I don't think I could handle any more caffeine today. But thanks for the offer.

M: Sure . . . So, what brings you here?

W: It's my roommate. She's driving me crazy. I need a new place, preferably a single. Can you help me?

M: Whoa, whoa . . . Slow down a little. I need a little more information about why your roommate is, uh, making you crazy. And we don't have too many singles just to give away. How about giving me a few more details, and then I'll see what I can do for you?

W: Sure. Sorry about that . . . It's just that I've been on edge the last couple of weeks from living with her.

M: Try to calm down, and tell me all about it.

W: Okay. I'm a transfer student here. I'm a sophomore. So as you know, I didn't get a chance to choose my roommate since it's my first semester here.

M: Right.

W: Well, the roommate I got assigned is, well, she's like my polar opposite. Not only do we have absolutely nothing in common, but our lifestyles are complete opposites, too.

M: How so?

W: My roommate is a social butterfly. She's always got friends over. I think she's in one of the sororities here or something. But she never cracks a book. She's always chatting with her friends, watching TV, or listening to music.

M: And you?

W: ³Me? **I came here to study. That's all I do.** But it's really hard for me to study in my room when there are people coming in and out at all hours of the day and night. That's why I'd really love a single.

M: Hmm . . . Unfortunately, it's a little too late in the semester to get you a single. You're probably going to have to stay there and try to get along with her.

W: But what about my studies?

M: Have you tried the library? There are lots of seats there, and it stays open all night long.

W: But that's not fair! I'll be the one inconvenienced. Not her.

M: I understand how you feel, but you should've come here earlier. Come back again before winter break, and I'll see what I can do about getting you a new place for the spring semester.

Service Encounter

Reason for Visiting:	Result:
Is not happy about his number to select a dormitory room	Employee says that numbers are all determined randomly

Problem:	Solution:
Cannot get a single room because of his low number	Student needs to find a friend with a good number to use the buddy system

1 [Gist-Content Question]

The student complains about how her roommate always has friends over, which is why she then says, "It's really hard for me to study in my room when there are people coming in and out at all hours of the day and night."

2 [Detail Question]

The student complains about all of the problems that her roommate is causing her, so she is implying that her roommate is inconsiderate.

3 [Understanding Function Question]

When the student says that studying is all she does, it can be inferred that she is involved in no extracurricular activities at the school.

Summarizing ▶

The student visits the student housing office to complain about her roommate. She says that, because of her roommate, she needs a single dormitory room. The employee asks for more information. The student mentions that she transferred to the school so could not choose her roommate. And the roommate she has now never studies and always has friends visiting their room. This means that she cannot study, which is the only activity that she does. The employee tells her it is too late to give her a single, so she should study at the library. He then promises to help her try to get a new room for the next semester.

TOEFL Practice Tests C1

p.104

1 Ⓐ	2 Ⓐ, Ⓓ	3 Ⓒ	4 Happiness: [2], [4]
Word of Mouth: [1], [3]	5 Ⓒ	6 Ⓐ	

Script 02-058

M Professor: In the rest of my lecture, I'd like to examine the intricacies of why people buy what they buy. As I'm sure you are all aware, the business of marketing is to sell products and services. That's it. However, why people buy a certain product or use one service but not another depends upon many factors. Some people, for example, are attached to a brand name they prefer or believe is reliable. Others buy and use products and services because they're convenient. ⁶However . . . one of the main reasons people buy certain products comes from their perceptions of how these products will affect their lives.

W Student: Do you mean how these products will make their lives easier?

M: Well, that's certainly one aspect. After all, we use many products to make our lives easier. Take cars, for example. They help us get where we want to go, and they enable us to visit places faster than if we were to walk to them. But . . . why buy one car and not another? What is it that makes one person choose a luxury car while another chooses a pickup truck while yet another buys an old clunker?

There are actually a large number of reasons why people buy specific products. I'm going to go over a few of them in brief now. One reason people do this is simply to make themselves happy. I'm sure all of you have done this before, right . . .? Perhaps you saw a new coat at a department store and said to yourself that you just had to have it no matter what it cost. Okay . . . Maybe the price was somewhat important, but you understand what I'm saying, right? You simply believed that you couldn't live without that coat. When you bought it, you felt happy, didn't you? It made you look good, and that, in turn, brought you happiness. Well, happiness, or pleasure, has a lot to do with the things that we buy.

Let's see . . . Interestingly enough, word of mouth has a tremendous influence on which products people buy or which services they use. For instance, many people watch TV shows or see movies simply because a friend or family member recommended them. That's exactly what word of mouth is. Think about how many times you've visited a restaurant because of someone's suggestion. Or perhaps you tried a new product or purchased music from a new singer all because one of your friends told you that you ought to. I'd be willing to bet that word of mouth is one of the most influential factors in all of your purchases and expenditures.

Let's do an obvious one next . . . price. Of course, we all prefer to pay less for something. However, please note that people's perceptions of quality are closely related to price. If a product or service has a high price and high quality, people will be more willing to spend their money on it. You'd spend big dollars to get a Rolex watch or to stay at a five-star resort, wouldn't you . . .? If you had the money I mean. Sure you would. On the other hand, would you pay a hundred dollars for a meal at a fast-food restaurant . . .? Anyone . . .? Nope. Why not? High price plus low quality is simply not a winning combination for most people.

Culture, surprisingly, also affects what people buy. Simply put, some products just won't sell in certain markets. For instance . . . ah, let's stay with the fast-food restaurant example. Fast-food restaurants took a long, long time to break into the French market. The French people just didn't want them. Why is that?

Well, in French culture, food and food service are quite important. And fast-food restaurants offered service, or non-service I should say, that wasn't compatible with their culture. While fast-food restaurants have made some inroads as of late, the culture there pretty much dictates that they're losing ventures. Even here, there are lots of things that local culture dictates that people won't buy. I wouldn't try selling luxury cars in a blue-collar neighborhood, nor would I try to sell rap music to people who live in rural areas.

⁵**Okay. Let's do one more and then wrap things up.** Age affects consumer spending quite a bit. Children and teenagers are more apt to spend their money carelessly than senior citizens. Children are also pretty good . . . and I'm sure many of you have firsthand knowledge of this . . . at nagging their parents to get them to purchase things. In addition, the eighteen-to-forty-nine age group has a lot of buying power since these people tend to be prime income earners in most countries. Meanwhile, older consumers, as I just noted, tend to be more conservative in their spending, especially those who are on fixed incomes and can't afford certain products. They've also formed brand loyalty over the years, so they will often stick with the same brands or same products for decades.

1 [Gist-Content Question]

The professor says, "There are actually a large number of reasons why people buy specific products. I'm going to go over a few of them in brief now."

2 [Detail Question]

The professor states, "Word of mouth has a tremendous influence on which products people buy or which services they use," and, "Culture, surprisingly, also affects what people buy."

3 [Understanding Organization Question]

During the lecture, the professor goes over several topics that he feels are important factors in why people purchase products.

4 [Connecting Content Question]

According to the lecture, purchasing something because one feels that it must be owned and because it makes the person feel good both have to do with happiness. As for word of mouth, this happens when someone recommends watching a movie to another and when a person hears about a product's quality from other people.

5 [Understanding Function Question]

When the professor says that he wants to "wrap things up" after talking about something else, it means that he is going to finish class soon.

6 [Understanding Function Question]

When the professor says, "Well, that's certainly one aspect," he is saying that the student is correct; however, she is not completely correct. She has only gotten part of the answer.

TOEFL Practice Tests C2

p.106

1 Ⓓ   2 Ⓑ   3 Ⓐ   4 Ⓐ   5 Ⓑ   6 Ⓒ

Script 02-059

W Professor: Throughout history, the ease of moving people and goods long distances has profoundly affected progress. First, the domestication of the horse enabled entire civilizations to cross continents much like the Mongols did in the thirteenth century. The development of oceangoing cargo-hauling ships later led to the exploration of the world and the spread of European civilization. Next in line were the railways, which had an even greater impact on progress than ships did. Despite ships being able to sail around the world, they couldn't penetrate the interiors of continents. It was with the coming of the railroad that the vast interiors of the continents of Eurasia, the Americas, and Africa were all able to be exploited.

⁵A perfect example is the transcontinental railway in the United States. Upon completion, it opened the American West and connected the continent's east and west coasts. **But let's go back in time a bit first . . .** The first modern railway lines were laid in 1830 in both England and the United States. By the late 1850s, most of the eastern United States had an extensive railway network. Wherever trains went, progress and profits followed. Trains brought people and goods from centers of manufacturing and then returned bearing agricultural products and raw materials from the frontiers. By 1859, the eastern railways had reached as far as Council Bluffs, which was located on the eastern bank of the Missouri River in Iowa. From there, the decision was made by the American government to build a railway line across the prairie all the way to the Rocky Mountains. At the same time, a second railway line would be built from Sacramento, California, and it would traverse the mountainous terrain to meet the eastern railway in the middle in Utah.

⁶It was a bold decision. Nothing that ambitious had ever been attempted anywhere in the world. **Not only was the land between Sacramento and Council Bluffs rugged and full of potentially hostile Native Americans, but there were also hardly any settlers in the land in between the two places.** Railways were built to make profits by carrying cargo or passengers, but there were neither at that time. Well, they pressed on anyway, mostly at the insistence of President Abraham Lincoln, who was a strong supporter of the project.

The Civil War in the early 1860s interrupted things, but it also was a boon for the railways since the men who were in charge of building them learned a lot from the war, particularly how to manage large numbers of men. The project was funded by the government through the Pacific Railway Act of 1862. Two companies, the Union Pacific in the east and the Central Pacific in the west, were established by that act. The Central Pacific started building the California line in 1863 while the Union Pacific, which was forced to delay because of a lack of men and material due to the war, started its work in 1865. Despite colossal engineering problems and many interruptions, the transcontinental railway was completed by 1869.

To say that the transcontinental railway had an enormous impact on American history would be an understatement. The building of the railways was an enormous undertaking, and the steel mills of Pennsylvania reaped fortunes from providing the rail for the project. The thousands of items the railway needed came from factories in the east and were transported west to the builders. The items for the California line, on the other hand, had to be shipped around South America, which made profits for the shipping companies. Finally, tens of thousands of Irish and Chinese immigrants found work building the railways, and this gave these people the opportunity to earn a living.

Once the railway started running in 1869, the western prairies were opened to settlement. The railway ran through Nebraska, Wyoming, Utah, and Nevada, among other states. Through the latter half of the nineteenth century, settlers in the tens of thousands came to these empty lands by train. The journey from California to the east coast and vice versa no longer depended on a long sea voyage around South America. This fact alone encouraged the further settlement of California. All along the railway line, towns sprang up, and people settled the land while seeking their fortunes in farming, business, or mining.

Just to give you a few statistics on population so that you can see how much it changed, let's look at Nebraska and California first. In 1860, barely 20,000 people lived in Nebraska. By 1900, there were 1.2 million people living in this prairie state. California had 390,000 people in 1860, mostly because of the San Francisco gold rush, but by 1900, there were 1.5 million people residing in the state. There's no doubt that the railway had an impact on these numbers. Before the gold rush of 1849, barely 93,000 people lived in all of California, and in 1850, there were no statistics for any non-Native people living in Nebraska. So in a period of fewer than forty years, you can see how dramatically the populations of these two states changed. The other states that the railway passed through were no different either.

1 [Gist-Content Question]

The professor describes the effect of railways on the United States throughout the lecture.

2 [Gist-Purpose Question]

When talking about the transcontinental railway, the professor states, "The project was funded by the government through the Pacific Railway Act of 1862."

3 [Understanding Attitude Question]

When the professor says, "Next in line were the railways, which had an even greater impact on progress than ships did," she shows that she believes that railroads were more important than oceangoing ships.

4 [Understanding Organization Question]

The professor says, "Just to give you a few statistics on population so that you can see how much it changed, let's look at Nebraska and California first. In 1860, barely 20,000 people lived in Nebraska. By 1900, there were 1.2 million people living in this prairie state. California had 390,000 people in 1860, mostly because of the San Francisco gold rush, but by 1900, there were 1.5 million people residing in the state. There's no doubt that the railway had an impact on these numbers." She is trying to prove the influence of the transcontinental railway on the two states' increasing populations.

5 [Understanding Function Question]

When the professor tells the students that they need to "go back in time a bit first," she means that they have to discuss some events that happened prior to the completion of the transcontinental railway first.

6 [Understanding Attitude Question]

When the professor notes that the Native Americans were hostile and that there were hardly any people in the region, she is implying that at that time, there was little reason to build the transcontinental railway.

TOEFL Practice Tests C3

p.108

1 Ⓒ   2 Ⓑ   3 Ⓐ   4 Ⓓ   5 Ⓓ

Script 02-060

M Student: Good afternoon, uh . . . Ms. Howell. Are you busy? I'd like to discuss an issue that I have.

W Student Housing Office Employee: Sure. I can speak with you. What's going on?

M: It's about the upcoming selections for dormitory rooms for the next semester.

W: Oh, sure. You should have already been assigned a number for when you get to choose your dorm room. ⁵If

you don't know your number, then, if you give me your student ID card, I can find out for you.

M: No, no. I already know my number. That's not, er, actually why, uh, why I'm here.

W: Didn't get the number you were hoping for, did you?

M: Not at all! I got one of the lowest numbers in the entire school. By the time I get to choose a room, all the good spots will be gone. There's no way I'll ever get a single even though I'm going to be a junior next year. That's just not fair.

W: I'm sorry about that, but all numbers are randomly assigned. There's really nothing I can do about that.

M: Oh, yeah. I understand. You didn't do anything wrong. I'm just frustrated . . . But I have a question for you. And it's extremely important that I get an answer to this.

W: Go ahead.

M: You see, one of my friends got a really high number, and . . .

W: It sounds like your problem has just been solved. Just go together with him when you choose a room. If you use the school's buddy system, even if he chooses a single, you two can partner together so that you can select a single room next to him. That's the way the school designed the program. We like to let friends live close to each other even if they're going to be residing in singles.

M: Yes, that sounds great, but . . .

W: But what?

M: My friend is, uh, thinking of living off campus next year. In fact, he's already got an apartment picked out. So, um . . . is there any way he can transfer his number to me?

W: Sorry, but that is strictly against the rules. I can't permit that.

M: Oh . . . well, uh, how about if he, uh, if he chooses a single, which lets me also get a single, but then he decides not to take student housing next semester?

W: I'm sorry again, but I don't think that will work either . . . Well, okay, it would work, but I don't think you're going to like what I'm about to say. You see . . . if he chooses a room and then decides not to use it because he wants to live off campus, he'll have to pay a penalty.

M: ⁴How much?

W: Forty percent of the fee.

M: Yikes. **Say, you were right. I don't like what you just said.** I definitely think that won't work. I'm sure John's not willing to pay a fine on my behalf. So, uh, what you're telling me is I need to find a friend with a good number who's definitely going to stay on campus next semester? That is, if I want to have any shot at a single room.

W: Bingo. You've got it.

M: All right. I guess I'll have to start making some phone calls.

W: Good luck.

M: Thanks. I'm going to need it.

1 [Gist-Purpose Question]

The student tells the woman that he wants a single room next semester, and he asks her a number of questions about how he can manage to get one.

2 [Detail Question]

About the school's buddy system, the woman says, "If you use the school's buddy system, even if he chooses a single, you two can partner together so that you can select a single room next to him. That's the way the school designed the program."

3 [Understanding Organization Question]

The student brings up his friend with the high number because he wants to propose a possible solution to his problem to the woman and see what she thinks about it.

4 [Understanding Function Question]

The student makes that comment to lighten the mood by attempting some humor.

5 [Understanding Attitude Question]

When the woman knows what the student's problem is before he can even tell her, it can be inferred that she has gotten visits from other students who have complained about the same issue.

Vocabulary *Review*   p.110

1	Ⓑ	2	Ⓓ	3	Ⓒ	4	Ⓐ	5	Ⓐ
6	Ⓑ	7	Ⓓ	8	Ⓐ	9	Ⓒ	10	Ⓑ
11	Ⓐ	12	Ⓓ	13	Ⓔ	14	Ⓘ	15	Ⓙ
16	Ⓗ	17	Ⓒ	18	Ⓑ	19	Ⓕ	20	Ⓖ

Mastering Question Types with Lectures A1   p.112

| TYPES 1–4 |

TYPE **1** Ⓐ   TYPE **2** Ⓑ   TYPE **3** Ⓐ   TYPE **4** Ⓓ

Script 02-061

M Professor: Okay, the topic of today's lecture is the light spectrum. Well, I suppose I should be a little more specific and say that we're going to focus on the visible light spectrum. That's the narrow band of light that's located to the right of the infrared region and to the left of the . . . of the ultraviolet region. As you hopefully read in your text last night, you should know that electromagnetic waves exist in a broad range of wavelengths; however, human eyes are sensitive . . . which means we can detect light . . . only in a very narrow band. This is the band we refer to as the visible light spectrum, which is also known simply as "visible light" to some people.

Now, look all around you in the classroom . . . Check out the different colors . . . All of these colors have their own individual wavelength, and, since we can see them, they obviously fall into the visible light spectrum. How is it that we can see them? Simple. When light of a particular wavelength strikes the retinas in our eyes, we see it represented as a particular color. That's all there is to it.

I'm sure you've all heard about the famous experiment conducted several centuries ago by Sir Isaac Newton in which he demonstrated how light shining through a prism can be separated into different wavelengths. [4]In doing so, he showed the various colors that visible light is comprised of. This separation of light, by the way, is known as dispersion. **Please make sure you remember that term as it's one I will continuously refer to over the course of the semester.** Now, the dispersion of light results in the following colors: red, orange, yellow, green, blue, and violet . . . Okay, sure, many of you have been told that indigo is found in between blue and violet, but most scientists omit this color, which is why I didn't include it. Anyway, there are obviously many more colors than the ones I noted. A quick glance around this room tells us that. The colors closer to infrared . . . red, orange, and yellow that is . . . have long wavelengths while, unsurprisingly, those closer to ultraviolet have shorter wavelengths.

As we know, by using a prism, we can disperse light and thereby see all the colors of visible light. However, there's another way we can see all the colors of the spectrum. Can anyone tell me what it is?

W Student: A rainbow, right?

M: Exactly. A rainbow is nature's way of splitting light. Oh, I don't want to forget about two more, uh, colors we should discuss. They, of course, are white and black. Please understand that the phrase "white light" is nothing but a, well, a misnomer. White, in fact, is not a color since it has no wavelength but is simply a combination of all of the colors of visible light. The same applies to black, which is the opposite of white. Black, like white, isn't a color since it too has no wavelength. Black is actually the absence of any color or, shall we say, the absence of any wavelengths on the visible light spectrum.

TYPE 1 [Gist-Content Question]

The professor spends most of the lecture talking about the visible colors of light.

TYPE 2 [Detail Question]

About black, the professor states, "Black is actually the absence of any color or, shall we say, the absence of any wavelengths on the visible light spectrum."

TYPE 3 [Understanding Organization Question]

About Sir Isaac Newton, the professor states, "I'm sure you've all heard about the famous experiment conducted several centuries ago by Sir Isaac Newton in which he demonstrated how light shining through a prism can be separated into different wavelengths." He thus uses Newton to introduce the part of his lecture on prisms.

TYPE 4 [Understanding Function Question]

When the professor tells the students that he will continuously refer to that term during the semester, he is letting them know that it is important for them to understand what the term means.

Summarizing ▶

> The professor says he will talk about the visible light spectrum. He states that it is light with wavelengths between infrared and ultraviolet light. According to the professor, the eye's retina simply registers individual wavelengths as different colors. He then mentions Sir Isaac Newton and his work with prisms, which can divide light into all of its different colors. He notes that colors close to infrared have long wavelengths while those close to ultraviolet have short wavelengths. He briefly mentions that rainbows can split light like a prism. He finally notes that white is a combination of all colors while black is the absence of color.

| **TYPES 5–8** |

TYPE 5 Ⓐ   **TYPE 6** Ⓒ   **TYPE 7** Ⓑ   **TYPE 8** Ⓒ

Script 02-062

M Professor: The Earth consists of several layers. Moving from the inside out, at the very center is the core. It has two parts, which are called the inner and outer core. Beyond the core are the mantle, the upper mantle, and, finally, the crust, which is the outer part of the planet. Geologists, however, call the outer crust and the upper mantle together the lithosphere. Essentially, this is the solid part of the Earth. The, uh, depth of the lithosphere varies from place to place. Often, its thickness depends on whether the crust begins on the ocean floor or a continental landmass. Under the oceans, the lithosphere is typically about, oh . . . let's say around fifty to one hundred kilometers thick. However, underneath the continents, it can be anywhere from forty to two hundred kilometers thick. Keep in mind, though, that the crust comprises but a minor part of the lithosphere. Underneath oceans, the crust is usually about five to ten kilometers thick while it's approximately thirty to fifty kilometers thick beneath the continents. Where the crust ends, the upper mantle begins.

However, between the crust and the upper mantle lies a boundary that scientists refer to as the Moho Discontinuity. It's named after a Croatian expert on earthquakes, Andrija Mohorovicic . . . no, you don't have to spell his name properly, but you do need to know about the crucial research he did. In 1909, he discovered that earthquake waves increased in speed when they were at a certain depth underground. He surmised that this was the result of a change in the Earth's structure. He assumed the rocks were somehow chemically different from those above them. That's how he came up with the Moho Discontinuity. And just so you know, some geologists call it the Mohorovicic Discontinuity and use his full last name. Anyway, the Moho Discontinuity, as you would expect, varies in depth. Again, its depth depends on if it's underneath an ocean or a landmass since it's located right where the crust and the upper mantle meet. Now, please note that much of this work is theoretical since no one's been able to prove physically that either the Moho Discontinuity or the mantle actually exists. We simply haven't been able to drill that far down to find out.

Okay, so we've got the crust, the Moho Discontinuity, and the upper mantle. They're all in the lithosphere. What's beneath the lithosphere? It's a region of the mantle called the asthenosphere. It's different from the lithosphere in that it's not, um, as rigid. By that I mean that the rocks are less rigid, so they tend to move around by the convection that's generated by heat from the inner part of the Earth. Recall that much of the inner part of the planet is molten rock. This movement in the asthenosphere is what the theories of plate tectonics and continental drift are based on. The upper crust of the lithosphere isn't cohesive but is instead broken up into large plates, all of which essentially float on the asthenosphere. Since the asthenosphere is moving, the plates move along with it. They move slowly of course; however, over the course of millions of years, the continents wind up in very different locations.

TYPE 5 [Gist-Content Question]

In talking about certain aspects of the lithosphere, the professor is focusing on the upper layers of the Earth.

TYPE 6 [Understanding Attitude Question]

The professor states, "Andrija Mohorovicic . . . no, you don't have to spell his name properly, but you do need to know about the crucial research he did." This shows that the professor feels that Mohorovicic's work is important to know.

TYPE 7 [Connecting Content Question]

The professor notes, "Under the oceans, the lithosphere is typically about, oh . . . let's say around fifty to one hundred kilometers thick. However, underneath the continents, it can be anywhere from forty to two hundred kilometers thick. Keep in mind, though, that the crust comprises but a minor part of the lithosphere. Underneath oceans, the crust is usually about five to ten kilometers thick while it's approximately thirty to fifty kilometers thick beneath the continents. Where the crust ends, the upper mantle begins."

TYPE 8 [Making Inferences Question]

When describing the asthenosphere, the professor mentions, "It's different from the lithosphere in that it's not, um, as rigid."

Summarizing ▷

The professor describes the different layers of the Earth. He notes that the crust and upper mantle together are called the lithosphere because they are the Earth's solid part. He then describes the thickness of the lithosphere in various places. He states that the scientist Andrija Mohorovicic theorized the existence of the Moho Discontinuity, which runs between the crust and upper mantle. He stresses that it is only a theory and has not been verified. Then he proceeds to talk about the asthenosphere, which lies beneath the lithosphere. Less rigid than the lithosphere, the asthenosphere enables the plates in the lithosphere to move, which makes the continents change places.

Mastering Question Types with Lectures A2 p.114

| TYPES 1-4 |

TYPE 1 (D)   **TYPE 2** (D)   **TYPE 3** (A)   **TYPE 4** (C)

Script 02-063

M1 Professor: In recent years, there has been a big push in some quarters to find alternatives to fossil fuels. Burning coal, natural gas, and oil causes air pollution, and they are also nonrenewable resources, so we're eventually going to run out of them. It's therefore only logical to find new sources of energy before that day comes. However, our infrastructure is so heavily dependent upon fossil fuels that switching to other alternatives won't be easy. People still persist in searching for alternatives though. Of the many possibilities, one potential winner has emerged: biofuels.

Biofuels are made by creating energy from organic matter. Among the many kinds of biofuels, the most commonly used organic matter comes from corn, sugarcane, soybeans, and canola. Processing them results in either ethanol or biodiesel. There are both good and bad points to biofuels. For one, they produce much fewer carbon emissions than fossil fuels do when they're burned. Corn ethanol, for instance, produces 22% less carbon than does gasoline. Sugarcane ethanol does even better by producing 56% fewer carbon emissions. Biodiesel made from canola oil or soybeans is the best as it leads to, uh, 68% fewer carbon emissions. [4]There's no doubt these fuels are more environmentally friendly than fossil fuels.

M2 Student: Why don't we switch to biofuels then?

M1: I was about to get to that. There are several reasons why. First of all, don't forget that we're talking about using food as a fuel source. In a world with millions of starving people, many are horrified by using food as a fuel source. They'd much rather it went to feed the hungry masses. I can see their point. Second, there's simply not enough production of biofuels to meet the possible demand. Third, biofuels are expensive to produce, which often makes them cost more than gasoline. Be honest. Would you really be willing to pay more for biofuels if there were a cheaper alternative? Many people wouldn't.

Oh, there's another important reason. There's some disagreement as to whether or not biofuels actually help the environment. The reason is that the processes used to make biofuels require energy to transform the organic matter into fuel. This energy comes from burning other organic matter—like, say, the scrap from sugarcane—or even from electricity that's created by the burning of fossil fuels. Some argue that, ultimately, producing biofuels puts just as many . . . or maybe even more . . . carbon emissions into the atmosphere as fossil fuels do.

But all is not lost. There's a possible alternative: alga. Yeah, the stuff that grows in water. Some types of alga can produce oils or starches that can be converted into biofuels. The beauty of alga is that it can be grown in any type of water and requires little care to raise it, unlike, say, corn. It also has a short growing period and can be harvested anytime, not just once or twice a year as most crops are. Theoretically, one acre of algae could produce about 5,000 gallons of biofuel. Compare this with the 300 gallons of corn ethanol and the sixty gallons of soybean biodiesel that come from the same amount of land. But as I said, this is all theoretical since no large-scale algae biofuel production is going on anywhere right now.

TYPE 1 [Gist-Purpose Question]

The professor says, "There's a possible alternative: alga."

TYPE 2 [Detail Question]

The professor comments, "In a world with millions of starving people, many are horrified by using food as a fuel source. They'd much rather it went to feed the hungry masses."

TYPE 3 [Understanding Organization Question]

During the lecture, the professor first defines what biofuels are, and then he explains where some different kinds of biofuels come from.

TYPE 4 [Understanding Function Question]

When the student asks his question, he is implying that he does not understand why biofuels are not used more regularly since, according to the professor, they are more environmentally friendly than fossil fuels.

Summarizing ▶

The professor talks about the need to find alternative energy sources because fossil fuels are nonrenewable. He claims that biofuels, which come from organic matter, are a potential energy source. Some that are used to make energy are corn, sugarcane, soybeans, and canola. They produce fewer carbon emissions than fossil fuels. When asked why biofuels are not more common, the professor states that many people do not want to use food to produce as fuel. In addition, not enough biofuel is being produced, it is expensive, and it might not reduce carbon emissions. He then says that alga is a potential source of biofuel, but more research remains to be done on it.

| TYPES 5–8 |

Script 02-064

W Professor: Let's move on to some special types of weather phenomena. We'll start with monsoon weather patterns. These are typically associated with India and Southeast Asia, but monsoons also occur in East Asia, Australia, North America, and in a milder form, in parts of Western Europe. Monsoons, which occur seasonally, are characterized by heavy rains and strong winds. Some people think "monsoon" is the term for the rain that falls, but in actuality, the word refers to the wind instead.

The way monsoons develop is connected with the relationship between how both land and water heat up. Water absorbs heat more slowly than land because the heat from the sun goes down deep into the oceans. **[6]On land, therefore, heat gets released faster, which causes it to rise and to create a low-pressure system. Over the ocean, meanwhile, heat is released more slowly, so the air is cooler than the air over land. This makes the air pressure higher in comparison . . . Is everyone with me so far. . .?** Low pressure attracts high pressure, which moves the air from the ocean to the land and thus creates a breeze. During the summer, when the sun's rays hit the Northern Hemisphere more directly and for a longer period of time each day, the land heats up more rapidly, the pressure is lower, and the wind coming in from the ocean is stronger.

Okay, so now the moisture content of the oceans plays a role in the formation of heavy rain systems. As the wind blows from the ocean to the land, it brings lots of moisture with it. The moisture rises as it heats up over land and thus forms clouds. Sometimes a long line, or band, of clouds is formed. This band then moves slowly over the land and drops a huge amount of rain as it moves. These rainstorms can last four or five days and may drop several feet of rain. Naturally, when this occurs, flooding results.

In East Asia, China, Korea, and Japan receive their monsoon rains in summer, and there are always floods then. Flooding is a major problem in India as well, and every year, sad to say, people die, and there are massive amounts of property damage, too. India often gets hit hard by the monsoons because of the presence of the Himalaya Mountains in the north.

M Student: Why is that?

W: The mountains act like a wall, and, as the clouds try to rise over them . . . many are several thousand meters high, remember . . . well, as the clouds try to go over the mountains, they release their moisture, which causes huge amounts of rain to fall. Oh, remember that monsoons occur at different times of the year in various places, but they typically hit Asia from June to September.

You might think that monsoons are disliked by the people they affect, but that's not really the case. The rains provide relief from stifling heat, and they are also a boon for agriculture. Over thousands of years, people have adapted their agricultural needs to the monsoon rains. It should come as no surprise, therefore, that rice is a major staple grain in much of Asia.

[Gist-Content Question]

During most of the lecture, the professor explains to the students the process by which monsoons are created.

[Understanding Attitude Question]

When the professor asks, "Is everyone with me so far?" she means that she knows the material is complicated, so she would like to confirm that everyone understands what she is talking about.

[Connecting Content Question]

The professor says, "Over thousands of years, people have adapted their agricultural needs to the monsoon rains. It should come as no surprise, therefore, that rice is a major staple grain in much of Asia." From her comments, it can be inferred that rice actually grows well in lots of water since it is a staple grain throughout many parts of Asia.

[Making Inferences Question]

At the end of the lecture, the professor has described a couple of benefits of monsoons, so it is likely that she will continue by naming some more of their benefits.

Summarizing ▶

Monsoons are heavy winds and rains that occur seasonally in many parts of the world. Because of the way both the land and ocean absorb heat, moisture from the ocean comes on land and then falls as rain. The rain can last for many days and cause floods in a lot of places. In India, because of the Himalaya Mountains, the monsoons can drop an extreme amount of rain. The professor says it seems that people would dislike monsoons, but in fact, people like them for many reasons. The rains provide relief from the heat and help crops grow.

Mastering Question Types with Conversations A3

p.116

| TYPES 1–4 |

| TYPE 1 C | TYPE 2 B | TYPE 3 C | TYPE 4 A |

Script 02-065

M Professor: Overall, Melissa, the rough draft of the paper you wrote is really good work. Make the changes I mentioned, and you won't have any problems when you submit the paper for real next week.

W Student: Thank you so much, Professor Garber. I really appreciate you're offering to read over my paper and to comment on it.

M: It's not a problem at all. I don't mind lending

students a hand when they ask. Now, uh, before you leave, there's something I'd like to talk to you about.

W: Okay.

M: As you know, this is an upper-level astronomy class that I'm teaching. And for some reason, a large number of freshmen and sophomores have signed up for the class.

W: Huh. I thought some of the students in class looked a bit young. I don't talk to anyone in class though, so I wasn't sure about it.

M: Well, I'd like to give you a chance to change that.

W: Change what?

M: Talking to your classmates.

W: What do you mean?

M: I've been grading the test papers from Monday's exam. You got a ninety-nine by the way.

W: Oh, cool.

M: Don't tell anyone about your grade. I won't give them back until next week. Anyway, the grades were a lot lower than usual. And the lowest grades were made by the youngest students. Unfortunately, the date for dropping classes has already passed, so the students doing poorly don't have that option anymore.

W: All right.

M: I really don't want to have a class full of failing students, so I need someone to help tutor them. What do you say?

W: Me? Tutor? Um . . . I've never done it before, but I can give it a try.

M: Wonderful. I'll let the class know at the end of today's lecture. I hope you don't mind tutoring, hmm . . . how about six or seven students at a time?

W: Okay. I suppose I can do that. I have time on Monday, Tuesday, and Thursday evenings. Is doing it from seven to eight in the evening all right?

M: That's perfect. I really appreciate it. Oh, you're going to get paid for this. This isn't a volunteer gig that I'm asking you to do.

[Gist-Purpose Question]

The student says, "I really appreciate you're offering to read over my paper and to comment on it," so she visited the professor to get his comments on a paper she wrote.

[Detail Question]

About the class, the professor remarks, "And for some reason, a large number of freshmen and sophomores have signed up for the class."

TYPE 3 [Understanding Organization Question]

About the previous test, the professor states, "Anyway, the grades were a lot lower than usual."

TYPE 4 [Understanding Function Question]

The professor wants the student to assist some of her classmates, so he asks her about the possibility of her becoming a tutor in his class.

Summarizing ▶

The professor says that a paper the student wrote is good but that she should make a few changes to it. He then talks to the student about his class. He mentions that many freshmen and sophomores are taking his advanced astronomy class. He remarks that their grades on the recent test were poor, but they cannot drop the class now. He would therefore like the student to work as a tutor. The student states that she has never tutored before. However, she agrees to help and informs the professor that she can help on Monday, Tuesday, and Thursday evenings.

| TYPES 5–8 |

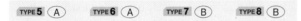

Script 02-066

M1 Student: Good morning. Are you the librarian on duty today?

M2 Librarian: I sure am. Is there something that I can help you with?

M1: I hope so. I'm trying to find this library book on the computer system, but I must be doing something wrong because I can't get any hits on it.

M2: Okay, let me take a look for you. Do you have the title of the book or at least the name of the author?

M1: Yes, I do. The title of the book is *Programming for the Absolute Beginner*. I really hope that the library has it because I need this book for one of my classes. I'm totally lost in my computer science class, and the professor told us that this book would help us catch up quickly if we read through it.

M2: Hmm . . . All right, let me type in the title here and see if it's available . . . Nothing. Do you know the author of the book?

M1: Yes, it's Jerry Lee Ford.

M2: Aha, I'm familiar with this book. I know that author's name because some other students have asked about this exact book in the past.

M1: Great. Then you know where it is.

M2: Well, yes and no.

M1: Huh? What do you mean?

M2: Simply that I know where it is, but I don't think you'll like the answer.

M1: Try me.

M2: We don't have this book at the library. I'm really sorry about that.

M1: Oh, no! What am I supposed to do now? I'll never pass my class.

M2: ⁸Hold on and let me finish. However, I do know for sure that the university bookstore across the street carries it, so you can go over there to buy it. It's under thirty dollars if I remember correctly, so it won't put a hole in your wallet.

M1: Okay. **I can live with that.**

M2: Sorry I couldn't help you out any more than that. But at least you know where you can find it now.

TYPE 5 [Gist-Content Question]

The student tells the librarian, "I'm trying to find this library book on the computer system, but I must be doing something wrong because I can't get any hits on it."

TYPE 6 [Detail Question]

The student says, "I'm totally lost in my computer science class," so he is not doing well in that class.

TYPE 7 [Understanding Attitude Question]

The librarian is very helpful and understanding of the student's situation, which makes him sympathetic to the student.

TYPE 8 [Making Inferences Question]

When the student says, "I can live with that," when the librarian tells him how much it will cost to purchase the book, he is implying that he will buy the book because he does not believe that it is too expensive.

Summarizing ▶

The student tells the librarian he is looking for a book on the computer system, but he cannot find it. The librarian asks for the title and looks it up himself. When he cannot find it, he asks the student for the author's name. Upon hearing the name, the librarian realizes the library does not have the book. The student is upset because he needs the book for a class he is having trouble with. The librarian then states that the student can purchase the book at the school bookstore for under thirty dollars, and the student implies that he will go and purchase it.

Mastering Topics with Lectures B1

p.118

1 (D) 2 (B) 3 (D)

Script & Graphic Organizer 02-067

M Professor: I'd like to move on now to talk about limestone. I know that some of you, like myself, are into spelunking, uh, caving, that is. There are actually quite a number of caves in this area, and a great many of them are limestone caves. In fact, this area is often referred to by professional spelunkers as TAG, which stands for Tennessee, Alabama, and Georgia. The reason is that these three states together have one of the largest limestone formations in North America, and as a consequence, they have one of the continent's biggest cave systems.

Now, spelunkers absolutely love limestone. The reason is that, uh, that due to its unique properties, it's much more likely than most other rocks to be formed into caves. Why's that, you may ask? Well, limestone is easily eroded by even the slightest bit of acidity in water. So, over the course of millions of years in some places, water seeps through limestone, which is quite porous, and eats away at the softer parts. This creates holes both large and small, and some of them eventually become cave systems. Many caves in the TAG area are found in the limestone layers that are beneath sandstone. Oh, for your information, the limestone begins in the Huntsville, Alabama area . . . that's in northern Alabama . . . and generally moves northeast into Tennessee along the Cumberland Plateau, where it slices into the northwest corner of Georgia along the way.

As for limestone itself . . . It's a sedimentary rock composed mostly of the mineral calcite, which is also known as calcium carbonate. As a sedimentary rock, it was originally formed from the bones and shells of sea animals that died millions of years ago. It's typically whitish in color, and very pure limestone is classified as marble, which is quite valuable in construction as well as sculpting. Limestone's color can vary depending upon what kind of impurities it has. Iron oxide, for instance, can make limestone brown, yellow, or red whereas carbon can make it black, gray, or even blue. Oh, in case you're curious, limestone formations with impurities are often called dirty limestone.

³Most limestone has some amounts of sand or silt, which is a byproduct of its formation at the bottom of ancient oceans. There's actually some speculation that many limestone formations that are found in places where oceans once existed were coral reefs. The reason is that many coral reefs today are composed of limestone. **That's just speculation though.** Anyway, be aware that any place where there's a great amount of limestone is an indicator that a large body of water, like an ocean, once existed there.

Of what use is limestone to people? One indirect benefit is that limestone helps improve the condition of the soil. Topsoil that lies over bedrock consisting of limestone is often quite fertile due to the calcium that frequently seeps into the soil from the limestone. This, in turn, helps farmers produce more crops. However, most people know limestone as a building material. It's used to make mortar and cement, and crushed limestone is utilized to make the grading for roads, so it's tremendously valuable to the construction industry.

But limestone's not nearly as strong as granite and sandstone are. As I mentioned, it's not only soft but is also susceptible to acidic water. That's not very ideal when you're trying to make a building from it. This is particularly important in many parts of the eastern U.S. since they get acid rain there. In fact, many buildings made of limestone on the east coast have suffered extensive damage and have had to be repaired at great expense because of the subsequent deterioration of the limestone used to make them.

Limestone

Limestone Characteristics:	Why It Forms Caves:
Is sedimentary rock Is composed of calcium carbonate Can be many colors	Its softness lets the acidity in water eat away parts of it
	What It Forms From: The bones and shells of sea animals that died millions of years ago
	How It Is Used: To make mortar and cement and to grade roads

1 [Understanding Organization Question]

The professor mentions, "As for limestone itself . . . It's a sedimentary rock composed mostly of the mineral calcite, which is also known as calcium carbonate."

2 [Making Inferences Question]

In the lecture, the professor says that areas with a lot of limestone were once located underwater. Since he states that the TAG area has a large number of limestone caves, it can be inferred that the TAG area was once underwater.

3 [Understanding Attitude Question]

When the professor notes that what he is saying is "just speculation," he means that the theory has not been verified as being true or false yet.

Summarizing ▶

The professor mentions that the TAG area has many limestone caves. He then notes why areas with a lot of limestone tend to have caves in them. He states that most limestone is comprised of calcium carbonate, which originally formed from dead animals millions of years ago. He also notes the different colors limestone may be. He claims that many areas with large amounts of limestone were once located underwater. The professor says that limestone is used to make buildings and to construct roads. However, because it is not very hard, some buildings made from limestone get worn down due to acid rain.

Mastering Topics with Lectures B2

p.119

1   2   3

Script & Graphic Organizer 02-068

W Professor: For decades, people have been harnessing the power of the sun in order to create energy. They do this by using solar panels, which capture the sun's energy, and then they use batteries to store the energy. What I'd like to discuss with you right now is how exactly this technology works. I mean, I'd like to note how these panels and batteries operate and go over some of the advantages and disadvantages of solar power.

Solar power systems work thanks to photovoltaic cells, or solar cells. In 1954, scientists at Bell Labs in the U.S. created the first solar cells. These cells use silicon that has trapped electrons. Photons of light then energize the electrons to the point where they are, um, they are able to create electricity. The electricity created is direct current, or DC, and is then stored in batteries. ³So a converter must be used for alternating current, uh, AC, applications. You remember the difference between the two, right . . .? Good . . . Of course, when the conversion occurs, some energy is, unfortunately, lost. **There's an excellent diagram in your textbook on page, uh, let's see, page 310, which shows the process very well . . .** Interestingly enough, the earliest applications for solar cells were on spacecraft. In addition, most first- and second-generation solar cells were quite inefficient and didn't produce enough energy at all. Even today, solar energy isn't nearly as environmentally friendly as people think it is because of, first, their inefficient nature, and, second, the amount of fossil-fuel-created electricity needed to create the cells in the first place.

Hundreds, perhaps even thousands, of solar cells comprise a single solar panel. Currently, solar panels are constructed of glass or silicon and are mounted on rigid metal frames. Some can rotate to face the sun, yet most are installed facing only one direction.

M Student: Could solar power supply a country's entire electrical needs?

W: Well . . . Theoretically, yes. But plans to make solar energy a significant part of any country's power grid often falter due to the sheer size and cost such a project would entail based on the current technology. Nevertheless, there are many large solar power plants all around the world, but the countries in which they're located must rely upon other ways to create electricity. In the U.S., for instance, solar power supplies less than one percent of the country's energy needs . . . Surprised about that, aren't you?

So, what are its good and bad points? Well, most of all, it's a renewable energy source. So long as the sun is shining, a home or a building designed to use solar power will have at least some energy. Additionally, despite the very high expense involved in purchasing the panels and setting up the systems, they do offer considerable energy savings. This happens over a matter of time though. Don't expect to recoup your investment in the first year or two. Think ten or fifteen years instead. Solar power is also quite environmentally friendly since, by virtue of using it, fewer carbon-producing fossil fuels are used to create electricity.

Now, what about its disadvantages . . .? Well, I think the most obvious one is that, without the sun, a solar panel system is utterly useless. So certain areas of the planet are simply never going to be able to use the existing technology to create solar energy. Even in places like, uh, say, Arizona, which has many areas that get more than 300 days of sun every year, there will still be some days when absolutely no solar energy can be created because of the presence of clouds. In addition, no energy gets created after the sun has set. Yet another disadvantage is that the panels themselves are not particularly efficient. It would take a huge number of panels to provide energy to an entire house, let alone a large building. My house, for instance, has solar panels on the roof, but all they do is heat the water. That's not particularly impressive.

Solar Power

Solar Power:	Advantages:
Is a way to harness the power of the sun to create energy by using solar cells on solar panels	Is renewable and offers long-term savings
	Disadvantages:
	Cannot be used on cloudy days or at night and is also very inefficient

1 [Gist-Purpose Question]

When the professor brings up solar cells, she then explains exactly how they are able to create energy from the sun.

2 [Detail Question]

The professor says, "Despite the very high expense involved in purchasing the panels and setting up the systems, they do offer considerable energy savings. This happens over a matter of time though. Don't expect to recoup your investment in the first year or two. Think ten or fifteen years instead."

3 [Understanding Function Question]

When the professor mention the page number in the book where the diagram is located, she is implying to the students that they should open their books and take a look at it.

Summarizing ▶

The professor notes when solar cells were first created. She explains how they work and tells the students to look at a diagram in their textbook. She says solar cells are placed on solar panels, which are aimed at the sun. She claims that solar power cannot be used to provide an entire country's energy needs and states it accounts for less than one percent of the U.S.'s energy. She says that one advantage of solar power is that it is renewable. It can also provide long-term energy savings. As for disadvantages, it cannot be used on cloudy days or at night. The panels are also somewhat inefficient.

Mastering Topics with Lectures B3   p.120

1 Ⓒ   2 Black Diamonds: ②, ③   Nanodiamonds: ①, ④   3 Ⓐ

Script & Graphic Organizer 02-069

M Professor: Diamonds are some of the world's most expensive gemstones and are also among the rarest. Yet even among diamonds, there are some types that are extremely rare. Two of these are black diamonds and nanodiamonds. However, while black diamonds are natural in origin, nanodiamonds are synthetic, so you won't be able to dig them up anywhere. Nanodiamonds are also incredibly small—hence their name—and may have potential uses in nanotechnology, such as in the delivery of medicines to various parts of the body.

Let's take a look at black diamonds first. They are sometimes called carbonado. That's C-A-R-B-O-N-A-D-O. They're only found in the Central African Republic and in Brazil in the alluvial deposits of rivers. Oh, that's the silt that's carried downriver and gets deposited near the river's mouth, which often forms a delta. Black diamonds are typically grayish or black, as their name implies, and they have occlusions, or imperfections, which give them this coloring. Extensive examinations of black diamonds have shown that they're the oldest diamonds on the planet as well as the hardest. Dating methods have revealed that black diamonds are around four billion years old . . . yes, billion, not million . . . whereas most diamonds are less than a billion years

old. Quite a difference, huh?

In some academic circles, there's speculation . . . valid, I think . . . that black diamonds are extraterrestrial in origin and may have come to Earth after an asteroid crashed into the planet. Now, before you ask how that's possible when black diamonds are found in both Africa and South America, remember that billions of years ago, the Earth's surface looked much different. At some time in the past, Africa and South America were adjacent to one another. So if an asteroid crashed there and brought these black diamonds with it, the subsequent movement of the continents would explain why they're now found in two separate places yet nowhere else on the Earth. It's possible they were buried deep underground and only surfaced after being washed downstream. Ah, another piece of evidence indicating their possible extraterrestrial origins is that black diamonds have hydrogen inside them whereas most diamonds are pure carbon. In addition, some black diamonds examined with infrared light showed a spectrum found only in a type of diamond that is known to come from space. I'd say that's pretty convincing evidence, wouldn't you?

Now, let's move on to nanodiamonds. As I stated, they're manufactured. How this happens is that they're created by the detonation of an explosion and are then formed from the carbon material caught in the explosion. To make them, researchers set off small explosives in a cooling medium such as water. Following the detonation, the material that remains is boiled in acid, which leaves only the nanodiamonds. Please be aware that, as their name implies, they are incredibly small. You need a powerful electron microscope to see them. Today, nanodiamonds have some commercial applications. They're used in polishing materials and dry lubricants. But the big hope is that someday they'll be used in medicine. This is what some doctors and researchers believe.

W Student: Could you explain a little more, please? I'm not sure I understand how nanotechnology in general is useful in medicine.

M: It would be my pleasure. Nanotechnology really is the future of medicine. Someday, small nanorobots will enter the body and attack an infection, virus, or other problem without doctors having to perform invasive surgery or do anything else to the body. Doctors hope to use nanodiamonds to create these nanorobots. So at some point in the future, for example, they'd be able to enter the body, find a cancerous tumor, and eliminate it. That would be an improvement over current radiation methods, which, while they kill tumors, also kill healthy cells in the body. Of course, the technology to do this doesn't exist yet, but it hopefully will in the near future.

Diamonds

Black Diamonds:	Nanodiamonds:
Are found in Africa and South America	*Are manufactured*
	Are created by explosions
Are four billion years old	*May be used in medical nanotechnology in the future*
May be from outer space	

1 [Gist-Content Question]

During the lecture, the professor discusses black diamonds and nanodiamonds, both of which are unique types of diamonds.

2 [Connecting Content Question]

According to the lecture, black diamonds are only found in two places on the Earth—in Africa and South America—and they may have come from outer space. As for nanodiamonds, they may have future uses in the field of medical nanotechnology, and they can be formed from manmade explosions.

3 [Making Inferences Question]

After the professor describes the theory that black diamonds come from outer space, he exclaims, "I'd say that's pretty convincing evidence, wouldn't you?" It can be inferred that he believes this theory on their origins is correct.

Summarizing ▶

The professor claims that black diamonds and nanodiamonds are extremely rare. Black diamonds are found in only two places. One is in Africa, and the other is in South America. They are also around four billion years old. He claims that they may have extraterrestrial origins and explains why people believe that. As for nanodiamonds, these can be made by humans by using explosives. He describes how this process occurs. He then mentions that nanodiamonds may have some use in the medical industry. However, this is not yet the case. Perhaps they will be used by doctors in the future.

Mastering Topics with Lectures B4

p.121

1 Ⓑ   2 Elliptical Galaxy: ① Spiral Galaxy: ③
Barred-Spiral Galaxy: ②, ④   3 Ⓓ

Script & Graphic Organizer 02-070

W Professor: Our galaxy, the Milky Way, is just one of the estimated millions, or perhaps hundreds of millions, or even billions, of galaxies in the universe. Despite there being huge numbers of other galaxies, it wasn't until 1924 that Edwin Hubble, an American astronomer, proved their existence. Space nebulae, which are large regions of gas and dust, had been observed prior to Hubble's time, but he proved that some of these nebulae contained stars and were, in fact, star clusters, that is, uh, galaxies, which were located outside the Milky Way.

As more and more galaxies were discovered over the years and more learned about them, astronomers began classifying them according to their size and shape. The smallest are called dwarf elliptical galaxies and contain a mere million stars. Next are spiral galaxies, which may have up to 300 billion stars. Yes, that's quite a difference from the dwarf elliptical galaxies, isn't it? There are also giant elliptical galaxies, which could have up to, um, ten trillion stars in them. The diameters of galaxies range from 3,000 light years for the smallest to perhaps half a million light years for the largest. As for the Milky Way, it's believed to have approximately 400 billion stars and to be 100,000 light years in diameter.

Another difference between galaxies is their shapes. The system Hubble devised to describe their shapes is still used today. He designated them with the uppercase letters E, S, and SB. E galaxies are elliptical and range from EO, which is almost spherical, to E7, which is very elongated. Oh, you'd better jot this down. It's not in your books, but I expect you to know it. S galaxies are spiral galaxies that spin like a disk and have extended arms composed of stars. S galaxies have sub-classifications of a, b, and c types. Oh, a, b, and c are lowercase here. Sa galaxies have tight spiral arms while Sb and Sc galaxies' arms are much less tight. Finally, SB galaxies . . . and now I mean a capital B . . . SB galaxies are barred-spiral galaxies, which comprise almost two-thirds of all spiral galaxies. These are spiral galaxies with very large arms but with a center more bar-shaped than circular. Again, SB galaxies are sub-classified as lowercase a, b, and c types depending on the tightness of the spirals.

Now, let's move on to galaxy formation. Following the Big Bang, the most widely accepted theory on the creation of the universe, the universe was mostly helium, hydrogen, and dark matter. Galaxies then formed from clumps of dark matter that cooled and combined during the early period of the universe. The clumps of dark matter had gravity and attracted more dark matter, thus letting them grow in size. The galaxies began to form a core and a halo. The core is the inner part, which is where most of the helium and hydrogen went, while the dark matter separated and ended up in the outer halo. The hydrogen and helium gases then began combining, which resulted in stars forming. Astronomers refer to a galaxy that's forming as a protogalaxy. It's estimated that the first protogalaxies formed around fourteen billion years ago. The initial process, which has been dubbed the Dark Ages, took around 500 million years before the first complete galaxies actually formed.

Once a galaxy was formed, it took another billion

years for its main features to be created. One feature is a massive central black hole. These black holes absorb matter and may control how large their galaxies can become. Some astronomers also believe that many large galaxies were once smaller galaxies that collided and then joined with one another. Yes, galaxies are always moving, and, sometimes, when they pass closely to one another, their gases may combine to create new stars. You know, the Milky Way and another galaxy are actually on a collision course. But don't worry too much . . . That won't happen for billions of years.

Galaxies and Their Formation

The Sizes of Galaxies:	The Shapes of Galaxies:
Dwarf elliptical galaxies have 1 million stars	Elliptical galaxies may be elliptical to spherical
Spiral galaxies have up to 300 billion stars	Spiral galaxies have extended arms
Giant elliptical galaxies have up to ten trillion stars	Barred-spiral galaxies have bar-shaped centers

1 [Detail Question]

The professor comments, "These black holes absorb matter and may control how large their galaxies can become."

2 [Connecting Content Question]

According to the lecture, elliptical galaxies can be almost spherical in appearance. Spiral galaxies may spin like a disk. And barred-spiral galaxies have very long arms and bar-shaped centers.

3 [Making Inferences Question]

The professor states, "As for the Milky Way, it's believed to have approximately 400 billion stars and to be 100,000 light years in diameter." According to the information that she gave previously about the number of stars and the sizes of different galaxies, it can be inferred that the Milky Way is a medium-sized galaxy.

Summarizing ▶

According to the lecturer, Edwin Hubble proved there were other galaxies in 1924. Now astronomers have seen enough other galaxies to classify them according to their size and shape. There are dwarf elliptical galaxies, spiral galaxies, and giant elliptical galaxies. She explains their characteristics. Galaxies also have different shapes. There are elliptical galaxies, spiral galaxies, and barred-spiral galaxies, all of which she then compares and contrasts. She mentions how galaxies were first formed and why they all are believed to have a massive black hole in their center. Finally, she notes that galaxies move and that some collide with each other.

Mastering Topics with Conversations B5 p.122

1 Ⓐ   2 Ⓑ   3 Ⓑ

Script & Graphic Organizer 02-071

W1 Student: Professor Stewart, do you mind if I come in and have a quick chat with you, please?

W2 Professor: Not at all, Amy. What's on your mind today? Are you having trouble understanding the poems we went over in class? Some of them were a little esoteric I think.

W1: Oh, actually, Yeats is one of my favorite poets. I've got several books of his poems at home, and I just love reading them. I find his work to be so . . . um, well. . . I guess unique and mysterious are the words I'm looking for.

W2: I couldn't agree with you more . . . Okay, then what would you like to talk about?

W1: Well, unfortunately, I've got a bit of bad news. I came to get you to sign this form so that I could drop your class.

W2: Drop my class? Whatever for?

W1: Well, as a senior, I really need to focus on my major before I graduate. I wouldn't want to mess up any of those classes. Plus, I'm doing several extracurricular activities this semester. I'm a member of the school's soccer team, and I write for the school newspaper and participate in student government as well.

W2: Goodness. I had no idea you were so involved in school activities. I guess I see your point. It's just that . . .

W1: What?

W2: Well, when you speak up in class, you always seem to make good contributions. I've also found some of your insights on poems to be quite original.

W1: Thank you for saying that.

W2: [3]I also really like the poems that you've written in class. Your free verse ones were quite good, but I was even more impressed with the sonnets you wrote.

W1: Oh? You liked them?

W2: Liked them? I loved them. They were so well written. I was quite impressed. I must say that losing you is going to be a tremendous loss for the class. Are you sure there's no way you could, oh, I don't know, drop an extracurricular activity or something?

W1: I don't really think that would be possible.

W2: Not even the newspaper?

W1: Oh, that's the most important activity of all. I'm thinking of trying to find work as a reporter when I graduate.

W2: I see. Well, in that case, I guess I have no choice but to sign the paper.

W1: Sorry about that. Here you are.

W2: Okay . . . Feel free to visit class anytime you want even though you won't be enrolled in it.

W1: I shall. And thanks for understanding. I hate to drop the class, but I just don't see any other options.

Office Hours

Reason for Visiting:	Result:
Needs to drop the professor's class	Asks the student to drop one of her extracurricular activities
Problem:	Solution:
Is too busy with extracurricular activities to take the class	Agrees to let the student drop the class

1 [Gist-Purpose Question]

The student tells the professor, "I came to get you to sign this form so that I could drop your class." Dropping the class would result in a change in her status in the class.

2 [Understanding Attitude Question]

Throughout the conversation, the professor says nice things to the student about her performance in her class. Thus, she is complimentary toward the student.

3 [Understanding Function Question]

When the student asks that question, her words as well as her tone of voice both indicate she is doubtful that the professor really liked the sonnets she wrote in class.

▶ Summarizing ▶

The student visits the professor's office to talk. The professor thinks the student is there to discuss some poems, but the student says she has come to drop the class. She explains that she is too busy with all of her extracurricular activities and needs to focus on her major classes prior to graduating. The professor expresses her disappointment because the student makes good contributions and writes excellent poems. When she tries to convince the student to stay in the class, the student says that is not possible. The professor agrees to let her drop the class and invites the student to visit her class anytime she wants.

Mastering Topics with Conversations B6 p.123

1 Ⓒ **2** Ⓐ **3** Ⓓ

Script & Graphic Organizer 02-072

M1 Student: Jeff, take a look at this new refrigerator I just got for my dorm room. I am so pleased to have this. I think I'm the only one on the entire floor who has one. Talk about lucky.

M2 Resident Assistant: Actually, Matt, there's a reason why you're the only one here in the dorm to have a refrigerator.

M1: Oh? What's that?

M2: Er, they're not allowed. I'm sorry, but you're not supposed to have that in your dorm room.

M1: You've got to be kidding me. How am I supposed to have cold drinks or keep food in my room without one?

M2: I totally understand where you're coming from . . . Believe me when I say that I'd love to have a fridge in my room as well, but it's not up to me. And as your RA, it's my job to enforce the school's regulations. I'm really sorry about this, but you're going to have to remove that from your room by this Friday.

M1: Seriously?

M2: Yeah, seriously. If you don't, I'll be forced to give you a fine and will also have to report you to the Student Housing Office.

M1: What would happen there?

M2: In a worst-case scenario, you'd get kicked out of student housing immediately and wouldn't be allowed to stay in the dorms for a complete year.

M1: Uh . . . I guess that I'll get rid of my fridge then.

M2: Good thinking. Let me know if you need some assistance. I've got a car, so I can take you and the fridge to someone's house off campus, and you can store it there.

M1: Okay, thanks for the offer. But . . . uh, hold on a second.

M2: What?

M1: You know, I actually got this fridge as a gift from one of my friends who graduated last semester. He lived in one of the on-campus apartments. Yeah . . . wait a minute . . . How come he was allowed to keep his fridge, but I can't?

M2: The on-campus apartments have different rules governing appliances.

M1: Oh, I didn't know that.

M2: Yeah, remember that this is a pretty old dorm

we're in. The electrical wiring's not as good as the more modern buildings. That's why there are no refrigerators allowed here. If every student had one, the electricity in this dorm would keep going out.

M1: Well, I guess my mind's made up then.

M2: How so?

M1: I'm moving into an on-campus apartment next semester. There's no way I'm going to live without cold drinks and food in my room anymore.

Service Encounter

Problem:	Solution:
Has a refrigerator that is not allowed in the dormitory	Must remove the refrigerator by Friday
Student's Reaction:	Student's Decision:
Does not understand why he must remove the refrigerator	Will find another place to live next semester

1 [Gist-Content Question]

The speakers are mostly talking about the fact that the student has a refrigerator in his dormitory room that is in violation of school regulations.

2 [Detail Question]

The resident assistant tells the student, "Remember that this is a pretty old dorm we're in. The electrical wiring's not as good as the more modern buildings. That's why there are no refrigerators allowed here. If every student had one, the electricity in this dorm would keep going out."

3 [Making Inferences Question]

The resident assistant says, "I'm really sorry about this, but you're going to have to remove that from your room by this Friday." He sympathizes with the student and understands how he feels, but he also knows that he has to follow the rules.

Summarizing ▶

The student tells his resident assistant about the refrigerator he just got. The resident assistant tells the student that refrigerators are not allowed in the dormitory and that he needs to remove it. The student wants to know what his punishment will be if he refuses. He learns he could be fined or kicked out of student housing. Then the resident assistant offers to drive the student to a place off campus to store the refrigerator. The student asks why refrigerators are not allowed in the dormitory, and the resident assistant says it is due to the electrical wiring in the building, which is old.

TOEFL Practice Tests C1
p.124

1 Ⓒ   2 Ⓐ   3 Ⓑ, Ⓒ   4 Ⓓ   5 Carbon-14 Dating Method: ⓵, ⓶   Potassium-Argon Dating Method: ⓷, ⓸   6 Ⓐ

Script 02-073

W Professor: Buried within the Earth are many objects from past civilizations, fossils, and, of course, rocks. When archaeologists and other scientists find one of these objects, one thing they want to determine is how old it is. For a manmade item, some typical ways to determine the date of its creation are to note the location where it was found, look for any inscriptions that might be on it, and take a look at the style of the object. For example, a recently excavated shipwreck in Asia proved to be a veritable goldmine of ancient artifacts. The ship had been carrying thousands of ninth-century Ming Dynasty bowls when it sank for some reason. How did the people who examined the find know that it was from the ninth century? First, many bowls had Chinese inscriptions on them that used the language from that period. Also, the bowls were made in a style popular at that time in a certain Chinese province. Finally, of the other items found in the shipwreck, one had a date inscribed on it.

Of course, it's not always that easy to ascertain something's date, especially when it comes to prehistoric objects. As a result, scientists have to resort to other methods. The most common form of testing they use is one that you've all most likely heard of. It's the carbon-14 dating method. You've heard of it, right . . .? Let me explain this method for you. Okay . . . Carbon is found in all living things. It has several isotopes, the most common being nonradioactive carbon-12 and carbon-13, which are both stable. Carbon-14, meanwhile, is an unstable radioactive isotope that is created by cosmic rays in the upper atmosphere. When carbon-14 falls to the Earth, it's absorbed by plants through the process of photosynthesis and is then taken in by animals and humans when they consume the plants. Thus, any organic material will have trace amounts of carbon-14 in it.

What does this have to do with dating objects? Good question. First, carbon-14 is unstable, as I just stated. That means it decays. All radioactive materials have what's called a half-life. The half-life is the rate at which something radioactive decays so that only half of it remains. For carbon-14, its half-life is 5,730 years, uh, give or take forty years. Right away, you can see that there's going to be some flux in the numbers, so nothing can be dated precisely by using the carbon-14 method. What it does, however, is provide close estimates, but it's not exact by any means.

Anyway, by using carbon-14 dating, an object can be

analyzed, and a date for the object can be determined. Unfortunately, there are two major problems with this method. First, it . . . It can only be used for objects from less than 60,000 years ago since the carbon-14 would have decayed beyond our ability to detect it on any older objects. Second, as I mentioned, it's only useful for organic objects . . . you know, uh, wood, plant matter, bones, clothing, and tools made from plants or animals, just to name a few . . . Then . . . how do we know the ages of fossils or rocks or, um, even the Earth, which is estimated to be around 4.5 billion years old, if we can't use carbon-14 dating?

Well, for older objects, we use potassium-argon dating. Potassium also has a radioactive isotope—potassium-40—that is found in many types of igneous rocks, which are those of volcanic origins. It has a half-life of 1.25 billion years. In addition, a little more than ten percent of the time, potassium decays into argon gas. This gas frequently gets trapped in the rock where the potassium decayed. However, if the rock is in molten form when the decay occurs, the argon gas can escape. Still, by comparing the amount of potassium and argon in rocks, scientists can determine when exactly the rock was formed. Rocks between 4.5 billion and 100,000 years old can be dated by using this method. Of course, this method is also limited since it's only useful for rocks formed from volcanoes.

Still, it has its uses. Here's an example. Say that, many years ago, a volcano erupted and managed to kill some primitive humans. It would have to have occurred over 100,000 years ago, right? So there weren't any cities or civilizations back then. Nevertheless, the eruption could have buried individuals or small groups of various humans or humanoids. Anyway, by using potassium-argon dating, scientists can learn when the people were killed and when exactly the volcano erupted. Oh, I almost forgot . . . Fossils can be dated with this method as well. But since it's limited, there is yet another dating method. This one uses isotopes of uranium to determine the ages of some other types of rocks.

1 [Gist-Content Question]

Throughout the lecture, the professor talks about some different methods that scientists use to determine how old various objects are.

2 [Gist-Purpose Question]

Before explaining the carbon-14 dating method, the professor says, "The most common form of testing they use is one that you've all most likely heard of. It's the carbon-14 dating method."

3 [Detail Question]

According to the professor, people can tell the date of something by looking "for any inscriptions that might be on it" and by taking "a look at the style of the object."

4 [Understanding Organization Question]

When describing how to determine the age of prehistoric objects, the professor describes both carbon-14 dating and potassium-argon dating.

5 [Connecting Content Question]

According to the lecture, the carbon-14 dating method is only accurate to a forty-year period and is used to date organic material. As for the potassium-argon dating method, it is used for volcanic rocks and can date objects as far back as 4.5 billion years in the past.

6 [Making Inferences Question]

At the end of the lecture, the professor states, "Oh, I almost forgot . . . Fossils can be dated with this method as well. But since it's limited, there is yet another dating method. This one uses isotopes of uranium to determine the ages of some other types of rocks." Thus, she will most likely discuss another type of dating method.

TOEFL Practice Tests C2

p.126

1 Ⓒ   2 Ⓑ   3 Ⓑ   4 Ⓒ   5 Central Regions: ②, ③, ④ Coastal Regions: ①   6 Ⓒ

Script 02-074

M1 Professor: When most people think of deserts, images of endless sand dunes shimmering in the heat often come to mind. Or perhaps they think of a long train of camels plodding along with their Bedouin masters swaying on top like sailors on ships in the desert. While there is some truth to these images, don't believe for a minute that all deserts look like that. In fact, a wide variety of deserts are found all over the world, and even Antarctica is classified as a desert. Yes, that's right. Now, first, let me explain how deserts are classified, and then I'll cover some ways that they form.

Technically speaking, a desert is any area that receives, on average, fewer than 250 millimeters of precipitation or an area that gets a greater amount of precipitation but has it evaporate so quickly that it's of little use for the growth of vegetation. In Antarctica, for example, there are low amounts of precipitation . . . snow, that is . . . and the little that falls remains frozen in ice and snow formations and thus would be of no use to any plants were they able to survive in the frigid conditions there.

6Now, forgetting about Antarctica for the time being, most deserts can be divided into hot and semi-arid deserts. Hot deserts have temperatures that vary a great deal between night and day. During the day, the temperatures may be very high, yet they can be quite low at night. Hot deserts also frequently lack almost any kind of vegetation, and they have areas with sand dunes as well as hard, rocky areas. The Sahara is the best example of a hot desert, but there are many more. Semi-arid deserts, on the other hand, experience less extreme temperature changes. They rarely fall below zero degrees Celsius at night, and many have some vegetation and animals as well. Parts of the deserts in the southwestern United States are considered semi-arid.

Many deserts are found in the central regions of continents. Again, the dry southwestern U.S. is an example as are the Gobi Desert in Mongolia and the enormous deserts found in central Australia. Due either to geographical circumstances or the location of prevailing storm systems, these regions all receive hardly any precipitation. Some may be in basins or on the far side of mountain ranges, as is the case with the deserts in the Southwest. Consider the Sierra Nevada Mountain Range. In the U.S., the prevailing weather conditions move from, uh, west to east. So many clouds dump rain or snow on the western side of the mountains before they continue eastward. The Sierra Nevada Mountains get more snowfall than any other place in the lower forty-eight states. Some places there can get around eighteen meters a year of snow. However, on the eastern side of the mountains, the Nevada Desert is practically as dry as a bone and rarely gets any precipitation. That's the rain-shadow effect, which is something we'll go over in a little more detail soon. Oh, and as for prevailing storm systems bringing no rain, the best example is in central Australia. Because of how the air currents there move, that area gets almost no precipitation.

Of course, not all deserts are found in inner locations. Some form along the coast. The Atacama Desert in Chile and the Namib Desert in southwest Africa are two examples. Yes, it seems odd for a desert to form along a coast since we often think of them as lush places. Yet in some places, very cold ocean currents near the coastline prevent the formation of rain-bringing storm systems. The Atacama Desert, for example, is considered by some to be the driest place on the Earth. Some places there have recorded no rainfall since at least the sixteenth century. Now that's truly incredible.

As if there aren't enough ways in nature to create deserts, humans can also be responsible for their creation. One way humans do this is by clearing forests. When people cut down trees but don't replace them by planting new ones, extensive soil erosion can occur. In most places, the life-giving topsoil is only a few feet deep and is thus easily subject to erosion through the actions of the wind and water. However, trees, bushes, grasses, and other forms of vegetation with extensive root systems act to hold the soil in place and prevent erosion. When there's no vegetation, however, the soil

can rapidly erode. Once that topsoil's gone, nothing can grow there, and a desert may be created.

M2 Student: Has this ever happened?

M1: It sure has. It has happened in China. In the far western part of the country, the desert keeps expanding every year. Two reasons are that the people living there are deforesting the region and that they also graze large herds of livestock on the land. With no trees and the grasses eaten, the topsoil gets blown away. In addition, every year, huge dust storms which form in this area take place for several months every spring. They not only affect China but also neighboring countries. There have been some attempts to plant trees and to stop the process of desertification, yet the desert areas there continue to increase in size.

1 [Gist-Content Question]

During the lecture, the professor goes over the different ways that deserts may form.

2 [Detail Question]

The professor states, "Some form along the coast. The Atacama Desert in Chile and the Namib Desert in southwest Africa are two examples."

3 [Understanding Attitude Question]

About the lack of rainfall in the Atacama Desert, the professor states, "Now that's truly incredible," which shows his amazement by this fact.

4 [Understanding Organization Question]

When mentioning that there are many types of deserts on the Earth, the professor says, "In fact, a wide variety of deserts are found all over the world, and even Antarctica is classified as a desert."

5 [Connecting Content Question]

According to the lecture, deserts in central regions may be formed by the rain-shadow effect, are often located next to mountain ranges, and often get very little precipitation. As for deserts in coastal regions, they are often created because of the effects of ocean currents.

6 [Understanding Function Question]

When the professor tells the class, "Now, forgetting about Antarctica for the time being," he implies that he is going to return to talking about Antarctica later in his lecture.

TOEFL Practice Tests C3   p.128

| 1 Ⓓ | 2 Ⓑ | 3 Ⓒ | 4 Ⓐ | 5 Ⓑ |

W Student: Hi, Professor Miller. Are you doing anything right now?

M Professor: Uh, hi, Stacy. Well, uh, I guess that I'm not too terribly busy. I'm just trying to go over this paper that I'm writing.

W: You still write papers? Isn't that something for, oh, students like me to do?

M: Well, this is a paper that I'm writing to submit to a scholarly journal. Along with my teaching duties here, I'm expected to do research as well and to publish in journals at least a couple of times each year. The school would even like me to publish a book or two, but that won't happen for a while.

W: I never knew that.

M: Yeah, that's why most of us professors only teach two or three classes a semester. We're supposed to use the rest of our time to research various topics . . . Okay, but enough about me. What have you come here to speak with me about?

W: Ah, yes. I was hoping that you could look over this essay that I'm writing. I'm having some problems narrowing down my thesis, and I thought that you might be able to help me out if you, uh, if you could just take a look at it.

M: Um, I'm confused. What paper? I haven't assigned a paper in your class. In fact, I wasn't planning on doing that until sometime next month.

W: Oh, this paper isn't for your class. It's for Professor Eagleton's class. But I know that you have the same interests that he does, so I thought that, uh, you know . . . maybe you could help me with it.

M: Haven't you tried talking with Professor Eagleton? It is his class after all.

W: Well, he's just so . . . uh, unapproachable I think is the best word. I tried to have a word with him after class today, but he kind of just brushed me off. He doesn't really seem to care too much about his students. You're different though.

M: Oh, uh, well . . . Thanks for saying that.

W: Well, it's true. So, uh, do you think you can help me with my paper?

M: I'd love to but . . .

W: You don't have enough time?

M: It's not that . . . It's just that it's not my class, so I don't want to, er, I don't want to offend anyone.

W: You mean that you don't want to upset Professor Eagleton if he finds out you've been helping me, right?

M: [6] I suppose that's one way of putting it.

W: Okay, I understand . . . I guess that I'll be going then.

M: Hold on. What's your topic about?

W: It's on the migration of settlers to the West in the nineteenth century. I'm trying to write about what made them go to uncharted and uncivilized territory . . . aside from the obvious reasons of course . . . and that's when I thought that you might be able to help.

M: Okay, that's a good topic. Hold on . . . Here . . . Take a look at this book. You might find it interesting.

W: Hmm . . . I've never seen this one before.

M: It's pretty old. There aren't many copies of it lying around. Still, it's got a lot of information in it that might help you with your paper. And if you have any more problems . . . hmm . . . why don't you send me an email or drop by my office during office hours, okay?

W: You're the best, Professor Miller. I really appreciate it.

---

1 [Gist-Purpose Question]

The student tells the professor, "I was hoping that you could look over this essay that I'm writing. I'm having some problems narrowing down my thesis, and I thought that you might be able to help me out if you, uh, if you could just take a look at it."

2 [Detail Question]

The professor gives the student a book to look at that should help her with the paper she is writing.

3 [Understanding Attitude Question]

About Professor Eagleton, the student says, "Well, he's just so . . . uh, unapproachable I think is the best word. I tried to have a word with him after class today, but he kind of just brushed me off. He doesn't really seem to care too much about his students."

4 [Making Inferences Question]

When Professor Miller lends the student the book and tells her to contact him if she has any more problems, it can be inferred that he is willing directly to help the student with her project.

5 [Understanding Function Question]

When the professor says, "Hold on," as the student is getting ready to leave, he is telling her that he has changed his mind and has decided to help her.

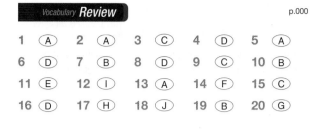
1 Ⓐ   **2** Ⓐ   **3** Ⓒ   **4** Ⓓ   **5** Ⓐ

6 Ⓓ   **7** Ⓑ   **8** Ⓓ   **9** Ⓒ   **10** Ⓑ

11 Ⓔ   **12** Ⓘ   **13** Ⓐ   **14** Ⓕ   **15** Ⓒ

16 Ⓓ   **17** Ⓗ   **18** Ⓙ   **19** Ⓑ   **20** Ⓖ

Chapter 06 | Physical Sciences 2 · Conversations

Mastering Question Types with Lectures A1   p.132

| TYPES 1–4 |

TYPE 1 Ⓒ   **TYPE 2** Ⓐ   **TYPE 3** Ⓑ   **TYPE 4** Ⓓ

Script 02-076

M1 Professor: I'm sure many of you are familiar with the children's song "Twinkle, Twinkle, Little Star," but how many of you have ever taken the time to consider the words and the science behind them? I'd wager that very few of you have. So tell me . . . Do stars really twinkle, and if so, why do they twinkle . . .? Andrew, I see you've raised your hand.

M2 Student: Yes, Professor Freeman, stars do twinkle. I'm not exactly sure why, but I remember hearing it has something to do with our seeing them through the Earth's atmosphere.

M1: Well done, Andrew. That's a good answer. And, yes, you're correct about the Earth's atmosphere. In fact, their twinkling has everything to do with the planet's atmosphere. ⁴Let me explain that right now. First of all, there's actually a scientific name for the twinkling of stars. It's stellar scintillation. **That's spelled S-C-I-N-T-I-L-L-A-T-I-O-N for those of you who are interested in the term.** Now, as I believe you all know, the Earth has many different layers of atmosphere. You know, like the troposphere, the stratosphere, and a couple of others . . . Anyway, as we view the stars from the ground and through these different layers, the stars appear to be blinking rapidly. That is, they're twinkling. The reason is that the atmosphere is moving.

Everyone's familiar with the term refraction, right . . .? Well, just to refresh your memories, refraction refers to the bending of light as it passes through the air and encounters small pockets of air. For instance, uh . . . Okay, if you've ever gone driving on a very hot day, you should be familiar with refraction. The hot air just above the surface of the road bends light more than the cooler air that is slightly above it. The result is that we see a shimmering veil of what appears to be water on

the road. At times, you can even see cars' reflections in the road. That's refraction. And it's refraction that causes this twinkling effect. As a star's light travels through the layers of the atmosphere, it gets bent in random directions many times, thus making it seem as though the star is twinkling. Oh, here's something else to remember: The more light travels through the atmosphere, the more it's refracted. Therefore, stars closer to the horizon appear to twinkle more than stars overhead since the light of stars near the horizon must travel through more air than the light of stars high in the sky.

Now, what about planets? Do they twinkle . . .? Anyone . . .? The answer is . . . yes, they do, but we usually can't detect it. Why not? You see, the planets are much closer to us than the stars are, so they appear bigger. They also reflect light and don't produce it like stars do. This mitigates the amount of twinkling they do. However, when the air is very turbulent, the planets may appear to twinkle. On these occasions, the air is moving so rapidly and, uh, randomly, that the planets appear to start twinkling. Oh, and the different compositions of the planets—rock for the inner planets and various gases for the outer ones—don't affect whether they appear to twinkle or not.

TYPE 1 [Gist-Content Question]

The professor goes over why the stars and other objects in the sky appear to twinkle when people look at them.

TYPE 2 [Detail Question]

The professor states, "However, when the air is very turbulent, the planets may appear to twinkle. On these occasions, the air is moving so rapidly and, uh, randomly, that the planets appear to start twinkling."

TYPE 3 [Understanding Organization Question]

The professor discusses the planets to note that they, like stars, twinkle, but their twinkling, unlike that of stars, is usually undetectable. Thus, he compares the twinkling of the two.

TYPE 4 [Understanding Function Question]

When the professor states, "For those of you who are interested in the term," he is indicating that the students are not required to know it, so it can be inferred that he will not test the students on it.

Summarizing ▶

The professor asks the students if stars really do twinkle. A student responds that they do, and he thinks it has something to do with the atmosphere. The professor tells the student he is correct. The professor then describes the event known as stellar scintillation. Because the light from stars must move through the different layers of the atmosphere, it appears to move. The reason is refraction. The movement of air causes the light to refract in many directions. This causes the twinkling effect. The professor then claims that planets twinkle, but it is hard to detect this except when there is turbulent weather.

| TYPES 5–6 |

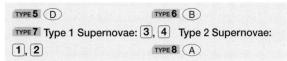

Script 02-077

W Professor: [6]In space, there are numerous phenomena, yet perhaps none is as wondrous as the supernova, which is, uh, well, it's basically a star that has exploded. When this happens, the intensity of its light can be brighter than an entire galaxy, and the energy it emits can be greater than that which our sun gives off in its entire lifetime. We're talking about billions of years. **Stop and consider that for a second . . .** Okay, there are two main types of supernovae, and each has several subtypes.

Type 1 supernovae occur when a white dwarf explodes. These were once large stars like our sun. However, upon exhausting their hydrogen supply, they expanded. In most cases, they turned red and then, after some time, collapsed and became very tiny white stars, hence the name white dwarf. However, if another star is near the white dwarf, it can accumulate a great deal of gaseous material from that nearby star. This compresses the white dwarf, which causes a chain reaction to start in its core. The subsequent massive nuclear reaction that takes places transforms the white dwarf into a supernova.

Type 2 supernovae, meanwhile, explode after a large star first implodes. That is, it collapses inward. Type 2 supernovae occur in stars that are, oh, about eight to fifteen times the size of the sun. What happens is that the huge star burns up all of its hydrogen and helium, so it then starts fusing carbon at its center. This builds up a massive, multilayered, and extremely dense core. When the star reaches a certain mass, called the Chandrasekhar Limit, it collapses onto its core. This causes the core to heat up and become even denser, and then the material that collapsed gets flung into space by literally bouncing off of the core as the star becomes a supernova. Sometimes, though, the star is so enormous that, instead of a supernova being formed, the star continues to collapse on itself, which creates a black hole. Little is known about black holes, but many astronomers believe that all galaxies have one at their center, and this prevents them, the galaxies, I mean, from becoming too large.

Occasionally, we can see supernovae from the Earth. There was one famous one in 1054 that people all over the world recorded seeing. They could actually see it during the day for about three weeks, and it shone at night for almost two years. That's how bright they can be. Anyway, when we see supernovae here, be aware that you're seeing light that has come to us after a long, long journey across the universe. By measuring the light when the supernova reaches its peak, astronomers can actually figure out how far it is, er, was, from the Earth and can therefore determine the distance of the galaxy where the supernova occurred. They can do this by measuring the red shift of the light source. If you'll recall, we studied that in last Thursday's lecture, so you should know what it means.

Okay, so why are supernovae important? Well, a supernova is believed to have been responsible for the creation of the sun and the solar system. I'd say that's a pretty important reason. Basically, material from an exploding supernova was gradually induced by gravity to form a spinning disk. This disk eventually became the sun at its center, and the planets formed in its outer parts.

TYPE 5 [Gist-Content Question]

During her lecture, the professor mostly covers the ways in which the two types of supernovae form.

TYPE 6 [Understanding Attitude Question]

When the professor tells the students, "Stop and consider that for a second," she wants them to think about the enormous amount of energy that gets released by a supernova.

TYPE 7 [Connecting Content Question]

According to the lecture, type 1 supernovae form from white dwarves and can be created when an exploding star takes gases from a nearby star. As for type 2 supernovae, they occur in stars that are much larger than the sun and occur when a star implodes.

TYPE 8 [Making Inferences Question]

At the end of the lecture, the professor notes that supernovae are important because one might have been responsible for forming the solar system. It is therefore likely that she will describe the process by which some people believe the solar system was created.

Summarizing ▶

The professor states that supernovae are some of the most wondrous phenomena in the galaxy and that they release huge amounts of energy. She says there are both type 1 and type 2 supernovae. Type 1 form from white dwarves. She explains how exploding white dwarves can take gases from nearby stars to help them explode and become supernovae. As for type 2 supernovae, they form from stars eight to fifteen times larger than the sun. She then explains the process by which they explode. She mentions that some supernovae can be seen from the Earth. Some are so bright that they can even be seen during the day.

Mastering Question Types with Lectures A2 p.134

| TYPES 1−4 |

TYPE 1 (B)   TYPE 2 (C)   TYPE 3 (B)   TYPE 4 (D)

Script 02-078

M Professor: There are three main types of rocks: igneous, sedimentary, and metamorphic rocks. All three have specific properties and are formed in distinct ways. Let's examine them one by one by covering how they form and also describing some examples of these rocks.

First, we'll take a look at igneous rocks. To understand them, we need to talk about magma. This is a molten substance created deep inside the Earth, uh, where high pressure and temperatures transform minerals into a liquefied state. As the minerals cool, rocks are formed both inside the mantle and the crust as well as on the surface. Igneous rocks that form underground are called intrusive igneous rocks, and those that form on the surface are extrusive igneous rocks. They also go by other names, uh, with those forming underground called plutonic igneous rocks and with those forming on the surface called volcanic igneous rocks. The main difference between the two types is how they cool and crystallize into rock formations. Underground, the cooling process is much slower because of the ever-present heat and pressure, so rocks form slowly and have large crystals. Those that form on the surface cool much faster as molten magma, now called lava, flows across the land and is exposed to cool air and sometimes even hit cold water. This faster cooling process creates much small crystals and therefore different types of rocks.

Intrusive igneous rocks also have coarser grains than extrusive igneous rocks due to their slower cooling. Some examples of intrusive igneous rocks include granite, diorite, and gabbro. Here on the screen . . . you can see some images of these rocks.

W Student: These rocks are commonly found on the surface, too, aren't they?

M: That's correct. Many intrusive igneous rocks can be found on the surface. The reason is that over a long period of time, the rocks are pushed up to the surface through the action of pressure and the movement of large land formations. In fact, the centers of many

mountains have large amounts of intrusive igneous rocks. Now, let's look at some extrusive igneous rocks. Common examples . . . take a look up here . . . include pumice . . . obsidian . . . and basalt . . . These rocks are normally found near active and dormant volcanoes, where they formed after lava flowed out of the volcanoes.

Okay, how about sedimentary rocks? These rocks form in layers when mineral and organic material accumulates and is then transformed into rocks through a process called cementation. Mineral materials in sedimentary rocks are created by the erosion and weathering of other rocks. As material is eroded, it's carried away by wind, water, and sometimes ice to new locations, where it settles and forms layers over time.

There are three main types of sedimentary rocks. We called them clastic, chemical, and organic sedimentary rocks. Clastic sedimentary rocks form from particles eroded from other rocks. Common examples are sandstone, mudrocks, and conglomerates. The main difference between these rocks are the sizes of the particles comprising them. Chemical sedimentary rocks form from minerals that dissolve in water and then later dry and form rocks. Limestone, halite, and gypsum are examples of these kinds of rocks. And lastly, organic sedimentary rocks are formed from dead plants and animals. Coal is the best-known example of this type. Many organic sedimentary rocks formed at the bottoms of former oceans and lakes that are now dry land.

Okay, let's look at metamorphic rocks, the third type, now.

TYPE 1 [Gist-Content Question]

During the lecture, the professor mainly talks about the formation of two different kinds of rocks.

TYPE 2 [Detail Question]

The professor says, "Igneous rocks that form underground are called intrusive igneous rocks, and those that form on the surface are extrusive igneous rocks," and adds, "Those that form on the surface cool much faster as molten magma, now called lava, flows across the land and is exposed to cool air and sometimes even hit cold water."

TYPE 3 [Understanding Organization Question]

The professor tells the class, "And lastly, organic sedimentary rocks are formed from dead plants and animals. Coal is the best-known example of this type."

TYPE 4 [Understanding Function Question]

About erosion, the professor remarks, "Clastic sedimentary rocks form from particles eroded from other rocks."

The professor says there are three main types of rocks: igneous, sedimentary, and metamorphic rocks. He says that igneous rocks are formed from high pressure and temperatures deep inside the Earth. Some rocks form underground while others form above the ground. The cooling process of both types makes these rocks different from one another. The professor says that many extrusive igneous rocks, such as pumice, obsidian, and basalt, are found near volcanoes. He then discusses sedimentary rocks. He says they form when mineral and organic matter accumulates and is then turned into rocks. He mentions clastic, chemical, and organic sedimentary rocks.

| TYPES 5–8 |

TYPE 5 (B)   TYPE 6 (C)

TYPE 7 The Underground Eroding of Rock: [2], [3]   The Action of the Sea: [4]   The Aboveground Eroding of Rock: [1]   TYPE 8 (D)

Script 02-079

W Professor: Caves are holes in the ground or ice and can be formed in many ways. However, there are four primary ways in which they are formed. They can be formed by the underground wearing away of soft rock such as limestone. They can be formed by the action of the sea or ocean as it erodes rocks in cliffs on the coast. The third way is through the eroding of hard rock either under or above the ground through the actions of water or wind. Finally, the fourth way is by the melting of ice in glaciers, which forms ice caves. The first three typically take years . . . thousands in some cases . . . yet they last a long time whereas ice caves can form quite rapidly yet disappear just as quickly.

Firstly, let me explain about caves formed underground in soft rock. As I just mentioned, limestone is the most common type of rock that caves form in. The reason is that the acidic content of rainwater causes the soft limestone to wear away much faster than it does, oh, say, granite or some other kind of hard rock. Limestone caves are renowned for their size, as some cave formations can stretch for hundreds of kilometers. In the U.S., some may even stretch beneath several different states. Many of these caves are also regarded for their beauty, as some of the most spectacular cave formations, especially large stalactites and stalagmites, are found in limestone caves.

M Student: I'm sorry, but what's the difference between those two?

W: Stalactites are long icicle-like formations that hang from the ceilings of caves while stalagmites are similar-looking ones that build up from cave floors. Both, however, are formed by the dripping of calcium carbonate in caves. Oh, in case you're curious, calcium carbonate is a byproduct of the eroding of limestone in acidic water. And both stalactites and stalagmites take years and years to form.

Now, let's move on to the second type of caves, those created by the sea or ocean. In many places along the coast, there are cliffs that have areas with both soft and hard rocks. [8]Near the water level, in both kinds of rocks, over time, the actions of waves can produce deep caves, which, since they're at water level, are often partially flooded, at least during high tide. These caves are nowhere near as large as limestone caves, yet some attract divers and explorers because the waters often create beautiful sights. If you get a chance to see one of these caves firsthand, go. **It's an experience you don't want to miss out on.**

The third way in which caves get formed is through the action of water and wind on hard rock. Please be aware that even the hardest stones may succumb to erosion. It just takes them longer to wear away. Now, these caves can be quite large and may be found deep underground or above the surface, such as on mountains. When they form in deserts, the wind typically blows sand, which acts like a, er, a sandblaster, and thus erodes even the hardest stones to create aboveground caves. In addition, when water starts eroding these caves, it can create them rather quickly, especially if it freezes in cracks in the rocks. Ice, you see, expands, and when that happens, it can break off huge chunks of rock overnight.

TYPE 5 [Gist-Purpose Question]

A student asks the professor what the difference between stalactites and stalagmites is, so the professor responds to this question.

TYPE 6 [Understanding Attitude Question]

When the professor tells the students that they do not want to miss out on that experience, it can be inferred that she has firsthand experience visiting this kind of cave, which is why she advises them to visit one of these caves themselves.

TYPE 7 [Connecting Content Question]

According to the lecture, the underground eroding of rock can happen in areas with limestone and may result in stalactites being formed. Meanwhile, the action of the sea can create caves that look beautiful. And the aboveground eroding of rock can happen because of either sand or ice.

TYPE 8 [Making Inferences Question]

At the beginning of her lecture, the professor notes that there are four primary ways in which caves are formed, yet she only describes three of them. It is therefore likely that she will describe the fourth way next.

The professor mentions there are <u>four ways</u> that caves may form. The first is that they are formed underground in <u>soft rock</u> such as limestone. Acid in water erodes the rocks, which creates caves. These caves often have <u>stalactites and stalagmites</u> in them. The next type of cave is formed by the actions of the sea or ocean. Hard or soft rock <u>on the coast</u> gets worn away and can create caves that look beautiful. <u>Water and wind</u> aboveground can make caves in mountains and in other places. This can happen over a long period of time or can happen fairly quickly with ice.

Mastering Question Types with Conversations A3

p.136

| TYPES 1–4 |

TYPE 1 (B)   TYPE 2 (D)   TYPE 3 (B)   TYPE 4 (A)

Script 02-080

M1 Student: Okay, thanks for clearing up that problem for me.

M2 Professor: It's no trouble at all, Chris. As your advisor, it's my job to help you get through your four years here as smoothly as possible.

M1: Well, you pay a lot more attention to me than some of my friends' advisors do to them, so I'm grateful for that.

M2: I thank you for the compliment. So, is there anything else you'd like to discuss?

M1: Actually, there is one small thing.

M2: I'm all ears.

M1: I've been thinking about signing up for Professor Reynolds's advanced Russian drama class next semester.

M2: An outstanding choice. You will definitely both enjoy and learn a tremendous amount in his class. I recommend it highly.

M1: Okay, but here's the thing . . .

M2: You haven't taken the requisite Russian courses, have you?

M1: That's correct, sir.

M2: Why don't you tell me about your background in the Russian language?

M1: Sure. Actually, I lived there for a couple of years when I was in junior high. My father was assigned to work in Moscow by his company, so the whole family went along with him. I picked up quite a bit of the language while I was there though.

M2: I see . . . Well, that was several years ago. How much Russian have you spoken since then?

M1: Not much to be honest.

M2: Then, I have a suggestion for you . . . How about signing up for Russian three or four next semester? You can take a placement class to see where exactly you belong. That should give you the knowledge you need to be able to handle the advanced drama class. ⁴A lot of the language used in those dramas is colloquial after all, so you definitely need to get a better grasp of the language than you have now.

M1: Do you really think I should wait another semester?

M2: Why not? You're only a sophomore. You've got plenty of time to take as many Russian drama classes as you like . . . so long as you improve your basic skills in the language first.

TYPE 1   [Gist-Purpose Question]

The student visits the professor to talk about a course he wants to take the next semester.

TYPE 2   [Detail Question]

The student says, "My father was assigned to work in Moscow by his company, so the whole family went along with him. I picked up quite a bit of the language while I was there though."

TYPE 3   [Understanding Organization Question]

The student brings up junior high school in response to the professor asking him about his background in the Russian language. It was during junior high school that the student lived in Russia and learned some Russian.

TYPE 4   [Understanding Function Question]

When the student asks if the professor really believes he should wait another semester to take the class, his words and his tone of voice indicate that he is disappointed with what the professor is telling him.

Summarizing ▶

The student thanks the professor for being <u>a good advisor</u>, and the professor responds that he is just doing his job. Then the student mentions he is thinking of taking an advanced <u>Russian drama class</u> the next semester. The professor says that is a good choice, but then they talk about the student's <u>Russian language skills</u>. The student lived in Russia for two years, but that was during <u>junior high school</u>. The professor tells the student he should take a Russian language class first and take the drama class later. The student is disappointed, but the professor says that the student, a sophomore, has <u>plenty of time</u> to take the class.

TYPE 5 Ⓒ   TYPE 6 Ⓐ   TYPE 7 Ⓒ   TYPE 8 Ⓐ

Script 02-081

M Housing Office Employee: Next . . . Yes, how may I be of service today?

W Student: Hello, I just checked into my dorm room and, uh, there's sort of a problem with it.

M: Okay, since the key is not working, just fill out this form here . . . and we'll get you a new one within twenty-four hours. This sometimes happens. Sorry.

W: Er . . . There's nothing wrong with my key. It works fine.

M: Huh? Uh, sorry. The last three people have been complaining about keys that don't work. I guess I expected you to do the same. I've got no idea what's going on with the keys this semester.

W: That's too bad. Anyway, I can get into my room all right. It's just that I have a problem with what's actually in . . . or, shall I say, not in, my room.

M: Is something missing?

W: Yes. There's no chair in my room.

M: Hmm . . . That's a new one for today. Have you reported it to the administration office in your dormitory?

W: Yes, I did, but the woman there told me to come here. I've got a copy of the complaint I filed at the office though.

M: Great. Let me take a look at that, please . . . Hmm . . . According to this, there was one chair in your room when there should have been two.

W: Correct. My roommate checked in first, so she got the chair. I got nothing. What do I need to do to get a chair?

M: ⁸I'd like you to fill out this form, please. It should only take a minute.

W: That's it?

M: For you, yes. Once you complete the form, I'll give it to my supervisor. She'll approve it, and then we'll go ahead and order a chair for you.

W: How long should that take?

M: It should be at your room by the end of the day. The school's got a big supply of extra furniture—you know, desks, chairs, beds—set aside in case things like this happen. All we have to do is tell them where to go.

W: Wow. I was expecting it to take a week or so. That's good to hear.

TYPE 5 [Gist-Content Question]

The student reports that there is a chair missing from her dormitory room, so what she needs to do to get a new chair is the main topic of their conversation.

TYPE 6 [Detail Question]

The student says that she went to the administration office in her dormitory, and the woman there told her to go to the office where she is now.

TYPE 7 [Understanding Attitude Question]

Throughout the conversation, the man is both friendly and sympathetic to the student and tries to help her as much as he can.

TYPE 8 [Making Inferences Question]

When the student asks, "That's it?" her words and her tone of voice indicate that she is surprised by how easy it will be for her to get a new chair. She had been expecting to have to do more to get one.

Summarizing ▶

The employee tells the student that if she fills out a form, she can get a new key in twenty-four hours. The student says she is not there for a key, and the employee apologizes. He says that many students have been asking for new keys. The student says that her dorm is missing a chair. She shows some paperwork she filled out, and the employee gives her another form to complete. Once she does that, the school will bring her a chair by the end of the day. The student seems pleased by this response.

Mastering Topics with Lectures B1   p.138

1 Ⓑ   2 Ⓑ   3 Ⓐ

Script & Graphic Organizer 02-082

W Professor: One hot topic nowadays is alternative energy sources. It's popular with people primarily because many of us are interested in reducing the number of pollutants and greenhouse gases that get released through the burning of fossil fuels. Now, who can tell me what I mean by the term alternative energy . . .? Yes?

M Student: Isn't that any kind of energy source that's not petroleum based?

W: That's part of it, but there's more to it.

M: Oh, yeah. Doesn't it have something to do with energy that's renewable?

W: Well done. That was the key word I was hoping to hear: renewable. Of course, it's also true that alternative energy sources are not petroleum based, but that's definitely not how I'd define them. There is a wide range of alternative energy resources. Let me see . . . There's solar power of course. Wind is another form. Hydroelectric energy and geothermal energy are two more. And those aren't the only types. What I'd like to do now is go over a few of these in brief just to make sure you know what I'm talking about, and then we're going to jump into the advantages and disadvantages of each one so that we can have a lively discussion at the end of class. Sound okay to everyone . . .? Good.

The first type of alternative energy I mentioned was solar power. As its name implies, this is energy that makes use of sunlight. Today, it's becoming more and more common as the technology used in the solar panels which capture the sun's rays is improving, so it's often utilized to heat water or air and even to produce electricity.

Wind is another form of alternative energy, and it's actually been used by people for centuries. Windmills, after all, harness the power of the wind, and they've been around for quite some time. Today, we call the more modern windmills wind turbines though. What happens is that the rotation of the blades on the turbines is used to create electricity by means of an electrical generator. Today, wind power is used not only by national electric grids but also by individual homes. And there's a lot of talk about establishing wind farms that will be able to generate huge amounts of energy . . . Er . . . so long as the wind is blowing, that is.

Next up is hydroelectric power, which is another form of energy people have been using for hundreds of years. Think of the big water wheels that were used to power the mills that would grind wheat and other grains into flour. That was one way people used the power of water. Today, however, people often use the force of either falling or flowing water to turn turbines that are connected to generators in order to produce electricity. Waterfalls, such as Niagara Falls, for example, are used for this purpose, but manmade dams are much more common places where hydroelectric power is produced. You might be surprised to know that around one-fifth of the world's electricity is produced in this manner today.

Geothermal energy uses the natural heat of the Earth to create energy. You all know about hot springs, right? Why are they hot? They're hot because the ground below them is hot. It could be because a volcano is nearby. Or it could just be a thermal vent. Whatever the case may be, both the steam and the hot water that are located underground can be used to generate electricity. Iceland is one country that makes extensive use of geothermal energy. You won't be surprised to learn, therefore, that Iceland is home to numerous volcanoes, both active and extinct, so it's a prime location for people to make use of geothermal energy.

Alternative Energy

Solar:	Wind:	Hydroelectric:	Geothermal:
Comes from the sun	Has been used for centuries	Is water power	Uses heat from the Earth
Technology for it is improving	Can be created by windmills	Uses falling water like in waterfalls	Is often used in places near volcanoes
	Is created by turbines today	Uses flowing water by damming rivers	Is common in Iceland

1 [Gist-Purpose Question]

The professor is describing various types of alternative energy in her lecture, and geothermal energy is one of those that she covers.

2 [Understanding Organization Question]

The professor first names several different types of alternative energy sources, and then she goes into detail on them.

3 [Making Inferences Question]

When the professor notes that wind energy is only possible as long as the wind is blowing, it can be inferred that there are some places where the wind does not blow, so wind power cannot be created in these locations.

Summarizing ▶

The professor begins by asking for a definition of alternative energy, which a student provides. She notes that the important word is renewable. Then, she begins by discussing several types of alternative energy. She first talks about solar power and says it is becoming more common. Next, she covers wind power and notes that while people in the past used windmills, modern people use turbines. After that is hydroelectric power, which comes from water. Finally, she describes geothermal energy, which uses heat from within the Earth to create electricity. She notes that volcanic places, such as Iceland, can often take advantage of geothermal energy.

Mastering Topics with Lectures B2   p.139

1 Ⓓ   2 Ⓐ   3 Ⓒ

Script & Graphic Organizer 03-083

M Professor: The Earth has seven continents, and, of course, there are also big islands, such as Greenland, but it's not considered a continent. Anyway, you might be surprised to learn that around, uh, about 300 million years ago, as scientists theorize, the Earth had only one continent. It was a German geologist named Alfred Wegener who came up with this theory, and he called this enormous continent Pangaea, which comes from a combination of Greek words meaning "all earth."

Anyway, in 1912, Wegener came up with the theory of continental drift. You should all already be familiar with it, but let me cover it just in case. It asserts that the world was once one large continent surrounded by a huge ocean and that it later broke up into the landmasses that exist today. Wegener theorized that the continents are comprised of fairly light rocks that sit atop heavier crusted material. Think of them as, oh, icebergs . . . huge ones of course . . . floating on the water. [3]Wegener also claimed that the continents aren't rigidly fixed to one location but are in fact slowly moving at a speed of about one yard per century. Obviously, continental drift doesn't happen in the blink of an eye but over the course of millennia.

Interestingly, when Wegener proposed his theory, he was met with widespread ridicule. However, over decades, more evidence was, uh, unearthed that suggested he was, well, correct and that the continents had at one time really been united. For instance, in the fossil record, remains of animals identical to one another were found in both Africa and South America. Mineral specimens found along the supposed break lines of some continents are also identical. Indeed, when most of you were young, you probably noticed just by looking at a globe how most of the continents, particularly Africa and South America, seemed as if they could fit together like pieces of a jigsaw puzzle.

Okay, so, uh, what is it that makes the theory of continental drift work? It's the makeup of the Earth itself that does it. The Earth has a core, a mantle, and a crust. The crust, which is the planet's outer layer, is divided into huge, thick plates that are drifting atop the mantle. These plates are formed from rock and vary in thickness. Now we're getting into plate tectonics, which was theorized in the 1960s and added to Wegener's own ideas. This theory states that the Earth's crust is divided into several large plates and many smaller ones. Geologists today have determined that the crust has seven major plates and as many as twelve smaller ones. These plates are the part of the crust that is actually moving. Their movements can cause earthquakes to occur, volcanoes to form and erupt, mountain ranges to rise and fall, and the very face of the planet to change.

W Student: How do they do this?

M: By moving. There are three types of plate movements. The first is divergent movement, which occurs when plates separate from one another. This often results in the formation of new oceanic crust. The second is convergent plate movement, which happens when two plates collide. If an oceanic plate collides with a continental one, the light oceanic plate will be forced underneath the heavier continental plate in what's called

subduction. If two oceanic plates collide, one might be pushed under, so magma from the mantle will rise, and volcanoes will be formed. And if two continental plates collide, mountain ranges will be created as the crust will get compressed and be pushed upward. The, uh, the third type of plate movement is lateral slipping. This happens when two plates move sideways against each other. The plates first slip and then stick as friction and pressure build up. Then, there is a sudden release of pressure, and the plates are suddenly jerked apart, which causes an earthquake.

The Formation of the Continents

Continental Drift:	*How Earth Once Looked:*
The theory that the continents slowly move around the Earth so that its shape is slowly but constantly changing	*Was one giant continent called Pangaea*
	Evidence for the Theory:
	Identical fossils and similar mineral specimens found on different continents
	Plate Tectonics:
	The Earth's crust is divided into 7 big plates and 12 minor ones that move around and cause changes

1 [Gist-Content Question]

The professor mostly covers various aspects of the theory of continental drift in his lecture.

2 [Detail Question]

The professor says, "If an oceanic plate collides with a continental one, the light oceanic plate will be forced underneath the heavier continental plate in what's called subduction."

3 [Understanding Function Question]

When the professor indicates that many people ridiculed Wegener's theory when he first proposed it, he implies that a lot of people did not believe in continental drift since they were making fun of it.

Summarizing ▶

The professor says that the land on the Earth was once one big continent called Pangaea. This comes from a theory proposed by Alfred Wegener. He called the theory continental drift. He believed the continents slowly moved across the face of the planet. At first, he was ridiculed, but later evidence proved that he was correct. This evidence was found in the fossil record and in mineral specimens. Wegener's ideas led to the theory of plate tectonics, which helps explain how earthquakes happen, how volcanoes form, and how mountain ranges are created. The professor then describes the various movements of plates that result in these events.

Mastering Topics with Lectures B3

p.140

1 Ⓐ 2 Ⓓ 3 Ⓒ

Script & Graphic Organizer 02-084

W Professor:[3]**One of the most controversial topics in the field of astronomy—or all science for that matter—is that of whether or not life is exclusive to Earth.** There are some who believe that Earth is not the only place with life, and thus they search for evidence of extraterrestrial life elsewhere. For many, this quest both begins and ends with Mars. So, I'm curious. Do any of you believe there are, uh, Martians or life in other star systems?

M Student: Sure. Why not? I'm not sure if there are Martians like how they're portrayed in movies and science fiction novels, but I'm pretty sure that Mars had some form of life that once existed on it and may even have some life today.

W: Not a bad answer. It shows that someone is using his head. Well, let's take a look at what is needed for life to exist on Mars. Oh, when I say that, I'm talking about carbon-based life. You know, what exists here on Earth. We have no way of knowing what other forms of life based on different elements would be like or what they would require, so I won't even begin to speculate on that.

Okay, so, if life is to exist on Mars—or any other planet for that matter—a variety of factors must occur. First, there needs to be a rocky planet orbiting a star that produces enough heat and light for life to survive. In addition, water in its liquid form would almost certainly have to be present along with very simple and complex organic compounds. Then, assuming that a planet has all these factors in place, there would have to be no major disruptions in the planet's temperature or its chemical composition for millions, no, billions, of years in order for the life forms to evolve.

So why do people often look to Mars for signs of extraterrestrial life? Well, despite the fact that Venus is often called Earth's "sister planet," of all the planets in the solar system, it's actually Mars that has the most similarities as Earth.

M: How so? I thought Venus and Earth were about the same size. Isn't that right?

W: That's correct, but that's about where the similarities end. For instance . . . Both Earth and Mars have similar temperatures. Yes, Mars, being farther from the sun than Earth, is colder, but the two have somewhat comparable temperatures. Today, conditions on Mars are too cold for liquid water to exist on the surface,

but there's strong evidence that Mars may have been much warmer in the past. Both Earth and Mars have atmospheres as well, but Mars's is much thinner than Earth's. Again, though, some experts believe that Mars's atmosphere was much thicker millions of years ago. As for the composition of the planet, like Earth, Mars has a rocky surface, which makes it easier for life to get a foothold as opposed to it trying to do so in a gassy environment where any life forms would, we assume, be floating about freely.

Oh, there's one more similarity between the two that I should mention. It's the presence of polar ice caps. On Mars, the ice caps expand and contract in accordance with the planet's seasons. While the ice on Mars is mostly frozen carbon dioxide, there's a strong possibility that water is present as well, which means that, just like Earth, Mars too could have a water cycle on the planet.

So you see, many of the conditions that life requires exist on Mars. That brings up the ultimate question: Will we find life on Mars? The answer is . . . Who knows? Okay, let me speculate on that for a second. If life indeed exists there, it's probably too cold for it to survive on the surface, so it would likely exist in the warmer areas belowground. There could be, for example, microorganisms living by hydrothermal vents near the planet's surface. That's just one possibility. But who knows what path evolution could have taken life on Mars?

Life on Mars

What Is Necessary for Life to Exist:	Similarities between Earth and Mars:
Must be a rocky planet	Have similar temperatures
Must orbit a heat- and light-bearing star	Have atmospheres
Must have liquid water and complex organic compounds	Are rocky planets
	Have polar ice caps

1 [Understanding Function Question]

In response to the student's answer, the professor says, "Not a bad answer. It shows that someone is using his head." She is implying that the student has thought about the answer that he gave her.

2 [Making Inferences Question]

At the end of the lecture, the professor starts to go into the types of life that might exist on Mars. She then asks, "But who knows what path evolution could have taken life on Mars?" It is likely that she will attempt to answer her own question, which she has already done in the lecture, and thus she will describe some possible life forms that may live on Mars.

3 [Understanding Function Question]

When the professor starts her lecture by indicating that

the question of whether or not life is exclusive to Earth is controversial, she is telling the students exactly what she is going to talk about in her lecture.

Summarizing ▶

The professor mentions that people looking for extraterrestrial life often focus on Mars. A student says that he thinks Mars likely had some life in the past or maybe even does today. The professor then explains what would be needed for carbon-based life to exist elsewhere. It includes a rocky planet with a heat and light-bearing star. Water and complex organic compounds are also necessary. She then mentions how similar Mars and Earth are. Their temperatures are similar, and they both have an atmosphere. Mars's is thinner, but it may not have been like that in the past. They both also have water around their polar caps.

Mastering Topics with Lectures B4　　　p.141

1 Ⓒ　　2 Ⓐ　　3 Dead Oil: ②, ③　Live Oil: ①, ④

Script 02-085

M Professor: How many of you came to class by means other than riding a bike or walking . . .? Hmm . . . Most of you I see. Cars, motorcycles, buses, trains, and subways. They all use petroleum. We're dependent on it. In fact, some estimate that the transportation sector of the economy utilizes up to 68% of all the petroleum that is produced. Quite an astonishing number, isn't it? Of course, we also use petroleum for a number of different reasons other than transportation. It's a common product in manufacturing. For instance, petroleum is required for the production of, uh, let's see . . . smartphones, cameras, toothpaste, ballpoint pens, and contact lenses, just to name a few of the myriad products it's used to make. I'd like to discuss petroleum right now. First, who can tell me what it is?

W Student: Isn't that another name for the oil that gets pumped from beneath the planet's surface?

M: That's a good answer, yet, while you just gave the common perception of, uh, of what petroleum is, you only gave me part of the answer. In actuality, the term petroleum covers a broad range of hydrocarbons that are found in their gaseous, liquid, and solid states beneath the Earth's surface. The two most common forms of petroleum are crude oil and natural gas.

W: I'm sorry, but did you say that petroleum can be found in its solid form? I've never heard of that.

M: Ah, yes. While we most commonly think of petroleum in its liquid form, it can be solid. Let me answer your question by asking one in return. How many of you have heard of the La Brea Tar Pits in the Los Angeles

area . . .? Okay, I see three or four hands. Well, it's most commonly known for being a place where numerous animals have been found preserved when they fell in the pits and drowned. But what is tar? Well, it's a solid form of petroleum.

Okay, we need to backtrack a little. Let's start at the beginning. Namely, how is petroleum formed? Well, a long, long time ago . . . and I'm talking about millions of years right now . . . Long before the dinosaurs roamed the Earth, there were oceans that covered most of the planet. These oceans were filled with tiny sea creatures and plants. When they died, they sank to the bottom of the ocean, and, over time, they were eventually covered by both sand and sediment. The sand and sediment eventually—again, over millions of years—transformed into sedimentary rock. Over time, the number of layers of rock increased, causing the rocks to press down harder and harder on the decaying matter—the dead plants and animals, that is—below them. Over a period of time that took ages, the heat from the Earth and the pressure from both the rocks and the water above them combined to turn those plants and animals into petroleum. That's actually the reason we call petroleum a fossil fuel: It literally originated from dead plants and sea animals. Of course, since the process of making petroleum takes millions of years, it's also a nonrenewable resource. Simply put, when it's gone, it's gone.

Oh, let me note that scientists often refer to two kinds of petroleum. These are known as dead oil and live oil. Dead oil is that which, due to the pressure applied to it during the formation process, no longer contains any gas within it. It's all been squeezed out. This includes viscous oil, asphalt, and tar. Live oil, on the other hand, contains dissolved gases. The most obvious example is natural gas. When being pumped, live oil is quite dangerous and must be handled and pumped very carefully to avoid the risk of explosions or fires. Let's get into how oil gets pumped or extracted from the ground now.

Petroleum

Formation of Petroleum:	Dead Oil:
Dead organic matter goes to the bottom of the ocean	No longer has any gas in it; includes viscous oil, asphalt, and tar
Is covered by sand and sediment	
Heat and pressure increase	Live Oil:
Transform it into petroleum	Has some gas in it; is natural gas; can be dangerous to handle and may explode easily

1 [Gist-Content Question]

During his lecture, the professor mostly covers the process by which petroleum is created.

2 [Understanding Organization Question]

The professor mentions sea creatures and plants because it was from their corpses that petroleum was created.

3 [Connecting Content Question]

According to the lecture, dead oil includes both tar and asphalt, and it has no gases in it. As for live oil, it is dangerous to the people who are handling it since it might explode, and it contains some dissolved gases.

Summarizing ▶

> The lecturer starts by noting the importance of petroleum for transportation as well as in manufacturing. He then gives a definition of petroleum and says that it can be found in gas, liquid, and solid forms. He says that its solid form is tar to respond to a student's question. He then describes the process by which decaying organic matter was converted into petroleum through heat and pressure millions of years ago. Because it comes from organic matter, that is why it is considered a fossil fuel. He also says petroleum is nonrenewable. He then describes the difference between dead oil and live oil.

Mastering Topics with Conversations B5   p.142

1 (B)   2 (B), (D)   3 (B)

Script & Graphic Organizer 02-086

> **W1 Student:** Professor Dillon, I've got a couple of questions about our class project. Would you mind if I spoke with you about them right now?
>
> **W2 Professor:** Not at all, Elaine. But you know that there are only three more weeks until the project is due, right? I hope you've at least gotten started on it.
>
> **W1:** Well, um, not exactly. You see, I'm . . . I'm not really sure about exactly, um, exactly what we're supposed to be doing.
>
> **W2:** What exactly is confusing?
>
> **W1:** Okay, according to the handout you gave us, we're supposed to be observing some different stages of child development. And then we need to make comments about what we observed, find some literature that explain what we observed, and then summarize it, right?
>
> **W2:** It sounds to me like you understood my directions perfectly. So what exactly is the problem? I'm afraid I don't understand what's wrong.
>
> **W1:** Um, I guess my question is, um, where are we supposed to observe kids? Are we supposed to go to a preschool or something because I don't even know where any preschools are around here?
>
> **W2:** Weren't you in class when I explained that?
>
> **W1:** Uh . . .
>
> **W2:** Okay. Apparently not. Okay, you were supposed to visit the Child Study Department and speak with the secretary. She has a list of the local preschools, nurseries, and other places that take care of children and are willing to let our school's students observe the children as they play and study.
>
> **W1:** I see.
>
> **W2:** Didn't any of your friends in class tell you about that?
>
> **W1:** I don't really hang out with anyone. I pretty much keep to myself. Sorry. So, um, what should I do?
>
> **W2:** Get to the Child Study Department as quickly as you can. That's what you need to do.
>
> **W1:** So do you think I've still got enough time to make some observations?
>
> **W2:** Sure, I think so. But I'm assuming that you start your observations tomorrow and do them virtually every day for the next two weeks.
>
> **W1:** Phew. That sounds like a lot of work.
>
> **W2:** True, but you wouldn't be in this position if you'd been doing your observations for the entire semester like all of the other students have been.
>
> **W1:** Er, yes. I, um, I see what you mean. Well, don't worry about me, Professor Dillon. I'll go over there right now and set something up. You know, I'm glad I came and spoke to you today.
>
> **W2:** That's true. If you had waited much longer, you'd be out of time and would likely have gotten a failing grade on this project . . . which means you'd probably have failed my class, too.
>
> **W1:** That's not going to happen. I'll make sure of that.

Office Hours

Reason for Visiting:	Result:
Needs information about a class project	Tells student to go to the Child Study Department immediately
Problem:	**Solution:**
Only has three weeks to complete her project	Must observe children every day and must work very hard

1 [Gist-Purpose Question]

The student tells the professor, "You see, I'm . . . I'm not really sure about exactly, um, exactly what we're supposed to be doing."

2 [Detail Question]

According to the professor, the student should watch young children as they play and study and should then go over and analyze the information that she has collected.

3 [Making Inferences Question]

When the professor tells the student that she could be in danger of failing the project, the student responds by saying, "That's not going to happen. I'll make sure of that." It can therefore be inferred that she intends to get a good grade on the project.

Summarizing ▶

The student wants to discuss her class project with the professor, who says it is due in three weeks and mentions she hopes the student has begun it. The student says she has not begun it because she is unclear on how she is supposed to observe the development of children. The professor says that she mentioned what to do in a previous class. Then, she explains that the student needs to visit the Child Study Department and make arrangements to visit a local preschool or other place with children. The professor notes that the student will have to work hard, but she can still do well on the project.

Mastering Topics with Conversations B6 p.143

1   2   3

Script 02-087

M Student: Good afternoon, ma'am. My name is Kyle Callahan. It's a real pleasure to meet you.

W Student Center Employee: Uh, nice to meet you, too, Kyle. What can I do for you this afternoon?

M: Actually, I'm here for the job.

W: Job?

M: Yes, the part-time job that's being advertised. You know, I'm really looking forward to working here at the student center. I had a weekend job at the library last semester, and it was simply awful. I thought that I'd get a chance to, you know, study or relax when I wasn't busy, but they were always making me shelve books. Talk about hard work.

W: Uh, I'm sorry to disappoint you Kyle, but I'm not really sure what you're talking about.

M: How so?

W: Well, to the best of my knowledge, we don't have any available positions right now. In fact, we just hired a couple of new student employees last week, and those were the last positions that we needed to get filled.

There aren't any more spots now.

M: Are you sure about that?

W: I'm pretty sure. Sorry.

M: Hmm . . . That's strange because I was talking last night to one of my friends who works here, and she told me that the student center needed a new employee to work in the game room area. You know, I'd be watching the pool tables, the ice hockey table, and the arcade games. Talk about a cool job.

W: That's odd. Who's your friend?

M: Her name's Melanie Stewart. I think she's got a pretty high position here. I'm not exactly sure, but that's the impression I get from speaking with her.

W: Actually, she's the student manager of the entire center. So, yes, she is pretty high up. Hmm . . . Okay, she might know what she's talking about, so let me check the computer here, Kyle, if you don't mind.

M: Of course not. Please take your time.

W: Okay, let me take a look here . . . No, there's nothing posted yet . . . Hmm . . . ³Aha. There's an internal memo that tells me exactly what you just said.

M: Sweet. So you mean that there is a job in the game room?

W: There sure is. And guess what, Kyle.

M: I give up.

W: I've got the power to hire new employees. So . . . as long as you're available to work every evening from six to nine from Monday to Friday, then the job's yours.

M: Let me just say that I look forward to seeing more of you in the future.

Service Encounter

Reason for Visiting:	Result:
Wants to apply for a job in the student center	Is unaware of any jobs being available at the moment
Student's Reaction:	Result:
Tells the woman about what his friend said to him	Student is offered a job by the woman and then accepts her offer

1 [Understanding Attitude Question]

The student is very polite to the woman. He speaks courteously, calls her "ma'am," and has a good attitude throughout the entire conversation.

2 [Making Inferences Question]

When the student says, "Let me just say that I look forward to seeing more of you in the future," it can be inferred that he is accepting the job and is going to work at the student center.

3 [Understanding Function Question]

When a person says, "Guess what," and the other person responds by answering, "I give up," the person who responds is indicating that he would like the person asking to continue speaking and to tell him what is going on.

Summarizing ▶

The student visits the student center to ask about a job, but the woman does not know what he is talking about. He says that there is a position available to work in the game room. He knows about it because a friend who works at the student center told him about it. The woman says she is not sure, but she looks for some information about the job. She discovers the student is correct about the job and that one is available. Then, she says that she has the power to hire him, so he can have the job if he wants it. The student accepts her offer.

TOEFL Practice Tests C1

1 Ⓒ   2 Ⓑ   3 Tambora: ①, ④   Krakatoa: ②, ③
4 Ⓓ   5 Ⓒ   6 Ⓓ

Script 02-088

W Professor: In Indonesia in 1815, there occurred the largest volcanic eruption ever experienced in recorded history. No, it wasn't Krakatoa, which many of you have undoubtedly heard of. Krakatoa came later. Instead, it was the Tambora Volcano, and it took place on an island called Sumbawa over the course of three days from April 10 to 12. It's estimated to have killed 92,000 people although only 10,000 of them died as a direct result of the eruption. The rest of the fatalities in the region happened due to the starvation and disease that resulted from the, well, the complete annihilation of local food supplies.

In actuality, the Tambora eruption may have been responsible for even more deaths in places all around the world. The reason is that, after it erupted, a cloud of ash and dust rose into the air and was subsequently carried all around the world, where it darkened skies and lowered temperatures as far away as America and even Europe. In history books, 1816 is often called "the year without a summer" because of these changes. You see, even a temperature change of just a few degrees can drastically affect crops. In 1816, there were crop failures in many lands and reduced yields on those crops that didn't die. ⁶There were famines in many countries, and large numbers of people also died of starvation.

M Student: That sounds horrific, but, uh, actually,

I had always been led to believe that the Krakatoa eruption was the biggest one ever recorded. Isn't that true?

W: That's a common misconception. However, while there were definitely similarities between Tambora and Krakatoa, Krakatoa wasn't as massive. But it's definitely the better known of the two. And it's actually what I was planning to discuss next. ⁵Now, Krakatoa was also on an Indonesian island . . . talk about a place with bad luck . . . and it too erupted for three days, from, uh, August 26 to 28, 1883, and it killed about 36,000 people. Many of the dead lost their lives in the tsunamis created by the eruption. There are even some reports of minor tsunamis appearing in England after the eruption, but the veracity of those claims is in question. Anyway, Krakatoa literally blew its top. Then, it collapsed and sank more than 1,000 feet below the island. Like after the Tambora eruption, Krakatoa hurled massive amounts of dust and ash in the air. Reports from back then say that there was a red color in the sky for the next few years, which made the sky even more beautiful. On the negative side though, there were more crop failures and thus indirect deaths caused by Krakatoa. While those were powerful eruptions, what has geologists worried is the possibility of an eruption even more massive than Tambora.

M: Has that ever happened?

W: Yes, but, mercifully, no one was around for it. It happened right in the area that is Yellowstone National Park, which is actually one big area of intense volcanic activity. Why do you think it has all of those geysers and hot springs? Anyway, most of the volcanic activity there today is minor, so the multitudes of tourists who visit every year aren't in imminent danger. Still, every 600,000 years or so, a supervolcano . . . yes, that's the correct term . . . erupts that makes Tambora look like, uh, look like a firecracker exploding. Oh, and it's been about, er, 600,000 years since the last eruption.

What's going to happen if or when the Yellowstone supervolcano erupts again? The direst predictions say that it will be an Earth extinction event. That means that the amount of ash and dust cast into the atmosphere will be so great and last for so long that many forms of life will cease to exist. First, plants will die from a lack of sunlight. Then, those animals that depend on plants as their food sources will die. Next, the carnivores will die. Finally, the humans who at least had the foresight to stock up on packaged goods for the event will likely die, too.

Don't be too shocked. The evidence shows that an extinction level event occurred in a manner similar to the one I just described about sixty-five million years ago. It was an asteroid or meteor, however, not a volcano, that did this and, in the process, wiped out the dinosaurs. Many species of plants in the fossil record from before sixty-five million years ago simply don't

Answers, Explanations, and Scripts | 91

exist afterward. Eventually, it's believed, mammals replaced the dinosaurs as the dominant species on the planet after this extinction event occurred.

Will any life survive a Yellowstone eruption? More than likely, yes. At a basic level, bacteria and perhaps some insect life will survive. And no one knows how sea life will be affected. Since the oceans are a very self-contained ecosystem, it's likely that at least some life in them would survive. As for those of us who dwell on land, the possibility of survival is, well, about as bleak as the sun will be after an eruption.

1 [Gist-Content Question]

During her lecture, the professor mostly talks about how various volcanic eruptions have changed the Earth's environment.

2 [Gist-Purpose Question]

The professor describes the aftereffects of the Tambora eruption as "the year without a summer," and she talks about how the eruption changed the weather all around the world.

3 [Connecting Content Question]

According to the lecture, the Tambora eruption caused "the year without a summer" and killed more people indirectly than it did directly. As for the Krakatoa eruption, it caused tsunamis that killed many people and made the sky look red for years afterward.

4 [Understanding Function Question]

About the asteroid that hit the Earth millions of years ago, the professor says, "Many species of plants in the fossil record from before sixty-five million years ago simply don't exist afterward." She therefore implies that not all of the plants living at the time were killed by the asteroid impacting on the Earth.

5 [Understanding Function Question]

When the professor notes, "The veracity of those claims is in question," she is indicating to the students that the reports of tsunamis appearing in England may not actually be true.

6 [Understanding Attitude Question]

When the student mentions that he thought the Krakatoa eruption was the biggest ever recorded, he is disputing what the professor said about the Tambora eruption and therefore indicating that he doubts what she just said.

TOEFL Practice Tests C2 p.146

1 Ⓐ **2** Ⓐ **3** Ⓑ, Ⓒ **4** Ⓒ **5** Ⓑ
6 Ⓓ

Script 02-089

M Professor: Ever since Pluto was first sighted by Clyde Tombaugh in 1930, it has been considered a planet. Okay, I suppose I should say "had" instead since, in 2006, the International Astronomical Union downgraded the status of Pluto to that of a dwarf planet. This, as one would expect, sparked a debate among astronomers as to what exactly constituted a planet. So to answer that question, I'm going to go over all of the various objects in the solar system, classify them, and explain some of their most defining characteristics. First and foremost in importance is the sun. It's the most important object in the solar system since, without it, no life on the Earth would exist. As we all know, the sun is a star that generates both heat and light through the nuclear reactions that occur inside it. The best estimate is that the sun will continue doing this for another, oh, four billion years or so, and then it'll die like all stars eventually do.

⁶Next are the planets, which are divided into the classical planets and dwarf planets. The debate about what each is lasted for years and wasn't settled until the 2006 conference. **And some, regrettably, still disagree with the results.** Anyway, at the conference, the members agreed that a classical planet is one that orbits the sun, has a round or nearly round shape, and has a, uh, a generally well-defined orbit that follows a regular path. The members thus concluded that there are only eight classical planets in the entire solar system as they rather unceremoniously dumped Pluto from that category.

As for what constitutes a dwarf planet, the members declared that while a dwarf planet also orbits the sun and has a round or nearly round shape, its orbit may be elliptical and not follow a regular path. Oh, there was one more stipulation. It was that a dwarf planet cannot be a satellite of a larger planet. This prevented some of the solar system's large satellites . . . Titan, which orbits Saturn, comes to mind . . . from being considered planets despite the fact that they may have some, uh, planet-like characteristics. Pluto was thus relegated to this category.

As for the rest of the objects in orbit around the sun, there was a third class created. These bodies are now referred to as small solar-system bodies. In this group are the various comets, asteroids, and other small objects that orbit the sun. Included in this group are all of the objects found in the Kuiper Belt. To refresh your memories, two weeks ago I briefly mentioned the Kuiper Belt. It's the donut-shaped region that extends to about fifty astronomical units from the sun. Remember that one astronomical unit is equal to the distance from Earth to the sun. Within the Kuiper Belt are an estimated 70,000 objects . . . though there could be many more for all we know . . . and most of them are over sixty miles in diameter. At least 800 of them have been named, and the six largest are more than 500 miles in diameter.

According to the members of the conference, Pluto and another dwarf planet—called Eris—are now considered part of the Kuiper Belt. There are a few other dwarf planets we know one. One is Ceres, and it lies within the asteroid belt that's between Mars and Jupiter. No space probes have ever visited any of these dwarf planets, so there's still a lot of speculation as to, well, as to what they're really like. But let me give you a few details about them so that you can understand why they're considered dwarf planets. Of course, one of the first things that comes to mind upon hearing the word "dwarf" is size, and, yes, they're quite small when compared to the eight classical planets. Eris is the largest of the three I've mentioned, and its diameter is only about 1,850 miles. Pluto's second at 1,485 miles, and Ceres is third at 588 miles. Compare this to Mercury, the smallest planet, which has a diameter of 3,032 miles. Clearly, the moniker "dwarf planet" is no misnomer.

One thing that has always stood out about Pluto has been its irregular orbit. While the classical planets have some slight irregularities . . . none of them orbits the sun in a perfect circle . . . Pluto's irregularities are quite pronounced, and its orbit is very elliptical. It takes 248 Earth years for Pluto to orbit the sun once. It does so from a mean distance of 3,647 million miles from the sun, yet it gets as close as 2,756 million miles to the sun. See what I'm saying? Oh, this lasts for about twenty years of Pluto's orbit, so now it's actually closer to the sun than Neptune is. And I should definitely mention that at Pluto's farthest point from the sun, it's 4,583 million miles away. Meanwhile, Eris also has an elliptical orbit while Ceres's orbit is quite regular. Here's one more fact about Pluto that's rather interesting. It has three satellites, but the largest, called Charon, is half as large as Pluto, and there is some speculation that it may someday be considered a dwarf planet as well.

1 [Gist-Content Question]

The professor goes over many of the objects that are found in the solar system during his lecture.

2 [Gist-Purpose Question]

About Pluto's orbit, the professor says, "One thing that has always stood out about Pluto has been its irregular orbit. While the classical planets have some slight irregularities . . . none of them orbits the sun in a perfect circle . . . Pluto's irregularities are quite pronounced, and its orbit is very elliptical."

3 [Detail Question]

According to the lecture, a dwarf planet "has a round or nearly round shape," and its orbit "may be elliptical and not follow a regular path."

4 [Understanding Organization Question]

In talking about the Kuiper Belt, the professor states, "Within the Kuiper Belt are an estimated 70,000 objects . . . though there could be many more for all we know."

5 [Connecting Content Question]

Concerning Eris and Mercury, the professor says, "Eris is the largest of the three I've mentioned, and its diameter is only about 1,850 miles. Pluto's second at 1,485 miles, and Ceres is third at 588 miles. Compare this to Mercury, the smallest planet, which has a diameter of 3,032 miles."

6 [Understanding Function Question]

When the professor notes that some people "regrettably" disagree with the results of the conference and then sighs, he is indicating that he disagrees with these people and agrees with the decision that was made at the conference.

TOEFL Practice Tests C3 p.148

1 Ⓑ 2 Ⓒ 3 Ⓓ 4 Ⓒ 5 Ⓑ

Script 02-090

M1 Student Activities Center Employee: Hello. Is there something that I can help you with?

M2 Student: I sure hope so.

M1: Okay, I'll do my best, but I hope this doesn't take too long. You see, uh, I've got a two-thirty appointment with a student, and since it's twenty-five after right now, I can only assist you until he gets here.

M2: Oh, you don't have to worry about that then. I'm your two-thirty appointment.

M1: James Vicker?

M2: That's me. It's nice to meet you. And you must be Keith Sanders, right?

M1: [5]Yes, yes. That's me. It's a pleasure to meet you. Please have a seat . . . Okay, James. Is it all right if I call you James?

M2: By all means. All my friends do.

M1: Great. Thanks. So, James, what did you schedule this meeting for?

M2: Well, I have just been elected the president of the school's debate club, so I'm here to . . . Is there a problem?

M1: I'm sorry, but did you say the school's debate club?

M2: Yes, I did.

M1: But we don't have a debate club.

M2: Ah, right. That's what I'm here for. I need to find out how to register a new club. See, a lot of my friends and I—and some other students, too—are really into debating. We had hoped to join the debate club, but imagine our surprise when we found out that there was no club.

M1: Go on.

M2: So we decided to, well, take matters into our own hands and start one up. So like I said, I got elected president. I'm not sure how that happened. Anyway, we were told that new clubs have to register at the Student Activities Office, so . . . here I am.

M1: Okay, well, you've definitely come to the right place. First, what you need is a faculty sponsor. Without one, you won't be allowed to form a club.

M2: We've already taken care of that. Professor Apulu in the Math Department has agreed to be our sponsor.

M1: Excellent. He has a wonderful reputation on campus and is a great public speaker. You've made a wise decision.

M2: Thank you for saying that. Everything that I've heard about him as well tells me that he'll be an active part of the club. He told me that there was some paperwork involved in setting up the club. You handle that, right?

M1: Yes, I do. And, yes, there are some forms you have to fill out, but they're mostly a formality once you have a faculty sponsor. Oh, you need a minimum of fifteen members. That's a school regulation. Do you have that?

M2: We have thirty-three people signed up.

M1: Wow, that's more than what a lot of even the longstanding clubs even have. It sounds like you're going to be off to a good start. Oh, you realize that once you are confirmed as an official club, you can apply for grants and other school funds, don't you?

M2: Oh, really? Would you happen to have some more information about that?

M1: Yes, but I'll have to print it for you. Say, why don't you get started on these forms, and I'll make some photocopies?

M2: That sounds like a plan. You wouldn't happen to have a pen that I could borrow, would you? I'm afraid I left mine at home.

1 [Gist-Content Question]

The student says, "That's what I'm here for. I need to find out how to register a new club," and that is what they mostly talk about.

2 [Detail Question]

The student mentions that he is the president of the debate club, which makes him one of the club's officers.

3 [Understanding Attitude Question]

When the student brings up Professor Apulu, the employee responds by saying, "Excellent. He has a wonderful reputation on campus and is a great public speaker. You've made a wise decision." He clearly thinks highly of Professor Apulu.

4 [Making Inferences Question]

At the end of the conversation, the employee asks the student, "Why don't you get started on these forms?" That is what the student is most likely going to do next.

5 [Understanding Function Question]

When the student responds that all of his friends call him James, he is showing that he is being friendly to the employee.

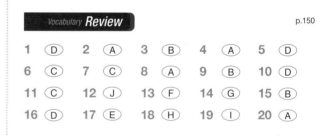

Vocabulary *Review*   p.150

1	Ⓓ	2	Ⓐ	3	Ⓑ	4	Ⓐ	5	Ⓓ
6	Ⓒ	7	Ⓒ	8	Ⓐ	9	Ⓑ	10	Ⓓ
11	Ⓒ	12	Ⓙ	13	Ⓕ	14	Ⓖ	15	Ⓑ
16	Ⓓ	17	Ⓔ	18	Ⓗ	19	Ⓘ	20	Ⓐ

Chapter **07** | Arts 1 · Conversations

Mastering Question Types with Lectures A1   p.152

| TYPES 1–4 |

TYPE **1** Ⓐ   TYPE **2** Ⓒ   TYPE **3** Ⓓ   TYPE **4** Ⓒ

Script 02-091

M1 Professor: I'd like to turn your attention to the roles of women in art. Unfortunately, this doesn't take us very far back in history. The reason is that, as far as we're aware, early artists were all men. Of course, there's always the possibility that a female artist passed herself off as a man, but we have no way of knowing that, do we? So it's not until during the Renaissance in the sixteenth century that we come across the first female artists whose names we actually know. Nevertheless, prior to this period, women played important roles in art.

Does anyone have an inkling of an idea as to what I'm speaking about? Adrienne, what do you think I mean?

W Student: Well, I know women were used as models by artists.

M1: Precisely. Even though women weren't the ones doing the actual creating of art, they still often served as sources of inspiration for the artists themselves by sitting and posing for them. Let me show you a slide that I'm pretty sure . . . no, uh, definitely sure, that you've all seen. Here it is . . . Ah, yes. The *Mona Lisa* by Leonardo da Vinci. Take a look closely as it was in this painting that Leonardo did something that, well, that no other portrait painter before him had ever done. Who would like to venture a guess as to what he did that was so unique? Alan, why don't you try?

M2 Student: Uh . . . Does it have something to do with her mysterious smile?

M1: That's a good guess, particularly since the most famous aspect of the painting is her smile, but it's not the answer I'm looking for. Anyone else . . .? Okay, I see several of you look like you're deep in thought. Let me give you the answer then. [4]What Leonardo did that was so unique was to paint this portrait from the front with her entire face showing. Yes, that was quite novel for the time. Before this, portraits of women showed them only in profile. **Oh, keep in mind that I'm referring to the Western art world and not art from other cultures.** So what was the reason that women were painted in profile? Well, it was considered inappropriate and too forward to paint a woman as if she were looking at the viewer and making direct eye contact, especially if the viewer happened to be a man . . . Yes, I know what you're thinking, but you have to consider the cultures of Leonardo's time and the ages before him. That's what they thought. Period . . . Now, the *Mona Lisa* was different. She's looking directly at the observer and seems to be welcoming people to look at her and to communicate with her. Unsurprisingly, the success of the *Mona Lisa* encouraged other artists from this period to start making their own frontal portraits of women, and these soon became the norm.

Now, I just mentioned that women were prevented from directly producing art and weren't given any formal training. Fortunately for them, the Renaissance brought about new ways of thinking, so that's when we first start seeing female artists. The first I'd like to speak about is Properzia, who worked in the early sixteenth century.

TYPE 1 [Gist-Content Question]

During his lecture, the professor focuses on the roles of women in early art.

TYPE 2 [Detail Question]

The professor states, "Unsurprisingly, the success of the *Mona Lisa* encouraged other artists from this period

to start making their own frontal portraits of women, and these soon became the norm."

TYPE 3 [Understanding Organization Question]

During his lecture, the professor asks questions. He then allows the students to answer the questions, and he uses their observations to guide him along in his lecture.

TYPE 4 [Understanding Function Question]

When the professor says that he is only talking about Western art and not art from other cultures, he implies that in some art from some other cultures, women were painted from the front.

Summarizing ▶

The professor begins by saying that women have not had a long role in the world of art as artists. However, he does note that they were used as models by artists. He then shows them a picture of the *Mona Lisa* and notes that Leonardo da Vinci did something unique with the painting. The professor says that Leonardo was the first Western artist to paint a woman from the front and not in profile. He says the reason had to do with the culture of that time. Then, he notes that because the *Mona Lisa* became popular, other artists began to imitate Leonardo's style.

| **TYPES 5–8** |

TYPE 5 Ⓑ   **TYPE 6** Ⓒ

TYPE 7 The Hudson River School Artists: [4] William Bliss Baker: [1], [2], [3]   **TYPE 8** Ⓒ

Script 02-092

W Professor: Over the course of time, there have been countless movements in the world of art. It seems as if new ones sprout up all the time while older ones either disappear or morph into something else. Naturalism is one such movement. Simply put, in the world of art, Naturalism refers to the depiction of objects as they exist in reality. The naturalist strives to present his or her works as they actually look. This movement actually started during the Renaissance. It was during that period that artists stopped exclusively painting pictures of a religious nature and instead looked to create works of art that depicted other topics. Anyway, Naturalism went in and out of vogue during the Renaissance, but it began anew in the nineteenth century.

M Student: What was the reason for that?

W: A combination of reasons. To begin with, part of the Naturalist movement, which is also called Realism by some people, was a response to the Romantic Age that had preceded it. The Romantics mostly produced art that was idealistic, and the Naturalists were pushing back against this. [8]In addition, consider the historical context of the nineteenth century. It was an age of science. As a whole, society during this period . . . **I'm speaking about both sides of the Atlantic Ocean here . . .** society was clearly interested in the study of science and the laws of nature as well as the objective observation of facts. Scientists like, uh, like Charles Darwin were capturing the imaginations of people in America and Europe. In fact, Darwin proved to be fairly influential in the Naturalist movement, which not only incorporated art but also included literature, philosophy, and the theater.

Unsurprisingly, Naturalist artists often created landscapes. Making landscapes was one of the easiest ways for them to, well, for them to depict nature as it was in reality. Yes, Tom? You have a question for me?

M: So does this include the painters in the Hudson River School? I know they painted lots of landscapes during the nineteenth century.

W: Actually, no. Those painters aren't considered Naturalists. Romanticism was what influenced them. If you look closely at their paintings, you can see how idealized their works are and how they don't actually reflect reality. So please don't be mistaken. No, when I refer to Naturalists, I'm talking about artists such as William Bliss Baker. He was an American, and he produced some of the most brilliant landscapes of the entire movement. *Fallen Monarchs*, *Woodland Brook*, and *Morning after Snow*, which happens to be my personal favorite painting by any artist, are three of his most famous and most impressive works. Oh, he also painted in the Hudson River Valley although he consciously made an effort to depict his works realistically, unlike the members of the Hudson River School. If you take a look at some of their paintings, you'll be able clearly to see the difference between the two styles. To be brief about it, Baker painted nature as he saw it in reality while the Hudson River School artists depicted nature as they wanted it to be. There was quite a difference not just in the thought process but also in the result.

TYPE 5 [Gist-Content Question]

The professor mostly talks about the Naturalist Art Movement during her lecture.

TYPE 6 [Understanding Attitude Question]

The professor implies that she prefers Naturalist art to Romantic art when she says, "No, when I refer to Naturalists, I'm talking about artists such as William Bliss Baker. He was an American, and he produced some of the most brilliant landscapes of the entire movement. *Fallen Monarchs*, *Woodland Brook*, and *Morning after Snow*, which happens to be my personal favorite painting by any artist, are three of his most famous and most impressive works."

TYPE 7 [Connecting Content Question]

According to the lecture, the Hudson River School artists made idealized works since they were Romantics. As for William Bliss Baker, he was a Realist, so he painted scenes as they were in reality, he was a Naturalist, and he also painted *Fallen Monarchs*.

TYPE 8 [Making Inferences Question]

When the professor says that she is referring to "both sides of the Atlantic Ocean," she means that she is talking about both the United States and Europe. Thus, she implies that not only Americans but also Europeans were interested in science.

Summarizing ▶

The professor states that Naturalism began during the Renaissance. Artists began trying to create paintings that showed their subjects as they actually looked. It went out of style but then became popular again in the nineteenth century. One reason for its renewed popularity was that it was a response to the Romantic Age. It was also based on science and realism, which were important in that century. A student asks about the Hudson River School, but the professor says they painted in the Romantic style. She says William Bliss Baker was a Naturalist. She talks about his paintings and how they accurately reflected reality.

Mastering Question Types with Lectures A2   p.154

| TYPES 1–4 |

TYPE 1 (B)   **TYPE 2** (D)   **TYPE 3** (B)   **TYPE 4** (A)

Script 02-093

M Professor: Okay, I think we've covered enough of the basics of ancient Greek theater. [4]As you can surely see, it was from the ancient Greeks that modern theater has evolved. Of course, the majority of Western plays, from the time of the Greeks all the way to our modern age, have also been influenced by them. **There's no mistaking that.** Now, I'd like to give you some brief biographies of some of the most important ancient Greek playwrights. These are men whose works we'll be reading throughout the course of the semester.

Unfortunately, while we know about the existence of many playwrights, most of their plays are lost. That's something which happens all too often regarding the ancient world. Over time, manuscripts . . . of which there were usually very few, sometimes even just one or two copies . . . simply got lost, so the writers' works were lost forever. As for plays from this period, the majority of what we have—both in their complete and incomplete forms—comes from the works of four men. They are Aeschylus, Sophocles, Euripides, and Aristophanes.

Yes, I realize that these Greek names can be hard to spell, but all four of them are mentioned frequently in your textbook, so look them up and memorize their spellings. All right?

We'll start with Aeschylus. He wrote some of the world's oldest plays, most of which were tragedies. He is believed to have written somewhere around eighty plays, yet, sadly, a mere handful of them has survived. As an innovator, Aeschylus added a second actor—the antagonist—to interact on stage with the protagonist. His greatest achievement was his work the *Oresteia*. Its tale is of Agamemnon's triumphant return home from the Trojan War, his murder by his wife and her lover, and the subsequent revenge of Agamemnon's children Orestes and Electra. We'll be reading that play next week.

Sophocles was another major playwright from this period. Like Aeschylus, he too was an innovator as he added the second, uh, no, the third . . . Sorry. I misspoke. He added the third actor to the stage. Three was the final number of actors by the way. He also fixed the number of chorus members at fifteen. Previously, it had ranged anywhere from between three and fifty members. Sophocles was extremely prolific, writing more than a hundred tragedies, yet only seven have survived to the present. The *Oedipus* trilogy is by far his most famous work.

Euripides, meanwhile, changed some of the topic matter in the plays. Whereas most playwrights, including Aeschylus and Sophocles, wrote about the gods or kings, Euripides preferred to write about common people. For instance, the titles of his plays include *The Bacchantes* and *The Trojan Women*. Contrast this with Sophocles's *Oedipus the King* and Aeschylus's *Agamemnon*. Oh, and Euripides often examined the psychological motivations of the characters in his plays. That was novel for his time.

While these three writers mostly wrote tragedies, Aristophanes made a conscious effort to write comedies. In fact, he's considered the father of Greek comedy, which, essentially, makes him the father of all comedy. Among his works that we'll be reading this semester are *Lysistrata* and *The Birds*.

TYPE 1 [Gist-Content Question]

The professor talks about several of the most important Greek playwrights in the early history of the theater.

TYPE 2 [Detail Question]

According to the professor, Euripides wrote both *The Bacchantes* and *The Trojan Women*.

TYPE 3 [Understanding Organization Question]

The professor gives a short biography of some ancient Greek playwrights. This includes a description of the type of work they did, any of their innovations, and the titles of some of their plays.

TYPE 4 [Understanding Function Question]

When the professor says, "There's no mistaking that," he is stressing the fact that Western plays have been strongly influenced by the Greeks.

Summarizing ▶

The professor tells the students he wants to give them some biographies of a few important ancient Greek playwrights. He says that many works have been lost over the course of time. However, some of the plays of four important men still survive. The first is Aeschylus. He added a second actor to plays and authored the *Oresteia*. Sophocles added a third actor to the stage and wrote the *Oedipus* trilogy. Euripides focused on the lives of regular people instead of only writing about the gods and kings. And Aristophanes was the father of comedy since those were some of the plays that he wrote.

| TYPES 5–8 |

TYPE 5 (D)   **TYPE 6** (A)
TYPE 7 Lorsch Abbey: ③   Saint-Chapelle: ①, ②, ④
TYPE 8 (C)

Script 02-094

W1 Professor: Take a look at this slide . . . Beautiful, isn't it? This is what some people used to refer to as divine light, and I think you can see why stained-glass windows were and, uh, I guess still are, loved by many people. You may not be aware of this, but the history of colored glass can be traced all the way back to ancient Egypt and Mesopotamia. Of course, over the centuries, glass-making techniques evolved, and, by the ninth century, pictorial stained-glass windows were rather popular throughout Europe. We don't have any stained glass from that early though. The oldest surviving stained glass is . . . this . . . it's a head of Christ that was found in Lorsch Abbey in Germany. It dates back to the tenth century. Here are two more early stained-glass windows here . . . and here.

W2 Student: Professor Malkin, it seems that all of these windows show scenes of a religious nature. Why is that?

W1: A good question. But it's one that, if you stop to think about it for a second, really answers itself. Permit me to explain. Stained-glass windows were found almost exclusively in churches, cathedrals, monasteries . . . Well, basically in religious institutions. So it's only natural that their subject matter concerned the Bible. In addition, recall that during the Middle Ages, few people could actually read as the literacy rate was very low. And the Bible was written in Latin, not in the vernacular of whatever region the people were in, so it was even less accessible than other writings were. Therefore, people relied on visual stimulus instead. That's what these stained-glass windows did. They told stories from the Bible. See, here's one showing the Crucifixion of Christ . . . And here's another of Jonah being swallowed by the whale . . . So the windows showed people pictures of the stories that they had only heard, not read. Oh, and I mustn't forget to show you the famous windows of Saint-Chapelle in France. This was the chapel of King Louis IX, the great crusader king often referred to as St. Louis. Anyway, upon entering the chapel, it appears to be made entirely of stained glass. [8]Here's a picture. . . Phenomenal! The picture doesn't do Saint-Chapelle justice though. You have to go there to get the full effect. **It's breathtaking.** As you can see here . . . and here . . . the windows all relate scenes from the Old and New Testaments. In fact, they cover the events in the Bible from the Garden of Eden to the Apocalypse.

W2: That's all very impressive, Professor Malkin, but I have another question if you don't mind. How did they make stained glass? It looks like it must have been rather difficult.

W1: Essentially, stained glass is merely colored glass. However, when various metallic oxides are added to it while it's in its molten state, it gets the, uh, the stained effect. I believe that one of the first descriptions of how to make stained glass appeared in a manuscript written by a monk sometime around the year 1100 A.D. It was a fairly involved process that I'm not going to get into today. But if any of you are interested, I can prepare a short lecture on it. Today, though, I'd prefer to focus on showing you examples of stained-glass windows and describing them in detail.

TYPE 5 [Gist-Purpose Question]

The professor states, "In addition, recall that during the Middle Ages, few people could actually read as the literacy rate was very low. And the Bible was written in Latin, not in the vernacular of whatever region the people were in, so it was even less accessible than other writings were. Therefore, people relied on visual stimulus instead. That's what these stained-glass windows did. They told stories from the Bible."

TYPE 6 [Understanding Attitude Question]

The professor uses words like "phenomenal" and "breathtaking" when describing stained glass, so it is clear that she likes the way it looks.

TYPE 7 [Connecting Content Question]

According to the lecture, the oldest extant stained glass comes from Lorsch Abbey. As for Saint-Chapelle, it has scenes from the entire Bible in stained glass, it appears to be made completely of stained glass, and a French king used it as his personal church.

TYPE 8 [Making Inferences Question]

When the professor says, "It's breathtaking," after commenting that a person needs to visit Saint-Chapelle to "get the full effect," she is implying that she has been to Saint-Chapelle before.

Summarizing ▶

The professor begins by telling the students that stained-glass windows became popular in Europe around the ninth century. The oldest surviving stained glass comes from an abbey in Germany and was made in the tenth century. She tells the students that stained glass showed Biblical scenes and that most of it was found in religious buildings. In addition, since most people could not read, they needed visual stimulation. She shows them some pictures of Saint-Chapelle in France and says that upon entering, it seems as if the entire building is made of stained glass. She then says that she can explain how stained glass is made in another lecture if the students are interested.

Mastering Question Types with Conversations A3

p.156

| TYPES 1–4 |

Script 02-095

M Professor: Hi, Jen. How's it going? Goodness. What are you carrying with you?

W Student: It's a poster I made for the upcoming environmental conference. I know you're interested in environmental issues, so I thought I'd show it to you and get your opinion on it.

M: Well, thank you very much. And you're right . . . I am into environmental issues. Actually, I'm the co-chair of the conference.

W: Gee, I never knew that.

M: It's not something that I often publicize, but since I can tell how interested you are in the conference, I thought I'd let you know lest you get surprised when the conference starts and you see me up on stage making introductions. But enough about my role . . . Let's see what you've done to contribute.

W: It's not much, but I hope you like it. Take a look . . .

M: Hmm . . . Interesting.

W: Yes, you see, my personal goal is to encourage people to stop using Styrofoam cups. They're so bad for the environment since they take much longer to decompose than, say, paper cups.

M: That's all very true, Jen. I couldn't agree with you more.

W: So, uh . . . The poster? What do you think?

M: It's quite good.

W: Really? I was hoping you'd say that. [4]You have no idea how long I worked on it. I'm not really that good at art. It doesn't come naturally to me, so doing all the drawings was hard work.

M: Well, you could have fooled me.

W: I'm sorry?

M: I mean that this artwork is pretty impressive. It seems like you have quite a knack for drawing.

W: I-I-I . . . I don't know what to say. I wasn't expecting to hear that.

M: Actually . . . I'd like to feature this poster at the conference if you don't mind. This is exactly the kind of contribution I'm looking for from students, and that's what this conference is about: getting students involved in taking care of the environment. So do you mind if we feature your work?

W: Mind? Not at all. It would be an honor.

TYPE 1 [Gist-Purpose Question]

The student tells the professor, "It's a poster I made for the upcoming environmental conference. I know you're interested in environmental issues, so I thought I'd show it to you and get your opinion on it."

TYPE 2 [Detail Question]

The professor says, "Actually, I'm the co-chair of the conference," which means that he is in charge of the upcoming conference.

TYPE 3 [Understanding Organization Question]

The student brings up the upcoming conference to let the professor know why she made the poster that she is showing him.

TYPE 4 [Understanding Function Question]

When the professor responds, "You could have fooled me," after the student says that she is not good at art, he is giving her a compliment. He means that, in his opinion, she actually is good at art.

Summarizing ▶

The student visits the professor to show him a poster she made for an upcoming environmental conference. He tells the student that he is the co-chair of the event, which surprises her. Then, she shows him a poster that she made to encourage people to stop using Styrofoam cups since they are bad for the environment. She asks him what he thinks of it, and he responds that he likes it. He then tells the student that he is impressed by the poster and would like to feature it at the conference. The student is pleased that he is going to do that.

| TYPES 5–8 |

TYPE 5 (B)   TYPE 6 (D)   TYPE 7 (B)   TYPE 8 (D)

Script 02-096

W Student: [7]Good morning, Mr. Cleveland. How are you today?

M Art History Department Employee: I'm doing great, Annabeth. What can I do for you today?

W: I need to borrow a slide projector from the office.

M: A slide projector?

W: Yes, the professor in the class I have in ten minutes doesn't have one, so he asked me to come here and get one for him.

M: But why a slide projector? I mean, uh, there's a computer in the room. He can easily use it to put the pictures he wants the class to see on the big screen.

W: Yeah, I thought it was a bit of an odd request. I can't even remember the last time I have seen a professor use a slide projector. But that's what Professor Davidson wants, so I need to get him one.

M: Professor Davidson? Aha. Say no more. I get it.

W: Get what?

M: He's the newest professor in the department. I remember the head of the department telling me that Professor Davidson is not really big on technology. He only has slides to show the students.

W: Huh. That's interesting. Maybe someone can show him how to turn his slides into computer files.

M: I'll mention it to him that it's possible the next time he comes into the office.

W: Great. So, uh . . . the slide projector?

M: Right. I had almost forgotten. We keep it in the storage room connected to this office.

W: It? You only have one?

M: That's correct. We used to have a lot, but we got rid of almost all of them once the school started installing computers in the rooms. I guess I'll have to make sure that this one always works properly so that Professor Davidson can use it . . . Okay. Here you are.

W: That makes sense. Thanks. Oh, uh, do I need to sign out for it or anything?

M: Don't worry about it this time. I know exactly where it's going, so I'm not too terribly concerned about it not getting returned to the office. But please remind Professor Davidson that he needs to return it once class is over.

TYPE 5 [Gist-Content Question]

During the conversation, the student and the employee are mostly discussing a piece of machinery—a slide projector—that the student needs.

TYPE 6 [Detail Question]

At the end of the lecture, the employee tells the student, "But please remind Professor Davidson that he needs to return it once class is over."

TYPE 7 [Understanding Attitude Question]

The student addresses the employee by his name: Mr. Cleveland. Then, the employee responds, "I'm doing great, Annabeth." Since the employee knows the student's name, it can be inferred that he has spoken with her in the past.

TYPE 8 [Making Inferences Question]

At the end of the lecture, the employees says, "Here you are," indicating that he is giving the student the slide projector. It can therefore be inferred that she will take the equipment to a classroom next.

Summarizing ▶

The student visits the Art History Department office and asks the employee there if she can borrow a slide projector for a class. The employee is surprised because he expects professors to use the computers in their classrooms. The student agrees but adds that Professor Davidson requested it. The employee responds that the professor is new, is not big on technology, and only has slides. He tells the student that there is only one slide projector left, and he lets her borrow it. He then reminds the student to tell the professor to return it to the office after class.

Mastering Topics with Lectures B1

p.158

1 Fact: ②, ④   Not a Fact: ①, ③   2 ⓒ   3 Ⓐ

M Professor: You all have some kind of paper on your desks to write on. But can anyone tell me what was used before the development of paper? Anyone . . .?

W Student: Parchment, right?

M: That's correct, and that's what I'd like to take a look at. A long, long time ago, the first writing was done on clay tablets, but sometime around the year 3000 B.C., the Egyptians developed papyrus, which they used to write on. However, since papyrus reeds didn't grow in other countries, its production was limited to Egypt, which resulted in it being extremely expensive, and thus only a few people utilized it.

[3]Additionally, around 150 B.C., Pharaoh Ptolemy V of Egypt suddenly refused to sell papyrus to King Eumenes of Pergamon, a city located in what's now western Turkey . . . **Okay. Bear with me through this history lesson, and in a second, you'll see where I'm going with this.** Back then, Pergamon, along with Alexandria, the home of the great library and learning center, was one of the two great cities in the Western world that was established during the time of Alexander the Great. Now, Eumenes was determined to establish the world's greatest library, so he meant to outdo the one in Alexandria. What a shame that we don't have more people like him today. Anyway, Eumenes did everything he could . . . even resorting to the theft of manuscripts . . . to increase the number of texts in his library.

Ptolemy, meanwhile, was interested in preventing Eumenes from exceeding Alexandria, so he quit selling him papyrus. Eumenes subsequently ordered his men to find another medium upon which words could be written. Necessity being the mother of invention, they succeeded. At that time, Pergamon had a huge wool industry, which, naturally meant there were many sheep. So people began looking at using the sheepskins to write upon. Through what basically came down to a, uh, a pickling process, the sheepskins were cured to the point where it was possible to write upon them, and thus Pergamon, and others who made use of the new development, was no longer dependent upon papyrus. Unfortunately for Eumenes, though, sheepskin was much more expensive than papyrus, so it's not as if the use of papyrus completely stopped.

Well, the use of parchment began to spread, so people anywhere near where sheep were raised could make at least a small amount of it. People in Europe actually utilized both parchment and papyrus until around the fifth century, when the Roman Empire fell. After that, the Europeans rarely traded with Egypt, so papyrus use essentially came to a halt. Since there were a limited number of sheep as well, people began looking into using the skins of other animals. Eventually, goatskins and calfskins were used. Oh, calfskin is often called vellum. There are some who say that vellum and parchment are the same while others claim only calfskin is vellum. I'm not really concerned with that argument, but you should be aware it exists and that calfskin is much better material than sheepskin.

So parchment continued to be used until around the 1400s, when paper, which had been developed by the Chinese centuries before, became more common. One interesting aspect of parchment is that it can be reused. Don't misunderstand and think that you can easily erase it like a blackboard, but it is possible. Thus writing was sometimes washed away by using a mixture of milk and oat bran. And the surface was sometimes physically scraped away by using pumice. Why is this important? Modern technology . . . by which I mean digitized imaging, multispectral imaging, X-ray fluorescence imaging, and optical character imaging . . . well, these techniques have enabled us to read what has been scraped away. Some texts once thought lost have been found, and who knows what will turn up in the future as more parchments get analyzed and technology improves even further?

Parchment

Reason Was First Made:	Material Is Made From:
Egyptian pharaoh refused to sell papyrus to king of Pergamon	The cured skins of sheep, calves, and goats
King of Pergamon wanted the world's greatest library	**Advantages:**
Ordered his people to find a medium to write upon	Can be erased; can be reused
	Disadvantages:
	Is expensive; requires a large number of sheep or other animals

1 [Detail Question]

According to the lecture, writing on parchment can be erased while the parchment is then reused, and parchment was more expensive to make than papyrus. Those are the facts. However, parchment was not first made from calfskin, nor was it developed during the Middle Ages.

2 [Understanding Organization Question]

About modern technology, the professor states, "Modern technology . . . by which I mean digitized imaging, multispectral imaging, X-ray fluorescence imaging, and optical character imaging . . . well, these techniques have enabled us to read what has been scraped away. Some texts once thought lost have been found, and who knows what will turn up in the future as more parchments get analyzed and technology improves even further?"

3 [Understanding Function Question]

When the professor tells the students, "Bear with me through this history lesson," he is indicating that even though it might be a little boring, what he is saying is important, so they ought to listen to him.

Summarizing ▶

The professor begins by talking about how the Egyptians developed papyrus to write on around 3000 B.C. He states that the Egyptian pharaoh refused to sell papyrus to the king of Pergamon around 150 B.C. since both were competing to create the world's greatest library. The king's people then developed parchment. They used the cured hides of sheep to write on. It was effective but expensive. People later used goatskins and calfskins, which are sometimes called vellum. Parchment was used until around the 1400s. Modern technology now lets people read texts that had been written, erased, and then written over, so it is possible that many lost texts may soon be found.

Mastering Topics with Lectures B2   p.159

1 Ⓒ   2 Ⓐ   3 Tuva Throat-Singing: ②, ③   Inuit Throat-Singing: ①, ④

Script & Graphic Organizer 02-098

W1 Professor: I'm aware that many of you, as Music majors, belong to various singing groups or organizations and that some of you perform solo. I believe most of you sing, well, I guess you'd call it standard music. But I know you're aware that there are more, uh, exotic forms of music. Take, for example, throat-singing. Have any of you ever tried that?

W2 Student: Oh, Professor Kristoff, I saw a documentary about throat-singing the other night. It looked so, uh, so amazing. But I don't think I could ever try it.

W1: Ah, I was wondering if any of you had caught that show on TV. How about the rest of you . . .? No? Only Jessica . . .? That's too bad. Okay, today, I'm going to tell you a little about throat-singing. It's actually one of the world's oldest forms of music and is a guttural style of singing and chanting. When throat-singing, some singers are actually able to produce two or more notes simultaneously, and they can create unusual textured timbres by using special vocalization techniques.

Throat-singing is an ancient tradition that developed, it's believed, among the nomadic tribesmen of Central Asia. These are people like the Mongols, or the Huns before them, who lived in the steppes of Central Asia and who had a close, almost spiritual, relationship with nature. Traditionally, throat-singing was always done outdoors; it's only recently that throat-singers have started to perform indoors. Basically, it started when the singers began mimicking the sounds they were hearing in the natural world. For instance, they reproduced the whistling of birds, the bubbling of streams, the howling of wolves, and the blowing of the wind. Those sorts of things. It was most commonly done by men due to superstitions among the tribes that women who did any throat-singing would become infertile. Today, however, old superstitions are being abandoned, and females are now learning and performing this style of music.

One spot where throat-singing has attained a place of great importance is Tuva, a rural region in Russia that's located northwest of Mongolia. Throat-singing there is called *khoomei*, which, appropriately enough, comes from the Mongolian word for throat. In Tuva, the throat-singers utilize a form of circular breathing, which enables them to sustain multiple notes for long periods of time. While it was once a folk tradition practiced only on the steppes, today, it's embraced as a symbol of the Tuvan people's identity, and professionals often give performances in formal settings. You should really try to catch a performance if you can. Tuvan throat-singers can produce two, three, and even four pitches at the same time, which creates an effect that, hmm . . . I suppose you could compare it with the sound produced by bagpipes. The Tuvans have developed a number of different styles of throat-singing and even have some stringed instruments to accompany it.

But don't think that Central Asia is the only place where throat-singing is practiced. The Inuit in northern Canada do it, too, and it's actually an important part of their cultural heritage. You might be interested in learning that it's Inuit women, not men, who almost exclusively practice it. In addition, the Inuit make throat-singing more of a communal activity, which is something that the Tuvans don't do. The Inuit commonly perform in groups of two or more women. The Inuit also don't produce extra notes like the Tuvans do. Instead, the Inuit rely more on short, sharp, rhythmic inhalations and exhalations of breath. They traditionally sang babies to sleep with it or performed it during games that women played while the men were away hunting.

Now, I'm going to play a few samples of throat-singing for you. First, we're going to listen to some Tuvan songs, and then we'll hear some Inuit samples.

Throat-Singing

Characteristics:	Tuva Style:
Is a guttural style of singing and chanting	*Uses circular breathing; can make two to four pitches at the same time; is sometimes accompanied by the music of string instruments*
Mimics sounds from outdoors	
Was traditionally done by men	**Inuit Style:**
	Women often perform in groups; don't produce extra notes; use short, sharp, rhythmic inhalations and exhalations of breath

1 [Gist-Content Question]

During the majority of the lecture, the professor describes the differences in throat-singing by the Tuva and the Inuit.

2 [Understanding Organization Question]

The professor states, "Tuvan throat-singers can produce two, three, and even four pitches at the same time, which creates an effect that, hmm . . . I suppose you could compare it with the sound produced by bagpipes."

3 [Connecting Content Question]

According to the lecture, Tuva throat-singing is often performed only by men, and the singers can sound two or more pitches at the same time. As for Inuit throat-singing, there are often two or more people performing at the same time, and they rely upon short, sharp breaths.

Summarizing ▶

The professor asks the students if they know anything about throat-singing. One student says she saw a documentary about it recently. The professor says that throat-singing developed in Central Asia as people tried to imitate the sounds they heard in the wild. At first, only men did it, but now some women do it, too. The Tuva people do a lot of throat-singing. They can create two to four different pitches at the same time and sometimes accompany their singing with music. The Inuit also do throat-singing. Women typically do it in groups of two or more singers. Their style of throat-singing differs from the Tuva's.

Mastering Topics with Lectures B3   p.160

 1 ⓒ   **2** ⑧   **3** ⑩

M Professor: In medieval France, there were two popular types of poetry: the chanson and the romance. Chansons were a part of the oral tradition in France and were once thought to have been the forerunners of the romances. However, nowadays, most scholars believe that chansons and romances existed pretty much simultaneously. Interestingly, only a few of the little more than 100 chansons that have survived to the present predate the year 1150 while the first romances date from around the year 1160.

Chansons had many different forms, but the best known of them was the *chanson de geste*, which translates as "song of heroic deeds." As you can likely guess, these were poems written in the style of epics and which told tales of heroic deeds of various historical or fictional figures. In essence, they were about chivalry, which was the code of honor many medieval knights lived by. You therefore shouldn't be surprised when I tell you that the development of chansons coincided with calls throughout Europe for knights to go on crusades to free the Holy Land from Muslims. Christianity and its defense were central themes in most chansons as were honor and loyalty, two integral characteristics of the chivalric knight. Chansons were also usually written about historical figures. Charlemagne, the ninth-century Holy Roman Emperor, and his descendants and predecessors, were frequent subjects. The most famous of all chansons is *The Song of Roland*, which tells the tale of Roland, one of Charlemagne's warriors, and his battles against the Muslim Saracens. The earliest known version of *The Song of Roland* dates from 1098, but the oldest extant manuscript is no older than 1140.

Please remember that most people in medieval times were illiterate. Only members of the clergy and some noblemen could read and write, and books were scarce. So chansons were either sung or spoken tales that were often related by traveling minstrels, otherwise known as bards. This surely accounts for the numerous versions of chansons that have come down to us over time. *The Song of Roland* itself has countless versions. The bards often changed the chansons slightly, so when the chansons were finally written down, they all had slight differences.

There is one question regarding chansons that medieval scholars are still arguing about. It concerns the relationship between chansons and romances. Some posit that the chansons gave birth to romances while others believe that they existed in parallel and had either little or no influence on one another. I belong to the latter camp. But let me tell you why. Chansons and romances existed almost simultaneously, and they both had different structures. This, to me, suggests that they developed separately as literary forms. Chansons came from the oral tradition and had fixed narrative schemes and themes. On the other hand, romances were more of what we would, oh, I guess what we'd call literature today despite being written in verse, not prose. Romances told tales of love and chivalry, and are often divided into two groups: those relating to Rome and those relating to Britain. Those concerning Rome weren't always set in the Roman Empire though. Some were set in the time of Alexander the Great while others were set in the Byzantine Empire, which was the eastern half of the Roman Empire.

The romances relating to Britain often focused on the Arthurian legends. They told tales about King Arthur and his Knights of the Round Table. While the Arthurian legends originated in Britain, there were many French romances about them. Many of these focused on characters other than Arthur, including Lancelot, Guinevere, and Galahad, and they told tales of their adventures and deeds. Of course, the most famous work about Arthur was *Le Morte d'Arthur*, or *The Death of Arthur* in English, which was written by Sir Thomas Mallory and printed in the late fifteenth century.

Medieval French Poetry

Chansons:	Romances:
Were often "songs of heroic deeds"	May have been influenced by chansons
Themes were Christianity and chivalry	Were often about ancient Rome
Were often about Charlemagne	Were also about Britain, especially King Arthur and his Knights of the Round Table
Most famous one was The Song of Roland	

1 [Gist-Purpose Question]

The professor brings up *The Song of Roland* first to note that it is the most famous chanson, and then he mentions what it is about.

2 [Detail Question]

About the French romance writers, the professor comments, "Many of these focused on characters other than Arthur, including Lancelot, Guinevere, and Galahad, and they told tales of their adventures and deeds."

3 [Making Inference Question]

The professor says, "You therefore shouldn't be surprised when I tell you that the development of chansons coincided with calls throughout Europe for knights to go on crusades to free the Holy Land from Muslims." Thus, it can be inferred that some knights were inspired by these chansons, so they went on crusades.

The professor mentions that chansons and romances were both popular in medieval France. The most famous kind of chanson was the *chanson de geste*, which is a "song of heroic deeds." These chansons often focused on Christianity and chivalry. *The Song of Roland*, which concerned one of Charlemagne's warriors, was the most famous chanson. Romances may have been influenced by chansons, or they may have developed independently. There is still a debate on that topic. Romances were often either about ancient Rome or Britain. Those that were about Britain usually focused on stories about King Arthur and his Knights of the Round Table.

Mastering Topics with Lectures B4　　p.161

1 Ⓓ　2 Ⓒ　3 Ⓑ

Script & Graphic Organizer 02-100

W Professor: Vaudeville is a form of entertainment that was popular in the United States from the late nineteenth century up to around the 1930s, when sound motion pictures pretty much took away vaudeville's audience. Vaudeville was a stage performance that had numerous variations. Basically, it consisted of many types of entertainment that were all staged one after the other. For instance, there was singing, dancing, music, comedy . . . It was similar to what we'd term a variety show today. It must have been such great fun. During its heyday, vaudeville was easily the most popular form of entertainment in America.

Entertainment in the U.S. in the mid-nineteenth century was quite varied. There were, well, let me see . . . stage plays, minstrel shows, Wild West shows, burlesque shows, and circuses, among others. The ones I just listed were the most popular. At the venues where these events were held, alcohol was often sold, and most patrons were men. Oh, that doesn't include circuses, which women and children frequently attended. Still, women and children were mostly absent from the other performances. However, Tony Pastor, a New York City theater owner, decided to offer less bawdy and more polite entertainment at his theater in order to attract families. He refused to sell alcohol, and he removed any lewdness from the acts performed in his theater. The date October 4, 1881, when he held his first show, is typically regarded as the beginning of vaudeville. As you might have guessed, its claim to being a polite and, uh, clean form of entertainment was the primary reason it became so wildly popular. Before that time, there was a huge audience of families that wanted to be entertained, but until vaudeville came along, there were no live performances that appealed to them.

Once it started, vaudeville attained a level of popularity similar to what motion pictures have today. Nevertheless, in its early days, there was little organization, and acts had to book performances wherever they could find a place to host them. Then, Bostonian B.F. Keith made changes that helped improve the vaudeville industry. Keith got started in the circus, but in . . . um, 1885 I believe, he began building and purchasing chains of vaudeville theaters all across the country. This essentially created the vaudeville circuit. Troupes of performers were contracted to travel from city to city, where they would perform several shows at each stop before moving to the next place. This enabled some vaudeville performers to become nationally known, and the genre subsequently took off in popularity.

For the next few decades, vaudeville, well, uh, it simply dominated American entertainment. But the rise of motion pictures made it inevitable that vaudeville would eventually decline. This became even more evident when talkies, that is, motion pictures with sound, were introduced in the 1920s. Many vaudeville stars recognized what was going to happen, so they embraced motion pictures and even began acting in them. Famed vaudeville acts such as the Marx Brothers, W.C. Fields, and Buster Keaton, as well as newcomers such as Bob Hope, found great fame and fortune by appearing on the silver screen.

While some claim it was movies that, er, did in vaudeville, some historians of the genre believe it was already in decline before sound was introduced to motion pictures. Their reasoning is that vaudeville theater owners realized the potential for reaping more profits from motion pictures than from live performances. Oh, I should mention that movies were often screened in vaudeville theaters. Anyway, with vaudeville, the owners had to use live acts, pay salaries, and deal with performers on a daily basis. With movies, they merely rented the films and showed them to a paying audience. The overhead was much less while the potential profits were greater. At first, vaudeville acts were combined with screenings of short films, but, eventually, most vaudeville theaters switched exclusively to motion pictures. The Great Depression was the final nail in the coffin of vaudeville since people simply lacked the funds to attend live performances while motion pictures were much less expensive.

Vaudeville

Characteristics:	Tony Pastor:
Included singing, dancing, music, and comedy	Held the first vaudeville performance at his theater
Was like a modern variety show	**B.F. Keith:**
Was entertainment for families	Owned many vaudeville theaters and created the vaudeville circuit
Was not bawdy like much other entertainment was	*Sound Movies:*
	Caused vaudeville to disappear as a form of entertainment

1 [Gist-Content Question]

The professor describes the rise in popularity of vaudeville and then what led to its decline and eventual disappearance.

2 [Detail Question]

When talking about B.F. Keith, the professor says, "Bostonian B.F. Keith made changes that helped improve the vaudeville industry. Keith got started in the circus, but, in . . . um, 1885 I believe, he began building and purchasing chains of vaudeville theaters all across the country. This essentially created the vaudeville circuit."

3 [Understanding Attitude Question]

When she starts talking about vaudeville shows, the professor exclaims, "It must have been such great fun." It is therefore possible to tell that she believes vaudeville shows must have been entertaining.

Summarizing ▶

The lecturer notes that vaudeville had a number of different acts and resembled a variety show. She mentions that much entertainment in the nineteenth century was for men only and involved alcohol. But in 1881, Tony Pastor put on the first vaudeville performance, which was a family-oriented affair. Vaudeville quickly became popular. Later, B.F. Keith began purchasing or building vaudeville theaters and started the vaudeville circuit, where entertainers went from city to city to perform. With the advent of movies, which were often shown in vaudeville theaters, vaudeville began to lose popularity. Finally, when movies with sound came out and the Great Depression began, vaudeville essentially ended.

Mastering Topics with Conversations B5   p.162

1 Ⓐ   2 Ⓒ   3 Ⓐ

M Professor: Hello there. Are you waiting outside to speak with me, or are you just standing around there until a friend shows up?

W Student: Er, actually, I was waiting to talk with you, Professor Reid. It just looked like you were, uh, really engrossed in that book you were reading, so I didn't want to disturb you.

M: Oh, I see. Yes, I do tend to get focused too much on what I'm doing.

W: So, uh . . .

M: Yes, yes. Please come in and have a seat . . . There you go. Now, what's on your mind, Miss . . .

W: Jenkins. Sally Jenkins.

M: Ah, yes. Miss Jenkins. Very well. What can I do for you?

W: Actually, Professor Reid, I'm a student in your Greek philosophy class. But I'm, uh, I'm here because . . . well, I need to drop the class.

M: Whatever for?

W: Well, I have to be completely honest with you. I have no clue what you were talking about yesterday. And that was just the first day of class. What's it going to be like when we're halfway through the semester and I'm totally lost?

M: Hmm . . . Would you mind telling me what exactly you didn't understand?

W: Everything! I mean, you covered so much information and named so many different philosophers. The only ones I'd ever even heard of were Socrates, Plato, and Aristotle, but you named a whole lot more like, uh, like . . . I can't even remember. Oh. And the terms. I don't even know how to spell them let alone understand what they mean.

M: [3]I see. Well, thank you, Miss Jenkins, for bringing that to my attention. Perhaps I erred and covered a little too much on the first day.

W: I'll say.

M: I sometimes get a little carried away on the first day. Philosophy is, you see, my life.

W: Yes.

M: But do you know what you ought to do?

W: What's that?

M: Stick with the course for a couple more weeks. I'll sign your drop slip now if you'd like, but I think you ought to stay with the class a little longer. See, I'll be going much more slowly in future classes. I was just trying to give an overview of the entire course yesterday. I can see now how that could be intimidating.

W: Well . . . I really am interested in the material, and if you say it's going to get easier . . . I guess it wouldn't hurt if I gave it another try.

M: Splendid. Then I shall see you bright and early tomorrow morning at nine.

Office Hours

Reason for Visiting:	Result:
Wants to drop the professor's class	Professor asks why she wants to drop the class
Problem:	**Solution:**
Could not understand the material covered in the first class	Will remain in the class since the lectures will become easier in the future

1 [Gist-Purpose Question]

The student goes to the professor to drop the class. To do that, the professor has to sign a form, which he calls a "drop slip."

2 [Making Inferences Question]

The student states, "I guess it wouldn't hurt if I gave it another try," from which it can be inferred that she will not drop the class for the time being but will continue taking it.

3 [Understanding Function Question]

When the student says, "I'll say," in response to the professor, she is agreeing with him that he covered too much material in the first class.

Summarizing ▶

The student tells the professor that she is taking his Greek philosophy class but wants to drop it. He asks why, and she responds that she was very confused in yesterday's class, which was the first of the semester. The professor asks for more information, and she states that she had never heard of most of the philosophers he had mentioned and that she did not know any of the terms. He says he covered a lot to give the students an overview of what they were going to learn. He asks the student to stay in class a little longer because the classes will get easier. She agrees to do so.

Mastering Topics with Conversations B6   p.163

1 Ⓐ   2 Ⓐ   3 Ⓒ

Script & Graphic Organizer 02-102

W Student: Excuse me, but is it all right if I come into the lab?

M Laboratory Assistant: Sure. You can come on in.

Are you here for the class that's supposed to meet here at one thirty? Congratulations. You're the first student of the day. You're a little early since it's not even one though.

W: Oh, no. I'm not in any lab class. I was just looking for a professor, but there doesn't seem to be anyone on the entire floor here except for you.

M: Ah, everyone must still be at lunch. There was some kind of a departmental meeting in the morning, and then most of the professors and staff members went out to eat afterward.

W: Oh, I see.

M: Well, who are you looking for?

W: I wanted to meet with Professor Miller. I'm a transfer student here, and I'm hoping to do some research on shellfish, so that's why I need to speak with him.

M: Professor Miller? He's an expert on sharks, not shellfish. If you want to conduct research on shellfish, you'd better speak with Professor Peters.

W: Is that so? My roommate told me the opposite.

M: No, your roommate is definitely wrong. I'm not only a lab assistant, but I'm also a graduate student here, and Professor Miller is my advisor. Trust me when I say that I definitely know what his specialty is. Anyway, talk to Professor Peters when he gets back from lunch.

W: Great. Thanks. Oh, one more thing . . .

M: Yeah?

W: Would you happen to know if there are any part-time positions around here? Like I said, I'm a transfer student. I'm a junior, so I don't really know anyone. I figure that getting a part-time job in the Biology Department would help me, you know . . .

M: Make some friends in your major and help you get to know your professors better?

W: Yeah, exactly. How'd you know that?

M: What do you think that I'm doing here? Working in the department is a great way to make a few extra dollars, to learn, and to get to know everyone better.

W: Totally. So are there any jobs available? Do you know?

M: ³I believe there's one spot open now. It involves cleaning the fish tanks in a couple of the labs. One of the labs belongs to Professor Peters by the way. **If I were you . . .**

W: Got it. So where can I apply?

M: Either speak with Professor Peters directly—that would be the best way—or talk to the departmental secretary.

W: You've been a really great help. Thanks, and I hope

to see you around more in the future.

Service Encounter

Reason for Visiting:	Result:
Is looking for a professor to speak with	Learns which professor he needs to talk to
Student's Question:	Result:
Asks about the availability of part-time jobs	Finds out there is a part-time job available cleaning fish tanks

1 [Detail Question]

The laboratory assistant tells the student, "If you want to conduct research on shellfish, you'd better speak with Professor Peters."

2 [Making Inferences Question]

The laboratory assistant tells the student to speak with Professor Peters or the departmental secretary. Since Professor Peters is currently not around but is at lunch, it is most probable that the student will visit the Biology Department office and speak with the secretary there.

3 [Understanding Attitude Question]

When the laboratory assistant says, "If I were you," and then pauses for a moment, he is telling the student that he ought to speak with Professor Peters. The reason is that the student wants to work with shellfish and wants to find a job, and Professor Peters both works with shellfish and needs a student employee.

Summarizing ▶

The student visits the laboratory, and the assistant mentions that she is <u>very early for her class</u>. The student then says that she is not in a class but is looking for a professor. She wants to speak with Professor Miller about <u>shellfish</u>. The assistant says that Professor Peters, not Professor Miller, knows about shellfish. The student then asks about <u>any part-time jobs</u> in the building. She wants to work there so that she can meet more people in her major and <u>to make some money</u>. The assistant says that there is a job available <u>to clean some fish tanks</u> and that the student should apply for it.

TOEFL Practice Tests C1

p.164

1 Ⓐ	2 Ⓒ	3 Ⓓ	4 Ⓐ	5 Ⓑ	6 Ⓑ

Script 02-103

M1 Professor: I'd like to turn our attention to glass. Glass has been around for millennia, even as far back as the Late Bronze Age. In fact, there was even a certain amount of trading of glass by Egypt and its neighbors during that period. In particular, the Egyptians traded glass ingots. These were raw pieces of glass, mind you—not actual glass vessels, cups, or containers. The ingots were typically thick, circular disks made in a wide variety of colors. One Egyptian glass workshop that has been excavated and dated back to around 1250 B.C. has provided modern scholars with a number of clues as to how glass was made back then. I'd like to share this method with you since I think you'll find it's, uh, it's quite fascinating.

In the Egyptian glass workshop uncovered at Qantir, which, along with most everything else of importance in Egypt, is near the Nile, archaeologists recently discovered some tools that Egyptian glassmakers used, and they were thus able to surmise the methods utilized to make glass. First, they believe, the artisans took sand with a large amount of quartz in it and then crushed it into fine dust. The workers then placed the dust in a ceramic vessel that was lined with lime so that the glass could be easily removed later . . . Yes, your hand is up?

M2 Student: Lime? As in the fruit?

M1: Huh? Oh, no. Not the fruit. ⁶The lime I'm referring to is a compound made mostly from calcium and is often found in limestone. Got it . . .? Okay, good. **Now, where was I . . .?** Ah, yes. I remember. Okay, so, the dust was in the ceramic vessel lined with lime. Then, the artisans heated the vessel to somewhere around 900 degrees Celsius, where the sand subsequently turned into glass. Once the glass cooled, the workers removed it from the vessel and then washed it to remove any impurities, such as salt, that had gotten on it.

This was the first step in the process. The second step in manufacturing the glass involved it being reheated, colored, and shaped. So, first, the glass was crushed into a powder. This glass dust was then poured into special crucibles, and then various elements were added to give it color. Most frequently, the colors were red, blue, purple, and turquoise . . . Oh, the elements? Well, for instance, cobalt made the glass blue, and copper turned the glass turquoise in color. In addition, clear glass was sometimes made, but it appears as though colored glass was more highly prized than clear glass. After the elements were added, the crucibles were heated to over 1,000 degrees Celsius, which caused the crushed glass and the coloring agents to melt and to combine to form almost pure glass ingots. Once they cooled, the crucibles were broken open, and the glass was removed. I should add that the crucibles too were lined with lime so that the ingots could be more easily removed.

From that point, the glass ingots either remained in Egypt or were traded elsewhere. In either case, the ingots went to expert glass craftsmen, who re-melted the glass and then shaped it into the forms they desired. Allen, you have an observation to make?

M2: Yes, I do. [5]I just think that's pretty unique. It's like the glass was, oh, a raw material of sorts.

M1: Hmm . . . That's a creative way of putting it. **I see your point.** After all, why make glass into a final form that people weren't interested in? Instead, the Egyptians let the people who bought the glass ingots determine the final shape of the glass. For the most part, glass in the Late Bronze Age was used to make colored beads, other forms of jewelry, and long-necked vessels for liquids such as perfumes. At that time, the technology to make panes of glass for windows didn't exist, so that wasn't an option. People then are also not believed to have used glass to drink liquids from. Cups and dishes were typically made of wood or ceramics for the lower classes and from ceramics or metal for the rich and royalty.

I should also mention that there's an ongoing debate concerning where glass was first made. The two leading, uh, candidates are Egypt and Mesopotamia. Archaeologists have found finished glass items in both areas dating to roughly similar time periods. One piece of evidence points to Egypt having learned glassmaking from the Syrians, who lived near the Mesopotamians. An inscription was found in Egypt stating that an Egyptian pharaoh won a victory over the Syrians and then brought some Syrian glassmakers back to Egypt. Perhaps the Egyptians captured them, brought them to Egypt, and then forced them to reveal their secrets. Who knows? Whatever the case may be, by the second millennium B.C., the Egyptians had somehow discovered how to make glass. Oh, while that Egyptian glass workshop at Qantir dates back to 1250 B.C., samples of glass found in Mesopotamia have been dated back to 1500 B.C. Yet we don't know the origins of this older glass. I suppose it's a mystery that will perhaps be revealed in the future.

1 [Gist-Content Question]

During his lecture, the professor mostly describes the process by which glass was made by the ancient Egyptians.

2 [Gist-Purpose Question]

About the debate concerning Mesopotamia and Egypt, the professor notes, "I should also mention that there's an ongoing debate concerning where glass was first made."

3 [Detail Question]

The professor says, "Cobalt made the glass blue."

4 [Making Inferences Question]

The professor states, "One piece of evidence points to Egypt having learned glassmaking from the Syrians, who lived near the Mesopotamians. An inscription was found in Egypt stating that an Egyptian pharaoh

won a victory over the Syrians and then brought some Syrian glassmakers back to Egypt." In saying this, he implies that the Syrians, not the Egyptians or the Mesopotamians, may have been the first people to have made glass.

5 [Understanding Function Question]

When the professor responds to the student by saying, "I see your point," he is admitting that the student's observation may be accurate.

6 [Understanding Attitude Question]

When the professor asks, "Where was I?" he means that he wants to stop talking about lime and get back to the main part of his lecture.

TOEFL Practice Tests C2

p.166

1 Ⓓ   2 Ⓑ   3 Ⓐ   4 Science-Fiction Works of Literature: ②, ③   Science-Fiction Movies: ①, ④
5 Ⓐ   6 Ⓓ

Script 02-104

M1 Professor: [5]One of my favorite genres of entertainment is science fiction. When I was young and saw *Star Trek* on TV for the first time, I fell in love with it. **Growing up, I read as much sci-fi literature as I could and saw virtually every sci-fi program on TV or movie.** The various interpretations of how the future will look were simply fascinating. Now, I'm sure most of you are aware that sci-fi novels and short stories are not quite the same as sci-fi TV programs and movies. In fact, they're two very different forms of expression.

First, science fiction differs from other forms of fiction in several very specific ways. It often deals with futuristic events and technology that hasn't been created or which may even be impossible to create, such as, uh, such as a time machine. Quite a lot of science fiction involves themes or storylines like interstellar travel, aliens—both friendly and unfriendly—time travel, and the expansion of humans throughout the universe. Some science fiction is exacting and detailed, and it offers plausible explanations for the technology used. This is more common in literature than in movies or TV shows though. In other instances, the reader or audience is simply given a situation and is expected to accept it on faith. For example, the hyperspace drive systems used in *Star Wars* and the warp drives used in *Star Trek* receive little technical explanation in the movies and TV shows.

M2 Student: Um, actually, Professor Patterson, in the novelizations of both *Star Trek* and *Star Wars*, the systems' details are better explained.

M1: Ah, yes, right. I was actually about to mention that.

However, on TV and in the movies, the audience is merely expected to believe that spaceships can travel at speeds several times that of light. After all, ships with FTL . . . uh, faster than light . . . drives are a useful plot device and help overcome the fact that space travel at present is extremely slow. So be aware that literature often gives more detailed descriptions than other media.

Another major difference is that literature provides deeper insights into humans and human nature than movies and TV programs. Novels and short stories can convey the authors' thoughts, feelings, and other ideas by relaying them through the characters or simply through the narration. In fact, some novels are so filled with these insights that, when they're adapted into movies, the major points of the novel get lost. Frank Herbert's *Dune* is a perfect example of this. A thick, thoughtful, beloved novel was turned into a poor movie that was little watched. Robert Heinlein's *Starship Troopers* was also dramatically altered from the original, and the entire point of the novel seems to have been missed by the director.

Movies and TV shows are visual media and, as such, depend more on the reactions of the actors to convey emotions and to reveal knowledge to the audience. In a book, the author can express necessary information by using as much space and as many words as are needed. But movies are short . . . you know, just two hours or so . . . so as much of the story and action as possible must be crammed into a limited amount of time. Therefore, this doesn't leave much time to examine why humans, er, colonized Mars, or why the aliens are attacking Earth, or how Luke Skywalker— to use a *Star Wars* reference—feels when his aunt and uncle are killed by the Empire.

Some science-fiction movies actually attempt to convey insights, but this isn't true for the vast majority. The trouble is that the few recent examples that have tried to express more human emotion and attain an understanding of human nature and our place in the universe have, um, bombed at the box office. I'm speaking of movies such as *Sphere* and *Mission to Mars*. With movies being so expensive to make, you have to follow the money. Cerebral sci-fi films simply don't do well. [6]On the other hand, movies with spaceships, exotic aliens, battles with laser guns, and plenty of explosions frequently do extremely well at the box office. The amount of money the numerous *Star Wars* films have made is proof of that. **The result is that there has been a, um, a dumbing down of both original science-fiction screenplays and movie adaptations of science-fiction literature that has detracted from their quality.** One need only watch the Will Smith movie *I, Robot* and then read the Isaac Asimov novel it was adapted from to see how different the two are.

Television, however, sometimes offers more of the elements of science fiction found in literature. For example, the original *Star Trek* TV program and its many descendants often tackled tough questions about humanity and our place in the universe. The main reason it could do this is that television has more time. A typical American TV program has between twenty-two and twenty-six half-hour or hour-long episodes per season. The writers thus need more material. And since TV programs lack the big budgets movies have, they need to rely more on the writing. The scripts for TV programs are frequently head and shoulders above those of movies, yet, in my opinion, neither comes close to the quality and depth offered by literature.

1 [Gist-Content Question]

Most of the professor's lecture is spent describing how the genre of science fiction differs depending upon if it is in book, movie, or TV form.

2 [Detail Question]

The professor states, "But movies are short . . . you know, just two hours or so . . . so as much of the story and action as possible must be crammed into a limited amount of time."

3 [Understanding Organization Question]

About *Dune*, the professor says, "Frank Herbert's *Dune* is a perfect example of this. A thick, thoughtful, beloved novel was turned into a poor movie that was little watched."

4 [Connecting Content Question]

According to the lecture, science-fiction literature often stresses human emotions and gives detailed descriptions of technology. As for science-fiction movies, they require people to accept a lot of information on faith and are focused primarily on making money for their creators.

5 [Understanding Function Question]

When the professor tells the students how much science-fiction literature he read and how much of it he watched on TV or at the movies, he is indicating to the students that he is intimately familiar with the genre.

6 [Understanding Attitude Question]

The professor notes that many screenplays and adaptations of science-fiction literature have been "dumbed down," so he is implying that he prefers science-fiction literature to movies since it can be assumed that the literature has not been "dumbed down."

TOEFL Practice Tests C3

p.168

1 Ⓓ   2 Ⓒ   3 Ⓐ   4 Ⓑ   5 Ⓓ

Script 02-105

M Professor: Good morning, Kelly, and thank you very much for coming in when I asked you to. Not every student is as prompt as you are, especially at eight thirty in the morning.

W Student: It's no problem, Professor Johnson. I'm actually curious about why you're interested in seeing me. I'm not in any trouble, am I? My grades are really good, and I made the Dean's List last semester after all.

M: Yes, that was quite impressive. Congratulations. The first semester of the freshman year is often the most difficult since students are trying to get adjusted to college, but you did quite well.

W: ⁵Thank you for saying that.

M: Oh, and no, you're not in any trouble.

W: That's a relief.

M: I just requested to speak with you because, as your student advisor, I want to make sure that you're on the right track and aren't experiencing any problems. Now, as you know, I was assigned to you when you got here, so chances are that I won't be your advisor for much longer . . . that is, unless you decide to major in Economics and then choose to keep me as your advisor. Are you considering that?

W: Actually, er, I was hoping to major in journalism. You see, I've started writing for the school newspaper . . . You know, the *Daily Digest* . . . And, well, journalism is just so much fun.

M: I hate to break this to you, Kelly, but we don't have a Journalism Department here.

W: Oh, well . . . Do you think I should transfer then?

M: Whoa. Slow down a little, Kelly. I remember when I was a freshman. I must have changed my mind about my major, gosh, four or five times before I settled on something.

W: Economics, right?

M: Wrong. I majored in history, but after graduating, I decided to pursue economics instead, and, well, here I am.

W: I see. So you're saying that I might change my mind about majoring in journalism in the next month or two?

M: There's a distinct possibility of that happening. So tell me . . . What else are you interested in?

W: Hmm . . . I enjoy the physics class I'm enrolled in, but I'm not interested in it as a major. But do you know what?

M: What?

W: I really enjoy this other class I'm taking. It's called Introduction to Political Science. I've always been into politics, so I think that this might be something I could pursue as a major.

M: That sounds quite promising.

W: ⁶Do you think it would be a good choice?

M: Why not? **If you like something, you ought to keep studying it.** And you know, by the time you graduate, if you're still interested in becoming a journalist, you could always go to graduate school for that. And you'd have a leg up on the competition because you'd already have a lot of knowledge in another field.

W: Yeah, I see.

M: But, uh, why don't you take your time? After all, you've still got three and a half more years to go.

W: That's true. I'll be sure to keep you updated on what I'm thinking of studying though.

M: I appreciate that.

---

1 [Gist-Content Question]

During their conversation, the speakers are mostly talking about what the student thinks she might major on in the future.

2 [Gist-Purpose Question]

The professor tells the student, "I just requested to speak with you because, as your student advisor, I want to make sure that you're on the right track and aren't experiencing any problems."

3 [Making Inferences Question]

During the course of the conversation, it is possible to determine that the student is not sure what her major is going to be. In addition, at the end of the conversation, the student tells the professor, "I'll be sure to keep you updated on what I'm thinking of studying though," which implies that she has not made up her mind yet.

4 [Understanding Function Question]

When the student says, "That's a relief," she is expressing her happiness that the professor just told her that she is not in any trouble. She had been worried that there might have been a problem when the professor asked her to visit.

5 [Understanding Attitude Question]

When the professor tells the student, "If you like something, you ought to keep studying it," it can be inferred that the professor followed his own advice and majored in a subject that he enjoyed.

Chapter **08** | Arts 2 · Conversations

Mastering Question Types with Lectures A1 p.172

| TYPES 1–4 |

TYPE 1 Ⓑ   **TYPE 2** Ⓒ   **TYPE 3** Ⓑ   **TYPE 4** Ⓐ

Script 02-106

M Professor: Let's turn our attention to one of the most famous mistakes in the world. It's even on display for the entire world to see. You know, when you buy a pencil, there's almost always an eraser on one end so that you can remove your mistakes, but when you're building a tall tower that weighs around, say, sixteen thousand tons, it's not so easy to erase your mistake. Does anyone know what I'm speaking about?

W Student: It sounds to me like you're talking about the Leaning Tower of Pisa.

M: Indeed I am. Construction on the tower began in 1173. It was originally intended to be a bell tower for Pisa's cathedral. However, five years into the construction, just after the third floor had been completed, the tower began tilting downward. It seems as though the architect, Bonanno Pisano, had failed to consider the consequences of erecting a 185-foot-tall tower on top of a stone foundation a mere ten feet thick. Furthermore, this thin foundation was resting atop soft sand, rubble, and a dense clay mixture, which, as is clearly evident, is a recipe for disaster. These factors combined to be insufficient to support the tower.

In the hope that the soil would eventually settle and thus stabilize the tower, all construction on it was halted for approximately a century. ⁴Later, when construction on the project eventually resumed, the project leader . . . his name was Giovanni di Simone for your information . . . He managed to complete an additional four floors. **However, in an extremely misguided attempt to compensate for the leaning of the first three floors, the builders made each new tier a little higher on the short side.** The result was that the weight of the additional stone made the tower sink even more. By the time it was completed in 1350, the tower

was leaning a full four feet seven inches from vertical. Later, when the bells were installed in the belfry, the weight of the bells caused the tower to tilt even more. Talk about a comedy of errors, huh? Over the centuries, the tower continued to tilt so that, by the late twentieth century, it was leaning more than seventeen feet toward the south. It's a miracle it never fell over.

W: That sounds awful. Didn't anyone try to fix it?

M: Sure, people made attempts to straighten the Leaning Tower of Pisa practically ever since it was completed. They all made use of the knowledge and technology available to them at the time, but their efforts were futile. Here's an example for you . . . In the twentieth century, the Italians under Benito Mussolini tried fixing the tower. Mussolini ordered the tower's foundation to be filled with concrete, but the concrete sunk into the wet clay while the tower continued tilting. They would have been better off simply leaving it alone. Finally, in the late twentieth century, the tower was stabilized by a combination of counterweights, excavated soil, and slings. Naturally, visitors weren't allowed in the tower while it was being restored, but it's open to visitors nowadays since there has been no more tilting in recent years, and the tower appears, finally, to have stabilized.

TYPE 1 [Gist-Content Question]

The professor mostly covers the history of the Leaning Tower of Pisa from its construction to its current status.

TYPE 2 [Detail Question]

The professor notes, "It seems as though the architect, Bonanno Pisano, had failed to consider the consequences of erecting a 185-foot-tall tower on top of a stone foundation a mere ten feet thick. Furthermore, this thin foundation was resting atop soft sand, rubble, and a dense clay mixture, which, as is clearly evident, is a recipe for disaster."

TYPE 3 [Understanding Organization Question]

The professor talks about Benito Mussolini's failed attempt when he says this, "They all made use of the knowledge and technology available to them at the time, but their efforts were futile. Here's an example for you . . . In the twentieth century, the Italians under Benito Mussolini tried fixing the tower. Mussolini ordered the tower's foundation to be filled with concrete, but the concrete sunk into the wet clay while the tower continued tilting. They would have been better off simply leaving it alone."

TYPE 4 [Understanding Function Question]

When the professor states that the construction method was "extremely misguided," he is implying that the leader of the project was incompetent.

The professor begins by noting that not all mistakes can be erased and that some are in plain sight for everyone to see. He is referring to the Leaning Tower of Pisa. He then describes its construction. According to him, its thin foundation and the soil it was built on made it start to lean. Construction stopped, but when it resumed again, it began leaning more as it was built higher. People made many attempts to straighten the tower, but they all failed. Some, like Benito Mussolini's attempt in the twentieth century, made it worse. Recently, it has been stabilized, so visitors are allowed inside once again.

| TYPES 5–8 |

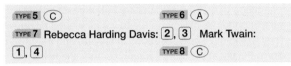

TYPE 5 Ⓒ   **TYPE 6** Ⓐ

TYPE 7 Rebecca Harding Davis: ②, ③   Mark Twain: ①, ④   **TYPE 8** Ⓒ

Script 02-107

M Professor: The years following the Civil War in the United States were tumultuous. Not only had the country been at war with itself, but it was also undergoing great societal changes. The U.S. was growing as literally millions of immigrants poured into the country from Europe and other countries around the world. The U.S. was also becoming more industrialized and more urbanized as people moved away from the farms and into urban centers, often in the west. There was a growing middle class as well. What did all this mean? Basically, it meant that the country was changing rapidly.

Literature was changing as well. During this time of extraordinary social changes, Rebecca Harding Davis and Mark Twain were two authors who wrote fiction that focused on the accurate representations of Americans in a variety of circumstances, particularly those I just mentioned. Their style of writing was known as Realism. It spans the time from the end of the Civil War, which happened in 1865, to around, oh, I believe 1910 is the accepted date. Incidentally, that's when both Davis and Twain died. It's fitting, I think, for the age of Realism to have ended with the deaths of two of its greatest writers. Anyway, the works of both authors focused on slavery, as well as other topics that frequently explored ordinary people having to make moral and ethical choices.

Let's take a quick look at Rebecca Harding Davis. Born in 1831 and dying in 1910, she often wrote about the dismal environment of her day. She was a proponent of social change and was particularly interested in aiding freed slaves, immigrants, and other, um, disadvantaged groups of people. Her works, as you might expect, reflected the social issues of the time. *Waiting for the Verdict* was an 1868 novel that concerned freed slaves and how they would, uh, adapt to life as free people. In 1874, she published *John Andross*, which was a novel about political corruption, something that was a common topic at that time due to the corruption of the administration of President Grant. We're going to read *Waiting for the Verdict* later in the semester as well as some of her short stories and essays, so hers is a name you need to remember.

As for the other major writer of this period, I expect you already know something about him. Born Samuel Clemens but known as Mark Twain, he was one of the greatest writers America has ever produced. His two most famous works are *Tom Sawyer* and *Huckleberry Finn*. Like Davis's works, his often focused on contemporary social issues. Slavery and slaves were also major themes in many of his works, including the two I just noted. [6]One thing that set Mark Twain apart from many authors was his actual writing style. He frequently wrote as people really spoke. That can make reading his works today somewhat difficult since he used a lot of expressions that were unique to his time. **Nevertheless, it gives his works a unique quality.** Of course, it also upset many of the critics of his day. Yet today we recognize the genius of Mark Twain, and we celebrate many of his works as both classics of American literature and Realist writing.

TYPE 5 [Gist-Content Question]

The professor mostly focuses on the writing styles of Rebecca Harding Davis and Mark Twain throughout his lecture.

TYPE 6 [Understanding Attitude Question]

When the professor says that Mark Twain's works have a "unique quality," he is indicating that Mark Twain wrote in a style that was individual to him.

TYPE 7 [Connecting Content Question]

According to the lecture, Rebecca Harding Davis wrote about political corruption and was interested in social causes, so she tried to help some groups of people. As for Mark Twain, he wrote under a penname, and he is also considered one of the greatest writers in America.

TYPE 8 [Making Inferences Question]

The professor states, "We're going to read *Waiting for the Verdict* later in the semester as well as some of her short stories and essays, so hers is a name you need to remember," when talking about Rebecca Harding Davis, so it can be assumed that his class will involve the study of Realist authors.

Summarizing ▶

The professor notes that the U.S. went through many social changes after the Civil War. Literature in this period also changed. He mentions that the style of writing called Realism lasted from 1865 to 1910. Two of its greatest writers were Rebecca Harding Davis and Mark Twain. Davis tried to help underprivileged groups of people and often wrote about the societal issues of her day. This included slavery and political corruption. Mark Twain wrote two very famous books: *Tom Sawyer* and *Huckleberry Finn*. He tried to write the same way that people speak, so it can make his books difficult. Still, he is recognized as one of America's greatest writers.

Mastering Question Types with Lectures A2 p.174

| TYPES 1–4 |

| TYPE **1** (A) | TYPE **2** (A), (D) |
| TYPE **3** (B) | TYPE **4** (C) |

Script 02-108

W Professor: Next on our list of famous artists is the Frenchman Paul Cezanne. He's known primarily for being both a painter in the school of Impressionism and for being the father of Cubism, which was later made famous by Picasso. He was born in 1839 and died in 1906. He came from the south of France and was born into a rather well-off family. Thus, Cezanne later inherited a great deal of money and never had to suffer any financial burdens during his life. His was most definitely not the life of a starving artist, which enabled him to commit himself to painting full time.

Cezanne suffered from bouts of depressions and feelings of inadequacy for most of his life. He had a dark, brooding personality, made few friends, and was reclusive in the later years of life. ⁴His temperament was not helped by, uh, by the fact that, in his early years as an artist, he endured lots of failure and rejection, especially when he was living in Paris. Yet in spite of depression, failure, and rejection, Cezanne managed to achieve late in his life a measure of fame and influence that was rare for a living artist. And though his style influenced a large number of artists, get this: **He so avoided the spotlight that some people doubted he was a real person.** His one true friend was the famed writer Emile Zola, with whom he had attended school as a child. Sadly, their friendship ended when Zola penned a novel in which the main character was a depressed artist. Cezanne felt that the character was based on him, so he terminated their friendship.

I think that's enough biographical information. Now, let's look at some slides of Cezanne's work. I'm going to keep talking as I click through them. Most of these pictures are easily found either in your book or on the Internet. Cezanne's best known for his landscapes, portraits—including several self-portraits—paintings of bathers, and still lifes. Here we see some of his still-life

work. This one has some fruit arranged on a table. Note the bright colors, the use of heavy brushstrokes, and the thick layers of paint. This one here is a portrait of Cezanne's father reading a newspaper. He painted it in 1866. Again, note the heavy brushstrokes and the, um, the simplicity of the picture. It's just a, uh, just an elderly man reading a newspaper while sitting in an armchair. Some contemporary critics suggested that Cezanne's work was too simple and thus boring, but for Cezanne, the mechanics of painting were more important than the subjects he actually painted.

By the, uh, the 1870s, Cezanne had turned toward Impressionism, but he later abandoned this form since it didn't conform to his ideas of solidity and structure. In the later years of his life, Cezanne painted more and more landscapes like this . . . this . . . and this. As you can see, his works started becoming dominated by geometrical figures. Notice in this painting the cylinders, spheres, and cones. Additionally, the heavy brushstrokes were sometimes placed seemingly at random. You can see evidence of that here in this picture that shows a house, road, and trees. This was painted in Cezanne's final days. After taking a look at this work, it should come as no surprise, I believe, that Cezanne is considered the father of Cubism.

TYPE 1 [Gist-Content Question]

The professor primarily describes Cezanne's life and some of his works.

TYPE 2 [Detail Question]

According to the professor, Cezanne used "heavy brushstrokes," and, "Cezanne's best known for his landscapes, portraits—including several self-portraits—paintings of bathers, and still lifes."

TYPE 3 [Understanding Organization Question]

About Cubism, the professor notes, "After taking a look at this work, it should come as no surprise, I believe, that Cezanne is considered the father of Cubism."

TYPE 4 [Understanding Function Question]

The professor notes that Cezanne "avoided the spotlight" and also says that some people even doubted his existence. She is thus noting how reclusive Cezanne was and how much he tried to avoid people.

Summarizing ▶

The professor begins with a biography of Paul Cezanne. She describes his life and notes that he was often depressed and had few friends. He also endured much rejection early in his career and was very reclusive. Cezanne painted landscapes, portraits, self-portraits, bathers, and still lifes. He used bright colors, heavy brushstrokes, and thick layers of paint. He was often accused of making simple work, but he focused more on the process than the subjects he painted. He painted in the Impressionist style, but his work changed in the last years of his life. He began painting in the Cubist style and is often considered the father of Cubism.

| TYPES 5–8 |

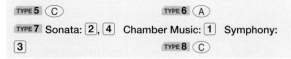

Script 02-109

M Professor: Some of the most brilliant music ever composed comes from a couple of centuries ago. I'm referring, of course, to classical music. Unfortunately, for many members of today's generation, the only times they listen to classical music is when they're put on hold on the telephone or when an occasional movie soundtrack makes use of one or two pieces of classical music. That really is unfortunate because there are so many wonderful pieces of classical music, and so much of it is superior to what is produced these days.

Before we go any further, let me tell you that classical music—in the broadest sense of the term—encompasses a number of styles of music and covers a period of, oh, around 700 years. Think about how many styles of music have waxed and waned in popularity over, uh, let's say the past two decades. And now consider how many changes there must have been over a period lasting seven centuries. A lot, right? So don't think that classical music is all the same because it most certainly isn't. In fact, musicologists have divided those 700 years into six different periods of music that are notable for their stylistic differences.

What we're going to focus on today is the fourth period, called the Classical Period, which has, as I'm sure you can surmise, given us the term classical music. The Classical Period refers to music written between the years 1750 and 1820. Basically, the music from this time was designed to be simple, balanced, and structured. The composers working during these decades wanted to, uh, they wanted to bring music down to Earth. They sought to control emotions. Their compositions were melodic and simple. The music was neither too loud nor too soft, and it was neither too fast nor too slow. Balance. That's the key. There were no extremes as the music was under control with no demonstrations of strong emotions. Even the size of the orchestra was kept to no more than forty musicians as it too was brought under control and balanced.

During the Classical Period, three distinct forms of music became popular. The most important was the sonata, which is sometimes called the ABA form. The beginning and ending of a sonata . . . that would be the A in the ABA form . . . are the same while only the middle is different. Again, you can see balance. The start and finish are balanced, and the only contrast comes in the middle. Sonatas were based on what was then a new kind of sound. It was called homophonic. Essentially, there was a melody played on top of harmonizing chords that had either supporting instruments or voices beneath it. Hmm . . . In modern terms, think of it as a vocalist singing along to the strumming of a guitar. Chamber music, from which evolved the string quartet, was another form of music popularized during this time. String quartets were where the violin became extremely popular. You really can't underestimate the popularity or the importance of the violin during this period.

Finally, the symphony was the third form stressed in this period. In case you don't know, a symphony is a musical work that has four movements. It was through their symphonies that many composers gained international fame. In fact, three of the most important of all classical music composers—Wolfgang Amadeus Mozart, Franz Joseph Haydn, and Ludwig van Beethoven—are all noted for their symphonies, among other works of course. Their compositions are timeless and continue to entertain people today.

TYPE 5 [Gist-Content Question]

The professor's lecture covers several of the defining features of the Classical Period.

TYPE 6 [Understanding Attitude Question]

The professor comments, "That really is unfortunate because there are so many wonderful pieces of classical music, and so much of it is superior to what is produced these days."

TYPE 7 [Connecting Content Question]

According to the professor, the sonata was based on homophonic sound and used the ABA form. Chamber music often featured the violin. And symphonies had four separate movements.

TYPE 8 [Making Inferences Question]

The professor mentions, "String quartets were where the violin became extremely popular. You really can't underestimate the popularity or the importance of the violin during this period."

Summarizing

The professor claims that few people these days listen to classical music. He then states that classical music covers a period of about 700 years, but he only wants to focus on the Classical Period, which was the fourth of six periods. The Classical Period lasted from around 1750 to 1820. It had music that was simple, balanced, and structured.

Balance was what the composers of this period strived for. The three main forms of music were sonatas, chamber music, and symphonies. There were also many composers, like Mozart, Haydn, and Beethoven, who lived during this time and became internationally famous from their work.

Mastering Question Types with Conversations A3

p.176

| TYPES 1–4 |

TYPE 1 Ⓓ   TYPE 2 Ⓐ   TYPE 3 Ⓒ   TYPE 4 Ⓓ

Script 02-110

M Student: Professor Gill, I know you've got class soon, but could I have a brief word with you?

W Professor: Sure, Gerald. What's on your mind?

M: It's the auditions for the play you're directing.

W: The auditions? But we held them last week. Weren't you aware of that?

M: Yes, I know they were last week, but I wasn't able to attend them. I, uh, I had a personal matter I had to attend to. It had to do with my family, so I was a hundred miles away for the entire weekend when the auditions were being held.

W: I'm terribly sorry to hear that, Gerald. I trust that all's fine now?

M: Oh, yeah. We got everything worked out. It was, uh . . . Well, it's not important. So, I was wondering about the auditions . . .

W: I hate to break the news to you, Gerald, but every position has been filled.

M: You're kidding? I was so looking forward to trying out for the role of Iago.

W: Yes, I'm sure you would have done a fine job, but Lee Wimberley is taking that role.

M: Oh . . . Does he have an understudy?

W: I'm afraid so. I chose Ray Chapman to be his understudy. I'm sorry, Gerald. I wish you'd gotten in touch with me before the auditions had begun. Then I could have done something for you. But now that everything has been decided, well . . . you know . . .

M: Yes, I understand. I don't want to put you in an uncomfortable position or anything.

W: Thanks for understanding. But, say, why don't you come and help out with the production? You could be a stagehand and help with the lights, the props, the costumes, and everything else like that.

M: That could be fun.

W: Not all fun. It'll be hard work, but it'll be a great learning experience as well.

M: Sure, I think I'll do that. I'd like to be associated with the play even if I don't get to act in it.

W: That's the right attitude, Gerald. And you know we'll be putting on another play next semester, so then you'll get a shot at acting.

TYPE 1 [Gist-Purpose Question]

When the professor asks the student what he would like to speak about, he answers, "It's the auditions for the play you're directing."

TYPE 2 [Detail Question]

The student responds to the professor by saying, "I, uh, I had a personal matter I had to attend to. It had to do with my family, so I was a hundred miles away for the entire weekend when the auditions were being held."

TYPE 3 [Understanding Organization Question]

The professor explains what a stagehand does so that she can give the student an idea of what role she would like him to fulfill when assisting with the play.

TYPE 4 [Understanding Function Question]

The student mentions his family problems to explain exactly why he did not attend the auditions.

Summarizing ▶

The student visits the professor to talk about the auditions for the school play. The professor says that they were held last week. The student acknowledges that he knows that but says he was dealing with family matters elsewhere, so he could not attend them. The professor says she would like to help him, but all of the roles have been filled. She will not make an exception for him either, but she offers him a job as a stagehand to help with the play's production. The student agrees and says that he would like to be associated with the play in some manner.

| TYPES 5–8 |

TYPE 5 Ⓒ   TYPE 6 Ⓑ   TYPE 7 Ⓓ   TYPE 8 Ⓑ

Script 02-111

M Student: Excuse me, but I need to speak with the person in charge, please.

W Student Services Employee: That would be me right now since there's no one else in the office. What can I do for you?

M: Well, I've got a big problem. You see, I got a parking ticket last Friday night.

W: Oh, sure. You can pay it off either with cash or a check.

M: No. I'm not here to pay my ticket. I'm here to protest it. There is absolutely no reason for me to have gotten a parking ticket.

W: Would you mind telling me the circumstances surrounding how you got your ticket?

M: Not at all. You see, my car got ticketed when it was in the school auditorium parking lot on Friday night. I was playing the cello in the student orchestra's performance, so that's why I was there.

W: Hey, I was at that performance. You all were pretty good.

M: Uh, thanks.

W: Okay, anyway, do you have a parking sticker? If you don't, that's probably why you got ticketed.

M: Yes, I have one. I've got one that lets me park in any student lots on campus for the entire semester.

W: Hmm . . . Oh, wait a second. I've got it. You're only allowed to park in the auditorium's lot until ten o'clock. Anyone parked there after ten will get a ticket and then have his or her car towed if it's not gone by midnight.

M: No, no. It can't be that. As you should be aware since you were there, the concert ended at eight thirty, and I was home before ten, so that can't be the reason.

W: Er, why don't you let me see the ticket? Then I can tell you what the problem is.

M: Oh, yeah. Why didn't I think of that? Here you are . . .

W: Aha. I know what the problem is. You see, when you parked your car, you were taking up two spaces. [8]That's what your ticket is for.

M: Oh . . . And I suppose I can't protest since it's my word against the police officer's, right?

W: Sorry. So . . . what'll it be? Cash or check?

TYPE 5 [Gist-Content Question]

The speakers are mostly discussing a parking ticket that the student received and about which he has come to complain.

TYPE 6 [Detail Question]

The student states, "You see, my car got ticketed when it was in the school auditorium parking lot on Friday night."

TYPE 7 [Understanding Attitude Question]

When the woman asks the student if he is going to pay with a cash or check, she means that he still has to pay his fine, which she would like for him to do now.

TYPE 8 [Making Inferences Question]

Throughout the conversation, it is very clear that the student is unhappy to have gotten the ticket.

Summarizing ▶

The student asks to speak with the person in charge, who is the woman. The student is upset about a ticket he got and would like to protest it. The woman says he probably got it because he has no parking sticker, but the student says he has one. Then, the woman suggests he was parked in the lot after ten, which is not allowed, but the student says he left earlier than that. When she looks at the ticket, she realizes that the student had taken up two parking spaces when he parked, so he was ticketed. Then, she tells the student that he still has to pay the fine.

Mastering Topics with Lectures B1   p.178

1 (A)   2 (C)   3 (B)

Script & Graphic Organizer 02-112

M Professor: The question I'd like to find the answer to this afternoon is this: Can an illustration be considered a work of art? First, permit me to clarify exactly what I mean by an illustration. Most illustrations are drawn with a pencil, charcoal, paint, or other writing utensils and are often done by hand although some today are done with computers. The subjects are not necessarily the dramatic poses or scenes found in paintings but can be virtually anything, even, uh, even, well, comic book panels. Illustrations are often used in school textbooks, technical journals, magazines, newspapers, and other public media. For example, the *Saturday Evening Post* cover designs by American illustrator Norman Rockwell are a prime example of illustrations.

Historically, illustrations are practically as old as humans. They date back to prehistory. The first caveman to paint on his cave wall was an illustrator. Millennia later, prior to the development of the printing press, books had to be hand-copied, and illustrations were typically added to provide images. During the Middle Ages, most books were of a religious nature, so these pictures usually showed scenes from the Bible. Called illuminated manuscripts, these books, like the *Book of Kells* for instance, have some of the most beautiful illustrations ever drawn. Later, woodcuts were used to print illustrations after the invention of the printing press in the fifteenth century. What the artist did was carve an image in a wood block. Then, the block was placed alongside the type to add an image to a book or a picture to a newspaper story.

The invention of photography in the middle of the nineteenth century took away some of the need for illustrations, most notably those printed in newspapers. But at the same time, the proliferation of journals for the masses gave new life to illustrations. At that time, most illustrations were still done in woodcuts, so adding color was difficult. However, by the turn of the, um, the twentieth century, improved printing methods enabled color to be added to the illustrations. The late nineteenth and early twentieth centuries thus comprised the prime age of illustrations in the U.S. and Europe. Remember that prior to the inventing of radios, movies, and televisions, most people got their news and entertainment from printed material. As the twentieth century continued, illustrations continued to be used, especially in mass-marketing campaigns.

Okay, but let me get back to my original question . . . Can an illustration be considered art? Does anyone want to take a stab at that?

W Student: I don't think we can consider illustrations to be on the same level as say, Vincent van Gogh or Picasso. Maybe we could say they're art if we compare them with, uh, I don't know, someone like . . . ah, like Andy Warhol.

M: You make a valid point, and it's one I happen to agree with. Illustrations aren't the same as the works of the master painters and might not even be on the same level as Andy Warhol's work. You know, pop art. However, in recent times, art galleries have been holding exhibits of illustrations. Clearly some curators think differently. Additionally, collectors are seeking illustrations from the past, including famous advertisements, magazine illustrations, and Norman Rockwell covers, and are paying enormous sums of money for them in some cases. Does this therefore qualify illustrations as art? I would say yes, but I'd characterize them as a, er, a special form of art.

W: What about computer-generated illustrations? Are they art?

M: Hmm . . . It's hard to say. If we state that art is only what is made by human hands, then I'd say that they aren't art. Then again, computers were made by human hands, and the tools used on a computer to make an illustration were operated by human hands. And the ideas for these illustrations came from the human brain. So considering all of these factors, I'd have to argue that even computer-generated illustrations really should be considered art.

Illustrations

Characteristics:	Illustrations as Art:
Drawn with various writing utensils	Are not classic art but are like pop art
Appear in many forms of media	Computer-Generated Illustrations as Art:
Date back to prehistory	Are made through the actions of humans so should be considered art
Have been in books and newspapers	

1 [Gist-Content Question]

At the beginning of the lecture, the professor tells the class, "The question I'd like to find the answer to this afternoon is this: Can an illustration be considered a work of art?"

2 [Detail Question]

The professor comments, "The invention of photography in the middle of the nineteenth century took away some of the need for illustrations, most notably those printed in newspapers."

3 [Understanding Organization Question]

Concerning Norman Rockwell, the professor says, "For example, the *Saturday Evening Post* cover designs by American illustrator Norman Rockwell are a prime example of illustrations."

Summarizing ▶

The professor states he wants to know whether illustrations are art or not. He then describes what illustrations are made with. He notes that cave art drawings were illustrations, books in the Middle Ages had illustrations, and many newspapers also had illustrations. Photography's invention caused illustrations to be used less in newspapers, but they were still popular in the nineteenth and twentieth centuries. A student says that illustrations are not classic art but are more like pop art, and the professor agrees. He says that computer-generated illustrations should also be considered art despite being made by computers.

Mastering Topics with Lectures B2   p.179

1 Ⓒ   2 Ⓐ, Ⓒ   3 Ⓑ

Script 02-113

W Professor: Throughout history, students have often learned art by studying it with masters. The master-student relationship was the cornerstone of learning for the majority of the medieval period and was especially prevalent in the eighteenth and nineteenth centuries in

Europe. Most of the time, masters and students worked together in an art studio that the French called an atelier. That's A-T-E-L-I-E-R. The height of the art atelier movement was in the nineteenth century and was centered on Paris, France. Many students went there from other countries to learn from French masters. Once they acquired sufficient mastery of a particular subject, they often returned to their home countries and opened their own ateliers. Sadly, the advent of the twentieth century saw a movement toward keeping art instruction primarily at large universities, and the art atelier movement declined. Many modern art historians are quick to note that the demise of the art atelier brought about a decline in the quality of art being produced.

The art atelier has its roots in the medieval European guild system, in which a master craftsman trained apprentices in the special skills necessary to become a professional. Guilds were strictly controlled by local laws and customs. Art ateliers developed along these lines as master artists took in students and taught them art. Typically, students' families had to pay a fee to the master to cover art supplies and instruction. Sometimes the master and his students lived together and would spend all day working on various projects in a studio.

M Student: How many years did a student typically study at an atelier?

W: It varied from student to student. However, three to six years was common. Many students began studying as children or teens. Later, in the nineteenth century, adults started joining ateliers, especially some of the more famous ones in Paris. At first, novice students weren't permitted to touch paint or to work on sculptures. Most of their first year or so was dedicated to learning to draw. They especially focused on drawing two-dimensional figures and making them appear lifelike. These drawings were done in charcoal. The subjects that students drew were still-life objects and live models. The goal was to have students develop the ability to draw forms in correct proportions so as to represent their subjects as realistically as possible. Only when they mastered drawing were they allowed to begin painting and sculpting. Interestingly, many masters wouldn't permit students to sign their paintings if they believed the works were unsatisfactory.

One of the more common techniques employed at ateliers was the sight-size method. Students would place their drawing paper upright on an easel so that whatever subject they were drawing and the paper were both in their line of vision. Then, students measured their subject with various tools, such as, uh, string and sticks or rulers. This enabled students to know the exact size of each part of the subject. Using this information, students then drew their subjects with the exact proportions they had measured. The placement of drawing paper in relation to the subject was crucial so that when viewed together, the object students drew

and their finished drawings were identical in size.

While the sight-size method likely restricted students' artistic skills and imaginations, the goal of instruction at ateliers was to provide a foundation in art methods so that students could later become either professional artists or teachers themselves. At some ateliers, there was more freedom to draw and paint by using methods other than the sight-size one.

One person whose name you should know is Leon Bonnat, a French artist in the nineteenth century. He ran an atelier and encouraged his students to use a variety of methods as well as their imaginations. Among his students were famed artist such as John Singer Sargent, Henri Toulouse-Lautrec, and Thomas Eakins.

Ateliers

Characteristics:	Paris:
Had its roots in the medieval European guild system	Was the center of the atelier movement in the nineteenth century
Students lived and worked with a master artist	
Students learned various art techniques to become professional artists or teachers	Techniques:
	Taught students to draw with charcoal
	Used the sight-size method
	Some focused on having students use their imagintions

1 [Gist-Content Question]

The professor mostly talks about how ateliers were used to provide instruction to students.

2 [Detail Question]

The professor tells the students, "Most of their first year or so was dedicated to learning to draw. They especially focused on drawing two-dimensional figures and making them appear lifelike. These drawings were done in charcoal," and, "The goal was to have students develop the ability to draw forms in correct proportions so as to represent their subjects as realistically as possible."

3 [Understanding Organization Question]

About Leon Bonnat, the professor states, "He ran an atelier and encouraged his students to use a variety of methods as well as their imaginations."

Summarizing ▶

Ateliers were art studios modeled on medieval guilds. A master artist took in apprentices and trained them to become artists or art teachers. Most students studied for around three to six years. At first, they drew with charcoal, but as they learned more skills, they could paint and sculpt. Students often used the sight-size method. This taught them to paint objects with the exact proportions. While this method restricted skills and imaginations, it provided students with a good foundation in art methods. Some ateliers gave students more freedom. For instance, Leon Bonnat taught many styles and encouraged students to use their imaginations.

Mastering Topics with Lectures B3

p.180

1 **2** Ⓒ **3** Ⓓ

Script 02-114

> **W Professor:** Before we finish, there's one last thing I need to cover. It has to do with how the artists in the Italian Renaissance were able to be so prolific. During the Renaissance, artists were considered to be in the, uh, I guess you could call it the service industry. They had patrons who commissioned exactly what they wanted from artists, who would then produce it. These commissions covered a wide range of artwork that included portraits, landscapes, altarpieces, murals, and frescoes for churches, homes, and other buildings. Additionally, sculptures and architectural works were commissioned. In fact, Leonardo da Vinci's published brochure advertising his services shows just how much of an industry there really was at one time. Included in it were no fewer than thirty-six services he claimed to be able to perform. Talk about a real Renaissance man. Anyway, no one man, not even Leonardo, could do everything by himself, and thus was born the apprentice system.
>
> Artists required assistants to complete their tasks, so they took on apprentices and trained them. These apprentices were usually anywhere from seven to twelve years of age when they started their training, and a typical apprenticeship lasted for twelve years, which is, perhaps not so coincidentally, the same number of years our children take to complete their initial schooling.
>
> What happened was that parents contracted with an artist to take on their son and to train him. Sorry, ladies, but girls were excluded from this system until the late sixteenth century. Yet since parents paid for their son's tuition, which the artist then pocketed, a boy's apprenticeship didn't come without cost. It wasn't unheard of for the most famous artists to have as many as thirty apprentices at any one time. First-year apprentices had very humble tasks. They swept, ran errands, prepared panels and canvases for painting, and ground and mixed pigments. As they progressed and learned more from their master, they were given more responsibilities. They would move on to drawing sketches, copying paintings, casting sculptures, and assisting in the simpler aspects of creating artwork.
>
> While apprentices all started out doing menial work, they often . . . unless they were totally lacking in ability . . . progressed to more skilled tasks quite quickly.
>
> **M Student:** Why did they do that?
>
> **W:** Well, most masters saw their apprentices as assistants who could help them make more money. The more work the apprentices did on real art projects, the faster their masters could complete their projects and get paid for their work. Of course, don't think that the artists permitted incompetent apprentices to do their work. The ones lacking talent were encouraged to, uh, take up another profession. Those with great skills, however, were often called upon to assist their masters with important commissions. They might, for instance, paint the background and some minor figures while leaving the main figures for the master to complete. [3]There were many instances where the apprentices surpassed their masters in skill. **There is a famous, yet most likely apocryphal, story about Leonardo da Vinci, who was himself once an apprentice.** It's said that when he painted an angel that far surpassed the skill and ability of his master, his master broke his own paintbrushes and vowed never to paint again.
>
> Of course, in a sense, this is what every apprentice desired: to surpass his master and to be able to become a master painter himself . . . with his own apprentices, I might add. To accomplish this task, he had to complete his own masterpiece and then have it judged by his master's guild. Upon approval, the apprentice would be considered to have graduated and could then become a guild member, and master painter, himself.
>
> Okay, that's all we have time for today. Don't forget that your reports are due next class, so please bring them along if you haven't already submitted them. If there are no questions . . . very well. Class dismissed.

Apprentices

Apprentices:	Initial Tasks:
Were limited to males	Sweeping, running errands, preparing panels and canvases for painting, and grinding and mixing pigments
Were seven to twelve years old	
Trained for around twelve years	**Later Tasks:**
Could graduate and become masters themselves	Drawing sketches, copying paintings, casting sculptures, and assisting in the simpler aspects of creating artwork

1 [Understanding Attitude Question]

The professor describes many of the tasks that apprentices did for their masters, so it is clear that she feels that they were useful.

2 [Making Inferences Question]

About apprentices, the professor says, "Parents paid for their son's tuition, which the artist then pocketed." She also notes that some artists had up to thirty apprentices and that some of the apprentices helped the artists create works of art. Thus, it can be inferred that those artists with many apprentices earned a lot of money.

3 [Understanding Function Question]

When the professor notes that the story is "most likely apocryphal," she is letting the students know that it probably is not true, so the incident did not really happen.

Summarizing ▶

The professor mentions that Renaissance artists did whatever their patrons requested of them. These could be any number of tasks. Since they were often very busy, they required apprentices. These were young boys between the ages of seven and twelve who trained with the master for around twelve years. Their parents had to pay tuition for them to get the training. They started out just doing menial tasks like cleaning and preparing paint, but as they learned, they got to do more involved work. This included actually painting parts of pictures. Some, like Leonardo da Vinci, eventually became better than their masters.

Mastering Topics with Lectures B4
p.181

1 2 3

Script & Graphic Organizer 02-115

M1 Professor: Let me show you a few pictures very quickly. Take a look at this building in New York City. I'm sure you'll recognize it . . . And then this one . . . And now, finally, check out this picture of a couple of buildings down in Miami, Florida. These all belong to the same style.

M2 Student: That's Art Deco, isn't it, Professor Williamson?

M1: It sure is. But can you tell me what exactly Art Deco is?

M2: Uh . . . Well, er . . . I know it when I see it. Sorry, but that's about the best I can do.

M1: There's no need to apologize, Greg. As a matter of fact, despite having heard the term and being able to recognize Art Deco when they see it—like you just said—a lot of people are still unable to describe exactly what Art Deco is. That's interesting since it's considered to be o-o-o-ne of the most influential design

movements of the twentieth century. It also happens to be a personal favorite of mine. I make it a point to visit as many buildings done in the Art Deco style as I can whenever I travel.

Anyway, Art Deco was a fairly short-lived period. It began in the 1920s and continued into the 1930s. There was also something of a revival of the movement in the 1960s, but it didn't last very long. Despite the short period of time it lasted, Art Deco designs actually abound. Okay, so . . . what exactly are its characteristics? Art Deco involved a mix of modern decorative styles, but it was primarily based on the various avant-garde painting styles of the early twentieth century. While it was first considered to be highly functional, Art Deco, in its later years, evolved to be a purely decorative style, meaning that its main purpose was to be beautiful as well as ornamental. It tended to be abstract, distorted, and simplified. It also was characterized by geometric shapes and highly intense colors, all of which celebrated the rise of commerce, technology, and speed. It was definitely a style that was influenced by its historical period. We're talking about the Roaring Twenties, remember. It seemed like everyone was making money then. Everyone was amazed by the new technologies and advancements being made during that time. The twenties were fun, and so was Art Deco. In fact, in many Art Deco designs, like this one here . . . and this one, too . . . you can see the influence of machines as well as the streamlined forms—especially in the slide on the screen now—that were based on the principles of aerodynamics.

Now, one other interesting thing about Art Deco was how many different art styles it was influenced by. I just mentioned that avant-garde styles were its primary influence. However, there were several other influences on it as well. For instance . . . Far East and Middle Eastern designs, Greek and Roman motifs, and even ancient Egyptian and Mayan styles all influenced it. Art Deco borrowed from all of these styles and then modernized them. The result was, well, simply amazing. People considered Art Deco to be cool and sophisticated in both architecture and the arts. The Empire State Building, which I showed you first, incorporated Art Deco designs. So did part of the Chrysler Building in New York. I've got a picture of it here . . . Miami has the most Art Deco buildings in the country. But Art Deco wasn't just about architecture. Its influence was widespread and included furniture, pottery, glass, and jewelry. The objects produced in its style ranged from luxurious goods made from exotic materials and priced far beyond most people's ability to pay all the way to mass-produced goods made specifically for the growing middle class. Let me show you a few of the objects that I'm speaking about.

Art Deco

Characteristics:	Influences:
Used modern decorative styles	Avant-garde styles; Far East and Middle Eastern designs; Greek and Roman motifs; also ancient Egyptian and Mayan styles
Was abstract, distorted, and simplified	
Used geometric shapes	
Had bright colors	Notable Art Deco Examples:
	The Empire State Building; the Chrysler Building; many buildings in Miami

1 [Gist-Purpose Question]

The professor states, "We're talking about the Roaring Twenties, remember. It seemed like everyone was making money then. Everyone was amazed by the new technologies and advancements being made during that time. The twenties were fun, and so was Art Deco."

2 [Detail Question]

The professor mentions, "Far East and Middle Eastern designs, Greek and Roman motifs, and even ancient Egyptian and Mayan styles all influenced it," when talking about Art Deco.

3 [Understanding Attitude Question]

The professor claims, "It also happens to be a personal favorite of mine. I make it a point to visit as many buildings done in the Art Deco style as I can whenever I travel." So he definitely appreciates Art Deco as an art form.

Summarizing ▶

The professor shows some slides and asks the students to identify the style. A student says it is Art Deco but cannot explain what exactly it is. The professor says that Art Deco was popular in the 1920s and 1930s. It was first highly functional and then evolved to be decorative. It was abstract, distorted, and simplified. It resembled the Roaring Twenties and the attitudes that people in this time period shared. The professor says both the Roaring Twenties and Art Deco were fun. He mentions that many different cultures influenced it as well. Then, he names some buildings and places that employ the Art Deco style.

Mastering Topics with Conversations B5   p.182

1   2   3 Ⓑ

Script & Graphic Organizer 02-116

M Professor: Jane, I'm so glad that I happened to look

out in the hall just now and see you walking by.

W Student: Oh, good afternoon, Professor Nelson. Is there something that you'd like to talk to me about? I have some time if that's the case.

M: Indeed there is. Like I said, it's fortunate that I saw you right now; otherwise, this would have to have waited until next week, and that would have been, well, it definitely would have been to your disadvantage.

W: Hmm . . . I'm not quite sure what you're talking about . . .

M: Well, it concerns the abstract that you submitted to me the other day. You know, the abstract for the paper that you're planning to write.

W: Oh, yeah. I worked really hard to come up with that topic. So, did you like it, sir?

M: Yes and no.

W: Sorry?

M: Ah, I should be the one apologizing for being vague. Sorry about that. Yes, I did like the abstract that you submitted. It was clear to me that a lot of thought had gone into the writing process.

W: Great. I'm glad you liked it.

M: Unfortunately . . . I can't permit you to write on that topic in our class.

W: Huh? Why not? You just said it was a great topic.

M: That's true, but I also gave you explicit directions concerning your class research paper. If you will recall, I gave everyone a handout in class that had acceptable topics, and, I'm sorry to say, this topic wasn't on the list. Uh, you were in class that day, weren't you?

W: Yes, I was. I got the handout.

M: Then why didn't you follow my instructions? Don't you recall what I told you? I believe it was . . . And I quote . . . I will not accept papers written on topics other than these.

W: Yes, I remember that clearly. It's just that . . . well, those topics are so boring. Sorry to say that.

M: Well, they may be boring to you, but you still need to pick one and write about it.

W: There's no chance that you can, er, make an exception in my case? Even with that great new topic that I just thought up?

M: I've been saying the same thing to students who have asked that question of me for the past fifteen years. And the answer is that you need to follow my instructions. I will expect a new abstract to be submitted by the next time we have class.

W: Yes, sir. I understand completely.

M: Thanks. I'll talk to you later.

Office Hours

Reason to See Student:	Result:
Wants to talk about an abstract the student submitted	Professor says that the student did not follow his instructions

Request:	Result:
Make an exception for the student	Refuses to give the student any special treatment and asks for a new abstract

1 [Gist-Purpose Question]

The professor wants to speak with the student because the student did an assignment improperly, so the student needs to make a change in her work.

2 [Understanding Function Question]

The professor states, "I've been saying the same thing to students who have asked that question of me for the past fifteen years. And the answer is that you need to follow my instructions." In bringing up his past students, the professor is indicating to the student that she will not get any special treatment since students from the past did not get any special treatment either.

3 [Making Inferences Question]

When the student asks if she can use her own idea rather than one of the professor's, the professor rejects her idea and insists that the student write about an "acceptable topic" from the handout. Thus the professor is showing that he does not take input from students but insists upon doing everything his own way.

Summarizing ▶

The professor asks the student to come in and speak with him. He says that it is fortunate that he saw the student. He wants to speak with the student about the abstract she turned in. The professor says it is a good abstract, but the student cannot use it. The student asks why. The professor responds that it is not on the list of acceptable topics. The student asks for the professor to make an exception for her, but the professor refuses. He says that the student should submit a new abstract by the time the class meets again.

Mastering Topics with Conversations B6   p.183

1 Ⓑ   2 Ⓒ   3 Ⓐ

Script & Graphic Organizer 02-117

W Student: I really hate to bother you . . . Uh, I'm looking for a book, yet I can't seem to find it on the shelves. It's rather odd because, according to the computer, no one has checked it out, so it should still be in the library.

M Librarian: If it's not on the bookshelf where it belongs, then the chances are pretty good that another student is reading it somewhere in the library right now.

W: Oh, I see. Well . . . is there anything that I can do then?

M: If it's a book for a class you're taking, I suppose you could look around the library and see if you recognize any of your classmates. Perhaps one of them has it.

W: ³No, that won't do. There are over 300 students in the class. I doubt I'd recognize even a tenth of the students in the class.

M: Well . . .

W: Oh, I've got it. Where do people put books when they've finished reading them?

M: The students are supposed to put all books in the return slot whenever they've finished reading them.

W: Supposed to?

M: Well, not everyone does that of course. So that means a librarian has to go around to all of the tables and collect books that need to be reshelved. Then we get some of our student employees to take all of those books and put them back on the shelves where they belong.

W: Around how long does that take?

M: Normally, we go around the library every thirty minutes or so to collect books. But we're a little understaffed at the moment, so we don't look around that often nowadays.

W: What's going on?

M: One of our librarians is out with a broken leg. She tripped and fell during that awful storm we had just a few days ago, so she's still recovering in the hospital. We've also had a few student employees suddenly quit in the last week or so for a variety of reasons.

W: Say, does that mean that you've got some part-time positions to fill?

M: Er, yes, I believe that is correct.

W: How would I apply for one of them?

M: You should speak with Mrs. Richardson. She's in charge of hiring. But it might be tricky getting a job now since the semester is almost over.

W: I'm willing to give it a shot though. I could really use some extra pocket cash right now. Do you think you can tell me where she is?

M: Sure. She's sitting in that office over there by the reference section.

W: Aha. I see exactly where you're talking about.

Service Encounter

Problem:	Solution:
Cannot find a book she is looking for	Look around the library to see if another student is using it
Student's Question:	**Result:**
Asks about the availability of part-time jobs	Can talk to Mrs. Richardson to apply for a part-time job

1 [Detail Question]

When the student asks why books are not being put on the shelves very quickly at the moment, the librarian answers, "One of our librarians is out with a broken leg. She tripped and fell during that awful storm we had just a few days ago, so she's still recovering in the hospital. We've also had a few student employees suddenly quit in the last week or so for a variety of reasons."

2 [Making Inferences Question]

At the end of the conversation, the student asks about getting a job at the library and is told to speak with Mrs. Richardson. She then inquires about where her office is, and the librarian points it out to her. It is probable that she will speak with Mrs. Richardson next.

3 [Understanding Attitude Question]

When the librarian answers, "Well," and merely pauses, he is implying that he has run out of suggestions on how he can help the student.

Summarizing ▶

The student asks the librarian about a book. She mentions it is listed as available, but it is not on the shelves. The librarian says another student is probably reading it in the library. She asks when it will get returned. The librarian states that they normally put books back on the shelf quickly, but the library is understaffed at the moment. After that, she changes topics and asks about getting a part-time job at the library. The librarian says that some jobs are available and that she should speak with Mrs. Richardson. The student asks where her office is, and the librarian points it out to her.

TOEFL Practice Tests C1   p.184

1 Ⓐ   2 Ⓓ   3 Ⓓ   4 Ⓑ   5 Buon Fresco: ②, ③   Secco Fresco: ①, ④   6 Ⓑ

Script 02-118

M Professor: I don't think there's much more to say about that topic. Now, let's look at a similar style of painting called the fresco. It's a type of painting that's made by applying paint to wet plaster as it dries or by applying paint with an adhesive agent over plaster that has already dried. It's a method that dates back to ancient times. One of the great things about frescoes is that they can last an incredibly long time, so they often provide us not only with outstanding images from the past but also with important historical clues. One of the best-known frescoes is the ceiling of the Sistine Chapel in the Vatican Palace in Rome. This was painted by Michelangelo. Let me go over frescoes a bit, and then we'll get to his masterpiece.

There are two major types of frescoes: buon frescoes and secco frescoes. A buon fresco is one that is done directly onto wet plaster. Here's what the artist does . . . First, he puts an under layer of thin plaster on the wall or ceiling of the interior of a building and then lets it dry. After that, the artist may draw a rough sketch of the work—usually in red—so that he has an idea of where to paint when the thin layer of wet plaster gets applied on top. The artist then puts the wet plaster onto the wall or ceiling and, a short time later, begins to apply the paint. The paint is often a pigment mixed with water because, due to the physical properties of the plaster, which is often lime mortar, the paint will adhere to the plaster and become, uh, fused to it as it dries. That's all there is to it. As for the second major type of fresco, the secco fresco, well, it's done on dried plaster. The artist needs to wet the plaster though, so that the paint will adhere to it. During Michelangelo's time, egg whites or yolks were used, and so were various types of resins, glues, and even oils.

Each style has advantages and disadvantages. The major advantage of the buon fresco is that it lasts an extremely long time. In fact, it can survive for hundreds or even thousands of years in some cases. Yet its major drawback is that only a small bit of work can be done at one time since the plaster often dries too quickly . . . in less than a day in most cases. Therefore, for extremely large frescoes, like the ones done by Michelangelo in the Sistine Chapel, they must be done in sections. Sometimes the borders of these sections are visible, so the artist must cover them up by using the secco style. Also, any mistakes made when making a buon fresco must be done over the buon fresco in the secco style since hardened plaster cannot be changed. [6]A minor disadvantage is that, as the plaster dries, the colors sometimes change, too. Well, that's true mostly of the past. **It doesn't happen nowadays too often.** Anyway, blues often didn't turn out very well on buon frescoes, so they had to be done in the secco fresco style.

The main advantage of the secco style is that a large section of plaster can be prepared and then worked on at the artist's leisure. So artists can take their time correcting mistakes or simply do them right the first time since they're, uh, they're not in a hurry anyway. In addition, many colors can be used since they don't bind with the plaster and thus aren't chemically altered. On the other hand, secco frescoes don't last nearly as long as buon frescoes. Many of those from the Renaissance have deteriorated as the paint has flaked away from the plaster.

W Student: Which style did Michelangelo use in the Sistine Chapel?

M: The buon style. Thus he had to apply fresh plaster every day that he worked on it. In fact, some of his early work actually had to be redone since the chapel was damp and mold started growing on the ceiling. But fortunately for him . . . and the millions who have subsequently admired his work . . . he found a better type of plaster upon which mold didn't grow. To work on the ceiling, scaffolding was built under it and was attached to holes in the walls. Michelangelo then stood, sat, or even laid down to paint on the drying plaster on the ceiling. That must have been hard. He sometimes drew an outline or worked from small sketches he had made beforehand. And he may have used a grid system as well, but that's not confirmed.

The most famous of all his Sistine Chapel frescoes is the *Creation of Adam*, in which Adam and God are reaching out to touch each other's fingers. The *Creation of Adam* is one of the nine events from the Book of Genesis in the Bible that Michelangelo painted in the chapel. The others in the group include scenes showing the creation of Eve, the expulsion from the Garden of Eden, and Noah's ark.

1 [Gist-Content Question]

The professor mostly describes buon and secco frescoes during his lecture.

2 [Gist-Purpose Question]

When he describes how Michelangelo painted the Sistine Chapel, the professor states, "To work on the ceiling, scaffolding was built under it and was attached to holes in the walls. Michelangelo then stood, sat, or even laid down to paint on the drying plaster on the ceiling. That must have been hard."

3 [Detail Question]

The professor says, "He sometimes drew an outline or worked from small sketches he had made beforehand."

4 [Understanding Organization Question]

During his lecture, the professor mostly focuses on describing the two different types of frescoes that he speaks about.

5 [Connecting Content Question]

According to the lecture, buon frescoes involve the paint bonding with the plaster and take a long time to finish. As for secco frescoes, they may begin to flake after a while, and they are used to cover up mistakes that the painter has made.

6 [Understanding Function Question]

When the professor talks about paint changing color as the plaster dries, he comments, "It doesn't happen nowadays too often." It can therefore be implied that the quality of modern paints is better than it was in the past, which is why the colors do not change as the paint dries these days.

TOEFL Practice Tests C2 p.186

1 (A) 2 (B) 3 (C) **4 Stop-Motion Photography:**
1 Miniature: 2, 3, 4 5 (B) 6 (C)

Script 02-119

M Professor: [5]While many of you may find it hard to believe, special effects weren't always created by using the computer-generated images that are common today. **No, actually, I take that back.** If any of you have seen any classic movies from the thirties, forties, fifties, or even the sixties, you could definitely find that easy to believe. While modern movies use computers, most special effects in early movies were either merely photographic tricks or physical effects. By physical effect, I'm referring to the manipulation of the camera, the lens, or the film itself. For example, a camera operator once discovered, totally by accident, which seems to happen more often than not, that if he stopped the film briefly while shooting someone or something moving and then started the camera again, the resulting film made it appear as if a person or an object had disappeared and then, well, reappeared in another place. Meanwhile, other effects, such as making the background appear to come closer or to move farther away, could be done by using different camera lenses.

Although some photographic tricks were used, in the early days of moviemaking, physical effects were the most commonly utilized special effects. Physical effects include a number of things, like, uh, say, explosions, gunfire, bullet holes appearing in walls or even, er, people, and anything else that can be created in real time with the actors while the camera is rolling. Physical effects have been used virtually since the advent of the motion picture industry and are still quite common today. Of course, nowadays, these effects are carefully coordinated with stuntmen and women, firearms and pyrotechnic specialists, and the actors and actresses themselves. This wasn't always the case in the past though, so accidents sometimes happened. Well, they still do today, yet with much less frequency.

Another common type of special effect was the background screen. These screens were used both in movies and TV shows. Okay, now I see some of you are grinning, and I know why. You're thinking of those film shots with the two actors driving in a car while the obviously fake scenery goes behind them. That's called rear projection by the way. Anyway, don't laugh too much. They did the best with their technology, and background screens are still fairly common these days. They are particularly common with newscasters who want to present an image of their reporter being in a foreign locale when he's really nowhere close to that spot. I should also mention that the background screens used today are simple blue or green screens behind the actors. Later, the special effects are filled in during the post-production process of the movie or TV program.

Another type of special effect you're probably somewhat familiar with is stop-motion photography. You've heard of this before, right . . .? No . . .? Uh, okay. Anyway, stop-motion photography is used to make objects appear to be moving by shooting the film one frame at a time. Talk about a laborious process. For example, a movie with dinosaurs can't use real dinosaurs since, well, there aren't any around anymore. So what the filmmakers did was first build a model of a dinosaur. Then, they'd move its legs, arms, and head a little bit at a time while shooting one frame of film each time they moved the model. After doing this thousands of times, they'd have a few minutes of film with a dinosaur that appeared to be moving. There's something related to this called Claymation. It's a kind of animation that uses clay models that are moved and filmed in the same manner. If any of you have seen the *Wallace and Gromit* films, which are about a British man and his dog, then you've seen an example of Claymation.

Sometimes, moviemakers wanted to make something that was either impossible because of the limited technology of their time or extremely expensive to create. For instance, filming a scene with, say, Godzilla tromping through the streets of Tokyo or having a rocket fly to the moon was either impossible or expensive depending upon when they were filmed. When a script called for a scene like this, moviemakers had to rely on the use of miniatures. These are models , . . often very tiny ones . . . that are created with meticulous detail and represent something larger than they are. What happened was that the moviemakers built a city like Tokyo on a minor scale, and then an actor in a Godzilla suit got to walk around the set destroying the buildings and everything else. Sure, it looks really cheesy and fake today, but at the time it was filmed, it was really state-of-the-art special effects. And keep in mind that miniatures don't have to be buildings. [6]They can be, oh, vehicles, spaceships, warships . . . almost anything. In fact, virtually all of the older science-fiction movies involving space travel used miniatures to some extent. **And this brings us to movies like *Star Wars*, which came out in 1977.**

1 [Gist-Content Question]

The professor mostly describes some different types of special effects that moviemakers made use of in the past.

2 [Detail Question]

The professor says, "Physical effects have been used virtually since the advent of the motion picture industry and are still quite common today. Of course, nowadays, these effects are carefully coordinated with stuntmen and women, firearms and pyrotechnic specialists, and the actors and actresses themselves."

3 [Understanding Organization Question]

During his lecture, the professor talks about several different kinds of special effects that people have used to make movies.

4 [Connecting Content Question]

According to the lecture, stop-motion photography is a very meticulous way to make a film. As for miniatures, some were used in the *Godzilla* movies, they often appear to be fakes, and they utilize small-scale models.

5 [Understanding Function Question]

When the professor exclaims, "No, actually, I take that back," he is retracting the statement he just made and is going to make a correction.

6 [Making Inferences Question]

When the professor states, "And this brings us to movies like *Star Wars*, which came out in 1977," while he is talking about miniatures, he is implying that the filming of *Star Wars* made use of miniatures.

TOEFL Practice Tests C3   p.188

1 Ⓒ   2 Ⓒ   3 Ⓐ   4 Ⓐ   5 Ⓓ

Script 02-120

W Student: Professor Smith, how are you doing today?

M Professor: I'm doing quite well, Teresa. Thanks for asking. Is there anything that I can do for you this afternoon?

W: Yes, there is as a matter of fact. Uh, do you happen to have a few minutes though? This might take a while.

M: I have all the time in the world. Go ahead and ask whatever is on your mind.

W: Well, it concerns today's lecture about primitive art. There were a couple of things about the lecture that I just didn't understand.

M: Go ahead.

W: Okay, like, those cave paintings. Why did people actually paint them? I don't get it.

M: Well, as I stated in my lecture, it's something of a mystery to us, too. There are a few theories as to why they might have painted them, but no one exactly knows for sure.

W: And those theories are?

M: For one, it could have had something to do with religious purposes. Second, it could have been that the cave dwellers wanted to make records of their deeds. That would have been for instances when you saw pictures of people hunting the animals. And some art historians merely think that these cave drawings are just sketches or doodles made by people who were bored.

W: I see. Okay, that clears up one thing. But, uh, I've got another question.

M: Sure. I'm all ears.

W: Well, how can you actually tell what some of those pictures are supposed to be?

M: What do you mean?

W: For example, there was this one picture that you said was a deer. Uh, no. It looked absolutely nothing like a deer to me. So why do people think that's what it looks like?

M: That's a good question, and there are a few reasons why we can say that it's a deer. One is that art historians can compare that picture with those found in other caves. So while the deer that we saw in class today didn't really look like a deer, it resembled a more clearly drawn deer that was found in another cave.

W: Aha . . . I see. That makes sense. Because, well, I have to be honest. That deer picture just looked awful.

M: Okay, I have to agree with you. But you should also remember that you can't judge these pictures by modern standards.

W: What does that mean?

M: ⁴These are cavemen we're talking about, right? We can't expect them to have been able to, you know, make sophisticated drawings. It's not like they had proper paints or brushes or anything.

W: That's logical.

M: So is there anything else you need to know?

W: ⁵Well, I came here with a few more questions, but I think I'd like to think about what you told me first and then see if I can come up with the answers myself.

M: That's the kind of student I want in my classes. Good luck, and let me know if I can help you again later on. Please realize that I never mind lending a hand to students, especially when I see them trying to figure out things like you are obviously doing.

W: All right. I'll be sure to drop by when I get stumped by something in the future.

1 [Gist-Purpose Question]

In response to the professor's question, the student answers, "Well, it concerns today's lecture about primitive art. There were a couple of things about the lecture that I just didn't understand."

2 [Detail Question]

The professor says, "One is that art historians can compare that picture with those found in other caves."

3 [Making Inferences Question]

When the student tells the professor that she will "drop by" in the future, she is indicating that the conversation is over and that she is going to leave the professor's office.

4 [Understanding Function Question]

When the student says, "That's logical," she is acknowledging that what the professor just said makes sense to her, so she is agreeing with the professor.

5 [Understanding Attitude Question]

When the professor tells the student, "That's the kind of student I want in my classes," she is complimenting the student for saying that she wants to find out the answers on her own. The professor is thus pleased with what the student has decided to do.

Vocabulary Review　　　　　　　　p.190

1	Ⓐ	2	Ⓓ	3	Ⓑ	4	Ⓓ	5	Ⓒ
6	Ⓑ	7	Ⓑ	8	Ⓒ	9	Ⓐ	10	Ⓓ
11	Ⓐ	12	Ⓙ	13	Ⓖ	14	Ⓑ	15	Ⓔ
16	Ⓒ	17	Ⓓ	18	Ⓕ	19	Ⓗ	20	Ⓘ

Part C
Experiencing the TOEFL iBT Actual Tests

≡ Actual Test 01

Listening Set A
p.192

1 Ⓐ 2 Ⓒ 3 Ⓒ 4 Ⓐ 5 Ⓓ

6 Ⓒ 7 Ⓓ 8 Skeletal Muscles: ⬛1⬛, ⬛2⬛ Smooth
Muscles: ⬛3⬛, ⬛4⬛ 9 Ⓑ 10 Ⓐ 11 Ⓐ

12 Ⓐ 13 Ⓒ 14 Ⓑ 15 Ⓑ 16 Ⓓ
17 Ⓐ

| Questions 1–5 |

Script 03-03

M Professor: Julie, I'm so terribly sorry to have kept you waiting outside my office for so long. I just had to take that phone call. It was from overseas and had to do with a grant that I'm applying for. It would have been, uh, inappropriate for me to ask the man to call me back later.

W Student: Oh, that's no problem, Professor Barkley. I was just reading over some of my notes while I was waiting out here . . . So, uh, is it all right if I come in then?

M: Yes, yes. Please come in and have a seat. Here, let me clear all that stuff off of the chair. The clutter in this office just never seems to go away . . . ⁵Okay, so tell me what's going on.

W: Well, it's just that . . .

M: There's no need to be shy, Julie. **Just say what's on your mind.**

W: Okay . . . I'm thinking of changing the focus of my major.

M: Well, that's not what I was expecting to hear. May I ask why?

W: Sure. I, uh, I simply don't feel like having the flute as my primary instrument is working out for me anymore.

M: Why not?

W: It's just that . . . Well, I can't really say. But I don't feel very comfortable with it. I think I'd rather have something else as my primary instrument, like, uh, the piano maybe. I've been playing the piano ever since I was seven, and I'm not too bad at it you know.

M: That's true. You're quite an excellent pianist.

W: Oh, thank you for saying that. So anyway, I, uh, I have the form right here. If you sign it, then I can take

care of the rest of the paperwork . . .

M: But you're an exceptional flutist.

W: Huh?

M: I'm serious. Don't act so surprised.

W: But I've just been awful in class this semester. Playing the flute used to be so much fun, but now it's like . . . it's like, uh, it's like a chore instead. The flute used to feel so light when I picked it up to play, but now it's as heavy as a ton of bricks.

M: Okay, I've never heard anyone put it that way before. You sure do have a way with words, Julie.

W: Seriously. I don't think this is a laughing matter.

M: You're right. I apologize. Okay, look . . . I know you've had a rough semester, but the class you're taking now is for graduate-level students. It's rare that we even let seniors, let alone juniors like you, into the class.

W: Oh . . . I never realized that.

M: Yes, but we made an exception in your case and let you in. I think the last time we made an exception for a student to take a graduate-level class was during one of my first few semesters here, and I've been teaching at this school for more than fifteen years.

W: Really?

M: Absolutely. So don't get discouraged. Besides, you're still getting an A– in the class, and that's nothing to be ashamed of.

W: So you don't think I should change instruments then?

M: I would recommend against it. But here's what you ought to do . . . Wait until the semester finishes and see how you feel. If you still want to switch to the piano, I will wholeheartedly support you.

---

1 [Gist-Purpose Question]

The student mentions to the professor that she wants to change her primary instrument from the flute to the piano.

2 [Detail Question]

The professor tells the student, "The class you're taking now is for graduate-level students."

3 [Understanding Function Question]

The professor states, "Yes, but we made an exception in your case and let you in. I think the last time we made an exception for a student to take a graduate-level class was during one of my first few semesters here, and I've been teaching at this school for more than fifteen years." He also notes that the student is getting an A– in the class, so he is emphasizing how well the student is doing.

4 [Making Inferences Question]

By the end of the conversation, the professor has convinced the student to wait until the end of the semester before she makes a decision on changing her primary instrument.

5 [Understanding Attitude Question]

When the professor says, "Just say what's on your mind," he is indicating that the student should be honest and tell him exactly how she feels.

| **Questions 6–11** |

Script 03-04

W Professor: That should do it for the skeletal system. If there aren't any questions, then I'd like to proceed to the muscular system . . . Okay, now, please turn to page ninety-three in your text, which has a nice picture on the human muscular system I'd like you to look at . . . First, what do muscles do? To put it succinctly, they enable us to move, to breathe, to chew and digest our food, to eliminate body waste, and, uh, and to move blood throughout the body. There are more than 600 muscles in the body, and they fall into two main categories: skeletal and smooth muscles. Yes?

M Student: Isn't the heart also a muscle but not one of those two types you just mentioned?

W: Yes, the heart is a muscle—a very powerful one at that—but it actually has some characteristics of both smooth and skeletal muscles. However, you're right since it's been designated a cardiac muscle, but I'll get to the heart in just a couple of minutes. Okay? First of all, though, I'd like to mention some of the differences between skeletal and smooth muscles. Skeletal muscles are primarily found in the arms, the chest, the legs, the abdomen, the neck, and the face. That's, uh, well, it's most of the body. On the other hand, smooth muscles are primarily found in internal organs and blood vessels. Skeletal muscles, as you may have guessed, are attached to the skeleton and enable us to move our bodies. Smooth muscles, on the other hand, mostly digest food, eliminate waste, and move blood through the body.

But don't think that they differ only in their locations and functions, for they also differ in composition. Skeletal muscles consist of cells called muscle fibers and are found in bundles. They have alternating light and dark bands, which is something we call striation. Additionally, they're long and slender and have many nuclei to direct their movements. What happens is that the nuclei receive nerve impulses from the brain that direct the muscles in their movement. Smooth muscles, however, contain only one of these nuclei and are arranged in sheets in circular patterns in the stomach, the intestines, and blood vessels.

Pardon me. Another important aspect of skeletal muscles is that they must be attached to the skeleton in order to move the body. Tendons, which are white cords of tissue, connect many muscles to the skeleton while other muscles are directly attached to the bones. Now, as I just stated, it's nuclei that receive the impulse from the brain to make the muscle move. When this happens, some muscles contract while others lengthen. For example, try flexing your arm right now . . . Did you feel that? Your bicep contracted, didn't it? And at the same time, your triceps lengthened, right? And, as soon as you relaxed your arm, the exact opposite occurred. That's how skeletal muscles work. Oh, and most skeletal muscle movements are voluntary, so you can control them with your brain. Of course, you may have an involuntary reaction that's, uh, that's most commonly a response to a dangerous situation. For instance, hmm . . . touching a hot stove almost always results in an involuntary reaction in which people quickly pull their hands away. There's one more thing. Should the nerves be damaged or should the body suffer a spinal cord or brain injury, the skeletal muscles cannot operate, so paralysis may occur.

In opposition to skeletal muscles, the movement of smooth muscles is entirely involuntary. These muscles contract in a slow, rhythmic pattern when compared with skeletal muscles. They are also controlled by the body's automatic nervous system. Here's an example. We don't consciously digest our food or pass it through our intestines. Instead, our stomach and intestine muscles slowly move the food through the digestive tract, where enzymes break down the food to extract the necessary nutrients from them. [10]What's left over—the waste material—then moves to the bladder and . . . Sorry again. **It must be this dry weather we've been experiencing lately.** Anyway, the waste material goes to the bladder and the lower intestines—the bowels. When the waste is ready to be eliminated, the bowels and the bladder signal they're ready to be emptied, and then people use voluntary muscle movement to eliminate the waste. And in blood vessels, smooth muscles relax and contract in order to regulate the flow of blood. Now, muscles can either increase or decrease in size depending on the type and the amount of activity they undergo.

M: Can we control how big or small they are?

W: That's why people go to the gym, isn't it? [11]When people do bodybuilding, they're increasing the sizes of many of their major muscle groups. **Conversely, a lack of physical activity . . . something I believe many in the younger TV-and Internet-addicted generation sadly suffer from . . . well, a lack of activity can cause the muscles to shrink or atrophy.** Muscles require constant effort in order to maintain their size.

They can shrink, remain the same size, or expand depending upon the amount of use they get.

6 [Gist-Content Question]

During the lecture, the professor speaks about the muscles, which are the parts of the body that control movement.

7 [Detail Question]

When answering the student's question about the heart, the professor says, "Yes, the heart is a muscle—a very powerful one at that—but it actually has some characteristics of both smooth and skeletal muscles."

8 [Connecting Content Question]

According to the lecture, skeletal muscles are made of muscle fibers, and they also rely upon the spinal cord to function properly. As for smooth muscles, they are not controlled by the person, and they may also be found in the stomach and blood vessels as well as in other parts of the body.

9 [Making Inferences Question]

In the first part of the lecture, when the student asks about the heart, as part of her response, the professor says, "I'll get to the heart in just a couple of minutes. Okay?" Since the professor has finished talking about both skeletal and smooth muscles, you can assume that she will probably start talking about the heart next.

10 [Understanding Function Question]

The professor clears her throat several times during the lecture. After clearing her throat for the third time, she apologizes and mentions that the weather is making her throat dry, which explains the reason that her throat is irritated.

11 [Understanding Attitude Question]

When the professor makes that comment, she includes the word "sadly" and also sighs. Both of these imply that she dislikes how young people are idle nowadays.

| Questions 12–17 |

Script 03-05

> **M Professor:** ¹⁷Okay, everyone, please take your seats as quickly as you can . . . Okay . . . **Before we begin, let me remind you that we've got a test coming up the week after next, so I think that it's a pretty good idea for all of you to focus on this lecture and to take comprehensive notes.** All right? Now, if everyone is ready . . . Excellent. Let's get started.
>
> First, petroleum is just a more formal word for crude oil, which is the basic form of oil before it's transformed into one of its many derivatives. This includes, uh,

lubricants, heating oil, and the gasoline you put in your automobiles. You should also be aware that natural gas is often included in the term petroleum since both crude oil and natural gas are formed from the same process and both of them are made of hydrocarbons, which, as the name implies, are comprised of molecules of hydrogen and carbon.

Essentially, most scientists subscribe to the theory that petroleum was formed from the remains of vegetation and animals that died millions of years ago. Research suggests that the most common life form involved in this transformation was algae. After these life forms died, they fell to the bottoms of, oh, oceans, seas, and swamps, where they were buried by layers of sediment, which crushed them for a period of millions of years. Under heat and pressure, these decomposing materials were turned into petroleum. And just so you know . . . coal was formed in a somewhat similar manner. That's why both petroleum and coal are known as fossil fuels: They were created from the remains of decaying animals and plants.

The process of transforming organic matter into petroleum is quite complex, but I'm going to give you a simplified explanation due to a lack of time. So the decaying matter, after being subjected to heat and pressure, transformed into a material called kerogen. It's a wax-like substance that exists in four types depending upon how much hydrogen, carbon, and oxygen is in it. The first three types of kerogen are where most fossil fuels come from after, of course, the kerogen underwent more changes caused by heat and pressure. Let me see . . . Type 1 kerogen often produced liquid petroleum such as crude oil. Type 2 kerogen produced a mixture of liquid and gas petroleum. Type 3 kerogen is comprised mostly of cellulose from plant matter, and it most likely produced most of the coal on the Earth. It also sometimes produced gases, such as methane, which are frequently associated with coal deposits. Type 4 kerogen, meanwhile, produced neither petroleum nor coal.

Now, don't think that all that was required to make petroleum was for decaying organic matter to have had heat and pressure applied to it for an extended period of time. That's not right. In actuality, certain geological conditions had to have existed for petroleum first to form and then to be trapped underground. There must have been what geologists refer to as a hydrocarbon trap. This consists of three types of rocks. First, there must have been a layer of rock that was the source of the oil. For example, under the floor of both the North and Norwegian seas is a layer of mudstone rock that is ideal for the formation of petroleum. Second, there must have been a type of porous or permeable rock that allowed the petroleum to gather in one spot. Third, on top of that permeable rock, there must have been some kind of impermeable rock that acted as a capstone, or a lid, for the hydrocarbon trap. This, as I think you can see, prevented the petroleum from escaping.

So when all of these conditions were met, after some time, a pool of petroleum was created and then trapped underground. Nowadays, we typically find petroleum in three separate layers. The lighter gases form on top, the heavier crude oils are in the middle, and there is water beneath them. Petroleum found in hydrocarbon traps like this is known as conventional petroleum. However, you should be aware that petroleum isn't always found in formations like these. It can appear in other ways. One such example is bitumen sands, which are basically thick layers of sandy soil that is soaked in petroleum—mostly heavy crude oil—so that it resembles a thick, tar-like substance. Extracting the petroleum from the bitumen sands is an expensive process and is really only worthwhile in areas that have large reserves of bitumen and when petroleum prices are high. At least, that's the case when using the technology that exists today. And for those of you who are curious, the largest bitumen extracting operation going on right now is the Tar Sands Project in Alberta, Canada. Of course, should the price of extracting petroleum go down, you'll see projects of a similar scale start happening all around the world.

12 [Gist-Content Question]

The professor spends most of his lecture describing how petroleum is formed.

13 [Gist-Purpose Question]

Right before the professor begins explaining what a hydrocarbon trap is, he states, "Certain geological conditions had to have existed for petroleum first to form and then to be trapped underground."

14 [Detail Question]

About type 3 kerogen, the professor says, "Type 3 kerogen is comprised mostly of cellulose from plant matter, and it most likely produced most of the coal on the Earth."

15 [Understanding Organization Question]

The professor simply lectures about the formation of coal in a straightforward manner without asking the students any questions or answering any of their questions.

16 [Making Inferences Question]

About bitumen sands, the professor says, "Extracting the petroleum from the bitumen sands is an expensive process and is really only worthwhile in areas that have large reserves of bitumen and when petroleum prices are high. At least, that's the case when using the technology that exists today." When he notes that extracting oil is expensive with modern technology, he implies that it may become cheaper in the future. He

also says, "Of course, should the price of extracting petroleum go down, you'll see projects of a similar scale start happening all around the world," which further reinforces the notion that it may be more economically feasible to extract oil in the future.

17 [Understanding Attitude Question]

When the professor tells the students that they have a test approaching and that they should focus on the lecture and take good notes, he means that the students need to know the material that he will cover in the lecture since it is going to be covered on the test.

Listening Set B

p.201

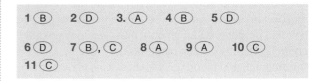

1 Ⓑ   2 Ⓓ   3. Ⓐ   4 Ⓑ   5 Ⓓ

6 Ⓓ   7 Ⓑ, Ⓒ   8 Ⓐ   9 Ⓐ   10 Ⓒ

11 Ⓒ

| **Questions 1–5** |

Script 03-07

W Student: Good morning, Professor Whittaker. I'm trying to figure out my schedule for next semester, but I could use a bit of help if you aren't too busy now.

M Professor: Of course, Natalie. I've always got time to speak to you. After all, you've taken quite a few of my classes in the past two years, and you've always excelled. I definitely don't mind speaking to outstanding students.

W: That's great. Thanks. And, uh, thanks for the kind words.

M: It's my pleasure.

W: So, um, I'm planning on taking five courses next semester. I've already got four of them figured out. But the fifth one . . . Well . . . that's the big problem.

M: How so?

W: Basically, what I want to learn doesn't exist as a class here.

M: I'm afraid I don't understand what you mean.

W: As you know, I'm double-majoring in History and Archaeology. Recently, I've become interested in the Middle Ages in Europe. We have lots of history classes covering the Middle Ages here. In fact, I'm going to take one next semester. But we don't have any classes in the Archaeology Department that cover medieval times.

M: Ah, yes. I believe most of the professors there specialize in Greek, Roman, and Egyptian archaeology. However . . .

W: Yes?

M: Do you know Professor Monroe?

W: Sure. I took a class with him last semester. He was an incredible lecturer. I really learned a lot in the class I took with him.

M: Ah, okay. I wasn't aware that you knew him. Anyway, in addition to doing Roman archaeology, he has an interest in medieval Europe. I believe he has even excavated a couple of castles in England which were built during the Middle Ages.

W: No way! That's exactly what I'd like to study.

M: Hmm . . . Are you aware you can create your own classes here?

W: You can?

M: I'll take that as a no. Yes, they're called directed study classes. Basically, you and a professor get together, come up with a course of study, and then register it as a class. In most cases, the professor assigns you some reading to do. You do the reading, report back to the professor once every week or two, and discuss what you read. Then, you get another reading assignment.

W: That sounds . . . intriguing.

M: It is. Those classes can be quite fun. Now, uh, you'd probably need some instruction on the history of the period. I could help you with that. And if Professor Monroe agrees, he could help you with the archaeological aspect. Would you like me to talk with him about it? I could get together with him either today or tomorrow and gauge his interest in the project.

W: I would love that. Thank you so much.

M: Well, it's not guaranteed. And if he does say yes, it will be lots of work. But you'll definitely learn plenty if you do it. Okay, I've got about ten minutes before my next class, so let me get in touch with Professor Monroe right now. I'll send you an email later today and let you know what's going on. Now, uh, I just need to find his number. I know I've got it somewhere . . .

1 [Gist-Content Question]

The students says, "Basically, what I want to learn doesn't exist as a class here."

2 [Understanding Attitude Question]

About Professor Monroe, the student remarks, "I took a class with him last semester. He was an incredible lecturer. I really learned a lot in the class I took with him."

3 [Detail Question]

The professor tells the student, "Anyway, in addition to doing Roman archaeology, he has an interest in medieval Europe. I believe he has even excavated a

couple of castles in England which were built during the Middle Ages."

4 [Making Inferences Question]

The professor tells the student, "Now, uh, you'd probably need some instruction on the history of the period. I could help you with that." So it can therefore be inferred that the professor is a member of the History Department.

5 [Making Inferences Question]

At the end of the conversation, the professor tells the student, "Okay, I've got about ten minutes before my next class, so let me get in touch with Professor Monroe right now. I'll send you an email later today and let you know what's going on. Now, uh, I just need to find his number." So he will probably make a telephone call next.

| Questions 6–11 |

Script 03-08

W Professor: Modern theater in the Western world owes its existence to Greek theater from the classical age. While the origins of Greek theater are not fully known . . . and probably never will be . . . it is known that by the sixth century B.C., theatrical performances were common enough that festivals were being held with regularity. What happened is that playwrights submitted their newest works to the festival, they were all judged, and then only a few of the plays were performed at the festival. Okay, here's some quick background for you . . . Athens was the center of Greek theater, and, unsurprisingly, the greatest playwrights and actors in ancient Greece came from Athens. What we think of as the golden age of Greek theater took place in the fifth century B.C., and playwrights like Euripides, Aristophanes, and Sophocles were at the forefront during this time.

Greek plays were staged outdoors. Here, I've got a picture for you . . . See . . . Plays were performed in massive theaters frequently built in natural amphitheaters, like in the sides of mountains. Look closely at this other picture here . . . The theater was shaped like a half-moon. The stage was on one side while the audience sat in seats built in rows and tiers that climbed high up the amphitheater's sides. And this spot between the stage and the seating . . . yes, this flat, circular area . . . was called the orchestra.

10A typical Greek play contained two major elements: the actors and the chorus. There were usually only three actors in a play as each actor would perform multiple roles. **They really earned their keep back then, didn't they?** Oh, and notice that I said "actors" and not "actresses." Only men acted in plays. The stage was forbidden to women, so men played women's roles when they appeared. Remember that women had very subservient positions in the ancient world. This was even the case in ancient Greece, particularly in Athens more so than other Greek city-states.

What was the chorus? It was a group that usually consisted of between twelve to twenty-four singers and dancers. The number of chorus members basically depended upon what type of play was being performed. Playwrights also kept changing the number of members as well. The chorus's job was simply to provide information to the audience in order to keep the play flowing smoothly. Think of the chorus as a kind of, uh, as a kind of narrator. The chorus relayed information by singing or having every member speaking simultaneously. In addition, the chorus had one more role: It was to represent the people of the city where the play was taking place. So if the play was set in Athens, the chorus members were Athenians. For a play set in Thebes, the members were Thebans. The reason they acted as the citizens is that the chorus was a representation of the public's conscience. They provided reactions to the unfolding events in the play. The chorus didn't perform on stage though. Instead, the members stood in the orchestra between the stage and the audience.

Okay, we've covered the stage, the actors, and the chorus. What's next? Props. I'm referring in particular to the use of masks although there were other props used. These masks often displayed extremely exaggerated emotions. There were masks for emotions like, uh, joy, sorrow, and anger. The reason for their exaggerated appearances was that they enabled the audience more clearly to identify with the emotions being expressed in the play.

M Student: Professor Halpern, I have a question. Weren't the masks also used to hide the actors' identities? I remember reading that somewhere.

W: That is correct, Joshua. Okay, but please don't misunderstand, class. This happened in sixteenth-century England, where actors were considered rogues and vagabonds. But regarding ancient Greece, there's a perfectly legitimate explanation as to why masks were used. It's simple, really. There were only three actors in a play, right? And they all played multiple roles. If they hadn't used masks, then the audience could have become confused. [11]When the same actor was playing the roles of Apollo, Heracles, and a princess, his face needed to be disguised. So the masks prevented the audience from identifying one actor with several characters in the play. **Thus, actors could play the roles of both the hero and the villain in the same performance.**

As for the structures of the plays, well, they were almost all identical. They started with a prologue in which one or two actors provided the background information necessary for the audience to follow what

was happening. The chorus then entered and sang and danced. Then came the first episode. I guess we'd call this the first act. Once the first episode ended, the actors left the stage, and the chorus again sang and danced while frequently retelling the events that had happened. Then, more episodes, or acts, would transpire until the story was told. The final part of the play was the exodus, which usually involved the chorus once again singing and dancing as its members exited the theater. Oh, and the songs often had words of wisdom concerning the moral lessons learned during the play itself.

6 [Gist-Content Question]

When beginning her talk about props, the professor mentions, "Props. I'm referring in particular to the use of masks although there were other props used. These masks often displayed extremely exaggerated emotions." Then, she states, "The reason for their exaggerated appearances was that they enabled the audience more clearly to identify with the emotions being expressed in the play."

7 [Detail Question]

According to the professor, the chorus "represent[ed] the people of the city where the play was taking place" and "provide[d] information to the audience in order to keep the play flowing smoothly."

8 [Understanding Attitude Question]

At the beginning of her lecture, the professor declares, "Modern theater in the Western world owes its existence to Greek theater from the classical age," which shows that she believes Greek theater has been highly influential on other forms of theater.

9 [Understanding Organization Question]

While talking about amphitheaters, the professor shows the students a couple of pictures of them and then describes what the amphitheaters looked like.

10 [Understanding Attitude Question]

When the professor notes that the actors performed multiple roles and then claims that they "really earned their keep," she is implying that the actors had impressive abilities since they could take on so many different roles.

11 [Understanding Function Question]

When the professor states that one actor could be both the hero and the villain in the same play, she implies that in some plays, the two main characters were never on stage together since it would be impossible for one man to play two different roles at the same time.

≡ Actual Test 02

Listening Set A

p.206

1 ⓒ	2 ⓓ	3 ⓑ	4 ⓑ	5 ⓒ
6 ⓓ	7 ⓓ	8 ⓑ	9 Fact: ②, ③	Speculation:
①, ④	10 ⓒ	11 ⓐ		

| Questions 1–5 |

Script 03-11

W Student: Hello. Are you Mr. Henderson?

M Guidance Counselor: Yes, I am. You must be Jennifer Nelson, right?

W: Yes, that's me. But I actually go by Jenny if you don't mind.

M: Not at all, Jenny. So . . . you scheduled an appointment with me. What would you care to discuss today?

W: Okay . . . I'm a freshman here, and I'm just having a hard time adjusting to this school. I've been thinking of applying to some other places to transfer, but my parents asked me to, you know, uh, come and speak with a counselor first. So, uh, here I am.

M: I see. Jenny, what exactly is it about this school that's making it so hard for you to adjust to life here?

W: The size! This school is so enormous that it freaks me out . . . Okay, hold on. Sorry. Let me tell you about myself. I'm from a small rural area in upstate New York. My town only has about, oh, I'd say no more than 3,000 people in it. And this school tops out at, what, uh . . .

M: There are more than 25,000 students attending classes here on a full-time basis.

W: Exactly! Talk about culture shock.

M: Well, that's something which is going to happen to you the rest of your life, Jenny. At some point in your life, you're going to have to get used to change. Unless, of course, you just go back to your hometown and stay there.

W: Okay, but that isn't the only thing about this school.

M: What else is wrong then?

W: It's just that—and I think this is connected to the school's size—everyone here is so distant and impersonal. I'm having a lot of trouble making friends.

M: How about your roommate?

W: She's a sophomore, so she's already got a bunch of friends from last year. We almost never hang out together.

M: Classmates?

W: I talk to some people in class, but that's about it. Once class is over, we always seem to go our separate ways.

M: Do you belong to any clubs or play intramural sports?

W: No, I don't really have time for those. I thought that, well, since it's my first semester here, I'd just focus on studying.

M: That makes perfect sense. Now, do you mind if I make a recommendation or two?

W: Not at all. That's why I'm here.

M: ⁵Thank you. Okay, I read your file before you came here so that I could learn as much about you as possible, and I noticed that you seem to be quite an accomplished violinist.

W: Oh, that's just a hobby.

M: A hobby? You won all kinds of awards for your playing. You know, the school has an orchestra. Why don't you try out with them? You'd be doing something you like, and you'd get a chance to meet people who share the same interests as you. That would go a long way toward helping you adjust to life here.

W: Okay. I guess I could log on to the school's website and find out how I can try out . . . Hmm . . . You know . . . You may be right. It would be nice to play the violin in a more formal setting and to meet some other musicians, too. Thanks.

1 [Gist-Content Question]

The student is speaking with the guidance counselor about how she is not succeeding at adjusting to life at school.

2 [Gist-Purpose Question]

The student is speaking with the guidance counselor because, as she says, "My parents asked me to, you know, uh, come and speak with a counselor first."

3 [Detail Question]

According to the student, there are fewer than 3,000 people in her hometown, which means that it is fairly small.

4 [Making Inferences Question]

The student says, "I guess I could log on to the school's website and find out how I can try out," which indicates that she will check out the school's website next.

5 [Understanding Function Question]

When the student claims that playing the violin is just a hobby, she is trying to disregard what the guidance counselor just said about her being an accomplished violinist.

W Professor: The second largest moon in the solar system is, appropriately enough, called Titan. It's second in size only to Jupiter's moon Ganymede, and it's even larger than the planet Mercury. Titan orbits Saturn and is notable because of its similarity to Earth. In a sense, you could almost call it Earth's twin. Hmm . . . I see some surprised looks on your faces. I suppose most of you haven't been keeping up with recent developments in astronomy. Okay, a couple of scientific probes sent to Titan have returned a wealth of information about it. Pictures sent from them show lakes, mountains, and many other geographical features that are similar to ones on Earth. Titan also happens to have an atmosphere. It's one of the very few bodies in our solar system that has one. But while Mars, Venus, and some other places have atmospheres, theirs are rather thin whereas Titan's is so thick and dense that it makes Titan seem bigger than Ganymede. Now, before I go any further, I'd like to give you some background information on Titan.

Titan was discovered in 1655 by the Dutch astronomer Christiaan Huygens. It's 3,200 miles in diameter and orbits Saturn at a distance of approximately 1,200,000 miles. It has a rotation period a little less than sixteen days and has an orbital period that's only, uh, about two hours shorter than its rotation period. Titan is so far from the sun that its surface temperature is around minus 280 degrees Fahrenheit. It's not the most hospitable of places. Most of its surface is comprised of methane, ethane, and other hydrocarbons. The air pressure on its surface is roughly fifty percent greater than that of Earth. Until recently, no one had ever seen Titan's surface because of its dense atmosphere. However, astronomers were aware it had a solid surface since it reflected and scattered radio waves.

Since the advent of both manned and unmanned rocket flight, a few probes have passed Titan, yet none got close to it until the *Cassini-Huygens* probe did in 2004 and 2005. They were actually two separate probes. [11]*Cassini* was the main one while *Huygens* was designed to visit Titan's surface. *Cassini-Huygens* arrived in the Saturn system in July 2004, where it orbited Saturn and passed among its satellites while taking pictures and gathering data until 2017.

M Student: It was active for that long?

W: Sure. These missions are designed to last years. *Voyager 1*, which was launched in 1977, is still functioning and transmitting information after all, and our technology today is much, much better than it was in the 1970s. *Cassini* was only supposed to last a few years, but it was extended a couple of times since it continued getting funded. So the *Huygens* probe was sent to Titan's surface in January 2005 and transmitted data suggesting that Titan's surface has similarities to Earth. Unfortunately, its batteries died after approximately two hours on Titan's surface, so it can no longer transmit data.

Still, what was learned was, well, simply remarkable. Between the two probes, enough data was gathered to show that Titan has bodies of liquids that resemble lakes. These lakes are filled with hydrocarbons though, not water, and are found mostly near Titan's poles. One area near Titan's north pole has seventy-five lakes, with the largest being over forty miles wide. There's speculation that Titan has all the necessary elements to sustain life but that its extremely low temperatures prevent this from happening.

Titan's atmosphere was one of the key focal points of the *Cassini-Huygens* probe. Measurements of its atmosphere vary, but it's between, oh, 200 to 800 miles thick. Compare this with Earth's atmosphere, which is roughly 100 miles thick. It's the thickness of the atmosphere that's responsible for the high air pressure on Titan's surface. And as for its composition, it's mostly nitrogen, but uh . . . as I mentioned earlier, there are smaller amounts of methane, ethane and, uh, other hydrocarbons, which are what make the atmosphere so thick.

What confuses scientists about Titan is that many believe that solar radiation should have evaporated its methane molecules long ago. That hasn't happened, but we don't know why. [10]Perhaps methane oceans or lakes on its surface are responsible for keeping its dense atmosphere intact, yet the *Huygens* probe landed near Titan's equator and found only dry lakes and river channels. **This has led some astronomers, like yours truly, to speculate that Titan has underground reserves of methane that periodically seep out and replenish the atmosphere.** Another theory is that lower levels of ethane in the atmosphere slow down the process of evaporation enough so that surface sources can keep it stable. At this point, we simply can't confirm either theory. Sadly, there's a lot about our solar system that we're in the dark about . . . I should also note that the methane on Titan acts like water does on Earth. It condenses, so methane rain falls on Titan's surface. If anyone ever gets caught in a methane storm there, that person had better make sure to have something stronger than an umbrella on hand.

6 [Gist-Content Question]

Throughout the lecture, the professor focuses on the physical characteristics of Titan.

7 [Detail Question]

The professor states, "Titan's [atmosphere] is so

thick and dense that it makes Titan seem bigger than Ganymede."

8 [Understanding Organization Question]

About methane, the professor states, "There are smaller amounts of methane, ethane and, uh, other hydrocarbons, which are what make the atmosphere so thick."

9 [Connecting Content Question]

According to the lecture, the facts about Titan are that its geography is similar to that of Earth, and its atmosphere is mostly nitrogen. What is speculation is that Titan can support life, and methane oceans on the surface are what cause its atmosphere to be so dense.

10 [Understanding Function Question]

When the professor says the phrase "like yours truly," she is letting the students know which of the theories about Titan she believes is correct.

11 [Understanding Attitude Question]

When the professor notes that the satellite arrived in 2004 and gathered data until 2017, the student answers by asking, "It was active for that long?" By his tone of voice, the student shows his surprise that the satellite was active for a period of many years.

Listening Set B

p.213

1 D	2 A	3 C	4 C	5 B
6 A	7 D	8 C	9 D	10 A	11 D

12 A   13 C   14 B   **15 Defensive Purposes:**
[2], [3] Trade: [1], [4]   16 C   17 C

| Questions 1–5 |

Script 03-14

W Student: Professor McDaniel, do you think I could have a moment of your time? I've got something I'd like to discuss with you.

M Professor: Sure, Emily. Why don't you come into my office, and then we can talk all about your grade on our most recent exam.

W: You know that's what I'm coming here for?

M: It seems to me to be the only reason you'd come to see me. Anyway, I was rather hoping that you'd visit so that I could figure out what went wrong. After all, you got A's on the first two tests, but you suddenly got a C on this one.

W: Yeah, I, uh . . .

M: So why don't you tell me what happened?

W: Um, well, I think that you graded me a little too harshly, Professor. I mean, take a look at my answer on cells here . . . Don't you think it deserves more than eight points out of fifteen?

M: Not at all. To be frank, you're lucky that you got as many points as you did. I think I must have been feeling generous when I graded your paper.

W: Huh? How so?

M: Emily, you left off a tremendous amount of information here. Yes, most of what you wrote on the test is correct. However, you simply didn't write enough about cells. Notice that the question also asks about various ways that cells can reproduce, but there isn't anything at all about cell reproduction in this answer.

W: Er . . .

M: I get the feeling that you didn't study as much for this test as you should have. Am I correct in my assumption?

W: Uh, I suppose that's part of the reason.

M: Is there anything you'd like to talk to me about? I mean, after all, you did so well on the first two tests that it seems a shame your grade is going to fall because of your, uh, abysmal performance on this one.

W: To be honest, I just haven't studied very much the past couple of weeks. I've had some, uh, personal issues that I've been dealing with.

M: I see.

W: But everything's fine now, so I'm back to working hard again.

M: That's good to know.

W: So, uh, is there anything I can do to improve my grade in this class? You know, like . . . write an extra report or something?

M: ⁵I'd like to give you that opportunity, but it just wouldn't be fair to the other students if they didn't get the same chance.

W: Okay. I can see the logic. **But how about if . . .?**

M: Yes?

W: How about if I get an A on the final test? Would you, uh, think about ignoring my grade on this one?

M: Hmm . . . That's an interesting proposal . . . Okay, I suppose that if you show significant improvement on the last test, I can forget about your dismal performance on this one. After all, that's what we're here for: to improve ourselves and to learn more.

W: That's music to my ears. I won't let you down on the next test, Professor. I'm going to get the highest grade in the class on it.

1 [Gist-Purpose Question]

The student goes to the professor to complain about the C she received on a recent test.

2 [Detail Question]

When the professor talks about the student's answer about cells on the test, he is showing the student how she gave an incomplete answer on the test. Thus, the professor is justifying the way that he graded the student's exam.

3 [Understanding Attitude Question]

When talking about the test, the professor says, "To be frank, you're lucky that you got as many points as you did. I think I must have been feeling generous when I graded your paper." He therefore implies that the student could have received a lower score than what she actually got.

4 [Making Inferences Question]

At the end of the conversation, the student says, "I won't let you down on the next test, Professor. I'm going to get the highest grade in the class on it." In stating this, she implies that she is going to study hard in the future.

5 [Understanding Function Question]

When the student says, "But how about if . . .," she is letting the professor know that she has come up with another idea.

| Questions 6–11 |

Script 03-15

M Professor: I'd like to take a few minutes to talk about the marine creature known as plankton. Plankton are tiny organisms that can live both in the salt water found in oceans and the fresh water in lakes. Plankton come in a wide variety, about which I'll examine in more detail shortly. Plankton also form a vital part of oceanic ecosystems, which, in turn, have a strong influence on ecosystems around the world. Finally, plankton play a crucial role in carbon dioxide capture and oxygen replacement. In essence, without plankton, the world would be much different.

First, how about the name plankton? Its name is derived from the Greek language and means drifter or wanderer. I'd say that's an apt name for plankton because they, well, they drift along in the water without any means of propulsion or ability to stop moving. They drift with tides and currents in the ocean and are at the mercy of those external propulsion forces. Those that live near the surface of the water are also propelled by strong winds. As a result, plankton can be found virtually everywhere there is moving water, but their

---

numbers vary from place to place. As a general rule, larger amounts are concentrated in areas where strong ocean currents move and converge.

For the most part, plankton are tiny creatures. Marine biologists distinguish them by their sizes and natures. Most are extremely tiny and can only be seen in detail when viewed with a microscope; however, others are larger and can be seen easily with the naked eye. Some plankton resemble animals whereas others are more plantlike. This distinction actually gives us the two basic groups of plankton: zooplankton and phytoplankton. Within each of those groups are a number of subgroups. I should also mention that plankton comes in two other varieties; they are bacteria and fungi plankton. Their main roles in water systems are to help convert dead organic material, such as fish that have died, into nutrients and to help fix nitrogen in the water, which helps phytoplankton grow.

Tiny phytoplankton are more plantlike and, uh, mainly live close to the surface of bodies of water because they rely on sunlight to produce nutrients through photosynthesis, just like plants that live on land do. Most of this doesn't happen on the surface though but around five to ten meters beneath the water's surface. Marine biologists believe that the intensity of sunlight is too strong for phytoplankton to endure by living at the surface of the water. There are also fewer nutrients in the water directly below the surface, which hinders that photosynthesis process. In addition, during photosynthesis, phytoplankton take in carbon dioxide and expel oxygen just like plants do.

W Student: [11]I read somewhere online that experts estimate that more than fifty percent of the world's supply of oxygen comes from phytoplankton. That sounds a bit too high. Or is the writer correct?

M: Actually, what you read is quite accurate. So you should be able to figure out that without phytoplankton, life on the Earth would be much different than it is today, and many species would likely not be alive. But hold that thought. We'll get back to it in a bit.

I'd like to say a few things about zooplankton first. Now, uh, zooplankton are larger types of plankton and derive nutrition by consuming phytoplankton. Some zooplankton are the eggs and small larvae of larger marine creatures such as mollusks and crustaceans. Others are similar to shrimp in their appearances. Of these plankton, krill is perhaps the most important since it forms as huge part of the diets of large marine creatures such as whales. Unlike phytoplankton, which are at the mercy of tides and currents, zooplankton possess some mobility. However, this is only on the vertical plane. They tend to move up to the surface of water to feed on phytoplankton during the night hours and then descend to deeper waters at dawn. This type of movement takes place in both saltwater and freshwater environments such as lakes.

As I mentioned earlier, plankton play a vital role as a keystone species in marine ecosystems and global ecosystems, too. Phytoplankton are basic lifeforms that are a vital link in the food chain. They're a food source for zooplankton, which, in turn, are food sources for many species of fish and mammals. That isn't the only thing that makes them a keystone species. Don't forget about how much oxygen they create. Without plankton, the oxygen content of the atmosphere would be much lower.

Now, uh, I want to do a bit of a thinking exercise now. Imagine a world without any plankton at all. Now, take a couple of minutes to think about how that world would be different from ours. What are some of the possible negative effects? How about positive ones? What do you think? Please write down some of your thoughts on a sheet of paper. Okay. Is everyone ready . . . ? Then please begin.

6 [Gist-Content Question]

Most of the lecture is about different types of plankton and their characteristics.

7 [Understanding Organization Question]

During the lecture, the professor first talks about phytoplankton and then discusses zooplankton.

8 [Connecting Content Question]

The professor mentions that phytoplankton is tiny and about zooplankton, he says, "Now, uh, zooplankton are larger types of plankton."

9 [Detail Question]

The professor says, "Zooplankton possess some mobility. However, this is only on the vertical plane. They tend to move up to the surface of water to feed on phytoplankton during the night hours and then descend to deeper waters at dawn."

10 [Making Inferences Question]

The professor tells the students to think about a world without plankton and to write down what they think will happen. The students will therefore probably think about a problem the professor suggested.

11 [Understanding Function Question]

The student mentions her doubt that fifty percent of the world's oxygen comes from plankton, but the professor says, "Actually, what you read is quite correct."
The professor therefore is confirming the student's information is right.

M Professor: All around the world, you can find cities in a number of geographical locations. Cities typically develop in one of three ways. They grow in a haphazard manner, in a carefully planned way, or in a combination of both methods. Most cities developed first as villages or towns and then grew larger in a haphazard way; however, in modern times, many of the more modern parts of cities were carefully planned. This is normal for cities that have been around for a while. I'm thinking of, you know, Rome, Paris, London . . . Of course, while the more modern sections of these cities have been carefully planned, their older districts lack this structure, which gives them a certain Old-World charm I suppose. Since most cities weren't planned, let's first look at some factors that led to people picking certain locations in which to live and determine why these locations eventually attracted enough people to become cities.

Historically, several factors have played roles in determining why people have chosen to gather in large numbers in certain places. First, most cities in the ancient world were located next to a water source, which, considering water's importance, shouldn't be surprising at all. Water is also vital for the irrigation of farmland and as a means of transportation. Keep in mind that in the ancient world, water was the easiest and fastest means of travel, and a large amount of trade was conducted by water-borne transport. In addition, ancient people needed relatively flat arable land nearby so that they could engage in agriculture in order to support their city's population. You may have noticed that a lot of ancient cities . . . especially the first ones . . . were founded on floodplains and were, uh, obviously near water and also had lots of fertile land nearby. For instance, the cities in the Indus River Valley in what's now India and Pakistan were built on floodplains. [17]These cities also are the oldest in the world that we know of—thanks to archaeological excavations—that show signs of careful city planning. You see, they typically had high walls, which protected the people from both floods and invaders. Many of their streets were also laid out in grid-like patterns. **Pretty advanced for ancient people, wouldn't you say?**

Now, let's think about how cities could be defended. High walls obviously helped, but there are other factors that strategists think about as well. For one, being on high ground is always desirable. Additionally, water or mountains provide obstacles attackers must somehow bypass, which makes some locations more preferable than others. Venice, for instance, was built on many islands after its people had been defeated and forced from their original homes on the Italian mainland. By locating their city on the water, it became easier to defend and harder to assault. Many other cities were originally fortresses that simply grew in size. London, for instance, was once a Roman fort. In Canada, Quebec was originally built as a fort by French colonists who wanted it to overlook the vital St. Lawrence River.

Trade is another vital factor in the growth of cities. Villages can expand into towns and then into cities by attracting people through the expansion of trade. A settlement's location near a vital water or trade route has led to the development of many cities. Hong Kong is a prime example of this. Located between Southeast and Northeast Asia, it serves as a gateway to the billion-plus population of China. Additionally, since the nineteenth century, the development of railways has led to the establishing of new cities all over the world. The American transcontinental railroad encouraged many cities to grow alongside it as it made its way from the Mississippi River west to California. Chicago, located slightly east of the Mississippi, was founded because it was situated in a strategic location between the eastern and western parts of the U.S., and thus many railroads eventually passed through it.

Finally, political considerations have caused some cities simply to be built where nothing once was. Washington, D.C. is one such example. A large part of it was once a mosquito-infested swamp, and politicians and other members of the populace actually tried to stay out of it as much as possible. Of course, it has grown into a, uh, a major city today, but the only reason for that is that it was made the capital of the U.S. Canberra, Australia, is another example of political considerations causing a city literally to emerge from nothingness. Decades ago, the people of Melbourne and Sydney both wanted their cities to become Australia's capital. Eventually, a compromise was reached, and the new city—Canberra—was planned, and construction began. While it's quite practical and has been planned well, many Australians find it, hmm . . . they find it artificial and claim it lacks the, uh, warmth and charm of places such as Sydney and Melbourne. This brings me to our next topic, which is a comparison of planned and mostly unplanned cities.

12 [Gist-Purpose Question]

About Venice, the professor states, "Venice, for instance, was built on many islands after its people had been defeated and forced from their original homes on the Italian mainland. By locating their city on the water, it became easier to defend and harder to assault." Thus, he talks about it to show the importance of defense to its founders.

13 [Detail Question]

The professor mentions, "Canberra, Australia, is another example of political considerations causing a city literally to emerge from nothingness."

14 [Understanding Organization Question]

The professor starts the lecture by mentioning the ways in which cities are founded, and then he goes into detail about them.

15 [Connecting Content Question]

According to the professor, London was an ancient Roman fort while Quebec was founded to "overlook the vital St. Lawrence River." Both of them were founded for defensive purposes. Meanwhile, Hong Kong was founded in a strategic area between Northeast and Southeast Asia and is a gateway to China while Chicago was also strategically located between the eastern and western parts of the U.S. These two cities were founded for trade reasons.

16 [Making Inferences Question]

At the end of the lecture, the professor says, "This brings me to our next topic, which is a comparison of planned and mostly unplanned cities," which shows that he intends to continue lecturing on a similar subject.

17 [Understanding Attitude Question]

When the professor says, "Pretty advanced for ancient people, wouldn't you say?" he is implying that the planning that went into these ancient cities was impressive.

Listening Set C   <small>p.221</small>

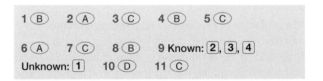

1 Ⓑ   2 Ⓐ   3 Ⓒ   4 Ⓑ   5 Ⓒ

6 Ⓐ   7 Ⓒ   8 Ⓑ   9 Known: ②, ③, ④

Unknown: ①   10 Ⓓ   11 Ⓒ

| Question 1–5 |

<small>Script 03-18</small>

M Student: Hi there. Is there someone here I can speak with?

W Newspaper Editor: Well, that depends on what you want to speak about.

M: Ah, good point. Sorry for being vague. I'm interested in becoming a reporter, so I guess I'd like to speak with, uh . . . I don't really know actually. An editor maybe?

W: Well, tonight's your lucky night. I just happen to be one of the editors here. I'm the only one in the office, and I don't have anything to do right now, so I've got some time to speak with you.

M: Excellent. That's good to hear.

W: So you want to be a reporter. How come?

M: Well, I guess reporter might not be the correct word. Reporters are just supposed to focus on the facts of the story, right?

W: Yes, that's true. We ask who, what, when, and where? Reporters—the good ones at least—keep their personal biases out of their articles and just give the facts.

M: Well, I don't know if that's the job for me then. I'm more interested in telling people my opinion and letting them know what I think.

W: In that case, you're referring to opinion columnists. Unfortunately, we don't have any positions available for them right now. They're pretty popular. Although . . . we do publish guest columns on occasion when something interesting comes up. You might want to inquire about that.

M: Well, to be honest, I'm actually here because I submitted an article, er, a column, I guess I should say, a couple of weeks ago, but I never heard back from anyone. [5]I don't care if my work gets published or not, but . . . No, that's not true. I do care. Otherwise, I wouldn't be here.

W: You didn't get a response? That's peculiar. What was your article about?

M: It was about the need to get more students involved in the physical sciences and some ways to attract more and better students into the Physics and Chemistry departments.

W: That was you?

M: Uh, yes. Oh, I take it that you got my article. So why didn't you respond?

W: Wow, we've been hoping you'd show up.

M: Couldn't you have just responded to me by email? That's how I submitted my article after all.

W: We couldn't because the person who opened your email downloaded the article and then accidentally deleted your letter. Since you didn't write your name on the article itself, we had no idea who you were. Uh, who are you by the way?

M: I'm Roydell Stewart. I'm a junior in the Physics Department.

W: Well, Roydell, I am so glad that you showed up here. You're no longer our mystery man.

M: That's a relief. So, uh, can I assume that you liked my article?

W: Oh, we all loved it. But we couldn't publish it until we had your permission, and since we didn't know who you were . . .

M: Ah, right.

W: [4]Tell you what. Why don't you come back tomorrow

afternoon? There will be more editors here. **We can talk about your column and about the ones we'd like for you to write in the future.**

M: Oh . . . Okay. I'll be back around three then.

1 [Gist-Purpose Question]

To explain why he is visiting the newspaper office, the student states, "Well, to be honest, I'm actually here because I submitted an article, er, a column, I guess I should say, a couple of weeks ago, but I never heard back from anyone."

2 [Detail Question]

When talking about opinion columnist positions, the editor says, "Unfortunately, we don't have any positions available for them right now."

3 [Understanding Attitude Question]

The editor states, "Well, Roydell, I am so glad that you showed up here," and she therefore shows that she is pleased to speak with him.

4 [Making Inferences Question]

When the editor makes the comment to the student about the columns she would like him to write in the future, she is hinting that she would like for him to write for the newspaper.

5 [Understanding Function Question]

When the editor asks, "You didn't get a response?" her tone of voice indicates that she is shocked by what he just said.

| Questions 6–11 |

Script 03-19

W Professor: Lou Gehrig is one of those few unfortunate humans who have a disease named after them. Gehrig was a famous baseball player for the New York Yankees in the 1920s and 1930s. As a matter of fact, he was one of the greatest men ever to play the game. Sadly, Gehrig became ill in 1939 and was diagnosed with ALS. He retired from the game and died from the disease two years later. Just so you know, ALS stands for amyotrophic lateral sclerosis, but it's commonly known as Lou Gehrig's disease. [11]It's a disease that affects the body's nervous system by preventing messages from the brain from, uh, from reaching the muscles throughout the body. Most patients who suffer from it die within five years of getting the disease.

M Student: But I thought that Stephen Hawking had ALS, yet he lived with the disease for more than fifty years. How was that possible?

W: True enough. Doctor Hawking, in case you don't know, was a famous British astrophysicist known for his research on the universe. He was also arguably the world's most famous ALS patient and managed to survive for more than half a century with the disease. However, he was confined to a wheelchair, had severe mobility problems, and was fully dependent upon care from others for his most basic needs. Nevertheless, he was still a rare example of a long-term ALS patient.

One of the tragedies of ALS is that as the muscles deteriorate, the brain and the higher cognitive functions still operate at normal capacity. The sufferer's senses of sight, hearing, touch, taste, and smell all remain unaffected. So the person fully recognizes that his or her bodily functions are collapsing. As for the signs of the disease, the initial symptoms are tingling and numbness in the extremities, a lack of strength, the unexpected dropping of things, and the occurrence of small accidents such as, uh, such as tripping or falling down. As the disease becomes more pronounced, the person becomes unable to walk and cannot make use of his or her arms. In the final stages, the sufferer loses all mobility in his or her body. Eventually, the individual becomes unable to speak and might not even be able to blink. How sad that must be. At some point near the end, the lungs cease functioning, and the patient can only survive by being put on a respirator. Should this not happen, death quickly ensues.

M: But what causes ALS? I've never heard anyone talk about that before.

W: It's the result of the motor neurons dying, and, as I said, uh, this prevents the brain from sending messages to the muscles. It's as simple as that. Oh, ALS typically occurs in people ages forty to seventy but can, of course, strike both older and younger people. Fortunately, it's fairly uncommon, as around, oh, I believe about 5,000 or so Americans get it every year. There are also two types: sporadic ALS and familial ALS. Sporadic ALS can strike anyone anywhere and at any time. It's the more common type. Familial ALS, however, is inherited, but it's quite rare as it's seen in around five to ten percent of patients.

While there's no known cure for ALS, doctors are currently working on finding one. Recent research has identified a gene responsible for a small percentage of familial ALS. This discovery has, fortunately, led to a renewed interest in research on ALS. Researchers also have some ideas about how ALS kills motor neurons. There are four possibilities . . . First, nearby cells, called glial cells, may produce toxins that can damage the motor neurons. Second, a neurotransmitter called glutamate, which is a substance that allows the brain to send and receive messages, may be produced in excessive quantities, which can lead to the death of cells. Third, in the motor neuron cells themselves, a breakdown in the protein that releases waste products

can lead to a buildup of toxins that kills the cells. Finally, problems can occur in the axon. That's A-X-O-N by the way . . . The axon is the long nerve that extends from the brain down the spinal cord and into the body. An accumulation of proteins called neurofilaments can occur. This strangles the flow of nutrients along the axon, and thus it prevents messages from reaching the muscles.

Despite the ongoing intensive research and these recent discoveries, the cause, or causes, of ALS is unknown. Why it strikes one person and not another remains a, well, it remains a mystery. There are some thoughts on the matter though. Some theorize that it's caused by a problem in the immune system. Others say it's the result of toxic substances, chemical imbalances in the body, or even a poor diet. In short, no one really knows. There is, however, hope for ALS sufferers. Some researchers believe that stem cells may prove useful. Experiments with mice have shown that stem cells can actually single out the damaged neurons, and they have then gone and replaced those very neurons. That's quite promising, but a lot more work remains to be done before a cure can be found.

6 [Gist-Content Question]

The majority of the lecture is spent describing the effects of ALS on sufferers' bodies.

7 [Understanding Attitude Question]

The professor states, "This discovery has, fortunately, led to a renewed interest in research on ALS. Researchers also have some ideas about how ALS kills motor neurons," which shows that she believes research on ALS should be pursued.

8 [Understanding Organization Question]

During the course of the lecture, the professor mentions a large number of facts about ALS.

9 [Connecting Content Question]

According to the professor, the types of ALS, the symptoms of ALS, and the effects of ALS are all known. However, its causes remain unknown.

10 [Making Inferences Question]

Since Stephen Hawking lived with ALS for more than fifty years, it can be inferred that he had a slowly progressive form of the disease.

11 [Understanding Function Question]

When the student responds to the professor's comment, he notes that Stephen Hawking lived with ALS for more than fifty years. So he disputes the professor's statement that most patients die from ALS within five years of getting the disease.

TOEFL® MAP

New TOEFL® Edition

Listening

Advanced